The Yiddish Dictionary Sourcebook

A Transliterated Guide to the Yiddish Language

The Yiddish Dictionary Sourcebook

A Transliterated Guide to the Yiddish Language

BY

HERMAN GALVIN

&

STAN TAMARKIN

KTAV PUBLISHING HOUSE, INC.,

HOBOKEN, 1986

Library of Congress Cataloging in Publication Data

Galvin, Herman.
    The Yiddish dictionary sourcebook.

    1. English language—Dictionaries—Yiddish.
2. Yiddish language—Dictionaries—English.
I. Tamarkin, Stan.   II. Title.
PJ5117.G34   1986   437'.947   86–1414

ISBN 0-87068-715-8

MANUFACTURED IN THE UNITED STATES OF AMERICA

For Freda and Janie

TABLE OF CONTENTS

Acknowledgments

We would like to thank the many students of both Yiddish and Jewish culture who have unselfishly helped to give life to this book. In particular, we owe a large debt to Jack Noskowitz, of the Workman's Circle in New York, who helped us as an editor and provided, in addition to his prodigious knowledge, an infectious enthusiasm. Bernard Scharfstein, our publisher, is someone to whom we also owe much. He has been generous with his patience and his sound advice. While a large part of what is useful in this work stems from those who have helped us, we alone are responsible for all errors and oversights.

H.G.
S.T.

YIDDISH LANGUAGE AND GRAMMAR

THE YIDDISH LANGUAGE

It would be highly satisfying for us to be able to report that Yiddish is alive and well, that it is a flourishing language, used daily by millions of Jews throughout the world, that it still is—as it was in its heyday—the language of a rich literature that ranged from traditional fiction to modernist poetry, from history and philosophy to linguistics and the social sciences. Unfortunately, we can not suggest that Yiddish is as widely used as it was at its zenith when an estimated eleven million people spoke what they affectionately called the *mame-loshn,* or "mother tongue," the everyday language of the home, the school, and the marketplace.[1]

Yiddish has demonstrably fallen on hard times, for since it reached its greatest heights immediately before the Second World War, it has been on a steady decline. The atrocities of Hitler's campaign to annihilate Europe's Jewish population which eventually resulted in the murder of six million Jews, government endorsed anti-Semitism in the Soviet Union, the single European country with a large Jewish population that survived the Holocaust, and the gradual tide of cultural assimilation of Jews throughout the Western Hemisphere into host societies that emphasized their own native languages and cultures, have all been heavy blows to the life of Yiddish. Even in the Jewish homeland of Israel, where much of the population at one time was Yiddish-speaking, the established language is Hebrew and Yiddish is considered to be somewhat of an anachronism.

Before writing off the survival of Yiddish, however, one must be cautious. There are still Jewish fraternal groups that propagate and nourish an interest in Yiddish; prestigious colleges and universities are giving courses in Yiddish language and literature, and Jewish children, especially in the Northeast, can attend Yiddish schools and camps; there are pockets of ultra-orthodox Jews throughout the world that use Yiddish as their normal mode of discourse; and, finally, there is a coterie of Yiddishists in countries as far apart culturally and geographically as America and the Soviet Union who are keeping alive the literary traditions of the *mame-loshen* by reading Yiddish newspapers, magazines, and journals. On a popular level, moreover, Yiddish has been steadily creeping into the mainstream of American culture where it has found a wide acceptance. Leo Rosten's popularization, *The Joys of Yiddish,* enjoyed a huge success a few years ago, and almost daily one hears a Yiddishism in a movie or on television. It would not be surprising nowadays either to hear a Gentile housewife in the midwest, far away from large Jewish centers of New York, Boston, or Philadelphia, call her hapless brother-in-law a *shlemil,* or to hear a beleaguered Gentile corporate executive complain that another trip cross country was "one *shlep* too many."

Perhaps the greatest recent measure of the vitality and success of Yiddish was the awarding of the 1978 Nobel Prize in Literature to Isaac Bashevis Singer. It is truly amazing for the world's most famous and distinguished prize to have been given to a writer who persists, even to the present day, to write in a language that has been undergoing such a struggle to survive! If nothing else, it is a tribute to Yiddish as well as to the prolific writer of novels, short stories, and memoirs, who has used the *mame-loshn* so beautifully and effectively. In his Nobel Prize acceptance speech, a speech in which he injected a few sentences in Yiddish, Singer tried to convey to the world the power of the *mame-loshn,* his conception of its character and emotional depth. "One can find in the Yiddish and in the Yiddish spirit," he wrote, "expressions of pious joy, lust for life, longing for the Messiah, patience and deep appreciation of human individuality." "There is a quiet humor in Yiddish," Singer continued, "and a gratitude for every day of life, every crumb of success, each encounter of love."[2]

There is general agreement among historical linguists that Yiddish has its roots in a mixture of dialects that was used in the Rhine valley of western Germany during the middle ages.[3] While there had apparently been a number of Jews living in Cologne as early as the fifth century A.D., the Jews that began to settle in large numbers in the Rhine valley during the ninth and tenth centuries—probably as a result of expulsions from northern France and Italy—were the first members of the Diaspora to use the language that is now known as Yiddish. Living north of the Pyranees and the Alps, in a region that Jews have long known as Ashkenaz, these Jewish settlers were the ancestors of the Jewish population of Europe which has been distinguished from the Sephardim, those Jews that inhabited the Iberian peninsula, Italy, and the lands that fringed the Mediterranean Sea. The Ashkenazim, as they have become to be called, moved both east and west, inhabiting the Low Countries, France, and Germany in the western part of Europe, and, later, Russia, Poland, Austria, and the Slovakian lands in the east. It is from the wide and varied cultures through which these migrating Jews moved over a period of centuries that Yiddish obtained its diverse characteristics. Building upon a base of tenth century Rhineland German and elements of Hebrew and Aramaic with which Jews in the Diaspora had long been familiar, Yiddish took on accretions from every language with which it came into contact and slowly evolved into a language of its own.

Since its "modern period," what the great Yiddish linguist Max Weinrich called the period from 1850 until the present, Yiddish's major components have been German, Hebrew, Russian, and Polish, yet there are also remnants of the Romance languages as well as Czech, Latvian, Lithuanian, and other European tongues.[4] Since the greatest concentration of Yiddish speakers for the last four hundred years have lived within the Pale of Settlement, that part of modern Russian and Poland where Russian Imperial decrees restricted Jewish settlement, the contributions of the eastern European languages have been the last to come into Yiddish. And the remnants of tenth century Rhineland German that formed the basis for as much as seventy-five per cent of the *mame-loshn,* although linguistically close relatives of modern Yiddish, seem far removed from the language as it is now spoken and written.

For centuries, until the flowering of Yiddish literature late in the nineteenth century, Yiddish has been scorned and ridiculed by Jews and Gentiles alike. To the Gentile Yiddish was a strange, disordered amalgam of languages spoken by an often alien and resented portion of humanity. It had no polish, no literature of its own, not even a proper grammar. Assimilated Jews who disliked the ethnic qualities associated with Yiddish conceived of the *mame-loshn* as proof of Jewish backwardness and ignorance, a graceless dialect that would only serve to delay and stymie Jewish integration into the Gentile societies of Europe. Down through the ages, in fact, the daily users of Yiddish held an ambivalent regard for Yiddish, an ambivalence that was reinforced by their reverence for their *loshn-Koydesh,* the sacred language of Hebrew, the practical need to know at least some of the native languages of the area in which they were living in order to communicate with their neighbors and government officials, and their own recognition that Yiddish, although perfect for casual conversation in the home and in the synagogue, was not suitable for intricate scientific and technical discourse. Written from right to left with a Hebrew orthography, hardly codified in terms of diction and spelling, Yiddish was often seen as a linguistic pastiche, the jargon of the Jews. Indeed since the end of the eighteenth century Jewish *maskilim,* Jewish intellectuals and assimilationists who were caught up in the spirit of the Enlightenment, called the *mame-loshn*—with a clear sense of deprecation—the *zhargon,* a name for Yiddish that was used for over a hundred years. In addition to this name, Yiddish has been variously called Judeo-German, *loshn-Ashkenas,* the language of the Ashkenazim, and *taytsh,* the Yiddish for "German" or "translation." According to Weinreich, in fact, the current name Yiddish is far younger than the language itself, for it apparently was not used widely until approximately the fifteenth century.[5]

While during its pre-history Yiddish was clearly a rough combination of medieval German and the languages that French and Italian Jews brought with them into the Rhineland (an Ur-language for which Weinreich has coined the name Laaz), there is little reason to equate Yiddish as it has been spoken for centuries with modern German.[6] Many of its roots are connotatively similar, of course, but in terms of denotative meaning and pronunciation in various Yiddish dialects, the connections between Yiddish and German have become distended and weakened. The Yiddish scholar Solomon A. Birnbaum has argued that by the time of the publication of the early Yiddish *Samuel Book,* an epic based on the biblical *Book of Samuel* that was probably composed in the fourteenth century and was published in 1544, the Yiddish of western Europe had become a language in its own right.[7] Many new words using German roots had been created, but on a Hebrew pattern, and there were elements from Romance and Semitic languages in Yiddish that bore no relation to German at all. Not only were there significant semantic changes between Yiddish and German, but the *mame-loshn* contained words with German roots that in their original language were either obsolescent or obsolete. Summing up the argument of modern linguists who conceive of Yiddish as a language, not a mish-mash, a tongue of the Askenaszic Jews, not a broken dialect of German, Uriel Weinrich has written that "the actual vocabulary of Yiddish therefore stands out as a *concrete historical formation* against the background of its potential sources." According to the greatest of all Yiddish linguists, "the end product could not, as it were, be predicted from a knowledge of the ingredients."[8]

The entry on the Yiddish language in the *Encyclopaedia Judaica* gives two clear examples that point up the similarity and dissimilarity shared by Yiddish and German. The well-known German word *Mensch* and the equally familiar Yiddish *mensh* are definitely related, yet there is a resonance to the Yiddish word that is not present in its German source. In German it means human being, man, person and individual, whereas in Yiddish it means much the same, but with richer associations. In the *mame-loshn, mensh* also suggests reliability, maturity, and, in one usage, the status of an employee. The example of the Yiddish word *unterzogn,* however, points out a dissimilarity, a relationship between the root language and its offspring that has been lost in time. In Yiddish this word means to breathe (or whisper) into another's ear in a prompting fashion, a definition that has no clear parallel in either the German prefix *unter,* which means "under," or the stem *sagen,* which means "to say." One can only guess at the various mutations that over the centuries created a distance between Yiddish and its many German antecedents, changes and shifts that evolved in the misty past, now long-buried in the Rhineland of the Middle Ages.[9]

The relationship between Yiddish and its borrowing from Hebrew and Aramaic are also a complex matter, for Yiddish had both borrowed and "corrupted," but often in a random manner. There are, as one would expect, a number of Yiddish words that are directly related to their Hebrew-Aramaic sources in the fields of prayer and religious learning, yet there are also Hebrew elements in Yiddish that are entirely neutral or even vulgar. There appears to be no firm basis for relating Yiddish and Hebrew-Aramaic in terms of form or function, so that while rules that govern or explain the Hebrew or Aramaic elements in the *mame-loshn* exist, they can not be taken as all-inclusive. As one might expect of a language whose speakers have known ghettoization, countless migrations, and a constant coexistence with a variety of legally established native tongues, Yiddish appears to be a linguistic quicksilver, a multifaceted tongue with a history and a linguistic structure that is extraordinarily complex.

In a consideration of Yiddish and its history it is most important to recognize that since the beginning of the Diaspora the Jewish people have been a bilingual people. This is not to suggest that every Jew at any time since the destruction of the Second Temple could speak both a native tongue and Hebrew, or a native tongue and a "Jewish" tongue, but a study of the Jewish experience through the ages demonstrates an astonishing number of languages that Jews could claim as their own, Jewish languages that were spoken in the midst of a "foreign" culture. Not only have linguists distinguished between such Diaspora languages as Aramaic, Judeo-Greek, Judeo-Arabic, Judeo-Latin, Judeo-Italian, Judeo-Provencal, Judeo-French, Judeo-Persian, and four varieties of Judeo-Spanish (Ladino, Romance, Judesmo, and Spaniolit), but they have isolated such esoteric Jewish languages as Bukharic of Central Asia, Tatic of the Caucasus, Yevanic of Egypt, Temanic of Asia, Crimchak of the Crimea, and the extinct Zarphatic of northern France, Catalanic of Iberia, and Shuadit of Provence.[10] Side by side with these Jewish tongues, of course, Jews prayed in Hebrew, studied in Hebrew (if they were literate), and introduced words from their Hebrew-Aramaic legacy into whatever vernacular they were using. Because the history of the Jewish people is so long, and the lands in which they have lived so numerous, it would be unwise to make a generalization about their ability to read, speak, and write Hebrew, yet it is probably safe to say that most Jewish men, down through the ages, could read the *loshn-koydesh* at least well enough to offer up Sabbath and festival prayers. Jewish literacy notwithstanding, Hebrew was always a presence for Jews in the Diaspora, a presence that inexorably enriched whatever Jewish vernacular that made up their normal mode of discourse.

Yiddish is an unusual language because of its pan-European history, for no other language could claim a territory that spread from the North Sea on the west to Kiev on the east, a territory that encompassed so many varying political, cultural, and national entities. While dialectic differences made the Yiddish of western Europe sound different from the way it was spoken in the east, and there were, indeed, even within the Pale of Settlement, many subtle linguistic differences, Ashkenazim spoke a language that was essentially familiar to all.[11] During the middle period of the history of Yiddish, from about the fourteenth century to the eighteenth, the bulk of Europe's Jewish population slowly migrated eastward. By the time of Europe's intellectual and social "Enlightenment" during the last half of the eighteenth century—a movement that Jews call the *Haskalah*—about eighty per cent of the Ashkenazim lived within the boundaries of the Pale of Settlement. Circumscribed by Imperial edict in 1791, the Pale contained approximately ninety-five per cent of the Russian Jewish population. Denied many basic civil rights, including freedom to travel, to attend universities, to own land, and to live in certain cities, Jews by an overwhelming margin lived in small towns, called *shtetls,* or in larger cities where they sometimes represented major portions of the urban population.[12] In the main they worked as artisans, shopkeepers, traders, business managers, or leaseholders of farm land which they were usually forbidden to own themselves. When it was necessary, they could speak a bit of Polish or Russian or whatever tongue was necessary to use on the market days when they would trade with Gentiles; and those members of the Jewish community that had regular intercourse with civil authorities were naturally more fluent in the local tongue. The very small percentage of the Jewish population that were successful in commerce or a profession to such a degree that they could attend universities and disregard many of the laws that controlled the lives of their co-religionists were well educated in Russian and Polish, yet the wide majority of the Jews in the Pale led lives that were insular and insulated.

The two forces that began to change the lives of Jews living in the Pale were the *Haskalah* and the rise of Hasidism, the pietistic religious movement. They were diametrically opposed, for the *Haskalah* turned Jewish life outward, especially in western Europe where it came earliest and had the greatest effect, and resulted in the adoption of modern modes of thought and action, while the *hasidic* movement led Jews to retain and conserve the traditional. Enlightened Jews shed their traditional garb, often were clean-shaven, and rejected orthodoxy in favor of rationalistic philosophical and religious ideals. Assimilation within the native cultures was the ethnic norm for the *maskilim,* as Jews of the *Haskalah* movement were called, and there was an increase in apostacy as social, political, and intellectual opportunities opened up—especially for those willing to change their religious confession. *Hasidism*, in some respects a reaction to the Enlightenment, was also a response to an entrenched rabbinate resistent to change, and favored religious fervour and immediacy that called for individual, direct experience and a deepened pietistic commitment to traditional religious values and ideals. Founded in Poland by Israel Baal-Shem (1698–1760), known as the Baal Shem Tov, the movement spread throughout the Pale, and soon many towns and *shtetlekh* could boast of their own *Hasidic* master, a learned and holy rabbi who served the community as a highly revered spiritual leader and supreme arbiter of the Law. The movement meant an enervating contribution to Yiddish, for while westernized *maskilim* were striving to orient themselves within essentially a non-Jewish (and non-Yiddish) world, the *Hasidim* denounced worldliness and emphasized the traditional virtues of Jewish life—life which meant a commitment to the *mame-loshn*, a language that was not tainted by modernism.

For the *maskilim* Yiddish was a reminder of their once unassimilated status, a reminder of a time when they were restricted to living in ghettoes, suffered from overt forms of anti-Semitism, and were excluded from the possession of ordinary civil rights. Unlike the Jews of the Pale who were cast into a "Jewish nation" by the civil authorities, a status that made their religious and ethnic identity that of a separate people within the Russian Imperial state, the Jews of western Europe had a more assimilated political and social status which allowed them to consider themselves, especially in the nineteenth century, not as "Jews," but as Frenchmen, Germans, and Austrians, for instance, who happened to be Jewish. This is not to say that anti-Semitism was absent in the west, an anti-Semitism that often prohibited their full acceptance within the social, political, and intellectual communities, yet the Jews of western Europe were clearly following a steady course during the Enlightenment period toward an assimilated existence. The German *Haskalah* leader Moses Mendelssohn (1729–1786), who translated the Bible into German written with a Hebrew orthography in order to modernize Jewish religious study, was a highly respected *maskil* who considered Yiddish to be an impediment to modernization. "I am afraid that this Jargon," he wrote of the *mame-loshn*, "has contributed not a little to the rudeness of the common man and I anticipate good results from the growing usage of the pure German vernacular among my brethren.[13]

While the Jews of western Europe allowed Yiddish to play a diminished role in their lives, the Jews living within the Pale—even the sizeable portion of *misnagdim*, those who rejected *Hasidism*—continued to use the *mame-loshn* as their main tongue. To be sure even Jews in the east, especially those living in urban centers like Warsaw or Vilna, were becoming "westernized" to some degree, yet the percentage of those who pursued an advanced secular education, became fluent in Russian or Polish, and abandoned fully traditional social and religious modes were small in number. Those intellectuals who wanted to enter the mainstream of the Russian and Polish cultures did write in these languages, and there was a number of intellectuals who chose to use Hebrew as a literary vehicle for poetry, philosophy, and history, but by and large the Jews of the Pale were uncultured in secular fields, and not prepared for the new intellectual and social values of the *haskalah*. It was not until the second half of the nineteenth century—after the emancipation of the serfs in Russia and the granting of new civil rights to Jews, after the changes brought by rapid industrialization, the trend toward urbanization, and the spread of republican ideals began to infiltrate even the smallest *shtetlekh* of the Pale— that Enlightenment values made a significant headway against traditionalism. Within a comparatively brief span of time, the five decades that spanned the Emancipation Proclamation of Czar Alexander II in 1862 and the beginning of the First World War in 1914, the Jews of the Pale encountered an onrush of new national, social, and political movements that included Zionism, trade unionism, and democratic socialism, as well as organizational offshoots such as the Polish and Russian Bund, the Haddassah society, Paole-Zion, and a variety of colonization groups. The changes in the Pale, however, were not accompanied by a pervasive renunciation of the *zhargon* as it had been in the west. Rather the *mame-loshn* was adopted as a vehicle for spreading the manifold gospels of change that accompanied the adoption of Enlightenment ideals in the east. Not only was Yiddish used to capture support for the new social and political "isms" that invaded the Pale, but it also became the language of a new "golden age" of Jewish literature, the tongue of a fresh outpouring of poetry, fiction, and drama that accompanied and reinforced the other directions that the *haskalah* was taking. The adoption of Yiddish by serious writers became a principal part of the "national revival of Russian Jewry" as Jewish intellectuals reached a greater number of readers than they had ever been able to reach before.[14]

The "golden age" of Yiddish had its antecedent in the modest number of publications that appeared over the centuries in the *mame-loshen,* a language that was never regarded as suitable for a body of serious literature. The reverence that Jews held for Hebrew as a holy language and the strictly religious education that was accorded Jewish males in the Jewish primary school, or *kheyder,* and in the more advanced school, or *yeshiva,* meant a disdain for

Yiddish and its relegation to being only appropriate for a literature read by women and girls, the members of the Jewish household that did not even receive a primary grade religious education. The earliest publications in Yiddish, those that appeared in the sixteenth century, were characteristically translations of the Bible, heroic legends and romances based on biblical and secular folk heroes, and ethical instruction for those who did not attend classes at the *kheyder*. An early classic of Yiddish literature that endured for over three hundred years was the *Bovo-Bukh* that appeared in 1507. Written by a Hebrew grammarian named Elijah Levita (1468/9–1549), known to his readers as Bokher, it was a collection of verse tales based on the Bible. It was followed by a number of Yiddish prayer books meant for women, and then in 1602, what became probably the best-known of all early Yiddish publications, the collection of folk tales and talmudic stories known as the *Mayse-Bukh*. The *Mayse-Bukh*, and then the *Tseno-Ureno* of Jabob ben Isaac Ashkenazi (1550?–1628), a rendition of the Pentateuch that became known as the "women's Bible," published in the 1590s, were the most widely read works in Yiddish until well into the nineteenth century. Other popular Yiddish publications were the allegorical fables and domestic prayers that were written by a variety of *hasidic* rabbis, particularly the tales of Rabbi Nakhman of Bratzlav (1772–1811) and the verse and prayers of Rabbi Levy Yitzchok of Berdichev (1740–1809). By the beginning of the nineteenth century, therefore, there was a foundation of Yiddish culture upon which later writers could build, but it was clearly non-secular. The Bible stories, ethical instruction, folk tales, and religious allegories that made up the bulk of Yiddish literature were distinctly Jewish, a literature that forced writers of the "golden age" to turn inward to folk sources if they wanted to draw upon their Yiddish literary tradition.

Although the increasing pressure for modernization that Russia experienced in the nineteenth century was the general impetus behind the flowering of Yiddish culture, the specific cause was the relaxation of censorship and other civil restrictions on Jews during the reign of Czar Alexander II from 1855 to 1881. With the freedom of the serfs and the liberal reforms that made cultural and political experimentation possible, Jewish writers began striking out in new directions. In the tradition of the *Haskalah,* some writers chose German, Polish, or Russian as vehicles for their new literary expressions; those steeped in religion often turned to the *loshon-koydesh* for their awakening interest in secular culture; and others, interested in widening the scope of their readership among Jews, published work in German written in Hebrew characters. Probably the best-known early effort to use the *mame-loshn* was Alexander Zeyderboym's (1816–1893) *Kol Mevaser,* a newspaper published from 1862 to 1871. Two years earlier he had experimented using a "quasi-Yiddish," German printed with Hebrew orthography, in his newspaper *Hamelits*, but with *Kol Mevaser*, all in Yiddish, he broke new ground and during the life of its run helped to establish some tentative standards for Yiddish grammar, orthography, and diction.

The adoption of Yiddish by serious writers of the Pale was not unopposed, for many well-known writers continued to argue that the *zhargon* was not sophisticated, that it was too uncultured for the fashioning of a successful literature. The Hebrew poet Y. L. Gordon, answering an invitation to submit his work to a Yiddish anthology, expressed the feelings of many Hebraists and cultural assimilations that decided the pretentions of Yiddish to be adequate for anything but folk stories and women's tales. "It is the badge of shame of the hounded wanderer," he wrote, "and I consider it the duty of every educated Jew to do what he can to see to it that it is gradually erased and vanishes from our midst." Gordon felt, furthermore, that the survival of Yiddish was "the most unfortunate phenomenon" of the Jewish people's "historical experience." Many of those who advocated social and political emancipation for Jews in the Pale, who shaped their hopes for Jewish culture on a western model, and who were opposed to religious orthodoxy, especially as it was represented by the *Hasidic* movement, agreed with Gordon's assessment. Even the Yiddishist Isaac Meyer Dik (1814–1893), a popular story teller from Vilna, recognized that *maskilim* would eventually abandon the *mame-loshn*. He considered Yiddish to be a "non-language," a "conglomeration" that had "gathered words and expressions from all languages like a beggar."[15]

The three most famous early champions of Yiddish, the writers who presided over its "golden age," were S. J. Abramovich, (1836–1917), known as Mendele Moykher Seforim, Solomon Rabinovich (1859–1916), known as Sholom Aleichem, and Y.L. Peretz (1852–1915). Able to write in Polish, well-versed in Hebrew, these three chose Yiddish for their mature writing because they felt that the *mame-loshn* was a liberating medium, a means both of reaching the widest possible audience and of utilizing the great panoply of folk material of Jews in the Pale that was best expressed in the vernacular. Although they were *maskilim,* Mendele, Sholom Aleichem, and Peretz responded to a need to express populist, romantic and nationalist ideals—not the trend toward acculturation that appeared to be the direction of most *maskilim.* As Jews who were consciously entering a world that was becoming increasingly modern, they looked backward to Yiddish folk material even as they looked forward to bringing Jewish culture of the Pale into the "enlightened," post-Emancipation, nineteenth century. Seizing the opportunity to find an audience among their co-religionists that would be far greater than those who could read Hebrew, Polish, or Russian, they appreciated—above all—the usefulness of the *zhargon* for reaching great numbers. Mendele Mokher Seforim explained that his "love for utility" overcame his "hollow pride." "Come what may," he wrote, "I will write in Yiddish, the cast-off daughter."[16]

While Mendele's career had been already launched before Sholom Aleichem and Peretz found their audiences, most historians of Yiddish literature agree that the "golden age" of Yiddish was inaugerated by the publication in 1888 and 1889 of Sholom Aleichem's *Yiddische Folks-Bibliotek,* the first significant modern publication entirely devoted to the *mame-loshen.* Gathering both established and new writers, many that heretofore had mainly used German, Polish, Russian, or Hebrew, Aleichem published an anthology of essays and stories that attempted to impart a literary authenticity to Yiddish literature, the notion that Yiddish could be used as a modern, sophisticated cultural medium. Although many established Jewish writers greeted the anthologies with hostility, either because they saw the use of Yiddish as a backwards step in terms of the *Haskalah,* or because they favored the use of their native languages, or Hebrew, for nationalistic reasons, the Yiddish writers recognized the usefulness of Yiddish for expressing what they conceived to be the heart of the common Jewish experience. According to Ruth R. Wisse, a contemporary literary critic of the "golden age" of Yiddish, the use of the *mame-loshn* by the early Yiddish writers gave them "the sizable artistic resources of a spoken vernacular."[17]

As the Russian empire ponderously entered the modern era, with a recalcitrance that made it appear to be one of the most backward of all European nations, Yiddish became extremely useful for expressing the newly awakening social and political aspirations of the Jewish people. The different branches of the Zionist movement within the Pale, as well as the artisans, trade unionists, socialists, and intellectuals that made up the Jewish Labor Bund of Russia and Poland, soon found Yiddish to be indispensable as a medium for spreading propaganda and for organizational efforts. Jewish assimilationists of varying political persuasions continued to condemn the *zhargon* as a backward tongue, but they could not deny its utility. Even Zionist extremists who advocated the use of Hebrew as a Jewish national language recognized that the language of the Ashkenazim was Yiddish—until that time when Jews were able to escape from their current settlement in eastern Europe. The results of the upsurge in national, social, and political advocacies, combined with the burgeoning "golden age" of Yiddish literature, was the rise of Yiddish publications in every format. In every *shtetl,* and in every metropolitan area within the Pale, one could find in the final decades of the nineteenth century and in the beginning of the twentieth, a tremendous number of pamphlets, newspapers, and journals, as well as fiction, poetry, and drama, written in Yiddish. Translations of classics and modern works appeared in Yiddish, and Jews within the Pale who did not have a secular education were able to read for the first time the works of Balzac and Dickens, of London and Twain.

During this "golden age," Yiddish literature went through a number of modes. The simple folk tales and morality tales of the *hasidic* masters were adapted by modern Yiddish writers, who soon invented their own style of ironic and realistic story-telling. The "classic" works of Mendele Mokher Seforim, Sholom Aleichem, and Y. L. Peretz were joined by a staggering avalanche of poetry, dramatic works, and political tracts that were written in a variety of literary styles. Yiddish literature passed through the phases that literatures throughout the world experienced as Jewish writers tried naturalism, imagism, and surrealism. Thirsty for more and better writing, Jews around the globe—from the center of the Jewish stage on New York's lower Second Avenue to the Jewish coffee shops of Warsaw, Vilna, and Berdichev—read and discussed the latest literary fashions. The Yiddish-reading public lionized their greatest writers, and when Peretz died in Poland and Sholom Aleichem in New York, estimated crowds of seventy-thousand mourners thronged their funerals. These giants of Yiddish literature were more than widely read writers—they were folk heroes of awesome dimensions, for their fiction and poetry in the *mame-loshon* caught the literary imagination of a generation. Their work was joined by the brilliant output of Sholem Asch, I. J. Singer, Abraham Reisen, and Joseph Opatashu, names that bring a spark of recognition to American and eastern European Jews who grew up before 1940, for these writers, and countless others, captured the attention of Yiddish readers on the two continents, the Jews of Cracow and the Jews of Odessa, the Jews of Brest-Litovsk and the Jews of New York's Lower East Side.

We started this introduction by admitting that Yiddish has fallen on hard times, and this is, we think, undeniable, yet it must also be said that the *mame-loshn* is a hardy tongue, as hardy as are the Jewish people themselves. In our popular American culture we continue to honor Sholom Aleichem through the world-wide popularity of *Fiddler on the Roof* and its hero, Tevye the Milkman. The famous YIVO Institute in New York maintains its huge archive of Yiddish material and continues to sponsor an extensive and ambitious research effort in Yiddish. The Workman's Circle, also in New York, continues its multi-faceted Yiddish programing, and one can still read the Jewish *Daily*

Forward. Jewish parents educate their children with Yiddish-related secular and religious material, like the well-known *Jewish Catalogue,* and just a few years ago the most popular course during the spring term at Tufts University was entitled "An Introduction to Yiddish Culture: From Shtetl to Suburbia."[18] Even the government of the United States has recently acknowledged the continuing significance of Yiddish. According to an article in the *New York Times,* the *mame-loshn* was named a language "worthy of credit at the Foreign Service Institute's highly demanding language school for State Department workers."[19] Fallen on hard times, yes, for Yiddish is strictly state-controlled in the Soviet Union and slowly losing more native speakers in America than it is gaining, but it is not dead, not, we hope, as this volume attests. In the words of Yiddish's Nobel prize laureate, "Yiddish has not yet said its last word." "It contains treasures that have not been revealed to the eyes of the world," said Isaac Bashevis Singer. "It was the tongue of martyrs and saints, of dreamers and cabalists—rich in humor and in memories that mankind may never forget. In a figurative way, Yiddish is the wise and humble language of us all, the idiom of the frightened and hopeful humanity."[20]

NOTES

1. Uriel Weinrich, "Yiddish Language," *Encyclopoedia Judaica,* Vol. 16 (1971), p. 790.

2. Isaac Bashevis Singer, "Text of the Nobel Lecture by Isaac Bashevis Singer," *New York Times,* December 9, 1978.

3. Max Weinreich, *History of the Yiddish Language,* trans. by Shlomo Noble, assisted by Joshua A. Fishman (1973), pp. 1–6, 328–346; see also Emanuel S. Goldsmith, *Architects of Yiddishism at the Beginning of the Twentieth Century: A Study in Jewish Cultural History* (1976), pp. 27–32, Max Weinreich, "Prehistory and Early History of Yiddish: Facts and Conceptual Framework," *The Field of Yiddish,* 1, ed. by Uriel Weinreich (1954), pp. 78f, and Yudel Mark, "The Yiddish Language: Its Cultural Impact," *American Jewish Historical Quarterly,* 59 (December, 1969): 202.

4. On the periodization of Yiddish, see M. Weinreich, *History of the Yiddish Language,* pp. 719–32; for a succinct description of the significant components of the Yiddish language, see U. Weinreich, "Yiddish Language," pp. 790f.

5. M. Weinreich, *History of the Yiddish Language,* pp. 315–320.

6. For a clear and concise explanation of this position, one held by most prominent Yiddish linguists, see Uriel Weinreich, "Yiddish Language," p. 790ff.

7. Solomon A. Birnbaum, *Yiddish: A Survey and a Grammar* (1979), pp. 50–51.

8. U. Weinreich, "Yiddish Language," p. 791.

9. *Ibid.*

10. Birnbaum, *Yiddish: A Survey and a Grammar,* pp. 14–15; Goldsmith, *Architects of Yiddishism at the Beginning of the Twentieth Century,* pp. 27–8; M. Weinreich, *History of the Yiddish Language,* pp. 45f.

11. The vast geographical area in which Yiddish has been and currently is being spoken, as well as the broad and intricate multi-lingual antecedents that serve as source material for Yiddish, make the problem of Yiddish dialects an extremely complex problem. Solomon A. Birnbaum, in *Yiddish,* offers a brief introduction to Yiddish dialects, pp. 94–105.

12. The history of Jewish life in the Pale has been studied by a growing number of historians in the past half-century. Unfortunately much of the historical work has been done in Yiddish, which has made it less accessible to modern American readers. The classic work on this subject is the multi-volume history by S. M. Dubnow, *History of the Jews in Russia and Poland from the Earliest Times until the Present Day,* translated by I. Friedlander (1920). Other useful works are *Russian Jewry: 1860–1917,* edited by J. Frumkin, a collection of essays in two volumes; *The Golden Tradition: Jewish Life and Thought in Eastern Europe,* edited by Lucy S. Dawidowicz (1967), a collection of essays that includes an excellent introduction by the editor; and *Class Struggle in the Pale* by Ezra Mendlesohn (1970).

13. Moses Mendelssohn, *Mendelssohns Schriften* (Leipzig, 1844), p. 5, quoted in Goldsmith, *Architects of Yiddishism,* p. 36. (Translations of sources quoted in this book are by Goldsmith unless otherwise noted.)

14. S. M. Dubnow, *History of the Jews in Russia and Poland,* Vol. 3, pp. 58–65.

15. I. M. Dik, *Di Eydele Rakhe* (Vilna, 1875), p. 19, quoted in Goldsmith, *Architects of Yiddishism,* p. 42.

16. Mendele Mokher Seforim, "Shtrikhn tsu Mayn Biografye," *Ale Verk,* 19 (Warsaw, 1928), p. 164f, translated by Gerald Stillman in Mendele Mocher Seforim, *The Parasite* (1945), pp. 10–11.

17. Ruth R. Wisse, ed., *A Stetl and Other Yiddish Novellas* (1973), p. 3.

18. Sol Gittleman reported the Tufts University class enrollment in *Yiddish,* 2 (1976): 114.

19. Francis X. Clines and Warren Weaver Jr., "Credit for Yiddish," *New York Times,* April 14, 1982.

20. Isaac Bashevis Singer, "Text of the Nobel Lecture by Isaac Bashevis Singer."

User's Note

We present this work as an introductory guide to the Yiddish language for the use of the English-speaking public. It is our hope that it will serve both as a reference tool for students and as an introduction for casual readers to a significant part of the cultural heritage of the Jewish people. We have tried to present Yiddish with all its *tam,* its flavor, so that our better than eight-thousand entries—words, popular expressions, idioms, and proverbs—will constitute a full representation of this rich and fascinating linguistic legacy.

Our work is unique, for nowhere can one find such an extensive listing of *transliterated* Yiddish. We have compiled a list of common words and expressions that includes (1) the English transliterations of the Yiddish; (2) the English equivalents of the Yiddish entries; (3) the phonetic renderings of the Yiddish pronunciation; and (4) the spelling of each entry in Yiddish using the appropriate Hebrew characters.

There is, unfortunately, too little about the definitions, spellings, and pronunciations of Yiddish words that can legitimately be called "standard." Notwithstanding the example of the YIVO Institute of New York, the leading establishment in the world for the study of Yiddish culture, scholars have long disagreed even about the most basic elements in Yiddish. The *Encyclopoedia Britannica* (Vol. II, 1959), for example, lists an alphabet of thirty-four characters, while other sources on the Yiddish language mention forty, forty-two, and forty-four characters in their Yiddish alphabets.

Given the lack of agreement, even among well-known Yiddishists, we have tried to follow a middle course. In places we have compromised, especially where common sense and the dictates of everyday usage have directed us to do so. For instances, we have chosen to transliterate the suffix *ayt* in words such as *krankayt* (illness), *sheynkayt* (beauty), and *frayhayt* (freedom) according to the style suggested by YIVO. In our pronunciation scheme for these words, however, we suggest that they be pronounced with an *eit* ending—a sound that rhymes with the English word "light." We agree with the cultural historian Irving Howe who commented in *The World of Our Fathers,* a study written largely from Yiddish sources, that "concessions to customary usage" should be made, that most Americans familiar with Yiddish would be more comfortable with the sound of *eit.*

17

We have attempted, moreover, to offer "standard" definitions while, at the same time, realizing that Yiddish speakers—or their descendants—from different parts of western or eastern Europe might disagree on the exact meaning or connotation of a word or phrase. Where confusion might arise, we have provided alternative meanings, and in some places specifying (with abbreviations) the context in which the entry is most likely to be used.

Not all words and phrases on the Yiddish-English side of the dictionary are cross-listed, for some Yiddish words simply do not allow for direct equivalents in English. We have, for example, listed *kishke* in Yiddish and offered "intestine" as a translation on both sides of the dictionary, but the alternative definition, "stuffed derma," can only be found on the Yiddish-English side. We felt it more likely that this dictionary would be used to look up the meaning and pronunciation of *kishke* than to find an equivalent in Yiddish for "stuffed derma."

We hope that this dictionary sourcebook becomes a useful reference took for everyone interested in Jewish culture and the Yiddish language. Yiddish provides all Jews with a rich social, religious, and intellectual legacy, a legacy that will always be deep within the heart and the history of a large part of the Jewish people.

YIDDISH PRONUNCIATION KEY

Printed Letter or Combination	*Script*	*Name*	*English translitera tion*	*English Sound Equivalent*	*English Example*
א	א	*shtumer alef*	none	silent	
אַ	אַ	*pasekh alef*	a	ah	f*a*ther
אָ	אָ	*komets alef*	o	aw	p*aw*
בּ	בּ	*beyz*	b	b	*b*oy
בֿ	בֿ	*veyz*	v	v	*v*ery
ג	ג	*giml*	g	g	*g*rey
ד	ד	*daled*	d	d	*d*ove
דזש	דזש	*daled-zayen-shin*	j	j	*j*azz
ה	ה	*hey*	h	h	*h*ot
ו	ו	*vov*	u	oo	b*oo*t
וּ	וּ	*melupm vov*	u	oo	b*oo*t
וו	וו	*tsvey vovn*	v	v	*v*ery
וי	וי	*vov yud*	oy	oy	t*oy*
ז	ז	*zayen*	z	z	ha*z*e
זש	זש	*zayen shin*	zh	zh	mea*s*ure
ח	ח	*khes*	kh	German *ach* Scottish lo*ch*	a*ch*-German o*ch*-Scottish
ט	ט	*tes*	t	t	*t*able
טש	טש	*tes shin*	ch	ch	tou*ch*
י	י	*yud*	i ee y	i ee y	t*i*n b*ee* *y*es
יִ	יִ	*khirek yud*	i	ee	b*ee*
ײ	ײ	*tsvey yudn*	ey	ay	h*ay*
ײַ	ײַ	*pasekh tsvey yudn*	ay	ei	st*ei*n

כ	ɔ	kof	k	k	*k*iss
כ	ɔ	khof	kh	German a*ch*	a*ch*-German
ך Final form	ʃ	langer khof	kh	Scottish lo*ch*	o*ch*-Scottish
ל	ʃ	lamed	l	l	*l*ove
מ	א	mem	m	m	*m*ist
ם Final form	ם	shlos-mem			
נ	⌐	nun	n	n	*n*o
ן Final form	I	langer nun			
ס	o	samekh	s	s	*s*o
ע	४	ayen	e	e	b*e*d
פ	ə̱	pey	p	p	*p*ill
פ̄	ō̱	fey	f	f	*f*ive
ף Final form	ʃ	langer fey			
צ	3	tsadek	ts	ts	ca*ts*
ץ Final form	ʃ	langer tsadek			
ק	ρ	kuf	k	k	*k*iss
ר	ɔ	reysh	r	r produced by trilling the tip of the tongue	*r*oad
ש	e˙	shin	sh	sh	*sh*oe
ש	e̊	sin	s	s	*s*o
ת	♫	tof	t	t	*t*able
ת	♫	sof	s	s	*s*uch

YIDDISH GRAMMAR

NOUNS

Nouns in Yiddish are either masculine, feminine, or neuter. The definite articles and adjectives must agree in gender and case:

Nominative

der zun	(the son)	=	masculine
di tokhter	(the daughter)	=	feminine
dos gesheft	(the business)	=	neuter

The definite article for all plural nouns is *di*.

di groyse aeroplanen   the large airplanes

The indefinite article scarcely changes. Before words that begin with consonants, the indefinite article is *a,* and before words that begin with vowels, it is *an.* Gender has no effect on indefinite articles.

a ponim	=	a face	*an ey*	=	an egg
a tate	=	a father	*an ort*	=	a place
a mame	=	a mother	*an epl*	=	an apple

Unfortunately plural endings of nouns are more complex than their counterparts in English. In essence, one must learn the plural ending as well as the gender of each noun. Here is a list that reflects most of the different possible endings. Because Yiddish has drawn upon so many other languages over the centuries, one will inevitably find irregularities and exceptions:

21

English	Yiddish Singular	Yiddish Plural	Change
pen	di feder	de feders	s is added
porch	der ganik	di ganikes	es is added
generation	der dor	di doyres	es is added*
bone	der beyn	di beyner	er is added
tongue	di tsung	di tsinger	er is added*
student	der talmid	di talmidim	im is added
friend	der khaver	di khaveyrim	im is added**
girl	di meydl	di meydlekh	ekh is added
menu	der menyu	di menyuen	en is added
eye	dos oyg	di oygn	n is added
scholar	der gelernter	di gelernte	r is dropped
apple	der epl	di epl	No change
head	der kop	di kep	Vowel change

* In addition to the ending a vowel is changed.
** In addition to the ending, both the stem and the vowel are changed.

The case endings of nouns do not present a problem, for most nouns in Yiddish only have two forms, one for the possessive and another for all the other cases. The possessive ending, for both singular and plural nouns, is simply an s.

A few Yiddish nouns, however, are exceptions and take special case endings. Here are a few examples:

Nominative:	tate	father	zeyde	grandfather
Possessive:	tatns	father's	zeydns	grandfather's
Accusative:	tatn	father	zeydn	grandfather
Dative:	tatn	father	zeydn	grandfather

PRONOUNS

As in English, the forms of the pronouns are variable:

Personal Pronouns: Nominative

	Singular		Plural
I	*ikh*	we	*mir*
you (familiar)	*du*	you	*ir*
you (formal)	*ir*	you	*ir*
he	*er*	they	*zey*
she	*zi*		
it	*es*		

Personal Pronouns: Accusative

me	*mikh*	us	*undz*
you	*dikh*	you	*aykh*
him	*im*	them	*zey*
her	*zi*		
it	*es*		

Personal Pronouns: Dative

me	*mir*	us	*undz*
you	*dir*	you	*aykh*
him	*im*	they	*zey*
her	*ir*		
it	*im*		

Personal Pronouns: Possessive

my	*mayn*	our	*undzer*
your	*dayn*	your	*ayer*
his	*zayn*	their	*zeyer*
her	*ir*		
its	*zayn*		

Interrogative Pronouns

who	*ver*	whom	*vemen*
whose	*vemens*	what	*vor*

Demonstrative Pronouns

this	*dos*	these	*di*
that	*yens*	those	*di*

Reflexive Pronouns

myself, herself, himself	*zikh*

Relative Pronouns

who	*vos*
which	*vos, velkher*
that	*vos*
whose	*vemes*
whom	*vos, vemen*

ADJECTIVES

Adjectives in Yiddish agree in gender, number, and case with the nouns that they modify. The only exception to note is the neuter singular, for here the adjective ending depends upon the presence or absence of the definite article. If there is a definite article preceding the adjective, then the adjective takes an ending. When the definite article is absent, then the adjective does not take an ending:

dos gute vort   the good word   *a gut vort*   a good word

Note also that the adjective ending when modifying a plural noun is always *e*.

Comparative adjectives take the endings *er* and *st*:

shver   heavy   *shverer*   heavier   *shverst*   heaviest

In addition to these simple endings, some adjectives in Yiddish also go through a vowel change in their comparative forms. Here are a few common examples:

kalt	cold	*kelter*	colder	*kelst*	coldest
groys	large	*greser*	larger	*grest*	largest
alt	old	*elter*	older	*eltst*	oldest
kleyn	small	*klener*	smaller	*klenst*	smallest
yung	young	*yinger*	younger	*yingst*	youngest

ADVERBS

Most adverbs are formed by the root of the adjective. There are also the usual adverbs of place and time:

vu	where	*do*	here	*dortn*	there
vuhin	where to	*aher*	to here	*ahin*	to there
ven	when	*a mol*	sometime	*keyn mol nit*	never

Adverbs of number are formed by adding the suffix *ns* to the number. Here are a few examples:

ersht	first	*ershtns*	firstly
tsveyt	second	*tsveytns*	secondly
drit	third	*dritns*	thirdly

VERBS

Most of the verb forms in the wordlist appear as transliterated infinitives. They end in either *-n* or *en*. The *-n* ending is more common. One usually finds the *en* suffix added to verb roots ending in *m, n,* (syllabic) *l, y, ng, nk,* vowels, or dipthongs.

Some are listed in their participial form, usually the past participle. This verb form is generally constructed by either adding the prefix *ge* and the suffix *t,* or by simply adding the suffix *en* or *n.*

The following examples demonstrate how some basic verb forms are constructed in Yiddish. Needless to say, it is far from exhaustive and therefore the interested student may consult a Yiddish grammar in order to appreciate the variety and complexity of Yiddish verb forms.

Present Tense

I say	*ikh zog*	We say	mir zogn
You say	*du zogst*	You say	ir zogt
He says	*er zogt*	They say	zey zogn
She says	*zi zogt*		
It says	*es zogt*		

Past Tense

I said	*ikh hob gezogt*	We said	mir hobn gezogt
You said	*du host gezogt*	You said	ir hot gezogt
She said	*zi hot gezogt*	They said	zey hobn gezogt
He said	*er hot gezogt*		
It said	*es hot gezogt*		

I came	*ikh bin gekumen*	We came	mir zaynen gekumen
You came	*du bist gekumen*	You came	ir zayt gekumen
He came	*er is gekumen*	They came	zey zaynen gekumen
She came	*zi iz gekumen*		
It came	*es iz gekumen*		

Future Tense

The future tense is formed by using the future forms of the auxillary verb *veln:*

I say	*ikh vel zogn*	We will say	mir veln zogn
You say	*du vest zogn*	You will say	ir vet zogn
She will say	*zi vet zogn*	They will say	zey veln zogn
He will say	*er vet zogn*		
It will say	*es vet zogn*		

NUMBERS AND THE CALENDAR

(The following calendar terms are all masculine, but in ordinary conversation the definite article is not used.)

DAYS OF THE WEEK

Sunday	zuntik	*zoon*-tik	זונטיק
Monday	montik	*mawn*-tik	מאָנטיק
Tuesday	dinstik	*deen*-stik	דינסטיק
Wednesday	mitvokh	*meet*-vawkh	מיטוואָך
Thursday	donershtik	*daw*-nehrsh-tik	דאָנערשטיק
Friday	fraytik	*frei*-tik	פֿרײַטיק
Saturday	shabes	*shah*-behs	שבת

MONTHS OF THE YEAR (English)

January	yanuar	*yah*-noo-ahr	יאַנואַר
February	februar	*fehb*-roo-ahr	פֿעברואַר
March	marts	mahrts	מאַרץ
April	april	ahp-*reel*	אַפּריל
May	may	mei	מײַ
June	yuni	*yoo*-nee	יוני
July	yuli	*yoo*-lee	יולי
August	oygust	oy-*goost*	אויגוסט
September	september	sehp-*tehm*-behr	סעפּטעמבער
October	oktober	awk-*taw*-behr	אָקטאָבער
November	november	naw-*vehm*-behr	נאָוועמבער
December	detsember	deh-*tsehm*-behr	דעצעמבער

MONTHS OF THE YEAR (Hebrew)

tishre	*tish*-reh	September-October	תּישרי
kheshvn	*khezh*-vn	October-November	חשוון
kislev	*kis*-lehv	November-December	כּיסלו
teyves	*tay*-vehs	December-January	טבֿת
shvat	sh-*vaht*	January-February	שבֿט
oder	*aw*-dehr	February-March	אָדר
nisn	*nis*-n	March-April	ניסן
iyer	*ee*-yehr	April-May	אײר
sivn	*siv*-n	May-June	סיוון
tamez	*tah*-mehz	June-July	תּמוז
ov	*awv*	July-August	אָבֿ
elul	*eh*-lool	August-September	אלול

Note: In a leap year the Hebrew calendar has two months called Oder: Oder Aleph and Oder Beyz.

SEASONS

Spring	friling	*free*-ling	פֿרילינג
Summer	zumer	*zoo*-mehr	זומער
Autumn	harbst	hahrbst	האַרבסט
Winter	vinter	*veen*-tehr	ווינטער

CARDINAL NUMBERS

one	eyns	ayns	אײנס
two	tsvey	tsvay	צוויי
three	dray	drei	דרײַ
four	fir	feer	פֿיר
five	finf	feenf	פֿינף
six	zeks	zehks	זעקס
seven	zibn	*zeeb*-n	זיבן
eight	akht	ahkht	אַכט
nine	nayn	nein	נײַן
ten	tsen	tsehn	צען

eleven	elf	ehlf	עלף
twelve	tsvelf	tsvehlf	צוועלף
thirteen	draytsn	*dreits*-n	דרײַצן
fourteen	fertsn	*fehrts*-n	פֿערצן
fifteen	fuftsn	*foof*-tsin	פופֿצן
sixteen	zekhtsn	*zehkhts*-n	זעכצן
seventeen	zibetsn	*zee*-behts-n	זיבעצן
eighteen	akhtsn	*ahkhts*-n	אַכצן
nineteen	nayntsn	*neints*-n	נײַנצן
twenty	tsvantsik	*tsvahn*-tsik	צוואַנציק
twenty-one	eyn un tsvantsik	*ayn*-oon-*tsvahn*-tsik	אײן און צוואַנציק
twenty-two	tsvey un tsvantsik	*tsvay*-oon-*tsvahn*-tsik	צוויי און צוואַנציק
thirty	draysik	*drei*-sik	דרײַסיק
forty	fertsik	*fehr*-tsik	פֿערציק
fifty	fuftsik	*foof*-tsik	פופֿציק
sixty	zekhtsik	*zehkh*-tsik	זעכציק
seventy	zibetsik	*zee*-beh-tsik	זיבעציק
eighty	akhtsik	*ahkh*-tsik	אַכציק
ninety	nayntsik	*nein*-tsik	נײַנציק
one hundred	hundert	*hoon*-dehrt	הונדערט
two hundred	tsvey hundert	tsvay-*hoon*-dehrt	צוויי הונדערט
one thousand	toyznt	*toy*-zint	טויזנט
two thousand	tsvey toyznt	tsvay *toy*-zint	צוויי טויזנט
one million	milyon	mil-*yawn*	מיליאָן
two million	tsvey milyon	tsvay mil-*yawn*	צוויי מיליאָן
one billion	bilyon	bil-*yawn*	ביליאָן
two billion	tsvey bilyon	tsvay bil-*yawn*	צוויי ביליאָן

ORDINAL NUMBERS

first	ershter	*ehr*-shtehr	ערשטער
second	tsveyter	*tsvay*-tehr	צווייטער
third	driter	*dree*-tehr	דריטער
fourth	ferter	*fehr*-tehr	פֿערטער

fifth	finfter	*feenf*-tehr	פינפטער
sixth	zekster	*zehks*-tehr	זעקסטער
seventh	zibeter	*zee*-beh-tehr	זיבעטער
eighth	akhter	*ahkh*-tehr	אַכטער
ninth	naynter	*nein*-tehr	נײַנטער
tenth	tsenter	*tsehn*-tehr	צענטער
eleventh	elfter	*ehlf*-tehr	עלפטער
twelftth	tsvelfter	*tsvehlf*-tehr	צוועלפטער

ENGLISH-YIDDISH DICTIONARY

a	a	ah	אַ
abandon, to	avekvarfn	ah-*vehk*-vahrf-n	אַוועקוואַרפֿן
	oplozn	*awp*-lawz-n	אָפּלאָזן
abandoned wife	di agune	ah-*goo*-neh	די עגונה
abdomen	der boykh	boykh	דער בויך
abide, to	blaybn	*bleib*-n	בלײַבן
ability	di feikayt	*feh*-ee-keit	די פֿעיִקייט
able (adj.)	feik	*feh*-ik	פֿעיִק
about (concerning)	vegn	*vehg*-n	וועגן
above (prep.)	iber	*ee*-behr	איבער
	hekher	*heh*-khehr	העכער
above (adv.)	oybn	*oyb*-n	אויבן
abroad	in oysland	in *oyss*-lahnd	אין אויסלאַנד
absent	felndik	*feh*-lin-dik	פֿעלנדיק
absorbed (in thought)	farklert	fahr-*klehrt*	פֿאַרקלערט
abundant	shefedik	*sheh*-feh-dik	שפֿעדיק
accent (stress)	der trop	trawp	דער טראָפּ
accent (speech)	der aktsent	ahk-*tsehnt*	דער אַקצענט
accident (mishap)	dos umglik	*oom*-gleek	דאָס אומגליק
accident (chance)	der tsufal	*tsoo*-fahl	דער צופֿאַל
accord	der heskem	*hehs*-kehm	דער הסכּם
account (calculation)	der khezhbn	*khehzh*-bn	דער חשבון
accountant	der khezhbn-firer	*khehzh*-bn-*fee*-rehr	דער חשבון־פֿירער
accurate	pinktlekh	*peenkt*-lehkh	פּינקטלעך
accusation	di bashuldikung	bah-*shool*-dee-koong	די באַשולדיקונג
accuse, to	bashuldikn	bah-*shool*-deek-n	באַשולדיקן
ache, to	vey ton	*vay* tawn	וויי טאָן
ache	der veytik	*vay*-tik	דער ווייטיק
acknowledge, to	bashtetikn	bah-*shteh*-teek-n	באַשטעטיקן
acquaintance	der bakanter	bah-*kahn*-tehr	דער באַקאַנטער
acquire, to	krign	*kreeg*-n	קריגן
across	ariber	ah-*ree*-behr	אַריבער
act, to	handlen	*hahnd*-lehn	האַנדלען
act, to (perform)	shpiln	*shpeel*-n	שפּילן
act, to (behave)	firn zikh	*feer*-n zikh	פֿירן זיך

act (deed)	di tuung	*too*-oong	די טוּונג
active	aktiv	ahk-*teev*	אַקטיוו
actor	der aktyor	ahk-*tyawr*	דער אַקטיאָר
actress	di aktrise	ahk-*tree*-seh	די אַקטריסע
actual	faktish	*fahk*-tish	פֿאַקטיש
adequate, to be	toygn	*toyg*-n	טויגן
address	der adres	*ah*-drehs	דער אַדרעס
admit, to (confess)	moyde zayn	*moy*-deh zein	מודה זײַן
admit, to (allow in)	araynlozn	ah-*rein*-lawz-n	אַרײַנלאָזן
adorable	tayer	*tei*-ehr	טײַער
adorn, to	batsirn	bah-*tseer*-n	באַצירן
adult (adj.)	dervaksn	dehr-*vahks*-n	דערוואַקסן
adult	der dervaksener	dehr-*vahk*-sehn-er	דער דערוואַקסענער
adultery	der nief	*nee*-if	דער ניאוף
advantage	di mayle	*mei*-leh	די מעלה
advice	di eytse	*ay*-tseh	די עצה
advise, to	eytsn	*ay*-tsehn	עצהן
advocate, to	shtitsn	*shteets*-n	שטיצן
affair (matter)	der inyen	*een*-yihn	דער ענין
affection	di libshaft	*leeb*-shahft	די ליבשאַפֿט
affectionate	varem	*vah*-rehm	וואַרעם
	liblekh	*leeb*-lehkh	ליבלעך
afford, to	farginen zikh	fahr-*gee*-nehn-zikh	פֿאַרגינען זיך
afraid	dershrokn	dehr-*shrawk*-n	דערשראָקן
afternoon	der nokhmitog	nawkh-*mee*-tawg	דער נאָכמיטאָג
after (prep.)	nokh	nawkh	נאָך
afterwards	dernokhdem	dehr-*nawkh*-dehm	דערנאָכדעם
again	vider	*vee*-dehr	ווידער
against	(a)kegn	(ah)*kehg*-n	(אַ)קעגן
agony	di yesurim	yih-*soo*-rim	די יסורים
agree, to	maskim zayn	*mahss*-kim zein	מסכים זײַן
agreement	der heskem	*hehs*-kehm	דער הסכם
aid, to	helfn	*hehlf*-n	העלפֿן
aim	der tsil	tseel	דער ציל
air	di luft	looft	די לופֿט
air conditioning	di luftkilung	*looft*-kee-loong	די לופֿטקילונג
air mail	di luftpost	*looft*-pawst	די לופֿטפּאָסט
airplane	der aeroplan	ah-eh-raw-*plahn*	דער אַעראָפּלאַן
airport	der fliplats	*flee*-plahts	דער פֿליפּלאַץ
alarm (fear)	di shrek	shrehk	די שרעק

alike	enlekh	ehn-*lehkh*	ענלעך
alive	lebedik	*leh*-beh-dik	לעבעדיק
all	gants	gahnts	גאַנץ
all (every)	ale	*ah*-leh	אַלע
all (everything)	alts	ahlts	אַלץ
all (entirely)	in gantsn	in *gahnts*-n	אין גאַנצן
allergy	di alergye	ah-*lehrg*-yeh	די אַלערגיע
allow,to	derloybn	dehr-*loyb*-n	דערלויבן
ally	der aliirter	ah-lee-*eer*-tehr	דער אַלייִרטער
Almighty, the	der eybershter	*ay*-behr-shtehr	דער אייבערשטער
almond	der mandl	*mahnd*-l	דער מאַנדל
almond bread	dos mandlbroyt	*mahnd*-l-broyt	דאָס מאַנדלברויט
almost	kimat	kee-*maht*	כמעט
alone	aleyn	ah-*layn*	אַליין
aloud	oyfn kol	*oyf*-n kawl	אויפֿן קול
already	shoyn	shoyn	שוין
also	oykh	oykh	אויך
alter, to	iberbaytn	*ee*-behr-beit-n	איבערבײַטן
although	khotsh	khawch	כאָטש
	hagam	hah-*gahm*	הגם
altogether	in gantsn	in *gahnts*-n	אין גאַנצן
always	ale mol	*ah*-leh-mawl	אַלע מאָל
	tomid	*taw*-mid	תּמיד
	shtendik	*shtehn*-dik	שטענדיק
am (first person sing.)	bin	been	בין
amazed	dershtoynt	der-*shtoint*	דערשטוינט
ambition	di ambitsye	ahm-*beets*-yeh	די אַמביציע
ambitious	ambitsyez	ahm-beets-*yehz*	אַמביציעז
ambulance	der ambulans	ahm-boo-*lahnss*	דער אַמבולאַנס
America	di amerike	ah-*meh*-ree-keh	די אַמעריקע
American	amerikanish	ah-meh-ree-*kah*-nish	אַמעריקאַניש
among	tsvishn	*tsveesh*-n	צווישן
amount to, to (monetarily)	batrefn	bah-*trehf*-n	באַטרעפֿן
amusement	di farvaylung	fahr-*vei*-loong	די פֿאַרווײַלונג
an	an	ahn	אַן
analyze, to	funanderklaybn	foo-*nahn*-dehr-kleib-n	פֿונאַנדערקלײַבן
ancestors	di oves	*aw*-vehs	די אבֿות
ancient	fartsaytik	fahr-*tsei*-tik	פֿאַרצײַטיק
and	un	oon	און

angel	der malakh	*mah*-lahkh	דער מלאך
angel of death	der malakh-amoves	*mah*-lahkh-ah-*maw*-vehs	דער מלאך־המוות
anger	der kaas	kahss	דער כּעס
angle	der vinkl	*veenk*-l	דער ווינקל
angry	broygez	*broy*-gehz	ברוגז
	beyz	bayz	בייז
anguish	di payn	pein	די פּײַן
animal	di khaye	*khah*-yeh	די חיה
ankle	dos knekhl	k-*nehkh*-l	דאָס קנעכל
anniversary	der yortog	*yawr*-tawg	דער יאָרטאָג
announce, to	onzogn	*awn*-zawg-n	אָנזאָגן
annoy, to	tshepen zikh tsu	*cheh*-pehn zikh tsoo	טשעפּען זיך צו
annual	yerlekh	*yehr*-lehkh	יערלעך
annuity	dos yorgelt	*yawr*-gehlt	דאָס יאָרגעלט
another	an ander	ahn *ahn*-dehr	אן אַנדער
another (one more)	nokh a	*nawkh* ah	נאָך אַ
answer, to	entfern	*ehnt*-fehr-n	ענטפערן
ant	di murashke	moo-*rahsh*-keh	די מוראַשקע
antibiotic	der antibiotik	ahn-tee-bee-*aw*-tik	דער אַנטיביאָטיק
anticipate, to	rikhtn zikh oyf	*rikht*-n zikh oyf	ריכטן זיך אויף
antique	der antik	ahn-*teek*	דער אַנטיק
anxiety	di umru	*oom*-roo	די אומרו
anxious	umruik	oom-*roo*-ik	אומרויִק
any (whatever)	abi velkher	ah-*bee vehl*-khehr	אַבי וועלכער
anybody, anyone	ver es iz	*vehr* ehs eez	ווער עס איז
anybody (anybody whosoever)	abi ver	ah-*bee* vehr	אַבי ווער
anything (anything whatever)	abi vos	ah-*bee* vawss	אַבי וואָס
anything (some thing)	vos es iz	*vawss* ehs eez	וואָס עס איז
anyway	say vi say	*sei* vee *sei*	סײַ ווי סײַ
anywhere	vu es iz	*voo* ehs eez	ווּ עס איז
apart	bazunder	bah-*zoon*-dehr	באַזונדער
apartment	di dire	*dee*-reh	די דירה
apologize, to	betn mekhile	*beht*-n meh-*khee*-leh	בעטן מחילה
apostate (Jewish)	der meshumed	meh-*shoo*-mehd	דער משומד
appalling	groylik	*groy*-lik	גרויליק
apparatus	der aparat	ah-pah-*raht*	דער אַפּאַראַט
appeal, to	apelirn	ah-peh-*leer*-n	אַפּעלירן

appear, to (in view)	bavayzn zikh	bah-*veiz*-n zikh	באַווײַזן זיך
appetite	der apetit	ah-peh-*teet*	דער אַפּעטיט
appetizer	der forshpayz	*fawr*-shpeiz	דער פֿאָרשפּײַז
apple	der epl	*eh*-pil	דער עפּל
applesauce	der epl-tsimes	*eh*-pil-tsee-mehs	דער עפּל־צימעס
apply, to (be fitting)	pasn	*pahs*-n	פּאַסן
appreciate, to	opshatsn	*awp*-shahts-n	אָפּשאַצן
approval	di haskome	hahss-*kaw*-meh	די הסכּמה
approve, to	haltn fun	*hahlt*-n foon	האַלטן פֿון
apricot	der aprikos	ahp-ree-*kawss*	דער אַפּריקאָס
April	der april	ahp-*reel*	דער אַפּריל
apron	der fartekh	*fahr*-tehkh	דער פֿאַרטעך
architect	der arkhitekt	ahr-khee-*tehkt*	דער אַרכיטעקט
are (2nd person sing.)	bist	beest	ביסט
area (region)	di gegnt	*geh*-gint	די געגנט
argue, to	taynen	*tei*-nehn	טענהן
arm (anat.)	der orem	*aw*-rehm	דער אָרעם
army	di armey	ahr-*may*	די אַרמיי
around	arum	ah-*room*	אַרום
arrange, to	aynordenen	*ein*-awr-deh-nehn	אײַנאָרדענען
arrest, to	arestirn	ah-rehs-*teer*-n	אַרעסטירן
arrive, to	onkumen	*awn*-koo-mehn	אָנקומען
arrogance	dos gadles	*gahd*-lehs	דאָס גדלות
art	di kunst	koonst	די קונסט
artery (anat.)	di arterye	ahr-*tehr*-yeh	די אַרטעריע
arthritis	der artrit	ahr-*treet*	דער אַרטריט
article (object)	der kheyfets	*khay*-fehts	דער חפֿץ
artificial	kinstlekh	*keenst*-lehkh	קינסטלעך
artisan	der bal-melokhe	bahl-meh-*law*-kheh	דער בעל־מלאכה
artist	der kinstler	*keenst*-lehr	דער קינסטלער
as (conj.)	beshas	beh-*shahss*	בשעת
as (prep.)	vi	vee	ווי
as (in the same way)	azoy vi	ah-*zoy*-vee	אַזוי ווי
as long as	abi	ah-*bee*	אַבי
	kol-zman	*kawl*-zmahn	כּל־זמן
ascend, to	shtaygn	*shteig*-n	שטײַגן
ash tray	dos ashtetsl	*ahsh*-teh-tsil	דאָס אַשטעצל
ashamed	farshemt	fahr-*shehmt*	פֿאַרשעמט

ask, to (inquire)	fregn	*frehg*-n	פֿרעגן
ask for, to (request)	betn	*beht*-n	בעטן
asparagus	di sparzhe	*spahr*-zheh	די ספֿאַרזשע
aspirin	di aspirin	ahss-pee-*reen*	די אַספּירין
assault, to	bafaln	bah-*fahl*-n	באַפֿאַלן
assembly	di farzamlung	fahr-*zahm*-loong	די פֿאַרזאַמלונג
assistance	di hilf	heelf	די הילף
association	der farband	fahr-*bahnd*	דער פֿאַרבאַנד
assure, to	farzikhern	fahr-*zee*-khehr-n	פֿאַרזיכערן
astonishment (object of)	der khidesh	*khee*-dehsh	דער חידוש
at (near)	lebn	*lehb*-n	לעבן
at (time)	in	in	אין
	tsu	tsoo	צו
at (place)	bay	bei	ביַי
at (occasion)	oyf	oyf	אויף
atom	der atom	*ah*-tawm	דער אַטאָם
atomic bomb	di atomishe bombe	ah-*taw*-mee-sheh *bawm*-beh	די אַטאָמישע באָמבע
attack, to	bafaln	bah-*fahl*-n	באַפֿאַלן
attempt, to	pruvn	*proov*-n	פּרוּוון
attic	der boydem	*boy*-dehm	דער בוידעם
attire	di kleyder	*klay*-der	די קליידער
attorney	der advokat	ahd-vaw-*kaht*	דער אַדוואָקאַט
attract, to	tsutsien	*tsoo*-tsee-en	צוציִען
audience	der oylem	*oy*-lehm	דער עולם
auditorium	der zal	zahl	דער זאַל
August	der oygust	oy-*goost*	דער אויגוסט
aunt	di mume	*moo*-meh	די מומע
	di tante	*tahn*-teh	די טאַנטע
author	der mekhaber	meh-*khah*-behr	דער מחבר
automobile	der oytomobile	oy-taw-maw-*beel*	דער אויטאָמאָביל
autumn	der harbst	hahrbst	דער האַרבסט
available	faranen	fah-*rah*-nehn	פֿאַראַנען
avenue	di evenyu	*eh*-veh-noo	די עוועניו
avert, to	farhitn	fahr-*heet*-n	פֿאַרהיטן
	oysmaydn	*oyss*-meid-n	אויסמיַידן
aviator	der flier	*flee*-ehr	דער פֿליִער
await, to	dervartn	dehr-*vahrt*-n	דערוואַרטן
awaken, to	oyfvekn	*oyf*-vehk-n	אויפֿוועקן

awareness	di visikayt	*vee*-see-keit	די וויסיקייט
away (absent)	nito	nee-*taw*	ניטאָ
away (from a place)	avek	ah-*vehk*	אַוועק
awe	der yires-hakoved	*yee*-rehss-hah-*kaw*-vihd	דער יראת־הכּבוד
awful	shreklekh	*shrehk*-lehkh	שרעקלעך
awhile	a vayle	ah *vei*-leh	אַ ווײַלע
awkward	umgelumpert	*oom*-geh-*loom*-pehrt	אומגעלומפּערט
axe	di hak	hahk	די האַק

baby	beybi	*bey*-bee	דער בייבי
bachelor	der bokher	*baw*-khehr	דער בחור
back	tsurik	tsoo-*reek*	צוריק
back (anat.)	der rukn	*rook*-n	דער רוקן
backward	oyf tsurik	oyf tsoo-*reek*	אויף צוריק
bacon	der beykon	*bay*-kawn	דער בייקאָן
bad	shlekht	shlehkht	שלעכט
bag (purse)	di tash	tahsh	די טאַש
baggage	der bagazh	bah-*gahzh*	דער באַגאַזש
bagel	der beygl	*bay*-gil	דער בייגל
bait, to (harass)	reytsn zikh mit	*rayts*-n zikh meet	רייצן זיך מיט
bake, to	bakn	*bahk*-n	באַקן
baker	der beker	*beh*-kehr	דער בעקער
bakery	di bekeray	beh-keh-*rei*	די בעקערײַ
bald	lise	*lee*-seh	ליסע
ball (toy)	di pilke	*peel*-keh	די פּילקע
ballot	dos shtimtsetl	*shteem*-tseht-l	דאָס שטימצעטל
ban	der kheyrem	*khay*-rim	דער חרם
banana	di banane	bah-*nah*-neh	די באַנאַנע
band (musical)	di kapelye	kah-*pehl*-yeh	די קאַפּעליע
bandage	der bandazh	bahn-*dahzh*	דער באַנדאַזש
bandit	der bandit	bahn-*deet*	דער באַנדיט
banjo	der bandzho	*bahn*-jaw	דער באַנדזשאָ
bank (shore)	der breg	brehg	דער ברעג
bank (financial)	der bank	bahnk	דער באַנק
banker	der bankir	bahn-*keer*	דער באַנקיר
bankruptcy	der bankrot	bahnk-*rawt*	דער באַנקראָט

banner	di fone	*faw*-neh	די פֿאָנע
banquet	der banket	bahn-*keht*	דער באַנקעט
baptize, to (a Jew)	shmadn	*shmahd*-n	שמדן
bar (saloon)	der bar	bahr	דער באַר
barber	der sherer	*sheh*-rehr	דער שערער
bare (nude)	naket	*nah*-keht	נאַקעט
barefoot	borves	*bawr*-vehs	באָרוועס
bargain	di metsie	meh-*tsee*-ih	די מציאה
bargain, to	dingen zikh	*deen*-gehn zikh	דינגען זיך
bark, to	biln	*beel*-n	בילן
barrel (cask)	di fas	fahss	די פֿאַס
baseball	der beysbol	*bays*-bawl	דער בייסבאָל
basement	der keler	*keh*-lehr	דער קעלער
bashful	shemevdik	*sheh*-mehv-dik	שעמעוודיק
basic	ikerdik	*ee*-kehr-dik	עיקרדיק
basket	der korb	kawrb	דער קאָרב
basketball	der koyshbol	*koysh*-bawl	דער קוישבאָל
bastard	der mamzer	*mahm*-zehr	דער ממזר
bat (animal)	di fledermoyz	*fleh*-dehr-moyz	די פֿלעדערמויז
bathhouse	di bod	bawd	די באָד
bathhouse (ritual)	di mikve	*meek*-veh	די מיקווה
bathe, to	bodn zikh	*bawd*-n zikh	באָדן זיך
bathing suit	der bodkostyum	*bawd*-kawst-yoom	דער באָדקאָסטיום
bathrobe	der bodkhalat	*bawd*-khah-laht	דער באָדכאַלאַט
bathroom	der vashtsimer	*vahsh*-tsee-mehr	דער וואַשצימער
bathtub	di vane	*vah*-neh	די וואַנע
batter (dough)	dos teyg	tayg	דאָס טייג
battery	di baterye	bah-*tehr*-yeh	די באַטעריע
be, to	zayn	zein	זײַן
beach	di plazhe	*plahzh*-eh	די פּלאַזשע
beam with pride, to	kveln	k-*vehl*-n	קוועלן
bean	dos bebl	*behb*-l	דאָס בעבל
	di fasolye	fah-*sawl*-yeh	די פֿאַסאָליע
bear, to (endure)	fartrogn	fahr-*trawg*-n	פֿאַרטראָגן
	oyshaltn	*oyss*-hahlt-n	אויסהאַלטן
bear, to (carry)	trogn	*trawg*-n	טראָגן
bear	der ber	behr	דער בער
bearable	nishkoshe	nish-*kaw*-sheh	נישקשה
beard	di bord	bawrd	די באָרד

beast	di khaye	*khah*-yeh	די חיה
beat, to	shlogn	*shlawg*-n	שלאָגן
beautiful	sheyn	shayn	שיין
beauty	di sheynkayt	*shayn*-keit	די שיינקייט
beauty parlor	der sheynkayt-salon	*shayn*-keit-sah-*lawn*	דער שיינקייט־סאַלאָן
because of	makhmes	*mahkh*-mehs	מחמת
	tsulib	tsoo-*leeb*	צוליב
because	vayl	veil	ווײַל
become, to	vern	*vehr*-n	ווערן
bed	di bet	beht	די בעט
bedbug	di vants	vahnts	די וואַנץ
bedding	dos betgevant	*beht*-geh-vahnt	דאָס בעטגעוואַנט
bedlam	di behole	beh-*haw*-leh	די בהלה
bedroom	der shloftsimer	*shlawf*-tsee-mehr	דער שלאָפֿצימער
bee	di bin	been	די בין
beehive	der binshtok	*been*-shtawk	דער בינשטאָק
beer	dos bir	beer	דאָס ביר
beet	der burik	*boo*-rik	דער בוריק
beet soup	der borsht	bawrsht	דער באָרשט
beetle	der zhuk	zhook	דער זשוק
before (prep.)	far	fahr	פֿאַר
before (conj.)	eyder	*ay*-dehr	איידער
before (adv.)	frier	*free*-ehr	פֿריִער
beg, to (**request**)	betn	*beht*-n	בעטן
beggar	der betler	*beht*-lehr	דער בעטלער
	der shnorer	*shnaw*-rehr	דער שנאָרער
begin, to	onheybn	*awn*-hayb-n	אָנהייבן
beginning	der onheyb	*awn*-hayb	דער אָנהייב
begrudge, to	nit farginen	nit fahr-*gee*-nehn	ניט פֿאַרגינען
begrudge, to not	farginen	fahr-*gee*-nehn	פֿאַרגינען
behind (prep.)	hinter	*heen*-tehr	הינטער
belch	der grepts	grehpts	דער גרעפּץ
belief	der gloybn	*gloyb*-n	דער גלויבן
believe, to	gleybn	*glayb*-n	גלייבן
bell	der glok	glawk	דער גלאָק
belly	der boykh	boykh	דער בויך
belong, to	gehern	geh-*hehr*-n	געהערן
beloved	balibt	bah-*leebt*	באַליבט

below (prep.)	unter	oon-tehr	אונטער
below (adv.)	untn	oont-n	אונטן
belt	der gartl	gahrt-l	דער גאַרטל
bench	di bank	bahnk	די באַנק
bend, to	beygn	bayg-n	בייגן
beneath (prep.)	unter	oon-tehr	אונטער
benefactor	der bal-toyve	bahl-toy-veh	דער בעל־טובה
benefit (usefulness)	der nuts	noots	דער נוץ
berry	di yagde	yahg-deh	די יאַגדע
beseech, to	betn zikh (bay)	beht-n zikh (bei)	בעטן זיך (בײַ)
beside	lebn	lehb-n	לעבן
	bay	bei	בײַ
besides (adv.)	(a) khuts dem	(ah) khoots dehm	(אַ) חוץ דעם
best	best	behsst	בעסט
bet	dos gevet	geh-veht	דאָס געוועט
bet, to	vetn zikh	veht-n zikh	וועטן זיך
betray, to	farratn	fahr-raht-n	פֿאַרראַטן
	aroysgebn	ah-royss-gehb-n	אַרויסגעבן
betroth, to	farlobn	fahr-lawb-n	פֿאַרלאָבן
better	beser	beh-sehr	בעסער
between	tsvishn	tsveesh-n	צווישן
beverage	dos getrank	geh-trahnk	דאָס געטראַנק
beware of, to	hitn zikh far	heet-n zikh fahr	היטן זיך פֿאַר
bewilder, to	tsetumlen	tseh-toom-lehn	צעטומלען
beyond	vayter fun	vei-tehr foon	ווײַטער פֿון
bible	di bibl	beeb-l	די ביבל
bicycle	der velosiped	veh-law-see-pehd	דער וועלאָסיפּעד
big	groys	groyss	גרויס
bigot	der fargleybter	fahr-glayb-tehr	דער פֿאַרגלייבטער
big deal (sl.)	der tsimes	tsee-mehs	דער צימעס
big shot	der knaker	k-nah-kehr	דער קנאַקער
bill (invoice)	der khezhbn	khehzh-bn	דער חשבון
bill of sale	dos farkoyf-tsetl	fahr-koyf-tseht-l	דאָס פֿאַרקויף־צעטל
billion	der bilyon	bil-yawn	דער ביליאָן
bind, to	bindn	beend-n	בינדן
bird	der foygl	foyg-l	דער פֿויגל
birth	di geburt	geh-boort	די געבורט
birthday	der geboyrn-tog	geh-boyr-n-tawg	דער געבוירן־טאָג
bit (wee bit)	dos pitsl	peets-l	דאָס פּיצל
bite, to	baysn	beis-n	בײַסן

bite	der bis	*beess*	דער ביס
bitter	bitter	*bee*-tehr	ביטער
black	shvarts	*shvahrts*	שוואַרץ
black woman/man	der/di neger/te	*neh*-gehr/teh	דער/די נעגער/טע
blackberry	di ozhene	*aw*-zheh-neh	די אָזשענע
blacksmith	der shmid	*shmeed*	דער שמיד
bladder	der penkher	*pehn*-khehr	דער פּענכער
blame, to	bashuldikn	bah-*shool*-deek-n	באַשולדיקן
blame	di shuld	*shoold*	די שולד
blank	pust	*poost*	פּוסט
blanket	di koldre	*kawld*-reh	די קאָלדרע
bleach, to	bleykhn	*blaykh*-n	בלייכן
	blyakirn	blah-*keer*-n	בליאַקירן
bleed, to	blutikn	*bloo*-teek-n	בלוטיקן
blend, to	tsenoyfgisn	tseh-*noyf*-gees-n	צונויפֿגיסן
bless, to	bentshn	*behnch*-n	בענטשן
blessing	di brokhe	*braw*-kheh	די ברכה
blind	blind	*bleend*	בלינד
blizzard	di zaverukhe	zah-veh-*roo*-kheh	די זאַווערוכע
blockhead	der bulvan	bool-*vahn*	דער בולוואַן
blond	blond	*blawnd*	בלאָנד
blood	dos blut	*bloot*	דאָס בלוט
blood vessel	di oder	*aw*-dehr	די אָדער
bloom, to	blien	*blee*-en	בליִען
blossom	di kveyt	k-*vayt*	די קווייט
blot, to	opklekn	*awp*-klehk-n	אָפּקלעקן
blouse	di bluze	*bloo*-zeh	די בלוזע
blow, to	blozn	*blawz*-n	בלאָזן
blow (hit)	der klap	*klahp*	דער קלאַפּ
blue	bloy	*bloy*	בלוי
blueberry	di yagde	*yahg*-deh	די יאַגדע
blueprint	der plan	*plahn*	דער פּלאַן
blunder	der grober feler	*graw*-behr *feh*-lehr	דער גראָבער פֿעלער
blush, to	reytlen zikh	*rayt*-lehn zikh	רייטלען זיך
board (plank)	di/dos bret	*breht*	די/דאָס ברעט
boast, to	barimen zikh	bah-*ree*-mehn zikh	באַרימען זיך
boat	dos shifl	*sheef*-l	דאָס שיפֿל
body (anat.)	der guf	*goof*	דער גוף
	der kerper	*kehr*-pehr	דער קערפּער
boil	dos geshvir	geh-*shveer*	דאָס געשוויר

boil, to	kokhn	*kawkh*-n	קאָכן
	zidn	*zeed*-n	זידן
bold	dreyst	drayst	דרייסט
bolt	der rigl	*reeg*-l	דער ריגל
bomb	di bombe	*bawm*-beh	די באָמבע
bone	der beyn	bayn	דער ביין
book	dos bukh	bookh	דאָס בוך
book (religious)	der seyfer	*say*-fehr	דער ספֿר
booklet	di broshur	braw-*shoor*	די בראָשור
boor	der zhlob	zhlawb	דער זשלאָב
boot	der shtivl	*shteev*-l	דער שטיוול
border	der grenets	*greh*-nehts	דער גרענעץ
border (edge)	der breg	brehg	דער ברעג
bore	der nudnik	*nood*-nik	דער נודניק
bore, badger, to	nudzhen	*nood*-jehn	נודזשען
born	geboyrn	geh-*boyr*-n	געבוירן
borrow (from), to	antlayen	ahnt-*lei*-en	אַנטלײַען
	borgn	*bawrg*-n	באָרגן
bosom	der buzem	*boo*-zehm	דער בוזעם
both	beyde	*bay*-deh	ביידע
bottle	di flash	flahsh	די פֿלאַש
bough	di tsvayg	tsveig	די צווײַג
boundary	der grenets	*greh*-nehts	דער גרענעץ
bowels	di gederem	geh-*deh*-rehm	די געדערעם
bowl	di shisl	*sheesh*-l	די שיסל
box	dos kestl	*kehst*-l	דאָס קעסטל
boy	der yingl	*yeeng*-l	דער ייִנגל
bracelet	der braslet	brahss-*leht*	דער בראַסלעט
brag, to	barimen zikh	bah-*ree*-mehn zikh	באַרימען זיך
braggart	der barimer	bah-*ree*-mehr	דער באַרימער
brain	der moyekh	*moy*-ehkh	דער מוח
brake	der tormoz	*tawr*-mawz	דער טאָרמאָז
branch	di tsvayg	tsveig	די צווײַג
brand-new	shpogl nay	*shpawg*-l nei	שפּאָגל נײַ
brandy	der konyak	*kawn*-yahk	דער קאָניאַק
brassiere	der stanik	*stah*-nik	דער סטאַניק
brazeness	di khutspe	*khoots*-peh	די חוצפּה
bread	dos broyt	broyt	דאָס ברויט
bread roll	di bulke	*bool*-keh	די בולקע
	der zeml	*zehm*-l	דער זעמל

breadwinner	der fardiner	fahr-*dee*-nehr	דער פֿאַרדינער
break, to	brekhn	*brehkh*-n	ברעכן
break up, to	tsebrekhn	tseh-*brehkh*-n	צעברעכן
breakfast	der frishtik	*freesh*-tik	דער פֿרישטיק
	dos iberbaysn	*ee*-behr-beis-n	דאָס איבערבײַסן
breast	di brust	broost	די ברוסט
breath	der otem	*aw*-tehm	דער אָטעם
breathe, to	otemen	*aw*-teh-mehn	אָטעמען
breeze	dos vintl	*veent*-l	דאָס ווינטל
bribe	der khabar	khah-*bahr*	דער כאַבאַר
bribe, to	unterkoyfn	*oon*-tehr-*koyf*-n	אונטערקויפֿן
brick	der tsigl	*tseeg*-l	דער ציגל
bride	di kale	*kah*-leh	די כּלה
bridegroom	der khosn	*khaws*-n	דער חתן
bridge (span)	di brik	breek	די בריק
brief	kurts	koorts	קורץ
briefcase	di teke	*teh*-keh	די טעקע
brilliant	brilyant	breel-*yahnt*	ברילּיאַנט
bring, to	brengen	*brehn*-gehn	ברענגען
brittle	krishldik	*kreesh*-l-dik	קרישלדיק
broad	breyt	brayt	ברייט
broil, to	brotn	*brawt*-n	בראָטן
broker	der mekler	*meh*-klehr	דער מעקלער
brooch	di brosh	brawsh	די בראָש
broom	der bezem	*beh*-zehm	דער בעזעם
brothel	dos hayzl	*heiz*-l	דאָס הײַזל
brother	der bruder	*broo*-dehr	דער ברודער
brother-in-law	der shvoger	*shvaw*-gehr	דער שוואָגער
brown	broyn	broyn	ברוין
bruise	der sinyak	seen-*yahk*	דער סיניאַק
brunette	brunet	broo-*neht*	ברונעט
brush	di barsht	bahrsht	די באַרשט
bubble, to	blezlen (zikh)	*blehz*-lehn (zikh)	בלעזלען (זיך)
bucket	der emer	*eh*-mehr	דער עמער
budget	der budzhet	boo-*jeht*	דער בודזשעט
buffalo	der bufloks	*boof*-lawks	דער בופֿלאָקס
bug	der zhuk	zhook	דער זשוק
build, to	boyen	*boy*-en	בויען
building	der binyin	*been*-yin	דער בנין
bulb (light bulb)	dos lempl	*lehmp*-l	דאָס לעמפּל

bull	der bik	beek	דער ביק
bullet	di koyl	koyl	די קויל
bump (blow)	der zets	zehts	דער זעץ
bunch	dos bintl	*beent*-l	דאָס בינטל
bundle	dos pekl	*pehk*-l	דאָס פּעקל
burden	di mase	*mah*-seh	די מאַסע
bureau (office)	dos byuro	*byoo*-raw	דאָס ביוראָ
bureau (chest)	der komod	kaw-*mawd*	דער קאָמאָד
burglar	der araynbrekher	ah-*rein*-breh-khehr	דער אַרײַנברעכער
burial	di kvure	k-*voo*-reh	די קבֿורה
burial shrouds	di takhrikhim	tahkh-*ree*-kheem	די תּכריכים
burn, to	farbrenen	fahr-*breh*-nehn	פֿאַרברענען
burn	der bren	brehn	דער ברען
burst, to	platsn	*plahts*-n	פּלאַצן
bury, to	bagrobn	bah-*grawb*-n	באַגראָבן
bus	der oytobus	oy-taw-booss	דער אויטאָבוס
business	dos gesheft	geh-*shehft*	דאָס געשעפֿט
busy	farnumen	farh-*noo*-mehn	פֿאַרנומען
busybody (sl.)	der kokhlefl	*kawkh*-leh-fehl	דער קאָכלעפֿל
but (conj.)	ober	*aw*-behr	אָבער
but (except) (prep.)	(a) khuts	(ah)-khoots	(אַ)חוץ
butcher	der katsev	*kah*-tsehv	דער קצבֿ
butter	di puter	*poo*-tehr	די פּוטער
butterfly	dos flaterl	*flah*-tehr-l	דאָס פֿלאַטערל
buttocks	der tokhes	*taw*-khehs	דער תּחת
button	dos knepl	k-*nehp*-l	דאָס קנעפּל
buy, to	koyfn	*koyf*-n	קויפֿן
by (via)	durkh	doorkh	דורך
by (near)	bay	bei	בײַ
by (prior to)	biz	beez	ביז
by heart	oysenveynik	*oys*-sehn-*vay*-nik	אויסנווייניק

cab	der taksi	*tahk*-see	דער טאַקסי
cabbage	dos kroyt	kroyt	דאָס קרויט
cabin of ship	di kayute	kah-*yoo*-teh	די קאַיוטע
cabinet	di shafe	*shah*-feh	די שאַפֿע
cabinet (ministers)	der kabinet	kah-bee-*neht*	דער קאַבינעט

cage	di shtayg	shteig	די שטײַג
cake	der lekekh	*leh*-kehkh	דער לעקעך
calculate, to	rekhenen	*reh*-kheh-nehn	רעכענען
calculation	der khezhbn	*khehzh*-bn	דער חשבון
calendar (Jewish)	der luakh	*loo*-ahkh	דער לוח
calendar	der kalendar	kah-lehn-*dahr*	דער קאַלענדאַר
calf (anat.)	di litke	*leet*-keh	די ליטקע
calf	dos kalb	kahlb	דאָס קאַלב
call, to	rufn	*roof*-n	רופֿן
calm	ruik	*roo*-ik	רויִק
calm, to	baruikn	bah-*roo*-ik-n	באַרויִקן
calorie	di kalorye	kah-*lawr*-yeh	די קאַלאָריע
camera	der aparat	ah-pah-*raht*	דער אַפּאַראַט
can (to be able)	kenen	*keh*-nehn	קענען
canary	der kanarik	kah-*nah*-rik	דער קאַנאַריק
cancer	der rak	rahk	דער ראַק
candelabra (religious)	di menoyre	meh-*noy*-reh	די מנורה
candidate	der kandidat	kahn-dee-*daht*	דער קאַנדידאַט
candle	dos likht	leekht	דאָס ליכט
candlestick	der laykhter	*leikh*-tehr	דער לײַכטער
candy	dos tsukerl	*tsoo*-kehr-l	דאָס צוקערל
cane	der shtekn	*shtehk*-n	דער שטעקן
canopy, wedding	di khupe	*khoo*-peh	די חופה
cantaloupe	di dinke	*deen*-keh	די דינקע
cantor (Jewish)	der khazn	*khahz*-n	דער חזן
cap (hat)	dos hitl	*heet*-l	דאָס היטל
capable	feik	*feh*-ik	פֿעיִק
caprice	der kapriz	kah-*preez*	דער קאַפּריז
capricious	kaprizik	kah-*pree*-zik	קאַפּריזיק
capture, to	khapn	*khahp*-n	כאַפּן
	fangen	*fahn*-gehn	פֿאַנגען
car	der oyto	*oy*-taw	דער אויטאָ
caraway (seeds)	der kiml	*keem*-l	דער קימל
card	dos kartl	*kahrt*-l	דאָס קאַרטל
care, to (be concerned)	arn	*ahr*-n	אַרן
care (concern)	di zorg	zawrg	די זאָרג
care for, to (be responsible)	farzorgn	fahr-*zawrg*-n	פֿאַרזאָרגן
careful	opgehit	*awp*-geh-heet	אָפּגעהיט

careless	opgelozn	*awp*-geh-lawz-n	אָפּגעלאָזן
carpenter	der stolyer	*stawl*-yehr	דער סטאָליער
carpet	der tepekh	*teh*-pehkh	דער טעפּעך
carriage (baby buggy)	dos vegele	*veh*-geh-leh	דאָס וועגעלע
carrot	di mer	mehr	די מער
carry, to	trogn	*trawg*-n	טראָגן
cart	der vogn	*vawg*-n	דער וואָגן
cash	dos mezumen	meh-*zoo*-mehn	דאָס מזומן
cashier	der kasirer	kah-*see*-rehr	דער קאַסירער
cast, to	varfn	*vahrf*-n	וואַרפֿן
casual	glaykhgiltik	*gleikh*-gil-tik	גלײַכגילטיק
cat	di kats	kahts	די קאַץ
catastrophe	di katastrofe	kah-tah-*straw*-feh	די קאַטאַסטראָפֿע
catch, to	khapn	*khahp*-n	כאַפּן
cattle	di beheymes	beh-*hay*-mehs	די בהמות
	dos fikh	feekh	דאָס פֿיך
cauliflower	der kalifyor	kah-leef-*yawr*	דער קאַליפֿיאָר
cause	di sibe	*see*-bih	די סיבה
caution, to	vorenen	*vaw*-reh-nehn	וואָרענען
cease, to	oyfhern	*oyf*-hehr-n	אויפֿהערן
ceiling	der sufit	soo-*feet*	דער סופֿיט
	di stelye	*stehl*-yeh	די סטעליע
celebrate	yoyvln	*yoyv*-lehn	יובֿלען
celebration, joyous	di simkhe	*seem*-kheh	די שׂימחה
celebrity	di barimtkayt	bah-*reemt*-keit	די באַרימטקייט
celery	di selerye	seh-*lehr*-yeh	די סעלעריע
cellar	der keler	*keh*-lehr	דער קעלער
cement	der tsement	tseh-*mehnt*	דער צעמענט
cemetery	der beys-oylem	bays-*oy*-lehm	דער בית־עולם
cereal (prepared food)	di kashe	*kah*-sheh	די קאַשע
ceremony	di tseremonye	tseh-reh-*mawn*-yeh	די צערעמאָניע
certain	zikher	*zee*-khehr	זיכער
	gevis	geh-*veess*	געוויס
certainly	avade	ah-*vah*-deh	אַוודאי
chain	di keyt	kayt	די קייט
chair	di shtul	shtool	די שטול
chance (opportunity)	di gelegnhayt	geh-*lehg*-n-heit	די געלעגנהייט
change, to	baytn	*beit*-n	בײַטן

English	Yiddish	Pronunciation	Hebrew
chap	der yat	yaht	דער יאַט
character (in a play)	der parshoyn	pahr-*shoyn*	דער פּאַרשוין
character (nature)	der kharakter	khah-*rahk*-tehr	דער כאַראַקטער
charge (accusation)	di bashuldikung	bah-*shool*-dee-koong	די באַשולדיקונג
charge (price)	der optsol	*awp*-tsawl	דער אָפּצאָל
charge account	di farrekhn-konte	fahr-*rehkh*-n *kawn*-teh	די פֿאַררעכן־קאָנטע
charity (alms)	di tsdoke	tseh-*daw*-keh	די צדקה
charm	der kheyn	khayn	דער חן
chase, to	nokhyogn	*nawkh*-yawg-n	נאָכיאָגן
chat	der shmues	*shmoo*-ehs	דער שמועס
chat, to	shmuesn	*shmoo*-ehs-n	שמועסן
chatter, to	plaplen	*plahp*-lehn	פּלאַפּלען
chauffeur	der shofer	shaw-*fehr*	דער שאָפֿער
cheap (inexpensive)	bilik	*bee*-lik	ביליק
	volvl	*vawlv*-l	וואָלוול
cheapskate (sl.)	der shnorer	*shnaw*-rehr	דער שנאָרער
cheat, to	opnarn	*awp*-nahr-n	אָפּנאַרן
check, to (prevent)	ophaltn	*awp*-hahlt-n	אָפּהאַלטן
check (bank check)	der tshek	chehk	דער טשעק
cheek	di bak	bahk	די באַק
cheer, to (applaud)	aplodirn	ah-plaw-*deer*-n	אַפּלאָדירן
cheer, to (gladden)	derfreyen	dehr-*fray*-ehn	דערפֿרייען
cheerful	freylekh	*fray*-lehkh	פֿריילעך
cheese	der kez	kehz	דער קעז
chemistry	di khemye	*khehm*-yeh	די כעמיע
cherish, to	tayer haltn	*tei*-ehr hahlt-n	טײַער האַלטן
cherry	di karsh	kahrsh	די קאַרש
chest (box)	der kastn	*kahsst*-n	דער קאַסטן
chest (anat.)	der brustkastn	*broost*-kahsst-n	דער ברוסטקאַסטן
chew, to	kayen	*kei*-en	קײַען
chewing gum	di kaygume	*kei* goo-meh	די קײַגומע
chick pea	der nahit	nah-*heet*	דער נאַהיט
chicken	di hun	hoon	די הון
chiefly	der iker	dehr *ee*-kehr	דער עיקר
child	dos kind	keend	דאָס קינד
childhood	di kindhayt	*keend*-heit	די קינדהייט
chilly	kil	keel	קיל
chimney	der koymen	*koy*-mehn	דער קוימען
chin	di gombe	*gawm*-beh	די גאָמבע
	der kin	kin	דער קין

choke, to	(der) shtikn	(dehr) *shteek*-n	(דער)שטיקן
cholera	di kholere	khaw-*leh*-reh	די כאָלערע
choose, to	(oys) klaybn	(*oyss*)-kleib-n	(אויס)קלײַבן
chopmeat	dos hakfleysh	*hahk*-flaysh	דאָס האַקפלייש
chopped	gehakte	geh-*hahk*-teh	געהאַקטע
Christian	der krist	kreest	דער קריסט
church	der kloyster	*kloyss*-tehr	דער קלויסטער
cigar	der tsigar	tsee-*gahr*	דער ציגאַר
cigarette	der papiros	pah-pee-*rawss*	דער פּאַפּיראָס
cinnamon	der tsimering	*tsee*-meh-ring	דער צימערינג
circle	der krayz	kreiz	דער קרײַז
circular	kaylekhik	*kei*-leh-khik	קײַלעכיק
circumcise, to	mal zayn	*mahl* zein	מל זײַן
circumciser	der moyel	*moy*-ehl	דער מוהל
circumcision ceremony	der bris	brees	דער ברית
circus	der tsirk	tseerk	דער צירק
citizen	der birger	*beer*-gehr	דער בירגער
city	di shtot	shtawt	די שטאָט
civil (polite)	eydl	*ayd*-l	איידל
civilization	di tsivilizatsye	tsee-vee-lee-*zahts*-yeh	די ציוויליזאַציע
clap, to	patshn	*pahch*-n	פּאַטשן
clarinet	der klarnet	klahr-*neht*	דער קלאַרנעט
clasp, to	arumnemen	ah-*room*-neh-mehn	אַרומנעמען
class	der klas	klahss	דער קלאַס
classroom	der klastsimer	*klahss*-tsee-mehr	דער קלאַסצימער
claw	di krel	krehl	די קרעל
clean, to	reynikn	*ray*-neek-n	רייניקן
	oysreynikn	*oyss*-ray-neek-n	אויסרייניקן
clean	reyn	rayn	ריין
clear	klor	klawr	קלאָר
clear one's throat, to	khraken	*khrah*-kehn	כראַקען
cleaver	der hakmesser	*hahk*-meh-sehr	דער האַקמעסער
clergyman (Gentile)	der galikh	*gah*-likh	דער גלח
clerk	der farkoyfer	fahr-*koy*-fehr	דער פאַרקויפער
clever	klug	kloog	קלוג
climate	der klimat	*klee*-maht	דער קלימאַט
climb, to	aroyfkrikhn	ah-*royf*-kreekh-n	אַרויפקריכן
cloak	der mantl	*mahnt*-l	דער מאַנטל

clock	der zeyger	*zay*-gehr	דער זייגער
clod (boor)	der zhlob	zhlawb	דער זשלאָב
close, to	farmakhn	fahr-*mahkh*-n	פֿאַרמאַכן
	shlisn	*shlees*-n	שליסן
close (adj.)	noent	*naw*-ehnt	נאָענט
closet	di shafe	*shah*-feh	די שאַפֿע
clothe, to	bakleydn	bah-*klayd*-n	באַקליידן
clothing	di klayder	*klay*-dehr	קליידער
cloud	der volkn	*vawlk*-n	דער וואָלקן
cloudy (overcast)	farvolknt	fahr-*vawl*-knt	פֿאַרוואָלקנט
	khmarne	kh-*mahr*-neh	כמאַרנע
club (cudgel)	der flokn	*flawk*-n	דער פֿלאָקן
club (society)	der klub	kloob	דער קלוב
coachman	der bale-gole	bah-leh-*gaw*-leh	דער בעל־עגלה
coal	di koyln	*koyl*-n	די קוילן
coarse	grob	grawb	גראָב
	prost	prost	פּראָסט
cock	der hon	hawn	דער האָן
cocktail	der kokteyl	*kawk*-tayl	דער קאָקטייל
cocoa	der kakao	kah-*kah*-aw	דער קאַקאַאָ
coconut	der kokosnus	*kaw*-kawss-noos	דער קאָקאָסנוס
coffee	di kave	*kah*-veh	די קאַווע
coffee pot	der kavenik	*kah*-veh-nik	דער קאַוועניק
coffin (Jewish)	der orn	*awr*-n	דער אָרון
coin	di matbeye	maht-*bay*-eh	די מטבע
coke	der koks	kawks	דער קאָקס
cold	kalt	kahlt	קאַלט
cold (low temperature)	di kelt	kehlt	די קעלט
cold cream	der hoytkrem	*hoyt*-krehm	דער הויטקרעם
cold (ailment)	di farkilung	fahr-*kee*-loong	די פֿאַרקילונג
collar	der kolner	*kawl*-nehr	דער קאָלנער
collect, to (a debt)	aynmonen	*ein*-maw-nehn	איינמאָנען
collect, to	zamlen	*zahm*-lehn	זאַמלען
collection	di zamlung	*zahm*-loong	די זאַמלונג
color	der kolir	kaw-*leer*	דער קאָליר
comb	der kahm	kahm	דער קאָם
combination	di kombinatsye	kawm-bee-*nahts*-yeh	די קאָמבינאַציע
come, to	kumen	*koo*-mehn	קומען
comfort	di treyst	trayst	די טרייסט

comfortable	bakvem	bahk-*vehm*	באַקװעם
comic (jester)	der komiker	*kaw*-mee-kehr	דער קאָמיקער
command	der bafel	bah-*fehl*	דער באַפֿעל
commandment	di mitsve	*mits*-veh	די מיצווה
	dos gebot	geh-*bawt*	דאָס געבאָט
comment	di bamerkung	bah-*mehr*-koong	די באַמערקונג
commodity	di skhoyre	*skhoy*-reh	די סחורה
common (usual)	geveyntlekh	geh-*vaynt*-lehkh	געוויינטלעך
commonplace	vokhedik	*vaw*-kheh-dik	וואָכעדיק
commotion	dos geruder	geh-*roo*-dehr	דאָס גערודער
communication (message)	di yedie	yeh-*dee*-eh	די ידיעה
communism	der komunizm	kaw-moo-*nee*-zim	דער קאָמוניזם
communist	der komunist	kaw-moo-*neest*	דער קאָמוניסט
community (the public)	der tsibur	*tsee*-boor	דער ציבור
companion	der bagleyter	bah-*glay*-tehr	דער באַגלייטער
company (guests)	di gest	gehst	די געסט
company (bus.)	di firme	*feer*-meh	די פֿירמע
compare, to	farglaykhn	fahr-*gleikh*-n	פֿאַרגלײַכן
comparison	der farglaykh	fahr-*gleikh*	דער פֿאַרגלײַך
compatriot	der landsman	*lahnds*-mahn	דער לאַנדסמאַן
competent	kompetent	kawm-peh-*tehnt*	קאָמפּעטענט
competitor	der konkurent	kawn-koo-*rehnt*	דער קאָנקורענט
complain, to	baklogn zikh	bah-*klawg*-n zikh	באַקלאָגן זיך
complain, to (sl.)	kvetshn	k-*vehch*-n	קװעטשן
complainer (sl.)	der kvetsh	k-*vehch*	דער קװעטש
complaint	di tayne	*tei*-nih	די טענה
complete	fulshtendik	*fool*-shtehn-dik	פֿולשטענדיק
compliment	der kompliment	kawm-plee-*mehnt*	דער קאָמפּלימענט
comprehend, to	bagrayf-n	bah-*greif*-n	באַגרײַפֿן
conceal, to	oysbahaltn	*oyss*-bah-hahlt-n	אויסבאַהאַלטן
conceited	haltn fun zik	*hahlt*-n foon zikh	האַלטן פֿון זיך
concert	der kontsert	kawn-*tsehrt*	דער קאָנצערט
conclusion	der sof	sawf	דער סוף
condemn, to (damn)	fardamen	fahr-*dah*-mehn	פֿאַרדאַמען
conduct	der oyffir	*oyf*-feer	דער אויפֿפֿיר
confess, to	moyde zayn zikh	*moy*-deh zein zikh	מודה זײַן זיך
confidence	der tsutroy	*tsoo*-troy	דער צוטרוי

confuse, to (mix up)	tsemishn	tseh-*meesh*-n	צעמישן
confused	tsemisht	tseh-*meesht*	צעמישט
	tsetumlt	tseh-*toom*-lt	צעטומלט
confusion	di tsemishung	tseh-*mee*-shoong	די צעמישונג
congratulate, to	gratulirn	grah-too-*leer*-n	גראַטולירן
congratulations	mazl-tov	*mahz*-l tawv	מזל־טובֿ
congregation	di kehile atsy	ke-*hee*-lih	דער קהילה
conscience	dos gevisn	geh-*vees*-n	דאָס געוויסן
conscious	bavustzinik	bah-*voost*-zee-nik	באַוווּסטזיניק
consequently	deriber	deh-*ree*-behr	דעריבער
consent, to	maskim zayn	*mahss*-kim zein	מסכּים זײַן
consider, to	batrakhtn	bah-*trahkht*-n	באַטראַכטן
considerable	nishkoshedik	nish-*kaw*-sheh-dik	נישקשהדיק
consolation	di nekhome	neh-*khaw*-meh	די נחמה
constant	keseyderdik	keh-*say*-dehr-dik	כּסדרדיק
constipation	di farshtopung	fahr-*shtaw*-poong	די פֿאַרשטאָפּונג
construct, to	boyen	*boy*-en	בויען
consult, to	meyashev zine zikh mit	meh-*yah*-shehv zein zikh mit	מישבֿ זײַן זיך מיט
contemplate, to	batrakhtn	bah-*trahkht*-n	באַטראַכטן
contempt	der bitl	*bee*-tl	דער ביטול
contemporary	haynttsaytik	*heint*-tsei-tik	הײַנטצײַטיק
contend, to	taynen	*tei*-nehn	טענהן
contents	der inhalt	*een*-hahlt	דער אינהאַלט
contest	der konkurs	*kawn*-koorss	דער קאָנקורס
continue, to	mamshikh zayn	*mahm*-shikh zein	ממשיך זײַן
continual	keseyderdik	keh-*say*-dehr-dik	כּסדרדיק
contraption	di makherayke	mah-kheh-*rei*-keh	די מאַכעריַיקע
contrary	farkert	fahr-*kehrt*	פֿאַרקערט
contribution	der tsushtayer	*tsoo*-shtei-ehr	דער צושטײַער
	der bayshtayer	*bei*-shtei-ehr	דער בײַשטײַער
contrive, to	fartrakhtn	fahr-*trahkht*-n	פֿאַרטראַכטן
controversy	der sikhsekh	*seekh*-sehkh	דער סיכסוך
convenient	bakvem	bahk-*vehm*	באַקוועם
convert (to Judaism)	der ger	gehr	דער גר
convert (to Christianity)	der meshumed	meh-*shoo*-mehd	דער משומד
conviction (belief)	di ibertsaygung	*ee*-behr-tsei-goong	די איבערצײַגונג
convince, to	aynredn	*ein*-rehd-n	אײַנרעדן
convulsion	di konvulsye	kawn-*vool*-syeh	די קאָנוווּלסיע

English	Yiddish	Pronunciation	Hebrew
cook, to	kokhn	*kawkh*-n	קאָכן
cooked medium	halb durkhgekokht	*hahlb doorkh*-geh-kawkht	האַלב דורכגעקאָקט
cooked rare	nit derkokht	nit-dehr-*kawkht*	ניט דערקאָקט
cooked well done	gut durkhgekokht	*goot doorkh*-geh-kawkht	גוט דורכגעקאָקט
cookie	dos kikhl	*keekh*-l	דאָס קיכל
cooking spoon	der kokhlefl	*kawkh*-leh-fehl	דער קאָכלעפל
cool	kil	keel	קיל
cool, to	kiln	*keel*-n	קילן
copper	dos kuper	*koo*-pehr	דאָס קופּער
copulate, to	porn zikh	*pawr*-n zikh	פּאָרן זיך
copy, to	nokhmakhn	*nawkh*-mahkh-n	נאָכמאַכן
copy	di kopye	*kawp*-yeh	די קאָפּיע
cordial	hartsik	*hahr*-tsik	האַרציק
cork	der korek	*kaw*-rehk	דער קאָרעק
corned beef	dos peklfleysh	*peh*-kil-flaysh	דאָס פּעקלפלייש
corner	der vinkl	*veenk*-l	דער ווינקל
corporation	di korporatsye	kawr-paw-*rahts*-yeh	די קאָרפּאָראַציע
corpse	der mes	mehs	דער מת
	der bar-menen	*bahr*-meh-nan	דער בר-מינן
correct	rikhtik	*reekh*-tik	ריכטיק
correspond with, to	korespondirn	kaw-rehs-pawn-*deer*-n	קאָרעספּאָנדירן
correspond, to (agree)	shtimen	*shtee*-mehn	שטימען
corset	der korset	kawr-*seht*	דער קאָרסעט
cosmetic	di kosmetik	kaw-*smeh*-tik	די קאָסמעטיק
cost, to	kostn	*kawsst*-n	קאָסטן
cost	der prayz	preiz	דער פּרײַז
costume	der kostyum	kawst-*yoom*	דער קאָסטיום
cotton	di vate	*vah*-teh	די וואַטע
	der bavl	*bahv*-l	דער באַוול
couch	di kanape	kah-*nah*-peh	די קאַנאַפּע
cough	der hust	hoost	דער הוסט
council	der rot	rawt	דער ראָט
counsel (attorney)	der advokat	ahd-vaw-*kaht*	דער אַדוואָקאַט
counsel (advice)	di eytse	*ay*-tseh	די עצה
counsel, to	eytsn	*ay*-tsehn	עצהן
count, to	tseyln	*tsayl*-n	ציילן
	rekhenen	*reh*-kheh-nehn	רעכענען
countenance	dos ponim	*paw*-nim	דאָס פּנים
counter (shop)	der tombank	*tawm*-bahnk	דער טאָמבאַנק

counterfeit	falsh	fahlsh	פֿאַלש
country	dos land	lahnd	דאָס לאַנד
	di medine	meh-*dee*-neh	די מדינה
countryman	der landsman	*lahnds*-mahn	דער לאַנדסמאַן
couple	di por	pawr	די פּאָר
coupon	der kupon	koo-*pawn*	דער קופּאָן
courage	der mut	moot	דער מוט
courteous	heflekh	*hehf*-lehkh	העפֿלעך
courtesy	di heflekhkayt	*hehf*-lehkh-keit	די העפֿלעכקייט
cousin	dos shvesterkind	shvehs-tehr-*keend*	דאָס שוועסטערקינד
cousin (masc.)	der kuzin	koo-*zeen*	דער קוזין
cousin (fem.)	di kuzine	koo-*zee*-neh	די קוזינע
cover, to	tsudekn	*tsoo*-dehk-n	צודעקן
cover	dos dekl	*dehk*-l	דאָס דעקל
cow	di ku	koo	די קו
	di beheyme	beh-*hay*-meh	די בהמה
coward	der pakhdn	*pahkh*-din	דער פּחדן
crab	der krab	krahb	דער קראַב
crack, to	shpaltn	*shpahlt*-n	שפּאַלטן
cradle	di vig	veeg	די וויג
craftsman	der bal-melokhe	bahl meh-*law*-kheh	דער בעל־מלאכה
cramp (med.)	der kramf	krahmf	דער קראַמף
crave, to	garn nokh	*gahr*-n nawkh	גאָרן נאָך
crazy	meshuge	meh-*shoo*-geh	משוגע
cream (sour)	di smetene	*smeh*-teh-neh	די סמעטענע
cream (sweet)	der shmant	shmahnt	דער שמאַנט
cream cheese	der shmirkez	*shmeer*-kehz	דער שמירקעז
create, to	bashafn	bah-*shahf*-n	באַשאַפֿן
creature (living being)	dos bashefenish	bah-*sheh*-feh-nish	דאָס באַשעפֿעניש
credit	der kredit	kreh-*deet*	דער קרעדיט
creek	dos taykhl	*teikh*-l	דאָס טײַכל
creep, to	krikhn	*kreekh*-n	קריכן
crepe, stuffed	di blintse	*bleen*-tseh	די בלינצע
crime	dos farbrekhn	fahr-*brehkh*-n	דאָס פֿאַרברעכן
criminal	der farbrekher	fahr-*breh*-khehr	דער פֿאַרברעכער
crimson	poms	pawms	פּאָמס
cripple	der/di kalike	*kah*-lee-keh	דער/די קאַליקע
crisis	der krizis	*kree*-ziss	דער קריזיס
crisp (brittle)	krukhle	*krookh*-leh	קרוכלע

criticize, to	kritikirn	kree-tee-*keer*-n	קריטיקירן
crook (thief)	der ganev	*gah*-nehv	דער גנב
	der zhulik	*zhoo*-lik	דער זשוליק
crooked	krum	kroom	קרום
cross (angry)	broygez	*broy*-gehz	ברוגז
cross over, to	aribergeyn	ah-*ree*-behr-gayn	אריבערגיין
cross	der tseylem	*tsay*-lehm	דער צלם
crowd	der oylem	*oy*-lehm	דער עולם
crowded	eng	ehng	ענג
crude	roy	roy	רוי
cruel	akhzoryesdik	ahkh-*zawr*-yehs-dik	אכזריותדיק
crumb	dos brekl	*brehk*-l	דאָס ברעקל
crumble, to	tsebreklen	tseh-*brehk*-lehn	צעברעקלען
crust	di skore	*skaw*-reh	די סקאָרע
crutch	di kulye	*kool*-yeh	די קוליע
cry	dos geshrey	geh-*shray*	דאָס געשריי
cry, to (weep)	veynen	*vay*-nehn	וויינען
cry out, to	shrayen	*shrei*-en	שרייען
cucumber	di ugerke	*oo*-gehr-keh	די אוגערקע
culture	di kultur	kool-*toor*	די קולטור
cunning	khitre	*kheet*-reh	כיטרע
cup	der kubik	*koo*-bik	דער קוביק
cupping-glasses (med.)	di bankes	*bahn*-kehs	די באַנקעס
curb, to	tsamen	*tsah*-mehn	צאַמען
cure	di refue	reh-*foo*-eh	די רפואה
curious	naygerik	*nei*-geh-rik	נייגעריק
curiosity	di naygerikayt	*nei*-geh-ree-keit	די נייגעריקייט
curl	dos grayzl	*greiz*-l	דאָס גרייזל
curse	di klole	*klaw*-lih	די קללה
curse, to	shiltn	*shelt*-n	שילטן
	zidlen	*zeed*-lehn	זידלען
curtain (drape)	der forhang	*fawr*-hahng	דער פאָרהאַנג
cushion	der kishn	*keesh*-n	דער קישן
customer	der koyne	*koy*-neh	דער קונה
cut, to (in pieces)	tseshnaydn	tseh-*shneid*-n	צעשניידן
cut, to	shnaydn	*shneid*-n	שניידן
cutlet	der kotlet	kawt-*leht*	דער קאָטלעט

dad	der tate	*tah*-teh	דער טאַטע
dainty	delikat	deh-lee-*kaht*	דעליקאַט
dairy	di milkhikeray	mil-khee-keh-*rei*	די מילכיקערײַ
dairy (adj.)	milkhik	*meelkh*-eek	מילכיק
daisy	di margeritke	mahrg-eh-*reet*-keh	די מאַרגעריטקע
damn, to	farshiltn	fahr-*sheelt*-n	פֿאַרשילטן
damp	faykht	feikht	פֿײַכט
dance, to	tantsn	*tahnts*-n	טאַנצן
danger	di sakone	sah-*kaw*-neh	די סכּנה
	di gefar	geh-*fahr*	די געפֿאַר
dangerous	sakonedik	sah-*kaw*-neh-dik	סכּנהדיק
	geferlekh	geh-*fehr*-lehkh	געפֿערלעך
dark (in color)	tunkl	*toonk*-l	טונקל
dark (without light)	fintster	*feents*-tehr	פֿינצטער
darkness	dos finsternish	*feents*-tehr-nish	דאָס פֿינצטערניש
darn, to (mend)	tsireven	*tsee*-reh-vehn	צירעווען
date (calendar)	di date	*dah*-teh	די דאַטע
date (fruit)	der teytl	*tayt*-l	דער טייטל
daughter	di tokhter	*tawkh*-tehr	די טאָכטער
daughter-in-law	di shnur	shnoor	די שנור
dawn	der kayor	kah-*yawr*	דער קאַיאָר
day (24 hour period)	der mes-les	mehs-*lehs*	דער מעת־לעת
day	der tog	tawg	דער טאָג
daylight	dos toglikht	*tawg*-likht	דאָס טאָגליכט
dead	toyt	toyt	טויט
dead (noun)	di meysim	*may*-seem	די מתים
deaf	toyb	toyb	טויב
deal, to (trade)	handlen	*hahnd*-lehn	האַנדלען
dealer	der soykher	*soy*-khir	דער סוחר
	der hendler	*hehnd*-lihr	דער הענדלער
dear (beloved)	tayer	*tei*-ehr	טײַער
debt	der khoyv	khoyv	דער חוב
debtor	der bal-khoyv	bahl-*khoyv*	דער בעל־חוב
deceased person	der nifter	*neef*-tehr	דער ניפֿטר
December	der detsember	deh-*tsehm*-behr	דער דעצעמבער
decent	laytish	*lei*-tish	לײַטיש
	onshtendik	*awn*-shtehn-dik	אָנשטענדיק

decide, to	bashlisn	bah-*shleesh*-n	באַשליסן
decision (judgment)	der bashlus	bah-*shlooss*	דער באַשלוס
deck of cards	dos peshl	*pehsh*-l	דאָס פּעשל
declare, to	derklern	dehr-*klehr*-n	דערקלערן
decorate, to (adorn)	baputsn	bah-*poots*-n	באַפּוצן
decrease, to	farklenern	fahr-*kleh*-nehr-n	פֿאַרקלענערן
deed	der akt	ahkt	דער אַקט
	di tuung	*too*-oong	די טוּונג
deep	tif	teef	טיף
deer	der hirsh	heersh	דער הירש
defeat	di mapole	mah-*paw*-leh	די מפּלה
defer, to	optretn	*awp*-treht-n	אָפּטרעטן
definite	bashtimt	bah-*shteemt*	באַשטימט
defy, to	antkegnshteln zikh	ahnt-*kehg*-n-shtehl-n zikh	אַנטקעגנשטעלן זיך
delay, to	farhaltn	fahr-*hahlt*-n	פֿאַרהאַלטן
deliberation	di batrakhtung	bah-*trahkh*-toong	די באַטראַכטונג
delicate	delikat	deh-lee-*kaht*	דעליקאַט
delicious	batamt	bah-*tahmt*	באַטעמט
delight	der tayneg	*tei*-nehg	דער תּענוג
delight, to	mekhaye zayn zikh	meh-*khah*-yeh zein zikh	מחיה זײַן זיך
deliver, to	tsushteln	*tsoo*-shtehl-n	צושטעלן
deluge	der mabl	*mahb*-l	דער מבול
demand, to (ask for)	fodern	*faw*-dehr-n	פֿאָדערן
democratic	demokratish	deh-maw-*krah*-tish	דעמאָקראַטיש
demon	der shed	shehd	דער שד
demonstrate, to	bavayzn	bah-*veiz*-n	באַווײַזן
dense	gedikht	geh-*deekht*	געדיכט
dentist	der tsondokter	*tsawn*-dawk-tehr	דער צאָנדאָקטער
deny, to	leykenen	*lay*-keh-nehn	לייקענען
depart, to (by vehicle)	avekforn	ah-*vehk*-fawr-n	אַוועקפֿאָרן
depart, to (by plane)	opflien	*awp*-flee-en	אָפּפֿליען
depart to (on foot)	aroysgeyn	ah-*royss*-gayn	אַרויסגיין
department store	di universal-krom	oo-nee-vehr-*sahl*-krawm	די אוניווערסאַל־קראָם
depend on, to	farlozn zikh	fahr-*lawz*-n zikh	פֿאַרלאָזן זיך
dependable	farlozlekh	fahr-*lawz*-lehkh	פֿאַרלאָזלעך
dependent upon, to be	onkumen tsu	*awn*-koo-mehn-tsoo	אָנקומען צו
deposit (fin.)	di ayntsol	*ein*-tsawl	די אײַנצאָל

depressed (mentally)	dershlogn	dehr-*shlawg*-n	דערשלאָגן
depression (econ.)	di depresye	deh-*prehs*-yeh	די דעפרעסיע
depression (sadness)	di more-shkhoyre	*maw*-reh *shkhoy*-reh	די מרה־שחורה
depth (deepness)	di tifkayt	*teef*-keit	די טיפקייט
derogatory	umkovedik	*oom*-kaw-veh-dik	אומכבודיק
descendants	di kindskinder	*keends*-keen-dehr	די קינדסקינדער
desert	di midber	*meed*-behr	די מידבר
deserted wife	di agune	ah-*goo*-neh	די עגונה
deserve, to	fardinen	fahr-*dee*-nehn	פאַרדינען
desire, to	farlangen	fahr-*lahn*-gehn	פאַרלאַנגען
desk	der shraybtish	*shreib*-tish	דער שרײַבטיש
desperate	fartsveyflt	fahr-*tsvay*-flt	פאַרצווייפלט
dessert	dos farbaysn	fahr-*beis*-n	דאָס פאַרבײַסן
destined	bashert	bah-*shehrt*	באַשערט
destiny	der goyrl	*goy*-rl	דער גורל
destruction	der khurbn	*khoor*-bn	דער חורבן
detour	der umveg	*oom*-vehg	דער אומוועג
devil	der tayvl	*teiv*-l	דער טײַוול
	der ruakh	*roo*-ahkh	דער רוח
devour, to	aynshlingen	*ein*-shleen-gehn	אײַנשלינגען
devout	frum	froom	פרום
dew	der toy	toy	דער טוי
diabetes	di tsukerkrenk	*tsoo*-kehr-krehnk	די צוקערקרענק
diamond	der diment	*dee*-mehnt	דער דימענט
diarrhea	der shilshl	*sheel*-shl	דער שילשול
dictate, to	diktirn	dik-*teer*-n	דיקטירן
die, to	shtarbn	*shtahr*-bn	שטאַרבן
die, to (animals)	peygern	*pay*-gehr-n	פגרן
diet	di diete	dee-*eh*-teh	די דיעטע
differ, to	zayn andersh	zein *ahn*-dehrsh	זײַן אַנדערש
difference	der untersheyd	*oon*-tehr-shayd	דער אונטערשייד
difficult	shver	shvehr	שווער
difficulty	di menie	meh-*nee*-eh	די מניעה
dig, to (excavate)	grobn	*grawb*-n	גראָבן
diligent	flaysik	*flei*-sik	פלײַסיק
dining room	der estsimer	*ehs*-tsee-mehr	דער עסצימער
dinner	der mitog	*mee*-tawg	דער מיטאָג
dip, to (immerse)	tunken	*toon*-kehn	טונקען
direction (course)	di rikhtung	*reekh*-toong	די ריכטונג

dirt (soil)	di erd	ehrd	די ערד
dirt (unclean matter)	dos shmuts	shmoots	דאָס שמוץ
dirty (soiled)	shmutsik	*shmoo*-tsik	שמוציק
disappear, to	farshvundn vern	fahr-*shvoond*-n *vehr*-n	פאַרשוווּנדן ווערן
disappoint, to	antoyshn	ahn-*toysh*-n	אַנטוישן
disappointment	di antoyshung	ahn-*toy*-shoong	די אַנטוישונג
disaster	dos umglik	*oom*-glik	דאָס אומגליק
disease	di krankayt	*krahn*-keit	די קראַנקייט
discount	di hanokhe	hah-*naw*-kheh	די הנחה
discover, to	oyfdekn	*oyf*-dehk-n	אויפדעקן
discussion	di diskusye	dis-*koos*-yeh	די דיסקוסיע
disgrace	der bizoyen	bee-*zoy*-en	דער בזיון
disguise	di farshtelung	fahr-*shteh*-loong	די פאַרשטעלונג
disgust	der ekl	*ehk*-l	דער עקל
disgusting	ekldik	*ehk*-l-dik	עקלדיק
	khaloshesdik	khah-*law*-shehs-dik	חלשותדיק
dish (food)	dos maykhl	*mei*-khl	דאָס מאכל
dishes (tableware)	di keylim	*kay*-lim	די כלים
dishonor	der umkoved	*oom*-kaw-vid	דער אומכּבוד
dislike, to	nit lib hobn	neet *leeb* hawb-n	ניט ליב האָבן
dismal	vist	veest	וויסט
disobey, to	nit folgn	neet *fawlg*-n	ניט פאָלגן
dispose of, to	poter vern fun	*paw*-tehr *vehr*-n foon	פטור ווערן פון
disposition (disposal)	di bazaytikung	bah-*zei*-tee-koong	די באַזייטיקונג
distant	vayt	veit	ווייַט
distinct	boylet	*boy*-leht	בולט
distorted (sour-faced)	farkrimt	fahr-*kreemt*	פאַרקרימט
distress	di noyt	noyt	די נויט
distribute, to	farteyln	fahr-*tayl*-n	פאַרטיילן
divide, to (make separate)	tseteyln	tseh-*tayl*-n	צעטיילן
divine	getlekh	*geht*-lehkh	געטלעך
divorce	der get	geht	דער גט
divorced woman	di grushe	*groo*-sheh	די גרושה
divorced man	der goyresh	*goy*-rehsh	דער גרוש
do, to	ton	tawn	טאָן
doctor	der dokter	*dawk*-tehr	דער דאָקטער

dog	der hunt	hoont	דער הונט
doll	di lyalke	*lahl*-keh	די ליאַלקע
dollar	der dolar	*daw*-lahr	דער דאָלאַר
domestic	inlendish	*een*-lehn-dish	אינלענדיש
donate, to	shenken	*shehn*-kehn	שענקען
donation	der bayshtayer	*bei*-shtei-ehr	דער בײַשטײַער
donation (alms)	di nedove	neh-*daw*-veh	די נדבֿה
donkey	der eyzl	*ayz*-l	דער אייזל
doom, to	farmishpetn	fahr-*meesh*-peht-n	פֿאַרמישפּטן
door	di tir	teer	די טיר
dose	di doze	*daw*-zeh	די דאָזע
dot	dos pintele	*peen*-teh-leh	דאָס פּינטעלע
double (adj.)	tsveyendik	*tsvay*-ehn-dik	צווייענדיק
doubt	der sofek	*saw*-fehk	דער ספֿק
doubtful	sofekdik	*saw*-fehk-dik	ספֿקדיק
doubtless	on sofek	*awn saw*-fehk	אָן ספֿק
dove	di toyb	toyb	די טויב
down	arop	ah-*rawp*	אַראָפּ
downstairs	untn	*oont*-n	אונטן
downward(s)	arunter	ah-*roon*-tehr	אַרונטער
dowry	der nadn	*nahd*-n	דער נדן
doze, to	dremlen	*drehm*-lehn	דרעמלען
dozen	der tuts	toots	דער טוץ
drag, to	shlepn	*shlehp*-n	שלעפּן
drain, to (dry)	optsapn	*awp*-tsahp-n	אָפּצאַפּן
drained	oysgeshept	*oyss*-geh-shehpt	אויסגעשעפּט
drama	di drame	*drah*-meh	די דראַמע
draw, to (pull)	tsien	*tsee*-en	ציִען
draw, to (sketch)	tseykhenen	*tsay*-kheh-nehn	צייכענען
drawer	der shuflod	*shoof*-lawd	דער שופֿלאָד
dreadful	eymedik	*ay*-meh-dik	אימהדיק
dream	der kholem	*khaw*-lim	דער חלום
dream, to	kholemen	*khaw*-lih-mehn	חלומען
dress	dos kleyd	klayd	דאָס קלייד
dress, to	onton zikh	*awn*-tawn zikh	אָנטאָן זיך
dressed up	oysgeputst	*oyss*-geh-pootst	אויסגעפּוצט
dresser	der komod	kah-*mawd*	דער קאַמאָד
dressing (food)	der sos	saws	דער סאָס
dried up	fardart	fahr-*dahrt*	פֿאַרדאַרט
drink, to	trinken	*treen*-kehn	טרינקען

drink	dos getrank	geh-*trahnk*	דאָס געטראַנק
drive, to (a vehicle)	firn	*feer*-n	פֿירן
drive, to	traybn	*treib*-n	טרײַבן
driver (chauffeur)	der shofer	shaw-*fehr*	דער שאָפֿער
driver (of horse)	der bale-gole	bah-leh-*gaw*-leh	דער בעל־עגלה
driver's license	der firlitsents	*feer*-lee-tsehnts	דער פֿירליצענץ
drop, to	faln	*fahl*-n	פֿאַלן
drown, to	dertrunken vern	dehr-*troon*-kehn *vehr*-n	דערטרונקען ווערן
drug	di meditsin	*meh*-dee-tseen	די מעדיצין
drum	di poyk	poyk	די פּויק
drunk (intoxicated)	shiker	*shee*-kehr	שיכּור
drunkard	der shiker	*shee*-kehr	דער שיכּור
dry (adj.)	trukn	*trook*-n	טרוקן
dry, to	trikenen	*tree*-keh-nehn	טריקענען
duck	di katshke	*kahch*-keh	די קאַטשקע
due (payable)	felik	*feh*-lik	פֿעליק
dull (boring)	nudne	*nood*-neh	נודנע
dumb (mute)	shtum	shtoom	שטום
dumb (stupid)	narish	*nah*-rish	נאַריש
dummy (blockhead)	der goylem	*goy*-lehm	דער גולם
dumpling	dos kneydl	k-*nayd*-l	דאָס קנײידל
dung	dos mist	meest	דאָס מיסט
dupe	dos nebekhl	*neh*-behkh-l	דאָס נעבעכל
during (prep.)	beshas	beh-*shahss*	בשעת
dusk	der farnakht	fahr-*nahkht*	דער פֿאַרנאַכט
dust	der shtoyb	shtoyb	דער שטויב
duty (obligation)	der khoyv	khoyv	דער חוב
duty-free	tsolfray	*tsawl*-frei	צאָלפֿרײַ
dwarf	der karlik	*kahr*-lik	דער קאַרליק
dwell, to	voynen	*voy*-nehn	וווינען
dwelling	di voynung	*voy*-noong	די וווינונג
dye, to	farbn	*fahrb*-n	פֿאַרבן
dysentery	di disenterye	dee-sehn-*tehr*-yeh	די דיסענטעריע

each (adj.)	yeder	*yeh*-dehr	יעדער
each one	yeder eyner	*yeh*-dehr *ay*-nehr	יעדער איינער
ear	der oyer	*oy*-ehr	דער אויער

earache	der oyer-veytik	*oy*-ehr-*vay*-tik	דער אויער־ווייטיק
earlock	di peye	*pay*-eh	די פּאה
earlier	frier	*free*-ehr	פֿריער
early	fri	free	פֿרי
earn, to	fardinen	fahr-*dee*-nehn	פֿאַרדינען
earnest	erntst	*eh*-rintst	ערנסט
earring	dos oyringl	*oy*-ring-l	דאָס אויירינגל
earth	di erd	ehrd	די ערד
earthquake	dos erd-tsiternish	*ehrd*-*tsee*-tehr-nish	דאָס ערד־ציטערניש
east	der mizrakh	*meez*-rahkh	דער מיזרח
eastern	mizrakhdik	*meez*-rahkh-dik	מיזרחדיק
easy (adj.)	gring	greeng	גרינג
eat, to	esn	*ehs*-n	עסן
eat greedily, to	fresn	*frehs*-n	פֿרעסן
eavesdrop, to	unterhern zikh	*oon*-tehr-*hehr*-n zikh	אונטערהערן זיך
echo	dos viderkol	*vee*-dehr-kawl	דאָס ווידערקול
economical	shporevdik	*shpaw*-rehv-dik	שפּאָרעוודיק
edge	di breg	brehg	די ברעג
education	khinukh	*khee*-nikh	חינוך
effective	efektiv	eh-*fehk*-teev	עפֿעקטיוו
efficient person	di berye	*behr*-yeh	די בריה
efficient	beryesh	*behr*-yehsh	בריהש
egg	dos ey	ay	דאָס איי
egotistic	egoistish	eh-gaw-*ees*-tish	עגאָיִסטיש
eight	akht	ahkht	אַכט
eighteen	akhtsn	*ahkhts*-n	אַכצן
eighth	akhter	*ahkh*-tehr	אַכטער
eighty	akhtsik	*ahkh*-tsik	אַכציק
either . . . or	oder . . . oder	*aw*-dehr . . . *aw*-dehr	אָדער . . . אָדער
elbow	der elnboygn	*ehl*-n-boyg-n	דער עלנבויגן
elect, to	derveyln	dehr-*vayl*-n	דערווויילן
election	dos valn	*vahl*-n	דאָס וואַלן
electricity	di elektre	eh-*lehk*-treh	די עלעקטרע
electric fan	der ventilator	vehn-tee-*lah*-tawr	דער ווענטילאַטאָר
electronics	di elektronik	eh-lehk-*traw*-nik	די עלעקטראָניק
elegant	elegant	eh-leh-*gahnt*	עלעגאַנט
elephant	der helfand	*hehl*-fahnd	דער העלפֿאַנד
elevate, to	oyfheybn	*oyf*-hayb-n	אויפֿהייבן
elevator	der lift	leeft	דער ליפֿט
eleven	elf	ehlf	עלף
eleventh	elfter	*ehlf*-tehr	עלפֿטער

eliminate, to	eliminirn	eh-*lee*-mi-nèer-n	עלימינירן
else (in addition)	nokh	nawkh	נאָך
else (different)	andersh	*ahn*-dehrsh	אַנדערש
else (otherwise)	anit	ah-*neet*	אַניט
elsewhere	andersh vu	*ahn*-dehrsh voo	אַנדערש װוּ
emaciated	oysgedart	*oyss*-geh-dahrt	אױסגעדאַרט
embarrass, to	farshemen	fahr-*sheh*-mehn	פֿאַרשעמען
embarrassment	di farlegnhayt	fahr-*lehg*-n-heit	די פֿאַרלעגנהײט
embittered	farbitert	fahr-*bee*-tehrt	פֿאַרביטערט
embittered person	der farbisener	fahr-*bee*-sehn-ehr	דער פֿאַרביסענער
embrace, to	arumnemen	ah-*room*-neh-mehn	אַרומנעמען
emergency	der noytfal	*noyt*-fahl	דער נױטפֿאַל
emotion	di emotsye	eh-*mawts*-yeh	די עמאָציע
emperor	der keyser	*kay*-sehr	דער קײסער
employ, to (use)	nitsn	*neets*-n	ניצן
employ, to	onshteln tsu	*awn*-shtehl-n tsoo	אָנשטעלן צו
empress	di keyserine	*kay*-seh-ri-neh	די קײסערינע
empty	pust	poost	פּוסט
	leydik	*lay*-dik	לײדיק
encounter, to	trefn	*trehf*-n	טרעפֿן
end, to	endikn	*ehn*-deek-n	ענדיקן
end	der sof	sawf	דער סוף
ending	der oysloz	*oyss*-lawz	דער אױסלאָז
endless	on a sof	*awn* ah sawf	אָן אַ סוף
endure, to	fartrogn	fahr-*trawg*-n	פֿאַרטראָגן
enema	di kane	*kah*-neh	די קאַנע
enemy	der soyne	*soy*-neh	דער שׂונא
engage, to (hire)	dingen	*deen*-gehn	דינגען
engaged (to be married)	farknast	fahr-*knahst*	פֿאַרקנסט
engagement (betrothal)	di farknasung	fahr-*knah*-soong	די פֿאַרקנסונג
engineer	der inzhenir	een-zheh-*neer*	דער אינזשעניר
enjoy, to	hanoe hobn fun	hah-*naw*-eh *hawb*-n foon	הנאה האָבן פֿון
enough	genug	geh-*noog*	גענוג
enter, to	arayngeyn	ah-*rein*-gayn	אַרײַנגײן
enterprise	di unternemung	*oon*-tehr-neh-moong	די אונטערנעמונג
entertain, to	farvayln	fahr-*veil*-n	פֿאַרװײַלן
entertainment	di farvaylung	fahr-*vei*-loong	די פֿאַרװײַלונג
enthusiasm	der entuzyazm	ehn-tooz-*yah*-zim	דער עטנוזיאַזם

entire	gants	gahnts	גאַנץ
entrance	der arayngang	ah-*rein*-gahng	דער אַרײַנגגאַנג
envelope	der konvert	kawn-*vehrt*	דער קאָנווערט
envy, to	nit farginen	nit-fahr-*gee*-nehn	ניט פֿאַרגינען
	mekane zayn	meh-*kah*-neh zein	מקנא זײַן
envy	di kine	*kee*-neh	די קנאה
epidemic	di epidemye	eh-pee-*dehm*-yeh	די עפּידעמיע
equal	glaykh	gleikh	גלײַך
erase, to	(oys)mekn	(oyss)*mehk*-n	(אויס)מעקן
eraser	der meker	*meh*-kehr	דער מעקער
errand	der gang	gahng	דער גאַנג
error	der grayz	greiz	דער גרײַז
	der toes	*taw*-ehs	דער טעות
escape	antloyfn	ahnt-*loyf*-n	אַנטלויפֿן
especially	spetsyel	spehts-*yehl*	ספּעציעל
essential	ikerdik	*ee*-kehr-dik	עיקרדיק
establish, to	oyfshteln	*oyf*-shtehl-n	אויפֿשטעלן
estimate, to	shatsn	*shahts*-n	שאַצן
eternal	eybik	*ay*-bik	אייביק
etiquette	der etiket	eh-tee-*keht*	דער עטיקעט
eulogy	der hesped	*hehs*-pid	דער הספּד
eve of	erev	*eh*-rehv	ערב
even (in spite of)	afile	ah-*fee*-leh	אַפֿילו
evening	der ovnt	*awv*-nt	דער אָוונט
event	di pasirung	pah-*see*-roong	די פּאַסירונג
ever (any time)	ven es iz	*vehn* ehs *eez*	ווען עס איז
ever (always)	tomid	*taw*-mid	תּמיד
everlasting	eybik	*ay*-bik	אייביק
every, (adj.)	yeder	*yeh*-dehr	יעדער
everybody	yeder eyner	*yeh*-dehr *ay*-nehr	יעדער איינער
everyone	yeder eyner	*yeh*-dehr *ay*-nehr	יעדער איינער
everything	altsding	ahlts-*deeng*	אַלצדינג
everywhere	umetum	*oo*-meh-toom	אומעטום
evidence	di raye	*rei*-eh	די ראיה
evident	kentik	*kehn*-tik	קענטיק
evil	beyz	bayz	בייז
evil eye	der eyn-ore	ayn-*haw*-reh	דער עין־הרע
exactly	punkt	poonkt	פּונקט
exaggeration	di guzme	*gooz*-meh	די גוזמה
exaggerate, to	megazem zayn	meh-*gah*-zehm zein	מגזם זײַן

example	der moshl	*mawsh*-l	דער משל
exasperated	oyfgekokht	*oyf*-geh-kawkht	אויפֿגעקאָכט
exhausted	oysgematert	*oyss*-geh-mah-tehrt	אויסגעמאַטערט
except	(a)khuts	(ah)khoots	(אַ)חוץ
exception	der oysnem	*oyss*-nehm	דער אויסנעם
excessive	iberik	*ee*-beh-rik	איבעריק
exchange, to	oysbaytn	*oyss*-beit-n	אויסבײַטן
excitable	hitsik	*hee*-tsik	היציק
excite, to	tsehitsn	tseh-*heets*-n	צעהיצן
exclaim, to	oysshrayen	*oyss*-shrei-en	אויסשרײַען
excommunication	der kheyrem	*khay*-rim	דער חרם
excrement	di tsoye	*tsoy*-eh	די צואה
excursion	di ekskursye	ehks-*koors*-yeh	די עקסקורסיע
excuse, to	antshuldikn	ahnt-*shool*-deek-n	אַנטשולדיקן
excuse	der terets	*teh*-rehts	דער תירוץ
execute, to (carry out)	oysfirn	*oyss*-feer-n	אויספֿירן
exile	dos goles	*gaw*-lehs	דאָס גלות
exist, to	eksistirn	ehk-sis-*teer*-n	עקסיסטירן
exit	der aroysgang	ah-*royss*-gahng	דער אַרויסגאַנג
expect, to	devartn	dehr-*vahrt*-n	דערוואַרטן
expectation	der aroyskuk	ah-*royss*-kook	דער אַרויסקוק
expel, to	aroystraybn	ah-*royss*-treib-n	אַרויסטרײַבן
expensive	tayer	*tei*-ehr	טײַער
expert	der mumkhe	*moom*-kheh	דער מומחה
	der meyvin	*may*-vin	דער מבֿין
explain, to	derklern	dehr-*klehr*-n	דערקלערן
explanation	di derklerung	dehr-*kleh*-roong	די דערקלערונג
explode, to	oyfraysn	*oyf*-reis-n	אויפֿרײַסן
expression	der oysdruk	*oyss*-drook	דער אויסדרוק
exquisite	mehuderdik	meh-*hoo*-dehr-dik	מהודרדיק
extensive	breyt	brayt	ברייט
extent	di greys	grays	די גרייס
extra	ekstre	*ehks*-treh	עקסטרע
extraordinary	umgeveyntlekh	*oom*-geh-vaynt-lehkh	אומגעוויינטלעך
extravagant	pazronish	pahz-*raw*-neesh	פּזרניש
extreme	ekstrem	ehkst-*rehm*	עקסטרעם
eye	dos oyg	oyg	דאָס אויג
eyebrow	di brem	brehm	די ברעם
eyeglasses	di briln	*breel*-n	די ברילן

English	Yiddish	Pronunciation	Hebrew
eyelash	di vie	*vee*-eh	די וויע
eyelid	dos ledl	*lehd*-l	דאָס לעדל
fabric (cloth)	der shtof	shtawf	דער שטאָף
face	dos ponim	*paw*-nim	דאָס פנים
fact	der fakt	fahkt	דער פאַקט
factory	di fabrik	*fah*-breek	די פאַבריק
faculty (ability)	di feikayt	*feh*-ee-keit	די פעיקייט
fade, to (lose color)	blyakirn	blah-*keer*-n	בליאַקירן
fail, to (not succeed)	durkhfaln	*doorkh*-fahl-n	דורכפאַלן
fail, to (miss)	farfeln	fahr-*fehl*-n	פאַרפעלן
faint, to	khaleshn	*khah*-leh-shn	חלשן
faint	shvakh	shvahkh	שוואַך
fair (just)	orntlekh	*aw*-rint-lehkh	אָרנטלעך
fair (pretty)	sheyn	shayn	שיין
fair (blond)	hel	hehl	העל
fair (passable)	nishkkoshedik	nish-*kaw*-shih-dik	נישקשהדיק
fair, a	der yerid	yah-*reed*	דער יריד
fairy	di feye	*feh*-yeh	די פעע
fairy tale	dos maysele	*mei*-seh-leh	דאָס מעשהלע
faith (creed)	di emune	eh-*moo*-neh	די אמונה
faith (confidence)	der bitokhn	bee-*tawkh*-n	דער בטחון
faithful	getray	geh-*trei*	געטרײַ
faker	der opnarer	*awp*-nah-rehr	דער אָפּנאַרער
faker, (sl.)	der trombenik	*trawm*-beh-nik	דער טראָמבעניק
fall (autumn)	der harbst	hahrbst	דער האַרבסט
fall, to	faln	*fahl*-n	פאַלן
false	falsh	fahlsh	פאַלש
falsehood	der lign	*leeg*-n	דער ליגן
familiar	bakant	bah-*kahnt*	באַקאַנט
family	di mishpokhe	mish-*paw*-kheh	די משפּחה
famous	barimt	bah-*reemt*	באַרימט
fantasy	di fantazye	fahn-*tahz*-yeh	די פאַנטאַזיע
far	vayt	veit	ווײַט
fare (money)	dos forgelt	*fawr*-gehlt	דאָס פאָרגעלט
farm	di farm	*fahr*-m	די פאַרם

farther	vayter	*vei*-tehr	װײַטער
fashion	di mode	*maw*-deh	די מאָדע
fast (secure)	fest	fehst	פֿעסט
fast, to	fastn	*fahst*-n	פֿאַסטן
fast (quick)	gikh	geekh	גיך
	shnel	shnehl	שנעל
fat	dos fets	fehts	דאָס פֿעטס
	dos shmalts	shmahlts	דאָס שמאַלץ
fat (adj.)	fet	feht	פֿעט
fat (sl.)	zaftik	*zahf*-tik	זאַפֿטיק
fate	der goyrl	*goy*-rl	דער גורל
father	der foter	*faw*-tehr	דער פֿאָטער
	der tate	*tah*-teh	דער טאַטע
father-in-law	der shver	shvehr	דער שװער
fatigue	di midkayt	*meed*-keit	די מידקייט
faucet	der kran	krahn	דער קראַן
fault (guilt)	di shuld	shoold	די שולד
fault (defect)	der khisorn	khee-*sawr*-n	דער חסרון
favor (kindness)	di toyve	*toy*-veh	די טובֿה
favorable	gintsik	*geen*-tsik	גינציק
fear	di moyre	*moy*-reh	די מורא
	der shrek	shrehk	דער שרעק
fear, to	moyre hobn	*moy*-reh *hawb*-n	מורא האָבן
fearful	moyredik	*moy*-reh-dik	מוראדיק
feast	di sude	*soo*-deh	די סעודה
feather	di feder	*feh*-dehr	די פֿעדער
featherbed	di perene	*peh*-reh-neh	די פּערענע
February	der februar	*fehb*-roo-ahr	דער פֿעברואַר
fee	der optsol	*awp*-tsawl	דער אָפּצאָל
feeble	shvakh	shvahkh	שװאַך
feeble-minded	shvakhkhepik	*shvahkh*-keh-pik	שװאַכקעפּיק
feel, to (touch)	tapn	*tahp*-n	טאַפּן
feeling	dos gefil	geh-*feel*	דאָס געפֿיל
fellow	der khevre-man	*khehv*-reh-mahn	דער חבֿרה-מאַן
feminine (adj.)	vayblekh	*veib*-lehkh	װײַבלעך
festival	der yontev	*yawn*-tehv	דער יום-טובֿ
fever	der fiber	*fee*-behr	דער פֿיבער
	di hits	heets	די היץ
few	vintsik	*veen*-tsik	װינציק
fiancé	der khosn	*khaws*-n	דער חתן

fiancée	di kale	*kah*-leh	די כּלה
field	dos feld	fehld	דאָס פֿעלד
fifteen	fuftsn	*foof*-tsin	פופֿצן
fifth	finfter	*feenf*-tehr	פֿינפֿטער
fifty	fuftsik	*foof*-tsik	פופֿציק
fig	di fayg	feig	די פֿײַג
figure	di figur	fee-*goor*	די פֿיגור
film	der film	feelm	דער פֿילם
filthy	shmutsik	*shmoo*-tsik	שמוציק
finagler	der dreyer	*dray*-ehr	דער דרײַער
final	letst	lehtst	לעצט
finally	lesof	leh-*sawf*	לסוף
find, to	gefinen	geh-*fee*-nehn	געפֿינען
fine (penalty)	di geltshtrof	*gehlt*-shtrawf	די געלטשטראָף
fine	fayn	fein	פֿײַן
finger	der finger	*feen*-gehr	דער פֿינגער
finish, to	endikn	*ehn*-deek-n	ענדיקן
finished	fartik	*fahr*-tik	פֿאַרטיק
fire	der fayer	*fei*-ehr	דער פֿײַער
fireman	der fayer-lesher	*fei*-ehr-*leh*-shehr	דער פֿײַער-לעשער
fireplace	der kamin	kah-*meen*	דער קאַמין
firm (business)	di firme	*feer*-meh	די פֿירמע
firm	fest	fehst	פֿעסט
first	ershter	*ehr*-shtehr	ערשטער
	ersht	ehrsht	ערשט
fish	der fish	feesh	דער פֿיש
fish, to	fishn	*feesh*-n	פֿישן
fisher	der fisher	*fee*-shehr	דער פֿישער
fist	di foyst	foyst	די פֿויסט
fit (suitable)	pasik	*pah*-sik	פּאַסיק
fitting, to be	pasn	*pahs*-n	פּאַסן
five	finf	feenf	פֿינף
fix, to	farrikhtn	fahr-*reekht*-n	פֿאַררייכטן
flag	di fon	fawn	די פֿאָן
flame	der flam	flahm	דער פֿלאַם
flank (cut of meat)	dos flanken	*flahn*-kehn	דאָס פֿלאַנקען
flash	der blits	bleets	דער בליץ
flash, to	derblitsn	dehr-*bleets*-n	דערבליצן
flatter, to	khanfenen	*khahn*-feh-nehn	חנפֿענען
flavor	der aromat	ah-raw-*maht*	דער אַראָמאַט

flee, to	antloyfn	ahnt-*loyf*-n	אנטלויפֿן
fleece	di fel	fehl	די פֿעל
flesh	dos layb	leib	דאָס לײַב
	dos fleysh	flaysh	דאָס פֿלייש
fling, to	shlaydern	*shlei*-dehr-n	שלײַדערן
flood	der mabl	*mahb*-l	דער מבול
floor (story)	der gorn	*gawr*-n	דער גאָרן
floor	di padloge	pahd-*law*-geh	די פּאַדלאָגע
	der dil	dill	דער דיל
flour	di mel	mehl	די מעל
flourish, to	blien	*blee*-en	בליִען
flourishing	bliendik	*blee*-ehn-dik	בליִענדיק
flower	di blum	bloom	די בלום
fluffy	pukhke	*pookh*-keh	פּוכקע
flute	di fleyt	flayt	די פֿלייט
fly, to	flien	*flee*-en	פֿליִען
fly	di flig	fleeg	די פֿליג
foe	der soyne	*soy*-neh	דער שונא
	der faynd	feind	דער פֿײַנד
fog	der nepl	*nehp*-l	דער נעפּל
fold (plait)	der kneytsh	knaych	דער קנייטש
follow, to	nokhgeyn	*nawkh*-gayn	נאָכגיין
folly	di narishkayt	*nah*-rish-keit	די נאַרישקייט
	dos tipshes	*teep*-shihs	דאָס טיפּשות
food	dos esnvarg	*ehs*-n-vahrg	דאָס עסנוואַרג
food (tasty dish)	dos maykhl	*mei*-khl	דאָס מאכל
food (conforming to dietary laws) (adj.)	kosher	*kaw*-shihr	כּשר
food (not conforming to dietary laws) (adj.)	treyf	trayf	טרייף
food (not kosher for Passover)	der khometz	*khaw*-mehtz	דער חמץ
food (neither dairy nor meat) (adj.)	parev(e)	*pah*-rehv-(eh)	פּאַרעוו(ע)
food store	di shpayzkrom	*shpeiz*-krawm	די שפּײַזקראָם
fool	der nar	nahr	דער נאַר
	der tipesh	*tee*-pesh	דער טיפּש
	der shoyte	*shoy*-teh	דער שוטה

fool (sl.)	der shmendrik	*shmehn*-drik	דער שמענדריק
	der shmegege	shmeh-*geh*-geh	דער שמעגעגע
foolish	narish	*nah*-rish	נאַריש
	tamevate	*ta-meh-vah-teh*	תּמעוואַטע
foolishness	di narishkayt	*nah*-rish-keit	די נאַרישקייט
	dos tipshes	*teep*-shihs	דאָס טיפּשות
foot (anat.)	der fus	fooss	דער פֿוס
for (prep.)	far	fahr	פֿאַר
for example	lemoshl	leh-*mawsh*-l	למשל
	tsum bayshpil	tsoom *bei*-shpil	צום ביַישפּיל
for spite	oyf tselokhes	oyf tseh-*law*-khehs	אויף צו להכעיס
forbid, to	awsern	*aw*-sir-n	אסר'ן
forbidden	awser	*aw*-sir	אסור
force (violence)	di gvald	*g-vahld*	די גוואַלד
force (power)	der koyakh	*koy*-ahkh	דער כּוח
forehead	der shtern	*shtehr*-n	דער שטערן
foreigner	der oyslender	*oyss*-lehn-dehr	דער אויסלענדער
forest	der vald	vahld	דער וואַלד
forever	oyf eybik	oyf *ay*-bik	אויף אייביק
forget, to	fargesn	fahr-*gehs*-n	פֿאַרגעסן
forgive, to	moykhl zayn	*moykh*-l zein	מוחל זיַין
forgiveness	di mekhile	meh-*khee*-lih	די מחילה
fork (eating utensil)	der gopl	*gawp*-l	דער גאָפּל
formerly	a mol	ah-*mawl*	אַ מאָל
fornication	di znus	znoos	זנות זה
forsake, to	farlozn	fahr-*lawz*-n	פֿאַרלאָזן
fortunate	mazldik	*mahz*-l-dik	מזלדיק
fortune	dos ashires	ah-*shee*-rehs	דאָס עשירות
fortune (luck)	dos mazl	*mahz*-l	דאָס מזל
forty	fertsik	*fehr*-tsik	פֿערציק
forward (adv.)	foroys	faw-*royss*	פֿאָרויס
foul	brudik	*broo*-dik	ברודיק
fountain pen	di kvalpen	k-*vahl*-pehn	די קוואַלפּען
four	fir	feer	פֿיר
fourteen	fertsn	*fehrts*-n	פֿערצן
fourth	ferter	*fehr*-tehr	פֿערטער
fowl	dos of	awf	דאָס עוף
fox	der fuks	fooks	דער פֿוקס
fracture	der brokh	brawkh	דער בראָך

fraud	der shvindl	*shveend*-l	דער שווינדל
free, to	bafrayen	bah-*frei*-en	באַפֿרײַען
free (gratuitous)	umzist	oom-*zeest*	אומזיסט
free (independent)	fray	frei	פֿרײַ
freedom	di frayhayt	*frei*-heit	די פֿרײַהייט
freeze	frirn	*freer*-n	פֿרירן
freeze, to	farfroyrn vern	fahr-*froyr*-n *vehr*-n	פֿאַרפֿרוירן ווערן
frequent	oft	awft	אָפֿט
fresh (new)	frish	freesh	פֿריש
Friday	der fraytik	*frei*-tik	דער פֿרײַטיק
fried	gepregelte	geh-*prehg*-ehlt	געפּרעגלט
friend	der fraynd	freind	דער פֿרײַנד
	der khaver	*khah*-vehr	דער חבֿר
friendly	frayndlekh	*freind*-lehkh	פֿרײַנדלעך
friendship	di frayndshaft	*freind*-shahft	די פֿרײַנדשאַפֿט
frighten, to	ibershrekn	*ee*-behr-shrehk-n	איבֿערשרעקן
frightened	dershrokn	dehr-*shrawk*-n	דערשראָקן
frog	der frosh	frawsh	דער פֿראָש
from	fun	foon	פֿון
front	der fornt	*fawr*-nt	דער פֿאָרנט
frost	der frost	frawst	דער פֿראָסט
frown, to	krimen zikh	*kree*-mehn zikh	קרימען זיך
frozen	farfroyrn	fahr-*froyr*-n	פֿאַרפֿרוירן
fruit	di frukht	frookht	די פֿרוכט
fry, to	preglen	*prehg*-lehn	פּרעגלען
frying pan	di skovrode	*skawv*-raw-deh	די סקאָווראָדע
fuel	dos brenvarg	*brehn*-vahrg	דאָס ברענוואַרג
fulfill, to	mekayem zayn	meh-*kah*-yehm zein	מקיים זײַן
full	ful	fool	פֿול
fun	di hanoe	hah-*naw*-eh	די הנאה
funeral	di levaye	leh-*vah*-yeh	די לוויה
funny	komish	*kaw*-mish	קאָמיש
fur	der pelts	pehlts	דער פּעלץ
	der futer	*foo*-tehr	דער פֿוטער
furious	oyfgekokht	*oyf*-geh-kawkht	אויפֿגעקאָכט
furnish, to	tsushteln	*tsoo*-shtehl-n	צושטעלן
furniture	dos mebl	*mehb*-l	דאָס מעבל
further (distance)	vayter	*vei*-tehr	ווײַטער
furthermore	dertsu	dehr-*tsoo*	דערצו
fuse	der korik	*kaw*-rik	דער קאָריק
fuss (commotion)	der tareram	tah-reh-*rahm*	דער טאַרעראַם

gain, to (win)	gevinen	geh-*vee*-nehn	געווינען
gall bladder	di gal	gahl	די גאַל
gallon	der galon	gah-*lawn*	דער גאַלאָן
galoshes	di kaloshn	kah-*lawsh*-n	די קאַלאָשן
gang	di bande	*bahn*-deh	די באַנדע
garage	der garazh	gah-*rahzh*	דער גאַראַזש
garbage	der opfal	*awp*-fahl	דער אָפּפֿאַל
	dos mist	meest	דאָס מיסט
garden	der gortn	*gawrt*-n	דער גאָרטן
gardener	der gertner	*gehrt*-nehr	דער גערטנער
garlic	der knobl	k-*nawb*-l	דער קנאָבל
garment	dos malbush	*mahl*-boosh	דאָס מלבוש
garter	dos zokn-bendl	*zawk*-n-behnd-l	דאָס זאָקן־בענדל
gas	der gaz	gahz	דער גאַז
gasoline	di gazolin	gah-zaw-*leen*	די גאַזאָלין
gasp, to	kaykhn	*keikh*-n	קײַכן
gate	der toyer	*taw*-yehr	דער טויער
gather, to	klaybn	*kleib*-n	קלײַבן
	zamlen	*zahm*-lehn	זאַמלען
gay	freylekh	*fray*-lehkh	פֿריילעך
gaze, to	onkukn	*awn*-kook-n	אָנקוקן
gem	der eydlshteyn	*ayd*-l-shtayn	דער איידלשטיין
general (adj.)	algemeyn	*ahl*-geh-mayn	אַלגעמיין
generation	der dor	dawr	דער דור
generosity	dos vatrones	vah-*traw*-nehs	דאָס וותרנות
generous	breythartsik	*brayt*-hahr-tsik	ברייטהאַרציק
genius	der goen	*gaw*-en	דער גאון
Gentile (masc.)	der goy	goy	דער גוי
Gentile (young male)	der sheygets	*shay*-gehts	דער שייגעץ
Gentile (fem.)	di goye	*goy*-eh	די גויע
Gentile (young fem.)	di shikse	*sheek*-seh	די שיקסע
gentleman	der dzhentlman	*jehn*-til-mahn	דער דזשענטלמאַן
genuine	ekht	ehkht	עכט
get, to	krign	*kreeg*-n	קריגן
get ready, to	ongreytn zikh	*awn*-grayt-n zikh	אָנגרייטן זיך

ghost	der gayst	geist	דער גײַסט
	der ruakh	*roo*-ahkh	דער רוח
giant	der riz	reez	דער ריז
gift (present)	di matone	mah-*taw*-neh	די מתּנה
ginger	der ingber	*eeng*-behr	דער אינגבער
girdle	der korset	kawr-*seht*	דער קאָרסעט
girl	dos/di meydl	*mayd*-l	דאָס/די מיידל
give, to (bestow)	gebn	*gehb*-n	געבן
give, to (deliver)	derlangen	dehr-*lahn*-gehn	דערלאַנגען
gizzard	der pupik	*poo*-pik	דער פּופּיק
glad	tsufridn	tsoo-*freed*-n	צופֿרידן
glance	der blik	bleek	דער בליק
glass	di gloz	glawz	די גלאָז
glitter, to	finklen	*feenk*-lehn	פֿינקלען
gloom	der umet	*oo*-meht	דער אומעט
gloom (depression)	di more-shkhoyre	*maw*-reh-*shkhoy*-reh	די מרה־שחורה
gloomy	farumert	fah-*roo*-mehrt	פֿאַראומערט
glove	di hentshke	*hehnch*-keh	די הענטשקע
glue	der kley	klay	דער קליי
gnaw, to	grizhen	*gree*-zhehn	גריזשען
go, to	geyn	gayn	גיין
go, to (ride)	forn	*fawr*-n	פֿאָרן
goad, to	untertraybn	*oon*-tehr-treib-n	אונטערטרײַבן
goal	der tsil	tseel	דער ציל
goat (fem.)	di tsig	tseeg	די ציג
goat (masc.)	der tsap	tsahp	דער צאַפּ
God	der got	gawt	דער גאָט
gold	dos gold	gawld	דאָס גאָלד
golf	der golf	gawlf	דער גאָלף
golf club	der golfshtekn	*gawlf*-shtehk-n	דער גאָלפֿשטעקן
gone	farbay	fahr-*bei*	פֿאַרבײַ
good	gut	goot	גוט
good deed	di mitsve	*mits*-veh	די מיצווה
good-by	zay(t) gezunt	*zei*(t) geh-*zoont*	זײַ(ט) געזונט
goodness	di gutskayt	*goots*-keit	די גוטסקייט
goods	di skhoyre	*skhoy*-reh	די סחורה
goose	di gandz	gahndz	די גאַנדז
gorgeous	prekhtik	*prehkh*-tik	פּרעכטיק
gossip (sl.)	di yente	*yehn*-teh	די יענטע
gossip, coarse (sl.)	di yakhne	*yahkh*-neh	די יאַכנע
government	di regirung	reh-*gee*-roong	די רעגירונג

English	Yiddish	Pronunciation	Hebrew
gown	dos kleyd	klayd	דאָס קלייד
grab	khapn	*khahp*-n	כאַפּן
graceful	gratsyez	grahts-*yehz*	גראַציעז
grade (class)	der klas	klahss	דער קלאַס
grain	di tvue	*tvoo*-ih	די תּבֿואה
grandchild	dos eynikl	*ay*-neek-l	דאָס אייניקל
grandfather	der zeyde	*zay*-deh	דער זיידע
grandmother	di bobe	*baw*-beh	די באָבע
grandparents	di zeyde-bobe	*zay*-deh-*baw*-beh	די זיידע־באָבע
grape	di vayntroyb	*vein*-troyb	די וויַינטרויב
grapefruit	der greypfrut	*grayp*-froot	דער גרייפּפֿרוט
grasp, to	onkhapn	*awn*-khahp-n	אָנכאַפּן
grass	dos groz	grawz	דאָס גראָז
grateful	dankbar	*dahnk*-bahr	דאַנקבאַר
gratification	di tsufridnkayt	tsoo-*freed*-n-keit	די צופֿרידנקייט
grave (earnest)	erntst	*eh*-rintst	ערנסט
grave	der keyver	*kay*-vehr	דער קבֿר
gravy	di yoykh	yoykh	די יויך
gray	groy	groy	גרוי
grease	dos fets	fehts	דאָס פֿעטס
great	groys	groyss	גרויס
great-grandchildren	di ureyniklekh	oor-ay-nik-lehkh	די אוראייניקלעך
great-grandmother	di elter-bobe	*ehl*-tehr-*baw*-beh	די עלטער־באָבע
great-grandfather	der elter-zeyde	*ehl*-tehr-*zay*-deh	דער עלטער־זיידע
greatness	di groyskayt	*groyss*-keit	די גרויסקייט
greedy	girik	*gee*-rik	גיריק
green	grin	green	גרין
greet, to	bagrisn	bah-*grees*-n	באַגריסן
greeting	der grus	groos	דער גרוס
	di bagrisung	bah-*gree*-soong	די באַגריסונג
grief	der tsaar	tsahr	דער צער
	dos ergernish	*ehr*-gehr-nish	דאָס ערגערניש
grieve, to	troyern	*traw*-yeh-rin	טרויערן
grim	farbisn	fahr-*bees*-n	פֿאַרביסן
grin, to	breyt shmeykhlen	*brayt shmaykh*-lehn	ברייט שמייכלען
grind, to	tsemoln	tseh-*mawl*-n	צעמאָלן
groan, to	krekhtsn	*krehkhts*-n	קרעכצן
grocery	di shpayzkrom	*shpeiz*-krawm	די שפּיַיזקראָם
ground	di erd	ehrd	די ערד
grow, to	vaksn	*vahks*-n	וואַקסן
grow, to (cultivate)	hodeven	*haw*-deh-vehn	האָדעווען

grow up, to	oyfvaksn	*oyf*-vahks-n	אויפֿוואָקסן
growl, to	vortshen	*vawr*-chehn	וואָרטשען
grown	dervaksen	dehr-*vahks*-n	דערוואָקסן
grumble, to	burtshen	*boor*-chehn	בורטשען
guarantee, to	garantirn	gah-rahn-*teer*-n	גאַראַנטירן
guarantor	der orev	*aw*-rehv	דער ערבֿ
guard, to	hitn	*heet*-n	היטן
guard	der shoymer	*shoy*-mehr	דער שומר
guess, to	trefn	*trehf*-n	טרעפֿן
guest	der gast	gahst	דער גאַסט
	der oyrekh	*oy*-rehkh	דער אורח
guide (leader)	der firer	*fee*-rehr	דער פֿירער
guilt	di shuld	shoold	די שולד
guilty	shuldik	*shool*-dik	שולדיק
guitar	di gitare	gee-*tah*-reh	די גיטאַרע
gullet	der gorgl	*gawrg*-l	דער גאָרגל
gum (anat.)	di yasle	*yahss*-leh	די יאַסלע
gun	di biks	beeks	די ביקס
guy	der khevre-man	*khehv*-reh-mahn	דער חבֿרה־מאַן

habit	di gevoynhayt	geh-*voyn*-heit	די געוווינהייט
hail	der hogl	*hawg*-l	דער האָגל
hair	di hor	hawr	די האָר
half (adv., adj.)	halb	hahlb	האַלב
half	di helft	hehlft	די העלפֿט
half-wit	der tam	tahm	דער תּם
hall	der koridor	kaw-ree-*dawr*	דער קאָרידאָר
halt, to	opshteln	*awp*-shtehl-n	אָפּשטעלן
hamburger	der kotlet	kawt-*leht*	דער קאָטלעט
hammer	der hamer	*hah*-mehr	דער האַמער
hand	di hant	hahnt	די האַנט
hand towel	dos hantekh	*hahn*-tehkh	דאָס האַנטעך
handkerchief	dos noztikhl	*nawz*-teekh-l	דאָס נאָזטיכל
handle	dos hentl	*hehnt*-l	דאָס הענטל
handsome	sheyn	shayn	שיין
hang, to	hengen	*hehn*-gehn	הענגען
happen, to	pasirn	pah-*seer*-n	פּאַסירן

English	Yiddish	Pronunciation	Hebrew
happily (luckily)	tsum glik	tsoom *gleek*	צום גליק
happiness	dos glik	gleek	דאָס גליק
happy	gliklekh	*gleek*-lehkh	גליקלעך
hard (difficult)	shver	shvehr	שווער
hard (not soft)	hart	hahrt	האַרט
hardly	koym	koym	קוים
hardship	di noyt	noyt	די נויט
harm, to	shatn	*shaht*-n	שאַטן
harsh	harb	hahrb	האַרב
Hasidic rabbi	der rebe	*reh*-beh	דער רבי
hasten, to	tsuayln	*tsoo*-eil-n	צואײַלן
hat	der hut	hoot	דער הוט
hat (traditional fur)	der spodik	*spaw*-dik	דער ספּאָדיק
hatchet	di hak	hahk	די האַק
hate, to	faynt hobn	*feint* hawb-n	פֿײַנט האָבן
hate	di sine	*see*-nih	די שׂנאה
hatred	der has	hahss	דער האַס
haul, to	shlepn	*shlehp*-n	שלעפּן
have, to	hobn	*hawb*-n	האָבן
have in mind, to	hobn in zinen	*hawb*-n in *zee*-nehn	האָבן אין זינען
hay	dos hey	hay	דאָס היי
he	er	ehr	ער
head (anat.)	der kop	kawp	דער קאָפּ
head (chief)	der rosh	rawsh	דער ראָש
headache	der kopveytik	*kawp*-vay-tik	דער קאָפּווייטיק
headlight	der fonar	faw-*nahr*	דער פֿאָנאַר
heal, to	heyln	*hayl*-n	היילן
healthy	gezunt	geh-*zoont*	געזונט
hear, to	hern	*hehr*-n	הערן
heart	dos harts	hahrts	דאָס האַרץ
heartache	der hartsveytik	*hahrts*-vay-tik	דער האַרצווייטיק
heartburn	dos harts-brenenish	*hahrts*-breh-neh-neesh	דאָס האַרץ־ברענעניש
hearty	hartsik	*hahr*-tsik	האַרציק
heat	di hits	heets	די היץ
heat, to	heytsn	*hayts*-n	הייצן
heave, to	heybn	*hayb*-n	הייבן
heaven	der himl	*heem*-l	דער הימל
heavy	shver	shvehr	שווער
Hebrew	dos hebreish	heh-*breh*-ish	דאָס העברעיש

heel	di pyate	pee-*ah*-teh	די פּיאַטע
height	di heykh	haykh	די הייך
heir	der yoyresh	*yoy*-rehsh	דער יורש
hell	dos gehenem	geh-*heh*-nehm	דאָס גהינום
hello	sholem-aleykhem	*shaw*-lehm-ah-*lay*-khehm	שלום־עליכם
help, to	helfn	*hehlf*-n	העלפֿן
help	di hilf	heelf	די הילף
Help!	gvald	g-*vahld*	גוואַלד
helpful	nutsik	*noo*-tsik	נוציק
helpless	ophentik	*awp*-hehn-tik	אָפּהענטיק
helpless person	dos nebekhl	*neh*-behkh-l	דאָס נעבעכל
hem	der zoym	zoym	דער זוים
hen	di hun	hoon	די הון
henceforth	fun itst on	foon eetst awn	פֿון איצט אָן
her	ir	eer	איר
	zi	zee	זי
herb	dos kraytekhts	*krei*-tehkhts	דאָס קרײַטעכץ
herd	di stade	*stah*-deh	די סטאַדע
here (in this locality)	do	daw	דאָ
here (in pointing)	ot	awt	אָט
here (hither)	aher	ah-*hehr*	אַהער
hereafter	lehabe	leh-*hah*-beh	להבא
hernia	di kile	*kee*-leh	די קילע
	der brokh	brawkh	דער בראָך
hero	der held	hehld	דער העלד
heroic	heldish	*hehl*-dish	העלדיש
heroine	di heldin	*hehl*-din	די העלדין
heroism	di gvure	g-*voo*-reh	די גבורה
herring	der hering	*heh*-reeng	דער הערינג
herself	zikh	zikh	זיך
hesitate, to	kvenklen zikh	k-*vehnk*-lehn zikh	קווענקלען זיך
hide	di fel	fehl	די פעל
hide, to	bahaltn	bah-*hahlt*-n	באַהאַלטן
hidden	farborgn	fahr-*bawrg*-n	פֿאַרבאָרגן
high	hoykh	hoykh	הויך
high school	di mitlshul	*meet*-l-shool	די מיטלשול
highway	der shosey	*shaw*-say	דער שאָסיי
hill	dos bergl	*behrg*-l	דאָס בערגל
him	im	eem	אים
himself	zikh	zikh	זיך

hip	di lend	lehnd	די לענד
hire, to	dingen	*deen*-gehn	דינגען
his	zayner	*zei*-nehr	זײַנער
	zayn	zein	זײַן
history	di geshikhte	geh-*sheekh*-teh	די געשיכטע
hit, to	shlogn	*shlawg*-n	שלאָגן
hoarse	heyzerik	*hay*-zeh-rik	הייזעריק
hoax	der opnar	*awp*-nahr	דער אָפּנאַר
hodge podge	der mishmash	*mish*-mahsh	דער מישמאַש
hog	der khazer	*khah*-zehr	דער חזיר
hold, to	haltn	*hahlt*-n	האַלטן
holdings	der farmegn	fahr-*mehg*-n	דער פֿאַרמעגן
hole	di lokh	lawkh	די לאָך
holiday	der yontev	*yawn*-tehv	דער יום־טובֿ
holy	heylik	*hay*-lik	הייליק
home	di heym	haym	די היים
homey	heymish	*hay*-mish	היימיש
homesick	farbenkt	fahr-*behnkt*	פֿאַרבענקט
homeward	aheym	ah-*haym*	אהיים
honest	orntlekh	*aw*-rint-lehkh	אָרנטלעך
	erlekh	*ehr*-lehkh	ערלעך
honesty	di erlekhkayt	*ehr*-lehkh-keit	די ערלעכקייט
honey	der honik	*haw*-nik	דער האָניק
honeydew	di tsesarke	tseh-*sahr*-keh	די צעסאַרקע
honor	der koved	*kaw*-vid	דער כּבֿוד
honor, to	opgebn koved	*awp*-gehb-n *kaw*-vehd	אָפּגעבן כּבֿוד
honorable	bekovedik	beh-*kaw*-veh-dik	בכּבֿודיק
hoof	di kopete	*kaw*-peh-teh	די קאָפּעטע
hook	der kruk	krook	דער קרוק
hope	di hofenung	*haw*-feh-noong	די האָפֿענונג
hope, to	hofn	*hawf*-n	האָפֿן
hopeful	ful mit hofenung	*fool* mit *haw*-feh-noong	פֿול מיט האָפֿענונג
hopefully	halevay	hah-leh-*vei*	הלװאַי
hopeless	on hofenung	*awn haw*-feh-noong	אָן האָפֿענונג
	farfalen	fahr-*fahl*-n	פֿאַרפֿאַלן
horn (mus.)	der trumeyt	*troo*-mayt	דער טרומייט
horrible	groylik	*groy*-lik	גרוילי
horse	dos ferd	fehrd	דאָס פֿערד
horseradish	der khreyn	khrayn	דער כריין
hosiery	dos zoknvarg	*zawk*-n-vahrg	דאָס זאָקנוואַרג

hospital	der shpitol	shpee-*tawl*	דער שפּיטאָל
host	der gastgeber	*gahst*-geh-behr	דער גאַסטגעבער
	der bale-bos	bah-leh-*bawss*	דער בעל־הבית
hostage	der orevnik	*awr*-ehv-nik	דער ערבניק
hostess	di gastgeberin	*gahst*-geh-behr-in	די גאַסטגעבערין
	di bale-boste	bah-leh-*bawss*-teh	די בעל־הביתטע
hostile	fayndlekh	*feind*-lehkh	פֿײַנדלעך
hot	heys	hays	הייס
hotel	der hotel	haw-*tehl*	דער האָטעל
hour	di sho	shaw	די שעה
house	dos hoyz	hoyz	דאָס הויז
	di shtub	shtoob	די שטוב
housewife	di bale-boste	bah-leh-*bawss*-teh	די בעל־הביתטע
how	vi	vee	ווי
how many	vifl	vifl	וויפל
however	fundestvegn	foon-*dehst*-*vehg*-n	פונדעסטוועגן
huckleberry	di tshernitse	*chehr*-nee-tseh	די טשערניצע
hug, to	haldzn	*hahldz*-n	האַלדזן
human	mentshlekh	*mehnch*-lehkh	מענטשלעך
human being	der mentsh	mehnch	דער מענטש
humanity	di mentshhayt	*mehnch*-heit	די מענטשהייט
humble	anivesdik	ah-*nee*-vehs-dik	עניוותדיק
humiliate, to	mevayesh zayn	meh-*vah*-yehsh-zein	מבייש זײַן
humiliation	der zilzl	*zeelz*-l	דער זילזול
humility	dos anives	ah-*nee*-vehs	דאָס עניוות
humor	der humor	hoo-*mawr*	דער הומאָר
hump	der horb	hawrb	דער האָרב
hunchback	der hoyker	*hoy*-kehr	דער הויקער
hundred	hundert	*hoon*-dehrt	הונדערט
hunger	der hunger	*hoon*-gehr	דער הונגער
hungry	hungerik	*hoon*-geh-rik	הונגעריק
hurry, to	ayln zikh	*eil*-n zikh	אײַלן זיך
hurt, to (**cause pain**)	vey ton	*vay* tawn	וויי טאָן
husband	der man	mahn	דער מאַן
hypocrisy	dos tsvies	*tsvee*-ehs	דאָס צביעות
hypocrite	der tsvuak	tsvoo-*ahk*	דער צבועק

I	ikh	eekh	איך
ice	dos ayz	eiz	דאָס אײַז
ice cream	der ayzkrem	*eiz*-krehm	דער אײַזקרעם
icy	ayzik	*ei*-zik	אײַזיק
idea	der aynfal	*ein*-fahl	דער אײַנפֿאַל
	di idee	ee-*day*-eh	די אידעע
identify	identifitsirn	ee-dehn-tee-fee-*tseer*-n	אידענטיפֿיצירן
idiot	der idiot	ee-dee-*awt*	דער אידיאָט
idle	pust un pas	*poost* oon *pahss*	פּוסט און פּאַס
idol	der gech	gehch	דער געטש
if	tomer	*taw*-mehr	טאָמער
	az	ahz	אַז
if (whether)	tsi	tsee	צי
if (supposing that)	oyb	oyb	אויב
ignoramus	der am-orets	ahm-*aw*-rehts	דער עם־האָרץ
	der grober-yung	*graw*-behr-yoong	דער גראָבער־יונג
ignorant	umvisndik	*oom*-vees-n-dik	אומוויסנדיק
ill	krank	krahnk	קראַנק
illiterate person	der analfabet	ahn-*ahlf*-ah-beht	דער אַנאַלפֿאַבעט
illness	di krankayt	*krahn*-keit	די קראַנקייט
illustration	di ilustratsye	ee-loo-*strahts*-yeh	די אילוסטראַציע
imagination	di fantazye	fahn-*tahz*-yeh	די פֿאַנטאַזיע
imitate, to	nokhmakhn	*nawkh*-mahkh-n	נאָכמאַכן
immediately	teykef	*tay*-kehf	תּיכּף
immigrant	der imigrant	eem-ee-*grahnt*	דער אימיגראַנט
impatience	di umgeduld	*oom*-geh-doold	די אומגעדולד
impediment	di menie	meh-*nee*-eh	די מניעה
impetuous	hastik	*hahs*-tik	האַסטיק
implore, to	betn rakhmim	*beht*-n *rahkh*-meem	בעטן רחמים
important	vikhtik	*veekh*-tik	וויכטיק
impossible	ummiglekh	*oom-meeg*-lehkh	אוממיגלעך
improve, to	farbesern	fahr-*beh*-sehr-n	פֿאַרבעסערן
impure	umreyn	*oom*-rayn	אומרײן
in (adv.)	arayn	ah-*rein*	אַרײַן
in (prep.)	in	in	אין

in-law (one's child's spouse's parent) (masc.)	der mekhutn	meh-*khoot*-n	דער מחותּן
in-law (one's child's spouse's parent) (fem.)	di mekheteneste	meh-kheh-*teh*-nehs-teh	די מחותּנסטע
incidentally	agev	ah-*gehv*	אגב
include, to	araynnemen	ah-*rein*-neh-mehn	אַרײַננעמען
inclination to good	der yeytser-tov	*yay*-tsehr-*tawv*	דער יצר־טוב
inclination to evil	der yeytser-hore	*yey*-tsehr-*haw*-rih	דער יצר־הרע
income	di hakhnose	hahkh-*naw*-seh	די הכנסה
income tax	der hakhnose-shtayer	hahkh-*naw*-seh-*shtei*-ehr	דער הכנסה־שטײַער
incorrect	nit-rikhtik	nit-*reekh*-tik	ניט־ריכטיק
increase, to	fargresern	fahr-*greh*-sehr-n	פֿאַרגרעסערן
indeed	take	*tah*-keh	טאַקע
indicate, to (suggest)	gebn tsu farshteyn	*gehb*-n tsoo fahr-*shtayn*	געבן צו פֿאַרשטײן
indicate, to	onvayzn	*awn*-veiz-n	אָנווײַזן
indifferent	glaykhgiltik	*gleikh*-gil-tik	גלײַכגילטיק
indigestion	di nit-fardayung	nit-fahr-*dei*-oong	די ניט־פֿאַרדײַונג
indoors	ineveynik	*een*-eh-vay-nik	אינעווייניק
industrious	flaysik	*fly*-sik	פֿלײַסיק
inept person	der shlimiel	shli-*meel*	דער שלימיעל
inexpensive	bilik	*bee*-lik	ביליק
infant	dos oyfele	*oy*-feh-leh	דאָס אויפֿעלע
infection	di infektsye	een-*fehk*-tsyeh	די אינפֿעקציע
inflammation	di ontsindung	*awn*-tsin-doong	די אָנצינדונג
inflation	di inflatsye	in-*flahts*-yeh	די אינפֿלאַציע
influence	di hashpoe	hah-*shpaw*-eh	די השפּעה
influenza	di influentsie	in-floo-*ehn*-tsyeh	די אינפֿלוענציע
inform, to	onzogn	*awn*-zawg-n	אָנזאָגן
imformation	di informatsye	in-fawr-*mahts*-yeh	די אינפֿאָרמאַציע
inherit, to	yarshenen	*yahr*-sheh-nehn	ירשענען
inheritance	di yerushe	yeh-*roo*-shih	די ירושה
injury	di vund	voond	די ווּנד
ink	di tint	teent	די טינט
inn	di kretshme	*krehch*-meh	די קרעטשמע
innocent	umshuldik	*oom*-shool-dik	אומשולדיק
inquiry	der onfreg	*awn*-frehg	דער אָנפֿרעג

insane	meshuge	meh-*shoo*-geh	משוגע
insect	der insekt	in-*sehkt*	דער אינסעקט
inside	ineveynik	*een*-eh-vay-nik	אינעווייניק
insignificant	nishtik	*neesh*-tik	נישטיק
inspect, to	onkukn	*awn*-kook-n	אָנקוקן
inspiration	di inspiratsye	in-spee-*rahts*-yeh	די אינספּיראַציע
instance (example)	der moshel	*maw*-shehl	דער משל
instant	di rege	*reh*-geh	די רגע
instantly	teykef	*tay*-kehf	תּיכּף
instead of	anshtot	ahn-*shtawt*	אַנשטאָט
instruct, to	onvayzn	*awn*-veiz-n	אָנוװײַזן
	lernen	*lehr*-nehn	לערנען
insufficient	nit-genugik	neet-geh-*noog*-ik	ניט־גענוגיק
insult	di baleydikung	bah-*lay*-dee-koong	די באַליידיקונג
insult, to	baleydikn	bah-*lay*-deek-n	באַליידיקן
insurance	di strakhirung	strah-*khee*-roong	די סטראַכירונג
	di farzikherung	fahr-*zee*-kheh-roong	די פֿאַרזיכערונג
insured	farzikhert	fahr-*zee*-khehrt	פֿאַרזיכערט
intelligence	di inteligents	in-teh-lee-*gehnts*	די אינטעליגענץ
intelligent	inteligent	in-teh-lee-*gehnt*	אינטעליגענט
intentionally	bekivn	beh-*keev*-n	בכּיוון
interesting	interesant	in-teh-reh-*sahnt*	אינטערעסאַנט
interfere, to	araynmishn zikh	ah-*rein*-meesh-n zikh	אַרײַנמישן זיך
interpret, to	oystaytshn	*oyss*-teich-n	אויסטײַטשן
interrupt, to	iberraysn	*ee*-behr-reis-n	איבעררײַסן
intestine	di kishke	*keesh*-keh	די קישקע
into (prep.)	in	in	אין
into (adv.)	arayn in	ah-*rein* in	אַרײַן אין
intolerable	nit tsu fartrogn	neet tsoo fahr-*trawg*-n	ניט צו פֿאַרטראָגן
introduce, to	bakenen	bah-*keh*-nehn	באַקענען
invalid	der khoyle	*khoy*-leh	דער חולה
invent, to	oysgefinen	*oyss*-geh-fee-nehn	אויסגעפֿינען
invention	dos oysgefins	*oyss*-geh-finss	דאָס אויסגעפֿינס
invest, to	investirn	in-vehs-*teer*-n	אינוועסטירן
investigate, to	oysforshn	*oyss*-fawrsh-n	אויספֿאָרשן
investigation	di oysforshung	*oyss*-fawr-shoong	די אויספֿאָרשונג
invitation	di farbetung	fahr-*beh*-toong	די פֿאַרבעטונג
invite, to	farbetn	fahr-*beht*-n	פֿאַרבעטן
iron (metal)	dos ayzn	*eiz*-n	דאָס אײַזן
iron (pressing)	dos presayzn	*prehs*-eiz-n	דאָס פּרעסאײַזן

is	iz	eez	איז
irritation (sarcastic dig)	der shtokh	shtawkh	דער שטאָך
island	der indzl	*eendz*-l	דער אינדזל
Israel	dos yizroel	yis-*raw*-ihl	דאָס ישראל
issue (controversy)	di plukte	*plook*-teh	די פּלוגתּא
it	es	ehs	עס
itch	dos baysenish	*bei*-sehn-ish	דאָס בײַסעניש
its	zayn	zein	זײַן
	zayner	*zei*-nehr	זײַנער
itself	zikh	zikh	זיך
ivy	der vilder vayn	*veel*-dehr vein	דער ווילדער ווײַן

jacket	di yak	yahk	די יאַק
	dos rekl	*rehk*-l	דאָס רעקל
jail	di turme	*toor*-meh	די טורמע
January	der yanuar	*yah*-noo-ahr	דער יאַנואַר
jar	der sloy	sloy	דער סלוי
jaw	der kayer	*kei*-ehr	דער קײַער
	der kin	kin	דער קין
jazz	der dzhez	jehz	דער דזשעז
jealous	eyferzikhtik	*ay*-fehr-zikh-tik	אײפֿערזיכטיק
jelly	der galaret	gah-lah-*reht*	דער גאַלאַרעט
	dos ayngemakhts	*ein*-geh mahkhts	דאָס אײַנגעמאַכטס
jerk (sl.)	der shnuk	shnook	דער שנוק
jest	der katoves	kah-*taw*-vehs	דער קאַטאָוועס
jester	der lets	lehts	דער לץ
Jew	der yid	yeed	דער ייִד
jewel	der brilyant	bril-*yahnt*	דער בריליאַנט
jewelry	dos tsirung	*tsee*-roong	דאָס צירונג
Jewish	yiddish	*yee*-dish	ייִדיש
job	di shtele	*shteh*-leh	די שטעלע
join, to	baheftn	bah-*hehft*-n	באַהעפֿטן
joke	der shpas	shpahs	דער שפּאַס
	der vits	veets	דער וויץ
joke, to	vitslen zikh	*veets*-lehn zikh	וויצלען זיך
jargon	der zhargon	zhahr-gawn	דער זשאַרגאָן

journal (periodical)	der zhurnal	zhoor-*nahl*	דער זשורנאַל
joy	di freyd	frayd	די פרייד
joyful	freydik	*fray*-dik	פריידיק
Judaism	di/dos yiddishkayt	*yee*-dish-keit	די/דאָס ייִדישקייט
judge	der rikhter	*rikh*-tehr	דער ריכטער
judge, to (consider)	paskenen	*pahs*-keh-nehn	פּסקענען
judge, to	mishpetn	*meesh*-peht-n	מישפּטן
judgement	der psak	p-*sahk*	דער פּסק
jug	der krug	kroog	דער קרוג
juice	der zaft	zahft	דער זאַפֿט
juicy	zaftik	*zahf*-tik	זאַפֿטיק
July	der yuli	*yoo*-lee	דער יולי
jump, to	shpringen	*shpreen*-gehn	שפּרינגען
June	der yuni	*yoo*-nee	דער יוני
junior	yinger	*yeen*-gehr	ייִנגער
junk food (sl.)	dos khazeray	khah-zehr-*ei*	דאָס חזירײַ
junk (mess)	dos khazeray	khah-zehr-*ei*	דאָס חזירײַ
jury	di zhuri	*zhoo*-ree	די זשורי
just (exactly)	punkt	poonkt	פּונקט
just (equitable)	yoysherdik	*yoy*-shihr-dik	יושרדיק
just (only)	bloyz	bloyz	בלויז
	nor	nawr	נאָר
just now (adv.)	akorsht	ah-*kawrsht*	אַקאָרשט
justice	di gerekhtikayt	geh-*rehkh*-tee-keit	די גערעכטיקייט
	der yoysher	*yoy*-shihr	דער יושר
justify, to	barekhtikn	bah-*rehkh*-teek-n	באַרעכטיקן

kashruth	dos kashres	*kahsh*-rehs	דאָס כּשרות
keen	sharf	shahrf	שאַרף
kerosene	der naft	nahft	דער נאַפֿט
kettle	der kesl	*kehs*-l	דער קעסל
key	der shlisl	*shlees*-l	דער שליסל
kick, to	briken	*bree*-kehn	בריקען
kick	der brike	*bree*-keh	דער בריקע
kidney	di nir	neer	דע ניר
kill, to	(der) hargenen	(*dehr*) *hahr*-geh-nehn	(דער)הרגענען

kindergarten	der kinder-gortn	*keen*-dehr-*gawrt*-n	דער קינדער־גאָרטן
kind (adj.)	frayndlekh	*freind*-lehkh	פֿרײַנדלעך
kindness	di frayndlekhkayt	*freind*-lehkh-keit	די פֿרײַנדלעכקייט
	di guthartsikayt	goot-*hahr*-tsi-keit	די גוטהאַרציקייט
king	der kinig	*kee*-nig	דער קיניג
kiss	der kush	koosh	דער קוש
kiss, to	kushn	*koosh*-n	קושן
kitchen	di kikh	keekh	די קיך
kite	di flishlang	*flee*-shlahng	די פֿלישלאַנג
kitten	dos ketsl	*kehts*-l	דאָס קעצל
knee	der kni	k-*nee*	דער קני
kneel, to	knien	k-*nee*-en	קניִען
knife	der meser	*meh*-sehr	דער מעסער
knit, to	shtrikn	*shtreek*-n	שטריקן
knitting	dos shtrikeray	shtree-keh-*rei*	דאָס שטריקערײַ
knock, to	klapn	*klahp*-n	קלאַפֿן
knot	der knup	k-*noop*	דער קנופ
know, to (acquaintance)	kenen	*keh*-nehn	קענען
know, to (knowledge)	visn	*vees*-n	וויסן
knowingly	visndik	*vees*-n-dik	וויסנדיק
known (familiar)	bavust	bah-*voost*	באַוווּסט

lack, to	feln	*fehl*-n	פֿעלן
ladder	der leyter	*lay*-tehr	דער לײַטער
lady	di dame	*dah*-meh	די דאַמע
lake	di ozere	*aw*-zeh-reh	די אָזערע
lamb	dos leml	*lehm*-l	דאָס לעמל
	di lam	lahm	די לאַם
lamb chop	der shepsen-kotlet	*shehp*-sehn-*kawt*-leht	דער שעפּסן־קאָטלעט
lame	lom	lawm	לאָם
lamp	der lomp	lawmp	דער לאָמפּ
land	dos land	lahnd	דאָס לאַנד
landowner	der porets	*paw*-rehts	דער פּריץ
landscape	di landshaft	*lahnd*-shahft	די לאַנדשאַפֿט

language	dos loshn	*lawsh*-n	דאָס לשון
	di shprakh	shprahkh	די שפּראַך
large	groys	groyss	גרויס
lascivious	oysgelasn	*oyss*-geh-lahs-n	אויסגעלאַסן
lash	der shmits	shmeets	דער שמיץ
lash, to	shmaysn	*shmeis*-n	שמײַסן
lash, to (tie)	tsubindn	*tsoo*-beend-n	צובינדן
last (adj.)	letst	lehtst	לעצט
last, to	gedoyern	geh-*daw*-yehr-n	געדויערן
late	shpet	shpeht	שפּעט
late (tardy)	farshpetikt	fahr-*shpeh*-tikt	פֿאַרשפּעטיקט
later	shpeter	*shpeh*-tehr	שפּעטער
laugh, to	lakhn	*lahkh*-n	לאַכן
laughter	dos gelekhter	geh-*lehkh*-tehr	דאָס געלעכטער
laundry	dos vesh	vehsh	דאָס װעש
lavatory	der vashtsimer	*vahsh*-tsee-mehr	דער װאַשצימער
law (religious)	der din	deen	דער דין
law (governing code)	dos gezets	geh-*zehts*	דאָס געזעץ
lawn	di lonke	*lawn*-keh	די לאָנקע
lawyer	der advokat	ahd-vaw-*kaht*	דער אַדװאָקאַט
lay, to	leygn	*layg*-n	לייגן
lazy	foyl	foyl	פֿויל
lead, to	firn	*feer*-n	פֿירן
leader	der firer	*feer*-ehr	דער פֿירער
leaf	der blat	blaht	דער בלאַט
leak, to	(oys)rinen	(oyss) *lehr*-nehn zikh	(אויס)רינען
lean, to	onlenen zikh	*awn*-lehn-en zikh	אָנלענען זיך
lean	moger	*maw*-gehr	מאָגער
	dar	dahr	דאַר
learn, to (find out)	dervisn zikh	dehr-*vees*-n zikh	דערװיסן זיך
learn, to (acquire knowledge)	(oys) lernen zikh	(oyss) *lehr* nehn zikh	(אויס/לערנען זיך
learned man	der lamdn	*lahm*-dn	דער למדן
learned (in Talmud)	der talmid-khokhem	*tahl*-mid-*khaw*-khehm	דער תּלמיד־חכם
leather	di leder	*leh*-dehr	די לעדער
leave, to (depart)	avekgeyn	ah-*vehk*-gayn	אַוועקגיין
leave, to (let remain)	iberlozn	*ee*-behr-lawz-n	איבערלאָזן

lecture	di lektsye	*lehkts*-yeh	די לעקציע
left	links	leenks	לינקס
leg	der fus	fooss	דער פֿוס
legacy	di yerushe	yeh-*roo*-sheh	די ירושה
legend	di legende	leh-*gehn*-deh	די לעגענדע
leisure	di fraye tsayt	*frei*-eh tseit	די פֿרײַע צײַט
lemon	di limene	*lee*-meh-neh	די לימענע
lemonade	der limenad	lee-meh-*nahd*	דער לימענאַד
lend (to), to	antlayen	ahnt-*lei*-en	אַנטלײַען
length	di leng	lehng	די לענג
leopard	der lempert	*lehm*-pehrt	דער לעמפּערט
less	vintsiker	*veen*-tsee-kehr	ווינציקער
	veyniker	*vay*-nee-kehr	וויניקער
lesson	di lektsye	*lehkts*-yeh	די לעקציע
lest	kedey nit	keh-*day* neet	כּדי ניט
let, to (permit)	lozn	*lawz*-n	לאָזן
let us	lomir	*law*-meer	לאָמיר
letter	der briv	breev	דער בריוו
letter (alphabet)	der/dos os	awss	דער/דאָס אות
lettuce	der salat	sah-*laht*	דער סאַלאַט
level	glaykh	gleikh	גלײַך
lewd	oysgelasn	*oyss*-geh-lahs-n	אויסגעלאַסן
liability	dos akhrayes	ahkh-*rah*-yis	דאָס אחריות
liar	der ligner	*leeg*-nehr	דער ליגנער
liberate, to	bafrayen	bah-*frei*-en	באַפֿרײַען
liberty	di frayhayt	*frei*-heit	די פֿרײַהייט
library	di bibliotek	bib-lee-aw-*tehk*	די ביבליאָטעק
lick, to	lekn	*lehk*-n	לעקן
lie	der lign	*leeg*-n	דער ליגן
lie, to (be located)	lign	*leeg*-n	ליגן
lie, to (prevaricate)	lign zogn	*leeg*-n *zawg*-n	ליגן זאָגן
life	dos lebn	*lehb*-n	דאָס לעבן
lift, to	heybn	*hayb*-n	הייבן
light (of little weight) (adj.)	gring	greeng	גרינג
light (bright) (adj.)	likhtik	*leekh*-tik	ליכטיק
light, to (ignite)	ontsindn	*awn*-tsind-n	אָנצינדן
lightning	der blits	bleets	דער בליץ
like, to	lib hobn	*leeb hawb*-n	ליב האָבן
like (similar)	enlekh	*ehn*-lekh	ענלעך

like (as)	vi	vee	ווי
lilac	der bez	behz	דער בעז
lily	di lilye	*leel*-yeh	די ליליע
limb	der eyver	*ay*-v̌ehr	דער אבֿר
lime (fruit)	der laym	leim	דער לײַם
limit	der gvul	g-*vool*	דער גבֿול
limp, to	hinken	*heen*-kehn	הינקען
lining	der untershlok	*oon*-tehr-shlahk	דער אונטערשלאָק
linoleum	dos linolyen	lee-*nawl*-yehn	דאָס לינאָלייען
lion	der leyb	layb	דער לײב
lip	di lip	leep	די ליפּ
lipstick	der lipnshtift	*leep*-n-shtift	דער ליפּנשטיפֿט
list	di reshime	reh-*shee*-meh	די רשימה
little (adj.)	kleyn	klayn	קלײן
little (not much)	a bisl	ah *bees*-l	אַ ביסל
little by little	bislekhvayz	*bees*-lehkh-veiz	ביסלעכווײַז
live (adj.)	lebedik	*leh*-beh-dik	לעבעדיק
live, to (reside)	voynen	*voy*-nehn	וווינען
live, to (be alive)	lebn	*lehb*-n	לעבן
lively	lebedik	*leh*-beh-dik	לעבעדיק
liver	di leber	*leh*-behr	די לעבער
living (livelihood)	di parnose	pahr-*naw*-seh	די פּרנסה
load	di mase	*mah*-seh	די מאַסע
loaf, to	geyn leydik	gayn *lay*-dik	גיין ליידיק
loan	di halvoe	hahl-*vaw*-eh	די הלוואה
loathsome	paskudne	pahs-*kood*-neh	פּאַסקודנע
lobster	der homar	haw-*mahr*	דער האָמאַר
locality	di gegnt	*geh*-gint	די געגנט
lock, to	farshlishn	fahr-*shlees*-n	פֿאַרשליסן
lock	der shlos	shlawss	דער שלאָס
log	der klots	klawts	דער קלאָץ
lone (single)	eyntsik	*ayn*-tsik	אײנציק
lonely/lonesome	elnt	*ehl*-nt	עלנט
	eynzam	*ayn*-zahm	אײנזאַם
	umetik	*oo*-meh-tik	אומעטיק
long	lang	lahng	לאַנג
long for, to	benken nokh	*behn*-kehn nokh	בענקען נאָך
look, to	kukn	*kook*-n	קוקן
look	der kuk	kook	דער קוק
look for, to	zukhn	*zookh*-n	זוכן

loose	loyz	loyz	לויז
lose, to	farlirn	fahr-*leer*-n	פֿאַרלירן
	onvern	*awn*-vehr-n	אָנווערן
lost	farloyrn	fahr-*loy*-rin	פֿאַרלוירן
	farfaln	fahr-*fahl*-n	פֿאַרפֿאַלן
lost (one's way)	farblonzhet	fahr-*blawn*-jeht	פֿאַרבלאָנדזשעט
lotion	dos shmirekhts	*shmeer*-ehkhts	דאָס שמירעכץ
loudmouth (sl.)	dos pisk	pisk	דאָס פּיסק
love	di libshaft	*leeb*-shahft	די ליבשאַפֿט
	di libe	*lee*-beh	די ליבע
love, to	lib hobn	*leeb* hawb-n	ליב האָבן
lover	der gelibter	geh-*leeb*-tehr	דער געליבטער
lover (of the arts)	der libhober	*leeb*-haw-behr	דער ליבהאָבער
low	niderik	*nee*-deh-rik	נידעריק
lower back (anat.)	di krizhes	*kree*-zhehs	די קריזשעס
luck	dos mazl	*mahz*-l	דאָס מזל
lucky	mazldik	*mahz*-l-dik	מזלדיק
ludicrous	shtusik	*shtoo*-sik	שטותיק
luggage	der bagazh	bah-*gahzh*	דער באַגאַזש
lullaby	dos viglid	*veeg*-lid	דאָס וויגליד
lumber	dos gehilts	geh-*heelts*	דאָס געהילץ
lump	dos shtik	shteek	דאָס שטיק
lunch	der lontsh	lawntsh	דער לאָנטש
	der onbaysn	*awn*-beis-n	דער אָנבײַסן
lung	di lung	loong	די לונג
luscious	mole-tam	*maw*-leh-tahm	מלא־טעם
lust	di tayve	*tei*-veh	די תּאווה
luxury	der luksus	*looks*-ooss	דער לוקסוס

machine	di mashin	mah-*sheen*	די מאַשין
mad	meshuge	meh-*shoo*-geh	משוגע
madness	dos meshugaas	meh-shoo-*gahss*	דאָס משוגעת
magazine	der zhurnal	zhoor-*nahl*	דער זשורנאַל
magic	der kishef	*kee*-shehf	דער כּישוף
magician	der kishef-makher	*kee*-shehf-*mah*-khehr	דער כּישוף־מאַכער
magnificent	glentsndik	*glehn*-tsin-dik	גלענצנדיק

maid (servant)	di dinst	deenst	די דינסט
maiden	di bsule	b-*soo*-lih	די בתולה
	di moyd	moyd	די מויד
mail	di post	pawst	**די פּאָסט**
mail, to	aroysshikn	ah-*royss*-sheek-n	אַרויסשיקן
major	hoypt	hoypt	הויפּט
make, to	makhn	*mahkh*-n	מאַכן
male	der zokher	*zaw*-khehr	דער זכר
man	der man	mahn	דער מאַן
manage, to	onfirn	*awn*-feer-n	אָנפֿירן
manicure	der manikur	*mah*-nee-koor	דער מאַניקור
mankind	di mentshhayt	*mehnch*-heit	די מענטשהייט
manners	di manirn	mah-*neer*-n	די מאַנירן
manufacturer	der fabrikant	fah-bree-*kahnt*	דער פֿאַבריקאַנט
many	fil	feel	פֿיל
	a sakh	ah *sahkh*	אַ סך
map	di karte	*kahr*-teh	די קאַרטע
	di mape	*mah*-peh	די מאַפּע
March	der marts	mahrts	דער מאַרץ
margarine	der margarin	mahr-gah-*reen*	דער מאַרגאַרין
mark (sign)	der simen	*see*-min	דער סימן
market	der mahrk	mahrk	דער מאַרק
marriage	di khasene	*khah*-seh-neh	די חתונה
marriage match	der shidekh	*shee*-dehkh	דער שידוך
marriage broker	der shadkhn	*shahd*-khn	דער שדכן
marriage contract	di ksube	k-*soo*-beh	די כּתובה
married	khasene gehat	*khah*-seh-neh geh-*haht*	חתונה געהאַט
marvel	der vunder	*voon*-dehr	דער וווּנדער
marvelous	vunderlekh	*voon*-dehr-lehkh	וווּנדערלעך
masculine	menlekh	*mehn*-lehkh	מענלעך
mass	di mase	*mah*-seh	די מאַסע
massage	der masazh	mah-*sahzh*	דער מאַסאַזש
master (one in authority)	der bale-bos	bah-leh-*bawss*	דער בעל־הבית
match (for lighting)	dos shvebele	*shveh*-beh-leh	דאָס שוועבעלע
material	der materyal	mah-tehr-*yahl*	דער מאַטעריאַל
matter (substance)	di materye	mah-*tehr*-yeh	די מאַטעריע
mattress	der matrats	maht-*rahts*	דער מאַטראַץ
matzoh ball	dos kneydl	k-*nayd*-l	דאָס קניידל
May	der may	mei	דער מײַ

maybe	efsher	*ehf*-shehr	אפשר
mayor	der birger-mayster	*beer*-gehr-*mei*-stehr	דער בירגער־מײַסטער
me	mikh	meekh	מיך
	mir	meer	מיר
meadow	di lonke	*lawn*-keh	די לאָנקע
meal	der moltsayt	*mawl*-tseit	דער מאָלצײַט
mean, to (**have in mind**)	meynen	*may*-nehn	מײנען
mean, to (**intend**)	oyssn zayn	me-*kha*-vn zein	מכוון זײַן
meanwhile	dervayl	dehr-*veil*	דערווײַל
measles	di mozlen	*mawz*-lehn	די מאָזלען
measure	di mos	mawss	די מאָס
measure, to	mestn	*mehst*-n	מעסטן
meat	dos fleysh	flaysh	דאָס פֿלײש
meat, made of	fleyshik	*flay*-shik	פֿלײשיק
mechanic	der mekhaniker	meh-*khah*-nee-kehr	דער מעכאַניקער
meddle, to	mishn zikh	*meesh*-n zikh	מישן זיך
medicine	di meditsin	meh-dee-*tseen*	די מעדיצין
meditate, to	klern	*klehr*-n	קלערן
meet, to (**be introduced**)	bakenen zikh mit	bah-*keh*-nehn zikh mit	באַקענען זיך מיט
meeting	di zitsung	*zee*-tsoong	די זיצונג
melancholy	melankholish	meh-lahn-*khawl*-eesh	מעלאַנכאָליש
melon	der melon	meh-*lawn*	דער מעלאָן
memorial	der denkmol	*dehnk*-mawl	דער דענקמאָל
memory	der zikorn	*zee*-kawr-n	דער זכרון
mend, to	farrikhtn	fahr-*reekh*-tin	פֿאַרריכטן
mention, to	dermonen	dehr-*maw*-nehn	דערמאָנען
menu	der menyu	*mehn*-yoo	דער מעניו
merchant	der soykher	*soy*-khihr	דער סוחר
mercy	dos rakhmones	rahkh-*maw*-nehs	דאָס רחמנות
mere	bloyz	bloyz	בלויז
merely	nor	nawr	נאָר
merit, to	fardinen	fahr-*dee*-nehn	פֿאַרדינען
merit	di mayle	*mei*-leh	די מעלה
	der zkhus	zkhoos	דער זכות
mess	der balagan	bah-lah-*gahn*	דער באַלאַגאַן
message	di yedie	yeh-*dee*-eh	די ידיעה
messenger	der sholiakh	shaw-*lee*-ahkh	דער שליח
Messiah	der meshiakh	meh-*shee*-ahkh	דער משיח

middle	der mitn	*meet*-n	דער מיטן
midnight	di halbe nahkht	*hahl*-beh nahkht	די האַלבע נאַכט
midwife	di akusherke	ah-koo-*shehr*-keh	די אַקושערקע
mighty (vast)	gvaldik	g-*vahl*-dik	גוואַלדיק
milk	di milkh	meelkh	די מילך
million	der milyon	mil-*yawn*	דער מיליאָן
mind, brain intellect	der moyekh	*moy*-ehkh	דער מוח
mine	mayner	*mei*-nehr	מײַנער
minister	der minister	*mee*-nees-tehr	דער מיניסטער
minister (clergy-man)	der galakh	*gah*-lahkh	דער גלח
	der gaystlekher	*geist*-lehkh-ehr	דער גײַסטלעכער
minor (lesser)	minervertik	*mee*-nehr-*vehr*-tik	מינערווערטיק
minute	di minut	mee-*noot*	די מינוט
miracle	der nes	nehs	דער נס
miraculous	nisimdik	*nees*-im-dik	נסימדיק
mirror	der shpigl	*shpeeg*-l	דער שפּיגל
miscellaneous	farsheydn	fahr-*shayd*-n	פֿאַרשיידן
mischief	dos shtiferay	*shtee*-feh-rei	דאָס שטיפֿערײַ
mischievous	shtiferish	*shtee*-feh-rish	שטיפֿעריש
miser	der kamtsn	*kahmts*-n	דער קמצן
miserable	tsoredik	*tsaw*-reh-dik	צרהדיק
misery	di tsores	*tsaw*-rehs	די צרות
misfortune	dos umglik	*oom*-gleek	דאָס אומגליק
mislay, to	farleygn	fahr-*layg*-n	פֿאַרלייגן
mislead, to	farfirn	fahr-*feer*-n	פֿאַרפֿירן
miss, to (long for)	benken nokh	*behn*-kehn nawkh	בענקען נאָך
Miss	fraylin	*frei*-lin	פֿרײַלין
missing	felndik	*fehl*-n-dik	פֿעלנדיק
mist	der nepl	*nehp*-l	דער נעפּל
mistake	der toes	*taw*-ehs	דער טעות
Mister	reb	rehb	רב
	her	hehr	הער
mistress (paramour)	di metrese	meht-*reh*-seh	די מעטרעסע
mitten	dos kulikl	*koo*-leek-l	דאָס קוליקל
mix, to	mishn	*meesh*-n	מישן
mix-up (confusion)	di tsemishung	tseh-*mee*-shoong	די צעמישונג
mixed-up (emo-tionally)	tsedreyt	tseh-*drayt*	צעדרייט
mob	der hamoyn	hah-*moyn*	דער המון

mock, to	makhn khoyzek fun	mahkh-n *khoy*-zehk foon	מאַכן חוזק פֿון
moderate	mesik	*meh*-sik	מעסיק
modern	modern	maw-*dehr*-n	מאָדערן
modesty	di basheydnkayt	bah-*shayd*-n-keit	די באַשײדנקײט
moist	faykht	feikht	פֿײַכט
moldy	farshimlt	fahr-*shee*-mlt	פֿאַרשימלט
moment	der moment	maw-*mehnt*	דער מאָמענט
Monday	der montik	*mawn*-tik	דער מאָנטיק
money	dos gelt	gehlt	דאָס געלט
monkey	di malpe	*mahl*-peh	די מאַלפּע
month	der khoydesh	*khoy*-dehsh	דער חודש
monument	der denkmol	*dehnk*-mawl	דער דענקמאָל
mood	di shtimung	*shtee*-moong	די שטימונג
moon	di levone	leh-*vaw*-neh	די לבֿנה
moonlight	dos levone-likht	leh-*vaw*-neh-likht	דאָס לבֿנה־ליכט
morale	di moral	maw-*rahl*	די מאָראַל
moral	di moral	maw-*rahl*	די מאָראַל
moral (adj.)	moralish	maw-*rah*-leesh	מאָראַליש
more	mer	mehr	מער
more (a lot more)	a sakh mer	ah *sahkh* mehr	אַ סך מער
more often	ofter	*awf*-tehr	אָפֿטער
morning	der frimorgn	*free*-mawrg-n	דער פֿרימאָרגן
morning prayer	di shakhris	*shahkh*-riss	די שחרית
morsel (of food)	der bisn	*bees*-n	דער ביסן
mortgage	di hipotek	hee-paw-*tehk*	די היפּאָטעק
mosquito	der komar	kaw-*mahr*	דער קאָמאַר
most	merste	*mehr*-steh	מערסטע
mostly	merstns	*mehr*-stns	מערסטנס
moth	der mol	mawl	דער מאָל
mother	di muter	*moo*-tehr	די מוטער
mother-in-law	di shviger	shvee-gehr	די שוויגער
mother tongue	mame-loshn	*mah*-meh-*lawsh*-n	מאַמע־לשון
motive	der motiv	maw-*teev*	דער מאָטיוו
motor	der motor	maw-*tawr*	דער מאָטאָר
mound	dos bergele	*behr*-geh-leh	דאָס בערגעלע
mountain	der barg	bahrg	דער באַרג
mourn, to	troyern	*traw*-yeh-rin	טרויערן
mourner's dox-ology	der kadish	*kah*-dish	דער קדיש
mournful	troyerik	*traw*-yeh-rik	טרויעריק

English	Yiddish	Pronunciation	Hebrew
mourning period	di shive	*shee*-veh	די שיבֿעה
mouse	di moyz	moyz	די מויז
moustache	di vontses	*vawnt*-sehs	װאָנצעס
mouth	dos moyl	moyl	דאָס מויל
move, to	rirn	*reer*-n	רירן
movie theatre	der kino	*kee*-naw	דער קינאָ
Mr.	reb	rehb	רב
	her	hehr	הער
Mrs.	froy	froy	פֿרוי
much	a sakh	ah sahkh	אַ סך
mud	di blote	*blaw*-teh	די בלאָטע
mumble, to	preplen	*prehp*-lehn	פרעפלען
murder	der mord	mawrd	דער מאָרד
murderer	der merder	*mehr*-dehr	דער מערדער
muscle	der muskl	*moosk*-l	דער מוסקל
muse, to	klern	*klehr*-n	קלערן
museum	der musey	moo-*zay*	דער מוזיי
mushroom	dos shveml	*shvehm*-l	דאָס שוועמל
music	di muzik	moo-*zeek*	די מוזיק
musician	der klezmer	*klehz*-mehr	דער קלעזמער
must	muzn	*mooz*-n	מוזן
mustard	der zeneft	*zeh*-nehft	דער זענעפֿט
mute	shtum	shtoom	שטום
mutter, to	burtshen	*boor*-chehn	בורטשען
mutton	dos shepsnfleysh	*shehps*-n-flaysh	דאָס שעפסנפֿלייש
my	mayn	mein	מײַן
myself	zikh	zikh	זיך
mysterious	misteryez	mees-*tehr*-yehz	מיסטעריעז
mystery	di misterye	mees-*tehr*-yeh	די מיסטעריע

English	Yiddish	Pronunciation	Hebrew
nag (sl.)	di klipe	*klee*-peh	די קליפה
nail (finger)	der nogl	*nawg*-l	דער נאָגל
nail (hardware)	der tshvok	chvawk	דער טשוואָק
naive	naiv	nah-*eev*	נאַיִוו
naked	naket	*nah*-keht	נאַקעט
name	der nomen	*naw*-mehn	דער נאָמען

nap (doze)	der dreml	*drehm*-l	דער דרעמל
napkin	di servetke	sehr-*veht*-keh	די סערוועטקע
narrow	shmol	shmawl	שמאָל
nasty	paskudne	pahs-*kood*-neh	פּאַסקודנע
native	der geboyrener	geh-*boy*-reh-nehr	דער געבוירענער
natural	natirlekh	nah-*teer*-lehkh	נאַטירלעך
naughty	shtiferish	*shtee*-feh-rish	שטיפֿעריש
navel	der pupik	*poo*-pik	דער פּופיק
near	noent	*naw*-ehnt	נאָענט
	lebn	*lehb*-n	לעבן
nearly	kimat	kee-*maht*	כּמעט
neat	tsikhtik	*tseekh*-tik	ציכטיק
necessary	neytik	*nay*-tik	נייטיק
necessity	di neytikayt	*nay*-tee-keit	די נייטיקייט
neck	der kark	kahrk	דער קאַרק
	der nakn	*nahk*-n	דער נאַקן
necklace	der haldzband	*hahldz*-bahnd	דער האַלדזבאַנד
necktie	der kravat	krah-*vaht*	דער קראַוואַט
	der shnips	*shneeps*	דער שניפּס
need	di noyt	noyt	די נויט
need, to	darfn	*dahrf*-n	דאַרפֿן
needle	di nodl	*nawd*-l	די נאָדל
needless	iberik	*ee*-beh-rik	איבעריק
neglect, to	farlozn	fahr-*lawz*-n	פֿאַרלאָזן
negotiation	di farhandlung	fahr-*hahnd*-loong	די פֿאַרהאַנדלונג
negotiable	farkoyflekh	fahr-*koyf*-lehkh	פֿאַרקויפֿלעך
neighbor (masc.)	der shokhn	*shawkh*-n	דער שכן
neighbor (fem.)	di shokhente	*shawkhen*-teh	די שכנה'טע
neighborhood	di shkheyneshaft	*shkhay*-neh-shahft	די שכנישאַפֿט
neither	nit der, nit yener	nit *dehr*, nit *yeh*-nehr	ניט דער, ניט יענער
nephew	der plimenik	plee-*meh*-nik	דער פּלימעניק
nerve (anat.)	der nerve	nehrv	דער נערוו
nervous	nervez	nehr-*vehz*	נערוועז
net	di nets	nehts	די נעץ
neutral	neytral	nay-*trahl*	נייטראַל
never	keyn mol nit	*kayn* mawl nit	קיין מאָל ניט
nevertheless (however)	fundestvegn	foon-*dehst*-vehg-n	פֿונדעסטוועגן
nevertheless (anyway)	meyle	*may*-leh	מילא

new	nay	*nei*	ניַי
news	di nayes	*nei*-ehs	די ניַיעס
newspaper	di tsaytung	*tsei*-toong	די צײַטונג
newsstand	der kiosk	kee-*awsk*	דער קיאָסק
next to	lebn	*lehb*-n	לעבן
nibble, to	nashn	*nahsh*-n	נאַשן
nice (agreeable)	voyl	voyl	ווויל
nickname	dos tsunemenish	*tsoo*-neh-meh-nish	דאָס צונעמעניש
niece	di plimenitse	plee-*meh*-neet-seh	די פּלימעניצע
niggardly	kamtsonish	kahm-*tsaw*-neesh	קמצניש
night	di nakht	nahkht	די נאַכט
nightgown	dos nakhthemd	*nahkht*-hehmd	דאָס נאַכטהעמד
nincompoop	der shmendrik	*shmehn*-drik	דער שמענדריק
nine	nayn	nein	ניַין
nineteen	nayntsn	*neints*-n	ניַינצן
ninety	nayntsik	*nein*-tsik	ניַינציק
ninth	naynter	*nein*-tehr	ניַינטער
no	nit	neet	ניט
	nisht	neesht	נישט
no (nay)	neyn	nayn	ניין
no (not any)	keyn	kayn	קיין
nobleman	der porets	*paw*-rehts	דער פּריץ
nobody	keyner nit	*kay*-nehr neet	קיינער ניט
nod, to	shoklen	*shawk*-lehn	שאָקלען
noise	der tuml	*toom*-l	דער טומל
noisy	tumldik	*toom*-l-dik	טומלדיק
none	keyn	kayn	קיין
	gornit	*gawr*-neet	גאָרניט
nonsense	der umzin	*oom*-zin	דער אומזין
	der shtus	shtoos	דער שטות
noodle flakes	di farfl	*fahrf*-l	די פאַרפל
noodles	di lokshn	*lawksh*-n	די לאָקשן
noon	mitogtsayt	*mee*-tawg-tseit	מיטאָגצײַט
normal	normal	nawr-*mahl*	נאָרמאַל
north	der tsofn	*tsawf*-n	דער צפון
northeastern	tsofn-mizrakhdik	*tsawf*-n-*meez*-rahkh-dik	צפון־מיזרחדיק
northern	tsofndik	*tsawf*-n-dik	צפונדיק
northwestern	tsofn-mayrevdik	*tsawf*-n-*mei*-rehv-dik	צפון־מערבדיק
nose	di noz	nawz	די נאָז
nostril	di nozlokh	*nawz*-lawkh	די נאָזלאָך

not	nisht	neesht	נישט
	nit	neet	ניט
not any	keyn	kayn	קיין
not anyone	keyner nit	*kay*-nehr neet	קיינער ניט
not anything	keyn zakh nit	kayn *zahkh* neet	קיין זאַך ניט
note (letter)	dos brivl	*bree*-vil	דאָס בריוול
	der tsetl	*tseht*-l	דער צעטל
note (musc.)	der ton	tawn	דער טאָן
notebook	di heft	hehft	די העפֿט
nothing	gornit	*gawr*-nit	גאָרניט
	gornisht	*gawr*-neesht	גאָרנישט
notice, to	bamerkn	bah-*mehrk*-n	באַמערקן
notion (idea)	der aynfal	*ein*-fahl	דער איינפֿאַל
nourishment	di dernerung	dehr-*neh*-roong	די דערנערונג
novel (book)	der roman	raw-*mahn*	דער ראָמאַן
November	der november	naw-*vehm*-behr	דער נאָוועמבער
now	itst	eetst	איצט
nowhere	in ergets nit	een *ehr*-gehts nit	אין ערגעץ ניט
numb	opgeteyt	*awp*-geh-tayt	אָפּגעטייט
number, to	tseyln	*tsayl*-n	ציילן
number	di tsol	tsawl	די צאָל
nun	di monashke	maw-*nahsh*-keh	די מאָנאַשקע
nurse	di krankn-shvester	*krahnk*-n-*shvehs*-tehr	די קראַנקן־שוועסטער
nurse, to (give treatment)	pileven	*pee*-leh-vehn	פּילעווען
nursery	der kinder-tsimer	*keen*-dehr-*tsee*-mehr	דער קינדער־צימער
nut	di nus	noos	די נוס
nutcracker	dos knaknisl	k-*nahk*-nees-l	דאָס קנאַקניסל
nutmeg	der mushkat	*moosh*-kaht	דער מושקאַט
nylon	der naylon	*nei*-lawn	דער נײַלאָן

oaf	der bulvan	bool-*vahn*	דער בולוואַן
oath	di shvue	*shvoo*-ih	די שבֿועה
obey, to	folgn	*fawlg*-n	פֿאָלגן
obituary	der nekrolog	nehk-raw-*lawg*	דער נעקראָלאָג

object	der kheyfets	*khay*-fehts	דער חפֿץ
object, to	aynvendn	*ein*-vehnd-n	אײַנווענדן
obligation	hiskhayvis	his-*khei*-viss	התחייבֿות
obscene	grob	grawb	גראָב
obscenity	di grobkayt	*grawb*-keit	די גראָבקייט
obscure	umklor	*oom*-klawr	אומקלאָר
obstinate	farakshnt	fahr-*ahksh*-nt	פֿאַרעקשנט
obvious	klor vi der tog	*klawr* vee dehr *tawg*	קלאָר ווי דער טאָג
ocean	der yam	yam	דער ים
o'clock	a zeyger	ah-*zey*-gehr	אַ זייגער
occasion	di gelegnhayt	geh-*lehg-n-heit*	די געלעגנהייט
occupation	der fakh	fahkh	דער פֿאַך
occupy, to (take possession of)	farnemen	fahr-*neh*-mehn	פֿאַרנעמען
occupy, to	voynen	*voy*-nehn	וווינען
October	der oktober	awk-*taw*-behr	דער אָקטאָבער
odd (strange)	modne	*mawd*-neh	מאָדנע
odor	der reyakh	*ray*-ahkh	דער ריח
of	fun	foon	פֿון
of course	avade	ah-*vah*-deh	אַוודאי
offend, to	baleydikn	bah-*lay*-deek-n	באַליידיקן
offense	der khet	kheht	דער חטא
offer	der forshlog	*fawr*-shlawg	דער פֿאָרשלאָג
office	dos byuro	byoo-*raw*	דאָס ביוראָ
officer (mil.)	der ofitsir	aw-fee-*tseer*	דער אָפֿיציר
officer (official)	der baamter	bah-*ahm*-tehr	דער באַאַמטער
often	oft	awft	אָפֿט
oh (pain, fright, impatience)	oy	oy	אוי
oh! (surprise)	take	*tah*-keh	טאַקע!
oil	der eyl	ayl	דער אייל
oil (edible)	der boyml	*boym*-l	דער בוימל
ointment	di zalb	zahlb	די זאַלב
	dos shmirekhts	*shmeer*-ehkhts	דאָס שמירעכץ
old	alt	ahlt	אַלט
old maid	di alte moyd	*ahl*-teh moyd	די אַלטע מויד
old man	der zokn	*zawk*-n	דער זקן
old wive's tale	di bobe mayse	*baw*-beh *mei*-seh	די באָבע־מעשׂה
olive	di masline	*mahss*-lee-neh	די מאַסלינע

English	Yiddish (transliteration)	Pronunciation	Yiddish
omelet	der omlet	awm-*leht*	דער אָמלעט
	der faynkukhn	*fein*-kookh-n	דער פֿײַנקוקן
omit, to	oyslozn	*oyss*-lawz-n	אויסלאָזן
on	oyf	oyf	אויף
on time	tsu der tsayt	*tsoo* dehr tseit	צו דער צײַט
once (formerly)	a mol	ah *mawl*	אַ מאָל
once (one time)	eyn mol	*ayn* mawl	אײן מאָל
one (someone)	me	meh	מע
	men	mehn	מען
one	eyns	ayns	אײנס
onion	di tsibele	*tsee*-beh-leh	די ציבעלע
only (single)	eyntsik	*ayn*-tsik	אײנציק
only (merely)	nor	nawr	נאָר
	bloyz	bloyz	בלויז
open	ofn	*awf*-n	אָפֿן
open, to	efenen	*eh*-feh-nehn	עפֿענען
opening	di efenung	*eh*-feh-noong	די עפֿענונג
operate, to	operirn	*aw*-peh-reer-n	אָפּערירן
operation (mil. or med.)	di operatsye	aw-peh-*rahts*-yeh	**די אָפּעראַציע**
operation (functioning)	di operirung	aw-peh-*ree*-roong	די אָפּערירונג
opinion	di meynung	*may*-noong	די מײנונג
opponent	der kegener	*keh*-geh-nehr	דער קעגענער
opposite (across from) (adv.)	antkegn	ahnt-*kehg*-n	אַנטקעגן
opposite (reverse)	der heypekh	*hay*-pehkh	דער היפּוך
opposition	di opozitsye	aw-paw-*zeets*-yeh	די אָפּאָזיציע
optimistic	optimistish	*awp*-tee-*mees*-tish	אָפּטימיסטיש
optometrist	der optiker	*awp*-tee-kehr	דער אָפּטיקער
or	oder	*aw*-dehr	אָדער
orange	oranzh	aw-*rahnzh*	אָראַנזש
orange (fruit)	der marants	mah-*rahnts*	דער מאַראַנץ
orange juice	der marantsn-zaft	mah-*rahnts*-n-zahft	דער מאַראַנצן־זאַפֿט
orchard	der sod	sawd	דער סאָד
orchestra	der orkester	awr-*kehs*-tehr	דער אָרקעסטער
orchid	di orkhidee	awr-khee-*day*-eh	די אָרכידעע
order (for merchandise)	di bashtelung	bah-*shteh*-loong	די באַשטעלונג
order (command)	der bafel	bah-*fehl*	דער באַפֿעל

order (orderliness)	di ordenung	*awr*-deh-noong	די אָרדענונג
ordinary	geveyntlekh	geh-*vaynt*-lehkh	געוויינטלעך
organ (anat.)	der organ	awr-*gahn*	דער אָרגאַן
origin	der moker	*maw*-kehr	דער מקור
orphan (masc.)	der yosem	*yaw*-sehm	דער יתום
orphan (fem.)	di yesoyme	yeh-*soy*-mih	די יתומה
other	anderer	*ahn*-deh-rehr	אַנדערער
otherwise	anit	ah-*neet*	אַניט
	andersh	*ahn*-dehrsh	אַנדערש
ought	darfn	*dahrf*-n	דאַרפֿן
our	undzer	*oon*-dzehr	אונדזער
ours	undzerer	*oon*-dzeh-rehr	אונדזערער
ourselves	zikh	zikh	זיך
out	aroys	ah-*royss*	אַרויס
out of one's mind	arop fun zinen	ah-*rawp* foon *zee*-nehn	אַראָפ פֿון זינען
outcast	der oysvorf	*oyss*-vawrf	דער אויסוואָרף
outdoors	in droysn	in *droys*-n	אין דרויסן
outhouse	der optret	*awp*-treht	דער אָפטרעט
outstanding	boylet	*boy*-leht	בולט
oven	der oyvn	*oyv*-n	דער אויוון
over (above) (adv.)	ariber	ah-*ree*-behr	אַריבער
over (prep.)	iber	*ee*-behr	איבער
over (adj.)	oys	oyss	אויס
overcast	farvolknt	fahr-*vawlk*-nt	פֿאַרוואָלקנט
overcoat	der mantl	*mahnt*-l	דער מאַנטל
overhear, to	unterhern	*oon*-tehr-*hehr*-n	אונטערהערן
overlook, to	farkukn	fahr-*kook*-n	פֿאַרקוקן
oversight	der farze	fahr-*zeh*	דער פֿאַרזע
overturn, to	iberkern	*ee*-behr-kehr-n	איבערקערן
overweight	ibervog	*ee*-behr-vawg	איבערוואָג
owe, to	shuldik zayn	*shool*-dik zein	שולדיק זײַן
own, to	farmogn	fahr-*mawg*-n	פֿאַרמאָגן
own	eygn	*ayg*-n	אייגן
own (one's own)	der eygener	*ay*-geh-nehr	דער אייגענער
ox	der oks	awks	דער אָקס
oxygen	der zoyershtof	*zoy*-ehr-shtawf	דער זויערשטאָף

pack, to	(ayn)pakn	(*ein*)*pahk*-n	(אײַן)פּאַקן
package	dos pekl	*pehk*-l	דאָס פּעקל
page	di zayt	zeit	די זײַט
pail	der emer	*eh*-mehr	דער עמער
pain	der veytik	*vay*-tik	דער ווייטיק
painful	veytikdik	*vay*-tik-dik	ווייטיקדיק
paint, to	farbn	*fahrb*-n	פֿאַרבן
paint, to (a picture)	moln	*mawl*-n	מאָלן
paint	di farb	fahrb	די פֿאַרב
painter (artist)	der moler	*maw*-lehr	דער מאָלער
painter (house)	der malyer	*mahl*-yehr	דער מאַליער
painting (picture)	dos gemel	geh-*mehl*	דאָס געמעל
pair	di por	pawr	די פּאָר
pajamas	di pizhame	pee-*zhah*-meh	די פּיזשאַמע
pal	der khaver	*khah*-vihr	דער חבֿר
pale	blas	blahss	בלאָס
palm (of hand)	di dlonye	*dlawn*-yeh	די דלאָניע
pan	di skovrode	*skawv*-raw-deh	די סקאָוואָראָדע
pancake	di latke	*laht*-keh	די לאַטקע
panic	di panik	*pah*-neek	די פּאַניק
pansy	dos khaneles eygele	*khah*-neh-lehs *ay*-geh leh	דאָס חנהלעס אייגעלע
pantry	di shpayzkamer	*shpeiz*-kah-mehr	די שפּײַזקאַמער
paper	dos papir	pah-*peer*	דאָס פּאַפּיר
paradise	der ganeydn	gah-*nayd*-n	דער גן־עדן
paralyzed	geleymt	geh-*laymt*	געליימט
parcel post	di peklpost	*peh*-kil-pawst	די פּעקלפּאָסט
pardon	di mekhile	meh-*khee*-leh	די מחילה
pardon, to	moykhl zayn	*moykh*-l zein	מוחל זײַן
pardon me	zayt moykhl	*zeit* moykh-l	זײַט מוחל
parents	di tate-mame	*tah*-teh-*mah*-meh	די טאַטע־מאַמע
park	der park	pahrk	דער פּאַרק
parrot	der papugay	pah-poo-*gei*	דער פּאַפּוגײַ
part, to	sheydn zikh	*shayd*-n zikh	שיידן זיך
part	der teyl	tayl	דער טייל
partner	der shutef	*shoo*-tehf	דער שותּף
pass, to (overtake)	iberyogn	*ee*-behr-*yawg*-n	איבעריאָגן

English	Yiddish	Pronunciation	Hebrew
passable (acceptable)	nishkoshe	nish-*kaw*-sheh	נישקשה
passenger	der pasazhir	pah-sah-*zheer*	דער פּאַסאַזשיר
passport	der pas	pahss	דער פּאַס
past (gone)	farbay	fahr-*bei*	פֿאַרבײַ
paste	der pap	pahp	דער פּאַפּ
pastry	dos gebeks	geh-*behks*	דאָס געבעקס
patch	di late	*lah*-teh	די לאַטע
path	der shteg	shtehg	דער שטעג
patience	dos geduld	geh-*doolt*	דאָס געדולד
patient (invalid)	der patsyent	pahts-*yehnt*	דער פּאַציענט
patient	geduldik	geh-*dool*-dik	געדולדיק
pauper	der kabtsn	*kahb*-tsehn	דער קבצן
	der evyen	*ehv*-yin	דער אביון
pause, to	blaybn shteyn	*bleib*-n *shtayn*	בלײַבן שטיין
paw	di lape	*lah*-peh	די לאַפּע
pawnshop	der lombard	*lawm*-bahrd	דער לאָמבאַרד
pay, to	(ba)tsoln	(*bah*)*tsawl*-n	(בֹּאַ)צאָלן
payment	di tsolung	*tsaw*-loong	די צאָלונג
pea	der arbes	*ahr*-behs	דער אַרבעס
peace	der sholem	*shaw*-lehm	דער שלום
peaceful	fridlekh	*freed*-lehkh	פֿרידלעך
peach	di fershke	*fehrsh*-keh	די פֿערשקע
peal, to	klingen	*kleeng*-en	קלינגען
peanut	di fistashke	fee-*stahsh*-keh	די פֿיסטאַשקע
pear	di barne	*bahr*-neh	די באַרנע
pearl	der perl	*pehr*-l	דער פּערל
peasant	der poyer	*paw*-yehr	דער פּויער
peasant, Russian	der muzhik	moo-*zheek*	דער מוזשיק
peculiar	modne	*mawd*-neh	מאָדנע
pedigree	der yikhes	*yee*-khis	דער ייחוס
peel, to	sheyln	*shayl*-n	שיילן
peer, to	aynkukn zikh	*ein*-kook-n zikh	אײַנקוקן זיך
pen	di pen	*pehn*	די פּען
penalty	di shtrof	shtrawf	די שטראָף
pencil	der blayer	*blei*-ehr	דער בלײַער
penis	der penis	*peh*-niss	דער פּעניס
pension	di pensie	*pehns*-yeh	די פּענסיע
people (persons)	di layt	leit	די לײַט
people (populace)	dos folk	fawlk	דאָס פֿאָלק
pepper	der fefer	*feh*-fehr	דער פֿעפֿער

perfect	perfekt	pehr-*fehkt*	פּערפֿעקט
perform, to (do)	durkhfirn	*doorkh*-feer-n	דורכפֿירן
perform, to (act)	oyftretn	*oyf*-treht-n	אויפֿטרעטן
perfume	der parfum	pahr-*foom*	דער פּאַרפֿום
perhaps	efsher	*ehf*-shehr	אפֿשר
	tomer	*taw*-mehr	טאָמער
peril	di sakone	sah-*kaw*-neh	די סכּנה
perjury	di falshe shvue	*fahl*-sheh *shvoo*-eh	די פֿאַלשע שבֿועה
permanent	shtendik	*shtehn*-dik	שטענדיק
permission	dos derloybenish	dehr-*loy*-beh-nish	דאָס דערלויבעניש
permit, to	derloybn	dehr-*loyb*-n	דערלויבן
permitted, to be	megn	*mehg*-n	מעגן
permitted, to not be	torn nit	*tawr*-n nit	טאָרן ניט
perpetual	doyresdik	*doy*-rehs-dik	דורותדיק
person	di perzon	pehr-*zawn*	די פּערזאָן
	der mentsh	*mehnch*	דער מענטש
personal	perzenlekh	pehr-*zehn*-lehkh	פּערזענלעך
perspire, to	shvitsn	*shveets*-n	שוויצן
persuade, to	iberredn	*ee*-behr-rehd-n	איבערעדן
pervert, to (distort)	farkrimen	fahr-*kree*-mehn	פֿאַרקרימען
pessimistic	pesimistish	*peh*-see-mees-tish	פּעסימיסטיש
pest (nuisance)	dos tsutshepenish	*tsoo*-cheh-peh-nish	דאָס צוטשעפּעניש
	der nudnik	*nood*-nik	דער נודניק
pester, to	dergeyn di yorn	dehr-*gayn* dee yawr-n	דערגיין די יאָרן
pet	der gletling	*gleht*-leeng	דער גלעטלינג
petition	di petitsye	peh-*teets*-yeh	די פּעטיציע
petticoat	dos unterkleyd	*oon*-tehr-klayd	דאָס אונטערקלייד
petty	nishtik	*neesh*-tik	נישטיק
pharmacist	der apteyker	ahp-*tay*-kehr	דער אַפּטייקער
pharmacy	di apteyk	ahp-*tayk*	די אַפּטייק
philanthropist	der bal-tsdoke	bahl-tseh-*daw*-keh	דער בעל־צדקה
philosophy	di filosofye	fee-law-*sawf*-yeh	די פֿילאָסאָפֿיע
photograph	di fotografye	faw-taw-*grahf*-yeh	די פֿאָטאָגראַפֿיע
piano	di pyane	pee-*ah*-neh	די פּיאַנע
pick up, to	oyfheybn	*oyf*-hayb-n	אויפֿהייבן
pickle	di zoyere ugerke	zoy-ehr-eh oo-gehr-keh	די זויערע אוגערקע
pickle, to	zayern	*zah*-yehr-n	זײַערן
picture	dos bild	beeld	דאָס בילד
pie	der pay	pei	דער פּײַ
piece (bit)	dos shtik	shteek	דאָס שטיק

English	Yiddish	Pronunciation	יידיש
piecemeal (adv.)	shtiklekhvayz	*shteek*-lehkh-veiz	שטיקלעכווײַז
pig	der khazer	*khah*-zehr	דער חזיר
pigeon	di toyb	toyb	די טויב
pile	di kupe	*koo*-peh	די קופּע
pill	di pil	peel	די פּיל
pillow	di kishn	*keesh*-n	די קישן
pilot	der pilot	pee-*lawt*	דער פּילאָט
pin	di shpilke	*shpeel*-keh	די שפּילקע
pinch, to	knaypn	k-*neip*-n	קנײַפּן
pineapple	di ananas	ah-nah-*nahs*	די אַנאַנאַס
pink (color)	rozeve	*raw*-zeh-veh	ראָזעווע
pious, saintly man	der tsadik	*tsah*-dik	דער צדיק
pipe (tobacco)	di lyulke	*lyool*-keh	די ליולקע
pipe	di rer	rehr	די רער
pistol	der pistoyl	pis-*toyl*	דער פּיסטויל
pit	di grub	groob	די גרוב
pitch, to	varfn	*vahrf*-n	וואָרפֿן
pitcher	der krug	kroog	דער קרוג
pity	dos rakhmones	rahkh-*maw*-nis	דאָס רחמנות
place	der ort	awrt	דער אָרט
	der plats	plahts	דער פּלאַץ
place, to	avekleygn	ah-*vehk*-layg-n	אַוועקלייגן
plague	di mageyfe	mah-*gay*-feh	די מגפה
	di make	*mah*-keh	די מכּה
plain, clear	klor	klawr	קלאָר
plain talk	di klore diburim	*klaw*-reh dee *boo* reem	די קלאָרע דיבורים
plan	der plan	plahn	דער פּלאַן
plan, to	planeven	*plah*-neh-vehn	פּלאַנעווען
plane	der aeroplan	ah-eh-raw-*plahn*	דער אַעראָפּלאַן
plant (factory)	di fabrik	fah-*breek*	די פֿאַבריק
plant	dos geviks	geh-*veeks*	דאָס געוויקס
plastic	der plastik	*plahss*-tik	דער פּלאַסטיק
plate (shallow dish)	der teler	*teh*-lehr	דער טעלער
platform	di platforme	*plaht*-fawr-meh	די פּלאַטפֿאָרמע
play, to	shpiln	*shpeel*-n	שפּילן
player	der shpiler	*shpee*-lehr	שפּילער
playing card	di kort	kawrt	די קאָרט
plaything	dos shpilekhl	*shpee*-lehkh-l	דאָס שפּילעכל
	di tsatske	*tsahts*-keh	די צאַצקע
plea	di bakoshe	bah-*kaw*-sheh	די בקשה

please, to	gefeln	geh-*fehl*-n	געפֿעלן
please	zayt azoy gut	*zeit* ah-zoy goot	זײַט אַזוי גוט
pleasure	der fargenign	fahr-geh-*neeg*-n	דער פֿאַרגעניגן
pleasure (mixed with pride)	dos nakhes	*nah*-khis	דאָס נחת
pledge	di havtokhe	hahv-*taw*-kheh	די הבֿטחה
plentiful	shefedik	*sheh*-feh-dik	שפֿעדיק
plenty	di shefe	*sheh*-feh	די שפֿע
pliers	di tsvang	tsvahng	די צוואַנג
pluck, to	flikn	*fleek*-n	פֿליקן
plum (fruit)	di floym	floym	די פֿלוים
pocket	di keshene	*keh*-sheh-neh	די קעשענע
point (dot)	dos pintele	*peen*-teh-leh	דאָס פּינטעלע
poison, to	farsamen	fahr-*sah*-mehn	פֿאַרסמען
poison	der sam	sahm	דער סם
pole	der slup	sloop	דער סלופ
police	di politsey	paw-lee-*tsay*	די פּאָליציי
police station	di politsey-stantsye	paw-lee-*tsay*-*stahnts*-yeh	די פּאָליציי-סטאַנציע
policeman	der politsyant	paw-leets-*yahnt*	דער פּאָליציאַנט
polish, to	polirn	paw-*leer*-n	פּאָלירן
polish	der polir	paw-*leer*	דער פּאָליר
polite	eydl	*ayd*-l	איידל
	heflekh	*hehf*-lehkh	העפֿלעך
pond	der stav	stahv	דער סטאַוו
pool (puddle)	di kaluzhe	kah-*loo*-zheh	די קאַלוזשע
poor (needy)	orem	*aw*-rehm	אָרעם
poor (unfortunate)	nebekh	*neh*-behkh	נעבעך
poorhouse	dos hekdish	*hehk*-deesh	דאָס הקדש
poor man	der oreman	aw-reh-*mahn*	דער אָרעמאַן
popcorn	di kokoshes	kaw-*kaw*-shehs	די קאָקאָשעס
porcelain	dos portselay	pawr-tseh-*lei*	דאָס פּאָרצעלײַ
porch	der ganik	*gah*-nik	דער גאַניק
pork	dos khazer-fleysh	*khah*-zehr-flaysh	דאָס חזיר-פֿלייש
porter	der treger	*trehg*-ehr	דער טרעגער
portion	der kheylek	*khay*-lehk	דער חלק
portrait	der portret	pawrt-*reht*	דער פּאָרטרעט
position (location)	di pozitsye	paw-*zeets*-yeh	די פּאָזיציע
possess, to	farmogn	fahr-*mawg*-n	פֿאַרמאָגן

possible	miglekh	*meg*-lehkh	מיגלעך
post (position)	der postn	*pawst*-n	דער פּאָסטן
post office	der postamt	*pawst*-ahmt	דער פּאָסטאַמט
postage stamp	di marke	*mahr*-keh	די מאַרקע
postage	dos postgelt	*pawst*-gehlt	דאָס פּאָסטגעלט
postman	der brivn-treger	*breev*-n-*trehg*-ehr	דער בריוון־טרעגער
postpone, to	opleygn	*awp*-layg-n	אָפּלייגן
pot roast	dos roslfleysh	*raws*-l-flaysh	דאָס ראָסלפֿלייש
pot (container)	der top	tawp	דער טאָפּ
pot (small)	dos tepl	*tehp*-l	דאָס טעפּל
potato	di bulbe	*bool*-beh	די בולבע
	der kartofl	kahr-*tawf*-l	דער קאַרטאָפֿל
pouch	dos zekl	*zehk*-l	דאָס זעקל
poultry	di oyfes	*oy*-fehs	די עופֿות
pound	der funt	foont	דער פֿונט
pour, to	(on)gisn	(*awn*)*gees*-n	(אָנ)גיסן
poverty	di oremkayt	*aw*-rehm-keit	די אָרעמקייט
powder (cosmetic)	der puder	*poo*-dehr	דער פּודער
power (strength)	der koyakh	*koy*-ahkh	דער כּוח
practical	praktish	*prahk*-tish	פּראַקטיש
practical purpose (result)	der takhlis	*tahkh*-lis	דער תּכלית
practice (custom)	di firung	*fee*-roong	די פֿירונג
praise, to	loybn	*loyb*-n	לויבן
pray, to	davenen	*dah*-veh-nehn	דאַוועננען
prayer book	der sider	*see*-dehr	דער סידור
prayer shawl	der talis	*tah*-lis	דער טלית
prayer	di tfile	t-*fee*-leh	די תּפֿילה
precarious	umzikher	*oom*-zee-khehr	אומזיכער
precious	tayer	*tei*-ehr	טײַער
predict, to	foroyszogn	fawr-*oyss*-zawg-n	פֿאָרויסזאָגן
preferable	bilkher	*beel*-khehr	בילכער
pregnant	shvanger	*shvahn*-gehr	שוואַנגער
prejudice	der forurtl	*faw*-roor-tl	דער פֿאָראורטל
prepare, to	tsugreytn	*tsoo*-grayt-n	צוגרייטן
prescription	der retsept	reh-*tsehpt*	דער רעצעפּט
present	di itstikayt	*eets*-tee-keit	די איצטיקייט
present (current)	itstik	*eets*-tik	איצטיק
present (gift)	di matone	mah-*taw*-neh	די מתּנה

present, to (intro-duce)	forshteln	*fawr*-shtehl-n	פֿאָרשטעלן
preserve, to	oyfhitn	*oyf*-heet-n	אויפהיטן
press, to (push)	drikn	*dreek*-n	דריקן
press, to (iron)	(oys)presn	*(oyss) prehs*-n	(אויס)פּרעסן
pressure	der druk	drook	דער דרוק
pretend, to	pretendirn	preh-tehn-*deer*-n	פּרעטענדירן
pretext	der oysred	*oys*-rehd	אויסרעד
pretty	sheyn	shayn	שיין
pretend, to	farhitn	fahr-*heet*-n	פֿארהיטן
	ophaltn	*awp*-hahlt-n	אָפּהאַלטן
previously	biz aher	beez-ah-*hehr*	ביז אַהער
price	der prayz	preiz	דער פּרייז
prick, to	shtekhn	*shtehkh*-n	שטעכן
pride	der shtolts	shtawlts	דער שטאָלץ
pride, to have	kveln	k-*vehl*-n	קוועלן
priest (Christian)	der galakh	*gah*-lahkh	דער גלח
	der prister	*prees*-tehr	דער פּריסטער
primary	ershtik	*ehr*-shtik	ערשטיק
prime	hoypt	hoypt	הויפּט
print, to	drukn	*drook*-n	דרוקן
printer	der druker	*droo*-kehr	דער דרוקער
prison	di turme	*toor*-meh	די טורמע
private	privat	pree-*vaht*	פּריוואַט
privilege	di privilegye	pree-vee-*lehg*-yeh	די פּריווילעגיע
probability	dos mashmoes	mahsh-*maw*-ehs	דאָס משמעות
probably	mistome	mee-*staw*-meh	מסתּמא
	mashmoes	mahsh-*maw*-ehs	משמעות
problem	di problem	prawb-*lehm*	די פּראָבלעם
procrastinator	der opleyger	*awp*-lay-gehr	דער אָפּלייגער
professor	der profesor	praw-*feh*-sawr	דער פּראָפֿעסאָר
profound	tif	teef	טיף
promise (pledge), to	tsuzogn	*tsoo*-zawg-n	צוזאָגן
promise	der tsuzog	*tsoo*-zawg	דער צוזאָג
promotion (advance)	di hekherung	*heh*-kheh-roong	די העכערונג
prompt	pinktlekh	*peenkt*-lehkh	פּינקטלעך
proof	der dervayz	dehr-*veiz*	דער דערווייז
proper	geherik	geh-*heh*-rik	געהעריק
prophet	der novi	*naw*-vee	דער נבֿיא

proposal	der forshlog	*fawr*-shlawg	דער פֿאָרשלאָג
prospect	der oyskuk	*oyss*-kook	דער אויסקוק
prosper, to	matsliakh zayn	mahts-*lee*-ahkh zein	מצליח זײַן
	gedayen	geh-*dei*-en	געדײַען
prosperous	bliendik	*blee*-ehn-dik	בליענדיק
prostitute	di zoyne	*zoy*-neh	די זונה
	di prostitutke	praws-tee-*toot*-keh	די פּראָסטיטוטקע
protect, to	oyshitn	*oyss*-heet-n	אויסהיטן
	bashitsn	bah-*sheets*-n	באַשיצן
protest, to	protestirn	praw-tehs-*teer*-n	פּראָטעסטירן
proud	shtolts	shtawlts	שטאָלץ
prove, to	dervayzn	dehr-*veiz*-n	דערווײַזן
provide, to	farzorgn	fahr-*zawrg*-n	פֿאַרזאָרגן
provide, to (make provision)	tsushteln	*tsoo*-shtehl-n	צושטעלן
province	di provints	praw-*veents*	די פּראָווינץ
prune	(di getriknte) floym	(geh-*treek*-n-teh) floym	די (געטריקנטע) פֿלוים
psychiatry	di psikhiatrye	p-see-khee-*aht*-ree-yeh	די פּסיכיאַטריע
psychoanalysis	der psikhoanaliz	p-see-khaw-*ahn*-ah- leez	דער פּסיכאָאַנאַליז
psychology	di psikhologye	p-see-khaw-*lawg*- yeh	די פּסיכאָלאָגיע
public (at large)	der klal	klahl	דער כּלל
publicity	der pirsum	*peer*-soom	דער פּירסום
pudding	der kugl	*koog*-l	דער קוגל
pulpit	di bime	*bee*-meh	די בימה
pulse	der deyfek	*day*-fehk	דער דפֿק
punch	der zets	zehts	דער זעץ
punctually	punkt	*poonkt*	פּונקט
punish, to	shtrofn	*shtrawf*-n	שטראָפֿן
punishment	di shtrof	shtrawf	די שטראָף
pupil	der talmid	*tahl*-mid	דער תּלמיד
pure	reyn	rayn	ריין
purity	di reynkayt	*rayn*-keit	די ריינקייט
purple	lila	*lee*-lah	לילאַ
purse	dos baytl	*beit*-l	דאָס בײַטל
pursue, to	nokhyogn	*nawkh*-yawg-n	נאָכיאָגן
pursuit	di yog	yawg	די יאָג
push, to	shtupn	*shtoop*-n	שטופֿן
put, to	shteln	*shtehl*-n	שטעלן
puzzle	di trefshpil	*trehf*-shpeel	די טרעפֿשפּיל

quaint	altfrenkish	ahlt-*frehn*-kish	אַלטפֿרענקיש
quake, to	tsitern	*tsee*-tehr-n	ציטערן
qualify, to	bagrenetsn	bah-*greh*-nehts-n	באַגרענעצן
quarrel	dos krigeray	*kree*-geh-rei	דאָס קריגעריַי
quarrel, to	krign zikh	*kreeg*-n zikh	קריגן זיך
quarter (one fourth)	dos fertl	*fehrt*-l	דאָס פֿערטל
queen	di kinigin	*keh*-nig-in	די קיניגין
	di malke	*mahl*-keh	די מלכּה
queer	modne	*mawd*-neh	מאָדנע
question	di frage	*frah*-geh	די פֿראַגע
question, to	fregn	*frehg*-n	פֿרעגן
quick	shnel	shnehl	שנעל
	gikh	geekh	גיך
quiet (adj.)	ruik	*roo*-ik	רויִק
	shtil	shteel	שטיל
quiet	di shtilkayt	*shteel*-keit	די שטילקייט
quilt	di (geshtepte) koldre	(geh-*shtehp*-teh) *kawld*-reh	די (געשטעפּטע) קאָלדרע
quit, to	oyfhern	*oyf*-hehr-n	אויפֿהערן
quota	di kvote	k-*vaw*-teh	די קוואָטע

rabbi (orthodox)	der rov	rawv	דער רבֿ
rabbi's wife	di rebetsn	*reh*-beh-tseen	די רביצין
rabbit	dos kinigl	*kee*-neeg-l	דאָס קיניגל
radical	der radikal	*rah*-dee-kahl	דער ראַדיקאַל
radio	der radyo	*rahd*-yaw	דער ראַדיאָ
radish	der retekh	*reh*-tehkh	דער רעטעך
rag	di shmate	*shmah*-teh	די שמאַטע
railroad	di ban	bahn	די באַן
railroad station	di stantsye	*stahnts*-yeh	די סטאַנציע
rain	der regn	*rehg*-n	דער רעגן
rain, to	regenen	*reh*-geh-nehn	רעגענען
rain heavily, to	plyukhen	*plyoo*-khehn	פּליוכען

rainbow	der regn-boygn	*rehg*-n-*boyg*-n	דער רעגן־בויגן
raincoat	der regn-mantl	*rehg*-n-*mahnt*-l	דער רעגן־מאַנטל
rainy	regndik	*rehg*-n-dik	רעגנדיק
raise, to (lift up)	oyfheybn	*oyf*-hayb-n	אויפֿהייבן
raisin	di rozhinke	*raw*-zhin-keh	די ראָזשינקע
ransom	dos oysleyzgelt	*oyss*-layz-gehlt	דאָס אויסלייזגעלט
ransom, to	oysleyzn	*oyss*-layz-n	אויסלייזן
rape, to	fargvaldikn	fahr-g-*vahl*-dik-n	פֿאַרגוואַלדיקן
rare (uncommon)	zeltn	*zehlt*-n	זעלטן
rascal	der yungatsh	yoon-*gahch*	דער יונגאַטש
	der kol-boynik	*kawl*-boy-nik	דער כּל־בוניק
raspberry	di malene	*mah*-leh-neh	די מאַלענע
rat	der shtshur	sh-*choor*	דער שטשור
rattle, to	gragern	*grah*-gehr-n	גראַגערן
rave, to (rant)	gvaldeven	g-*vahl*-deh-vehn	גוואַלדעווען
raw	roy	roy	רוי
rayon	di kunstzayd	*koonst*-zeid	די קונסטזײַד
razor	der golmesser	*gawl*-meh-sehr	דער גאָלמעסער
razor blade	dos golmesserl	*gawl*-meh-sehr-l	דאָס גאָלמעסערל
reach, to (extend)	greykhn	*graykh*-n	גרייכן
reaction	der opruf	*awp*-roof	דער אָפּרוף
read, to	leyenen	*lay*-eh-nehn	לייענען
ready	greyt	grayt	גרייט
really	beemes	beh-*eh*-mehs	באמת
	take	*tah*-keh	טאַקע
real estate	dos grunteygns	*groont*-ayg-nss	דאָס גרונטאייגנס
reason	der taam	tahm	דער טעם
reason (intellect)	der seykhl	*saykh*-l	דער שׂכל
recall, to (remember)	dermonen zikh	dehr-*maw*-nehn zikh	דערמאָנען זיך
receipt (bus.)	di kabole	kah-*baw*-leh	די קבלה
receive, to	bakumen	bah-*koo*-mehn	באַקומען
recently	anumlt	ah-*noom*-lt	אָנומלט
reception (wedding)	der kaboles-ponim	kah-*baw*-lehs-*paw*-nim	דער קבלת־פּנים
recipe	der retsept	reh-*tsehpt*	דער רעצעפּט
reckless	nit batrakht	nit bah-*trahkht*	ניט באַטראַכט
reckon, to	rekhenen	*reh*-kheh-nehn	רעכענען
recognize, to	derkenen	dehr *keh*-nehn	דערקענען
recommend, to	rekomendirn	reh-kaw-mehn-*deer*-n	רעקאָמענדירן
reconciled, to be	iberbetn zikh	*ee*-behr-*beht*-n zikh	איבערבעטן זיך

record (mus.)	di plate	*plah*-teh	די פּלאַטע
	der disk	deesk	דער דיסק
recover, to (get well)	gezunt vern	geh-*zoont*-vehr-n	געזונט ווערן
recover, to	tsurikkrign	tsoo-*reek*-kreeg-n	צוריקקריגן
red	royt	royt	רויט
reduce, to	(far)minern	(fahr) *mee*-nehr-n	(פֿאַר)מינערן
reflect, to (con-sider)	fartrakhtn zikh	fahr-*trahkht*-n zikh	פֿאַרטראַכטן זיך
refreshment	der kibed	*kee*-behd	דער כּיבוד
refrigerator	der fridzhider	free-jee-*dehr*	דער פֿרידזשידער
refugee	der polit	*paw*-leet	דער פּליט
regards (greeting)	der grus	groos	דער גרוס
registered	registrirt	reh-giss-*treert*	רעגיסטרירט
rejoice, to	freyen zikh	*fray*-en zikh	פֿרייען זיך
relative	der korev	*kaw*-riv	דער קרובֿ
release, to	oplozn	*awp*-lawz-n	אָפּלאָזן
reliable	farlozlekh	fahr-*lawz*-lehkh	פֿאַרלאָזלעך
religion	di religye	reh-*leeg*-yeh	די רעליגיע
religious	religyez	reh-leeg-*yehz*	רעליגיעז
remain, to	blaybn	*bleib*-n	בלייַבן
remainder	der resht	rehsht	דער רעשט
remark	di bamerkung	bah-*mehr*-koong	די באַמערקונג
remedy	di sgule	s-*goo*-leh	די סגולה
remember, to	gedenken	geh-*dehn*-kehn	געדענקען
remembrance	di dermonung	dehr-*maw*-noong	די דערמאָנונג
remind, to	dermonen	dehr-*maw*-nehn	דערמאָנען
reminder	di dermonung	dehr-*maw*-noong	די דערמאָנונג
remorse	di kharote	khah-*raw*-teh	די חרטה
remote	vayt	veit	ווייַט
remove, to	tsunemen	*tsoo*-neh-mehn	צונעמען
rent, to	dingen	*deen*-gehn	דינגען
rent	dos dire-gelt	*dee*-reh-gehlt	דאָס דירה־געלט
repair, to	farrikhtn	fahr-*reekht*-n	פֿאַרריכטן
repeat, to (reiterate)	iberkhazern	*ee*-behr-khah-zehr-n	איבערחזרן
repent, to	kharote hobn	khah-*raw*-teh hawb-n	חרטה האָבן
replace, to	farbaytn	fahr-*beit*-n	פֿאַרבייַטן
reply, to	entfern	*ehnt*-fehr-n	ענטפֿערן
reply	der entfer	*ehnt*-fehr	דער ענטפֿער
	di tshuve	*choo*-veh	די תּשובֿה

reproach, to	hobn taynes	*hawb*-n *tei*-nehs	האָבן טענות
reproach	di tayne	*tei*-neh	די טענה
request, to	betn	*beht*-n	בעטן
request	di bakoshe	bah-*kaw*-sheh	די בקשה
rescue, to	rateven	*rah*-teh-vehn	ראַטעווען
resent, to	hobn faribl	*hawb*-n fah-reeb-l	האָבן פֿאַריבל
reservation	di rezervatsye	reh-zehr-*vahts*-yeh	די רעזערוואַציע
residence	dos voynort	*voy*-nawrt	דאָס וווינאָרט
respect	der derekh-erets	*deh*-rehkh-*eh*-rehts	דער דרך־ארץ
respectable	laytish	*lei*-tish	לײַטיש
response	der entfer	*ehnt*-fehr	דער ענטפֿער
responsibility	dos akhrayes	ahkh-*rah*-yehs	דאָס אחריות
rest (repose)	di ru	roo	די רו
rest, to	opruen	*awp*-roo-en	אָפּרוען
restaurant	der restoran	rehs-taw-*rahn*	דער רעסטאָראַן
restless	umruik	*oom*-roo-ik	אומרויִק
restrain, to	aynhaltn	*ein*-hahlt-n	אײַנהאַלטן
restroom	der optret	*awp*-treht	דער אָפּטרעט
result	der takhlis	*tahkh*-lis	דער תכלית
retire, to (stop working)	tsuriktsien zikh	tsoo-*reek*-tsee-en zikh	צוריקציִען זיך
retreat, to	tsuriktsien zikh	tsoo-*reek*-tsee-en zikh	צוריקציִען זיך
return (adv.)	krik	k-*reek*	קריק
return to (give back)	umkern	*oom*-kehr-n	אומקערן
return, to	tsurikkumen	tsoo-*reek*-koo-mehn	צוריקקומען
reveal, to	oyszogn	*oyss*-zawg-n	אויסזאָגן
revenge	di nekome	neh-*kaw*-mih	די נקמה
revenue	di hakhnose	hahkh-*naw*-seh	די הכנסה
review, to	iberkukn	*ee*-behr-kook-n	איבערקוקן
reward	der skhar	skhahr	דער שכר
rhyme	der gram	grahm	דער גראַם
rib	di rip	reep	די ריפּ
rice	der rayz	reiz	דער רײַז
rich	raykh	reikh	רײַך
rich man	der gvir	g-*veer*	דער גביר
	der nogid	*naw*-gid	דער נגיד
riches	dos ashires	ah-*shee*-rehs	דאָס עשירות
riddle	dos retenish	*reh*-teh-nish	דאָס רעטעניש
ride, to	forn	*fawr*-n	פֿאָרן
ride	der for	fawr	דער פֿאָר

ridicule	der khoyzek	*khoy*-zehk	דער חוזק
ridiculous	lekherlekh	*leh*-khehr-lehkh	לעכערלעך
rifle	di biks	beeks	די ביקס
right (correct)	rikhtik	*reekh*-tik	ריכטיק
right (claim)	dos rekht	rehkht	דאָס רעכט
right (direction)	rekhts	rehkhts	רעכטס
ring, to	klingen	*kleeng*-en	קלינגען
ring (jewelry)	dos fingerl	*feeng*-ehr-l	דאָס פינגערל
ring (circle)	der ring	reeng	דער רינג
riot	di mehume	meh-*hoo*-meh	די מהומה
rip, to	raysn	*reis*-n	רײַסן
	trenen	*treh*-nehn	טרענען
ripe	tsaytik	*tsei*-tik	צײַטיק
rise, to (stand)	oyfshteyn	*oyf*-shtayn	אויפשטייַן
risk	dos aynshtelinish	*ein*-shteh-leh-nish	דאָס אײַנשטעלעניש
river	der taykh	teikh	דער טײַך
road	der veg	vehg	דער וועג
roam, to	arumblonken	ah-*room*-blawn-kehn	אַרומבלאָנקען
roast	dos gebrotns	geh-*brawt*-ns	דאָס געבראָטנס
roast, to	brotn	*brawt*-n	בראָטן
rob, to	bagazlen	bah-*gahz*-lehn	באַגזלען
robber	der gazlen	*gahz*-lehn	דער גזלן
robe	der khalat	khah-*laht*	דער כאַלאַט
rogue	der zhulik	*zhoo*-leek	דער זשוליק
roll, to	kayklen	*keik*-lehn	קײַקלען
roll (bread)	der zeml	*zehm*-l	דער זעמל
	di bulke	*bool*-keh	די בולקע
roof	der dakh	dahkh	דער דאַך
room (place) (space)	dos ort	awrt	דאָס אָרט
room (chamber)	der tsimer	*tsee*-mehr	דער צימער
rooster	der hon	hawn	דער האָן
rope	der shtrik	shtreek	דער שטריק
rose	di royz	royz	די רויז
rot, to	foyln	*foyl*-n	פוילן
rotten	paskudne	pahs-*kood*-neh	פּאַסקודנע
rotten (decayed)	farfoylt	fahr-*foylt*	פאַרפוילט
rouge	di shminke	*shmeen*-keh	די שמינקע
round	kaylekhik	*kei*-leh-khik	קײַלעכיק
route (army)	der marshrut	mahrsh-*root*	דער מאַרשרוט
rub, to	raybn	*reib*-n	רײַבן

rubber	di gume	*goo*-meh	די גומע
rubbers	di kaloshn	kah-*lawsh*-n	די קאַלאָשן
rubbish	dos mist	meest	דאָס מיסט
rude	grob	grawb	גראָב
rug	der divan	dee-*vahn*	דער דיוואַן
	der tepekh	*teh*-pehkh	דער טעפּעך
ruin, to	khorev makhn	*khaw*-rehv mahkh-n	חרוב מאַכן
rule, to (decide)	paskenen	*pahs*-keh-nehn	פּסקענען
rumor	di shmue	shmoo-eh	די שמועה
rush	dos yogenish	*yaw*-geh-nish	דאָס יאָגעניש
rush, to	ayln zikh	*eil*-n zikh	אײַלן זיך
rust	der zhaver	*zhah*-vehr	דער זשאַווער
rusty	farzhavert	fahr-*zhah*-vehrt	פֿאַרזשאַווערט

Sabbath bread	di khale	*khah*-lih	די חלה
Sabbath dish, tradi- tional	der tsholent	*chawl*-nt	דער טשאָלנט
sack	der zak	zahk	דער זאַק
sacred	heylik	*hay*-lik	הייליק
sacrifice, to (forego)	mevater zayn oyf	meh-*vah*-tehr zein oyf	מוותּר זײַן אויף
sad	umetik	oo-meh-tik	אומעטיק
saddle	der zotl	*zawt*-l	דער זאָטל
sadness	der umet	oo-meht	דער אומעט
safe (unharmed)	besholem	beh-*shaw*-lehm	בשלום
safety pin	di zikher-shpilke	zee-khehr-*shpeel*-keh	די זיכער־שפּילקע
sailor	der matros	maht-*raws*	דער מאַטראָס
salad	der salat	sah-*laht*	דער סאַלאַט
salary	di skhires	*skhee*-rehs	די שכירות
salmon	der laks	lahks	דער לאַקס
salt	di zalts	zahlts	די זאַלץ
salvation	di yeshue	yeh-*shoo*-ih	די ישועה
same	zelbik	*zehl*-bik	זעלביק
sand	dos zamd	zahmd	דאָס זאַמד
sandwich	der sendvitsh	*sehnd*-vitch	דער סענדוויטש
sane	baym zinen	beim *zee*-nehn	בײַם זינען
sardine	di sardinke	sahr-*deen*-keh	די סאַרדינקע

Satan	der sotn	*sawt*-n	דער שטן
sated (full)	zat	zaht	זאַט
satisfaction	dos nakhes	*nah*-khehs	דאָס נחת
satisfied	bafridikt	bah-*free*-dikt	באַפֿרידיקט
satisfy, to	bafridikn	bah-*free*-deek-n	באַפֿרידיקן
Saturday	der shabes	*shah*-behs	דער שבת
sauce	der sos	saws	דער סאָס
saucepan	dos fendl	*fehnd*-l	דאָס פֿענדל
saucer	dos tetsl	*tehts*-l	דאָס טעצל
sausage	der vursht	voorsht	דער וווּרשט
savage	vild	veeld	ווילד
save, to (rescue)	rateven	*rah*-teh-vehn	ראַטעווען
save, to (economize on)	shporn	*shpawr*-n	שפּאָרן
save, to (put away)	opshporn	*awp*-shpawr-n	אָפּשפּאָרן
saw	di zeg	zehg	די זעג
say, to	zogn	*zawg*-n	זאָגן
scale	di skale	*skah*-leh	די סקאַלע
scale (for weighing)	di vog	vawg	די וואָג
scalp	der skalp	skahlp	דער סקאַלפּ
scalp disease	der parkh	pahrkh	דער פּאַרך
scandal	der skandal	skahn-*dahl*	דער סקאַנדאַל
scarcity	der doykhik	*doy*-kheek	דער דוחק
scare, to	ibershrekn	*ee*-behr-shrehk-n	איבערשרעקן
scatter, to	tseshitn	tseh-*sheet*-n	צעשיטן
scent	der reyakh	*ray*-ahkh	דער ריח
scholar	der gelernter	geh-*lehr*-n-tehr	דער געלערנטער
school	di shul(e)	*shool*-(eh)	די שול(ע)
schoolroom	der klastsimer	*klahs*-tsee-mehr	דער קלאַסצימער
schoolroom, traditional religious	der kheyder	*khay*-dehr	דער חדר
science	di visnshaft	*vees*-n-shahft	די וויסנשאַפֿט
scissors	di sher	shehr	די שער
scold, to	musern	*moo*-sehr-n	מוסרן
scorn	der bitl	*beet*-l	דער ביטול
scoundrel	der oysvorf	*oyss*-vawrf	דער אויסוואָרף
scrambled eggs	di prazhenitse	*prah*-zheh-nee-tseh	די פּראַזשעניצע
scrap	dos brekl	*brehk*-l	דאָס ברעקל
scrape, to	shobn	*shawb*-n	שאָבן
scratch, to	kratsn	*krahts*-n	קראַצן

scream, to	shrayen	*shrei*-en	שרײַען
screw	der shroyf	shroyf	דער שרויף
screwdriver	der shroyfn-tsier	*shroyf*-n-*tsee*-ehr	דער שרויפֿן־ציִער
scrub, to	reybn	*rei*-bn	רײַבן
sea	der yam	yahm	דער ים
seam	di not	nawt	די נאָט
search, to	zukhn	*zookh*-n	זוכן
seasick	yam-krank	*yahm*-krahnk	ים־קראַנק
season	di sezon	seh-*zawn*	דער סעזאָן
seat	dos zitsort	*zeets*-awrt	דאָס זיצאָרט
second	tsveyter	*tsvay*-tehr	צווייטער
second (time unit)	di sekunde	seh-*koon*-deh	די סעקונדע
secret	der sod	sawd	דער סוד
seduce, to	farfirn	fah-*feer*-n	פֿאַרפֿירן
see, to	zen	zehn	זען
seem, to	dakhtn zikh	*dahkht*-n zikh	דאַכטן זיך
seize, to	onkhapn	*awn*-khahp-n	אָנכאַפן
seldom	zeltn	*zehlt*-n	זעלטן
select, to	(oys) klaybn	(*oyss*) *kleib*-n	אויסקלײַבן
self	zikh	zikh	זיך
selfish	egoistish	eh-gaw-*ees*-tish	עגאָיִסטיש
sell, to	farkoyf-n	fahr-*koyf*-n	פֿאַרקויפֿן
send, to	shikn	*sheek*-n	שיקן
send, to (away)	avekshikn	ah-*vehk*-sheek-n	אַוועקשיקן
senile	oyver-botl	*oy*-vehr-*bawt*-l	עובֿר־בטל
senior	elter	*ehl*-tehr	עלטער
sense (judgement)	der seykhl	*saykh*-l	דער שכל
sense (meaning)	der pshat	p-*shaht*	דער פשט
sentence, to	farmishpetn	fahr-*meesh*-peht-n	פֿאַרמישפטן
separate	bazunder	bah-*zoon*-dehr	באַזונדער
separate, to	opteyln	*awp*-tayl-n	אָפטיילן
separation	di tsesheydung	tseh-*shay*-doong	די צעשיידונג
September	der september	sehp-*tehm*-behr	דער סעפטעמבער
serious	ehrnst	*eh*-rintst	ערנסט
seriously	oyf an emes	oyf ahn *eh*-mehs	אויף אַן אמת
sermon, Jewish	di droshe	*draw*-sheh	די דרשה
servant (masc.)	der diner	*dee*-nehr	דער דינער
(fem.)	di dinst	deenst	די דינסט
seven	zibn	*zeeb*-n	זיבן
seventeen	zibetsn	*zee*-behts-n	זיבעצן

seventh	zibeter	*zee*-beh-tehr	זיבעטער
seventy	zibetsik	*zee*-beh-tsik	זיבעציק
several	etlekhe	*eht*-leh-kheh	עטלעכע
severe	shtreng	shtrehng	שטרענג
severity	di shtrengkayt	*shtrehng*-keit	די שטרענגקייט
sew, to	neyen	*nay*-en	נייען
sewing machine	di neymashin	*nay*-mah-shin	די ניימאַשין
sex	dos geshlekht	geh-*shlehkht*	דאָס געשלעכט
sexton, Jewish	der shames	*shah*-mehs	דער שמש
shade	der shotn	*shawt*-n	דער שאָטן
shadow	der shotn	*shawt*-n	דער שאָטן
shake, to	shoklen	*shawk*-lehn	שאָקלען
	treyslen	*trayss*-lehn	טרייסלען
shame	di shande	*shahn*-deh	די שאַנדע
	di bushe	*boo*-sheh	די בושה
shampoo	der shampu	shahm-*poo*	דער שאַמפּו
share (portion)	der kheylek	*khay*-lehk	דער חלק
share, to	teyln zikh mit	*tayl*-n zikh mit	טיילן זיך מיט
sharp	sharf	shahrf	שאַרף
sharpen, to	shlayfn	*shleif*-n	שלײַפֿן
shave, to	razirn zikh	rah-*zeer*-n zikh	ראַזירן זיך
shaving cream	di razirzeyf	rah-*zeer*-zayf	די ראַזירזייף
shawl	di shal	shahl	די שאַל
she	zi	zee	זי
shear, to	shern	*shehr*-n	שערן
shed, to	aropvarfn	ah-*rawp*-vahrf-n	אַראָפּװאַרפֿן
sheep	der sheps	shehps	דער שעפּס
sheet (bed)	der laylekh	*lei*-lehkh	דער לײַלעך
shelf	di politse	*paw*-lee-tseh	די פּאָליצע
shell (skin)	di sholekhts	*shaw*-lehkhts	די שאָלעכץ
shepherd	der pastekh	*pahs*-tehkh	דער פּאַסטעך
sherbert	der frukhtayz	*frookht*-eiz	דער פֿרוכטאײַז
shine, to (polish)	polirn	paw-*leer*-n	פּאָלירן
shine, to (give light)	shaynen	*shei*-nehn	שײַנען
ship	di shif	sheef	די שיף
shirt	dos hemd	hehmd	דאָס העמד
shiver, to	tsitern	*tsee*-tehr-n	ציטערן
shoe	der shukh	shookh	דער שוך
shoelace	dos shukhbendl	*shookh*-behnd-l	דאָס שוכבענדל
shoemaker	der shuster	*shoo*-stehr	דער שוסטער

shoot, to	shisn	*shees*-n	שיסן
shop, to	aynkoyfn	*ein*-koyf-n	אײַנקויפֿן
shop	di krom	krawm	די קראָם
short	kurts	koorts	קורץ
shortcut	der durkhveg	*doorkh*-vehg	דער דורכוועג
shorten, to	farkirtsn	fahr-*keerts*-n	פֿאַרקירצן
shortened	farkirtst	fahr-*keertst*	פֿאַרקירצט
shortly	bald	bahld	באַלד
shot (from firearm)	der shos	shawss	דער שאָס
should (ought)	zol	zawl	זאָל
should (would)	volt	vawlt	וואָלט
shoulder	di pleytse	*play*-tseh	די פּלייצע
	der aksl	*ahks*-l	דער אַקסל
shout, to	shrayen	*shrei*-en	שרײַען
shovel	der ridl	*reed*-l	דער רידל
show, to	vayzn	*veiz*-n	ווײַזן
shower (bath)	der shprits	shpreets	דער שפּריץ
shower (rain)	dos regndl	*rehg*-n-dil	דאָס רעגנדל
shrew	di klipe	*klee*-peh	די קליפּה
shriek, to	kvitshen	k-*vee*-chehn	קוויטשען
shrimp	dos rakl	*rahk*-l	דאָס ראַקל
shrouds, Jewish burial	di takhrikhim	tahkh-*ree*-kheem	די תּכריכים
shudder, to	oyftsitern	*oyf*-tsee-tehr-n	אויפֿציטערן
shut, to	farmakhn	fahr-*mahkh*-n	פֿאַרמאַכן
shy	shemevdik	*sheh*-mehv-dik	שעמעוודיק
sick	krank	krahnk	קראַנק
sick person	der khoyle	*khoy*-leh	דער חולה
sickness	di krenk	krehnk	די קרענק
side	di zayt	zeit	די זײַט
sidewalk	der tretar	treh-*tahr*	דער טרעטאַר
sigh, to	ziftsn	*zeefts*-n	זיפֿצן
sight (spectacle)	der spektakl	spehk-*tahk*-l	דער ספּעקטאַקל
sign (mark)	der simen	*see*-mehn	דער סימן
significant	bataytik	bah-*tei*-tik	באַטײַטיק
silence	di shtilkayt	*shteel*-keit	די שטילקייט
silent	shtil	shteel	שטיל
silk	di zayd	zeid	די זײַד
silly	narish	*nah*-rish	נאַריש
silver	dos zilber	*zeel*-behr	דאָס זילבער

silverware	di gopl-lefl	*gawp*-l-*lehf*-l	די גאָפּל־לעפֿל
similar	enlekh	*ehn*-lehkh	ענלעך
similarity	di enlekhkayt	*ehn*-lehkh-keit	די ענלעכקייט
simple (uninvolved)	poshet	*paw*-sheht	פּשוט
simpleton	der tam	tahm	דער תּם
	der yold	yawld	דער יאָלד
sin	di aveyre	ah-*vay*-reh	די עבֿירה
	di zind	zeend	די זינד
sin, to	zindikn	*zeen*-deek-n	זינדיקן
since (because)	vayl	veil	ווײַל
since (time)	zint	zeent	זינט
sincere	oyfrikhtik	*oyf*-rikh-tik	אויפֿריכטיק
sincerity	di oyfrikhtikayt	*oyf*-rikh-ti-keit	די אויפֿריכטיקייט
sing, to	zingen	*zeen*-gehn	זינגען
singer	der zinger	*zeen*-gehr	דער זינגער
single	eyntsik	*ayn*-tsik	איינציק
single (unmarried)	neet khasene gehat	*neet* khah-seh-neh geh-*haht*	ניט חתונה געהאַט
sink	der opgos	*awp*-gawss	דער אָפּגאָס
sink, to	zinken	*zeen*-kehn	זינקען
sinner	der zindiker	*zeen*-dee-kehr	דער זינדיקער
sip, to	zupn	*zoop*-n	זופֿן
sister	di shvester	*shvehs*-tehr	די שוועסטער
sister-in-law	di shvegerin	*shveh*-geh-rin	די שוועגערין
sit, to	zitsn	*zeets*-n	זיצן
sit down, to	zetsn zikh	*zehts*-n zikh	זעצן זיך
site (place)	dos ort	awrt	דאָס אָרט
six	zeks	zehks	זעקס
sixteen	zekhtsn	*zehkhts*-n	זעכצן
sixth	zekster	*zehks*-tehr	זעקסטער
sixty	zekhtsik	*zehkh*-tsik	זעכציק
size	di greys	grays	די גרייס
size (of garments)	der numer	*noo*-mehr	דער נומער
ski, to	nartlen zikh	nahrt-lehn zikh	נאַרטלען זיך
skimmed milk	di opgeshepte milkh	*awp*-geh-shehp-teh meelkh	די אָפּגעשעפּטע מילך
skin	di hoyt	hoyt	די הויט
skip, to (caper)	hopken	*hawp*-kehn	האָפּקען
skirt (garment)	dos rekl	*rehk*-l	דאָס רעקל
skull	der sharbn	*shahrb*-n	דער שאַרבן

sky	der himl	*heem*-l	דער הימל
slander	dos rekhiles	reh-*khee*-lehs	דאָס רכילות
slap	der patch	pahch	דער פּאַטש
	der frask	frahsk	דער פֿראַסק
slap, to	patshn	*pahch*-n	פּאַטשן
slaughterer, ritual	der shoykhet	*shoy*-kheht	דער שוחט
slave	der shklaf	*shklahf*	דער שקלאַף
slavery	dos shklaferay	shklah-feh-*rei*	דאָס שקלאַפֿעריי
sleep, to	shlofn	*shlawf*-n	שלאָפֿן
sleep	der shlof	shlawf	דער שלאָף
sleeve	der arbl	*ahrb*-l	דער אַרבל
slender	moger	*maw*-gehr	מאָגער
slice	der penets	*peh*-nehts	דער פּענעץ
slim	shlank	shlahnk	שלאַנק
slip (undergarment)	dos unterkleyd	*oon*-tehr-klayd	דאָס אונטערקלייד
slipper	der shtekshukh	*shtehk*-shookh	דער שטעקשוך
slippery	glitshik	*glee*-chik	גליטשיק
slob	der shlump	shloomp	דער שלומפּ
slow (not fast)	pamelekh	pah-*meh*-lehkh	פּאַמעלעך
slums	di dales-hayzer	*dah*-lehs *hei*-zehr	די דלות-הייזער
slumber, to	dremlen	*drehm*-lehn	דרעמלען
slurp, to	zhloken	*zhlaw*-kehn	זשליאָקען
sly	khitre	*kheet*-reh	כיטרע
small	kleyn	klayn	קליין
smallpox	di pokn	*pawk*-n	די פּאָקן
smart	klug	kloog	קלוג
smart (chic)	elegant	ehl-eh-*gahnt*	עלעגאַנט
smear, to	shmirn	*shmeer*-n	שמירן
smell, to	shmekn	*shmehk*-n	שמעקן
smell	der reyakh	*ray*-ahkh	דער ריח
smile	der shmeykhl	*shmay*-khil	דער שמייכל
smile, to	shmeykhlen	*shmaykh*-lehn	שמייכלען
smoke	der roykh	roykh	דער רויך
smoke, to	reykhern	*ray*-khehr-n	רייכערן
smooth	glat(ik)	*glaht*(ik)	גלאַט(יק)
smooth, to	oysgletn	*oyss*-gleht-n	אויסגלעטן
snack	der nash	nahsh	דער נאַש
snake	di shlang	shlahng	די שלאַנג
snap, to (crackle)	knakn	k-*nahk*-n	קנאַקן
sneaky	gneyvish	gah-*nay*-veesh	גנבֿיש

sneeze, to	nisn	*nees*-n	ניסן
sniff, to	shnapn	*shnahp*-n	שנאַפֿן
snobbish	snobish	*snaw*-beesh	סנאָביש
snore, to	khropen	*khraw*-pehn	כראָפֿען
snow	der shney	shnay	דער שניי
so (in order that)	kedey	keh-*day*	כדי
so (thus)	azoy	ah-*zoy*	אַזוי
soak, to	(ayn)veykn	(*ein*)*vayk*-n	(אײַן)װייקן
soap	di zeyf	zayf	די זייף
sob, to	khlipen	*khlee*-pehn	כליפּען
sober	nikhter	*neekh*-tehr	ניכטער
soccer	der fusbol	*fooss*-bawl	דער פֿוסבאָל
sock (hose)	der zok	zawk	דער זאָק
sofa	di sofe	*saw*-feh	די סאָפֿע
	der divan	dee-*vahn*	דער דיוואַן
soft	veykh	vaykh	װייך
soil, to	bashmutzn	ba-*shmutz*-n	באַשמוצ'ן
soldier	der zelner	*zehl*-nehr	דער זעלנער
	der soldat	sawl-*daht*	דער סאָלדאַט
sole (of shoe)	di padeshve	pah-*dehsh*-veh	די פּאַדעשװע
solemn	fayerlekh	*fei*-ehr-lehkh	פֿײַערלעך
some (a little)	a bisl	ah-*bees*-l	אַ ביסל
some (a few)	etlekhe	*eht*-leh-kheh	עטלעכע
somebody	emetser	*eh*-meh-tsehr	עמעצער
somehow	vi es iz	*vee* ehs *eez*	װי עס איז
someone	emetser	*eh*-meh-tsehr	עמעצער
something	epes	*eh*-pehs	עפּעס
somewhat	a bisl	ah *bees*-l	אַ ביסל
somewhere	ergets	*ehr*-gehts	ערגעץ
son	der zun	zoon	דער זון
song	dos lid	leed	דאָס ליד
son-in-law	der eydem	*ay*-dehm	דער איידעם
soon	bald	bahld	באַלד
sore throat	der haldzveytik	*hahldz*-vay-tik	דער האַלדזװייטיק
sorrow	der troyer	*traw*-yehr	דער טרױער
soul	di neshome	neh-*shaw*-meh	די נשמה
sound (healthy)	gezunt	geh-*zoont*	געזונט
sound (noise)	der klang	klahng	דער קלאַנג
soup	di zup	zoop	די זופ
sour faced person	der farkrimter	fahr-*kreem*-tehr	דער פֿאַרקרימטער

sour	zoyer	*zoy*-ehr	זויער
source	der moker	*maw*-kir	דער מקור
south	der dorem	*daw*-rim ן	דער דרום
southeastern	dorem-mizrakhdik	*daw*-rim-*meez*- rahkh-dik	דרום־מיזרחדיק
southern	doremdik	*daw*-rim-dik k	דרומדיק
southwestern	dorem-mayrevdik	*daw*-rim-*mei*-rehv- dik	דרום־מערבֿדיק
souvenir	der ondenk	*awn*-dehnk	דער אָנדענק
span	der shpan	shpahn	דער שפּאַן
spank, to	patshn	*pahch*-n	פּאַטשן
sparkle, to	finklen	*feenk*-lehn	פֿינקלען
speak, to	redn	*rehd*-n	רעדן
speaker	der redner	*rehd*-nehr	דער רעדנער
special	spetsyel	spehts-*yehl*	ספּעציעל
specialist	der mumkhe	*moom*-kheh	דער מומחה
spectacle	der spektakl	spehk-*tahk*-l	דער ספּעקטאַקל
spectacles	di briln	*breel*-n	די ברילן
spectator	der tsukuker	*tsoo*-koo-kehr	דער צוקוקער
speech	di rede	*reh*-deh	די רעדע
	di droshe	*draw*-sheh	די דרשה
speed (rapidity)	di gikhkayt	*geekh*-keit	די גיכקייט
spice	dos gevirts	geh-*veerts*	דאָס געווירץ
spill, to	fargisn	fahr-*gees*-n	פֿאַרגיסן
spinach	der shpinat	shpee-*naht*	דער שפּינאַט
spine	der ruknbeyn	*rook*-n-bayn	דער רוקנביין
spinster	di farzesene moyd	fahr-*zeh*-seh-neh moyd	די פֿאַרזעסענע מויד
spirit	der gayst	geist	דער גייַסט
spit, to	shpayen	*shpei*-en	שפּייַען
spite, for	oyf tselokhes	oyf tseh *law*-khehs	אויף צו להכעיס
splash, to	plyushken	*plyoosh*-kehn	פּליושקען
spleen (anat.)	di milts	meelts	די מילץ
split, to	shpaltn	*shpahlt*-n	שפּאַלטן
spoil, to (mar)	kalye makhn	*kahl*-yeh mahkh-n	קאַליע מאַכן
spoon (tablespoon)	der eslefl	ehs *lehf*-l	דער עסלעפּל
	der lefl	*lehf*-l	דער לעפֿל
spoon (teaspoon)	der teylefl	tay *lehf*-l	דער טייּלעפּל
	dos lefele	*leh*-feh-leh	דאָס לעפֿעלע
sponge	der shvom	shvawm	דער שוואָם
spot (place)	der plats	plahts	דער פּלאַץ
	dos ort	awrt	דאָס אָרט
spot	der flek	flehk	דער פּלעק

spread, to	tseshpreytn	tseh-*shprayt*-n	צעשפרייטן
spread out	tseshpreyt	tseh-*shprayt*	צעשפרייט
spring (season)	der friling	*free*-ling	דער פרילינג
spy	der shpyon	shpee-*awn*	דער שפּיאָן
squeeze, to	kvetshn	k-*vehch*-n	קװעטשן
squirrel	di veverke	*veh*-vehr-keh	די װעװערקע
squirt, to	shpritsn	*shpreets*-n	שפּריצן
stab, to	dershtekhn	dehr-*shtehkh*-n	דערשטעכן
stage	di bine	*bee*-neh	די בינע
stagger, to	vaklen zikh	*vahk*-lehn zikh	װאַקלען זיך
stain	der flek	flehk	דער פלעק
stairs	di trep	trehp	די טרעפ
stale	alt-gebakn	*ahlt*-geh-*bahk*-n	אַלט־געבאַקן
stammer, to	farkhiken zikh	fahr-*hee*-kehn zikh	פֿאַרהיקען זיך
	shtamlen	*shtahm*-lehn	שטאַמלען
stand up, to	oyfshteln zikh	*oyf*-shtehl-n zikh	אויפֿשטעלן זיך
stand, to	shteyn	shtayehn	שטײען
star	der shtern	*shtehr*-n	דער שטערן
starch	der krokhmal	*krawkh*-mahl	דער קראָכמאַל
stare, to	glotsn	*glawts*-n	גלאָצן
start, to	onheybn	*awn*-hayb-n	אָנהייבן
start	der onheyb	*awn*-heyb	דער אָנהייב
starve, to	shtarbn fun hunger	*shtahrb*-n foon *hoon*-gehr	שטאַרבן פֿון הונגער
state (govt.)	di medine	meh-*dee*-neh	די מדינה
statue	di statue	*stah*-too-eh	די סטאַטוע
status	der matsev	*mah*-tsihv	דער מצב
stay, to	blaybn	*bleib*-n	בלײַבן
steady	fest	fehst	פֿעסט
steak	der bifsteyk	*beef*-stayk	דער ביפסטייק
steal, to	ganvenen	*gahn*-veh-nehn	גנבֿענען
steam bath	der shvitsbod	*shveets*-bawd	דער שװויצבאַד
steer, to	kereven	*keh*-reh-vehn	קערעווען
step, to	tretn	*treht*-n	טרעטן
step (stair)	dos trepl	*trehp*-l	דאָס טרעפל
stepdaughter	di shtiftokhter	*shteef*-tawkh-tehr	די שטיפֿטאָכטער
stepfather	der shtiftate	*shteef*-tah-teh	דער שטיפֿטאַטע
stepmother	di shtifmame	*shteef*-mah-meh	די שטיפֿמאַמע
stepson	der shtifzun	*shteef*-zoon	דער שטיפֿזון
stick	der shtekn	*shtehk*-n	דער שטעקן

stiff	shtayf	shteif	שטײף
still (quiet) (adj.)	shtill	shteel	שטיל
	ruik	roo-ik	רויִק
still (adv.)	nokh	nawkh	נאָך
still (nevertheless) (conj.)	dokh	dawkh	דאָך
stomach ache	der boykhveytik	boykh-vay-tik	דער בויכווייטיק
storm	der shturem	shtoo-rehm	דער שטורעם
stout	balaybt	bah-leibt	באַלײבט
stove	der oyvn	oyv-n	דער אויוון
straight	glaykh	gleikh	גלײך
straighten, to	oysglaykhn	oyss-gleikh-n	אויסגלײכן
strain, to (filter)	zayen	zei-en	זײַען
strange (peculiar)	modne	mawd-neh	מאָדנע
strange (alien)	fremd	frehmd	פֿרעמד
stranger	der fremder	frehm-dehr	דער פֿרעמדער
strawberry	di truskavke	troos-kahv-keh	די טרוסקאַווקע
stray, to (roam)	blondzhen	blawn-jehn	בלאָנדזשען
street	di gas	gahss	די גאַס
strength	di gvure	g-voo-reh	די גבֿורה
	der koyakh	koy-ahkh	דער כּוח
stress	der druk	drook	דער דרוק
strike, to (hit)	shlogn	shlawg-n	שלאָגן
strike, to (stop work)	shtraykn	shtreik-n	שטרײַקן
string	dos shtrikl	shtreek-l	דאָס שטריקל
strive, to	shtrebn	shtrehb-n	שטרעבן
stroke, to	gletn	gleht-n	גלעטן
stroll, to	shpatsirn	shpah-tseer-n	שפּאַצירן
strong	shtark	shtahrk	שטאַרק
structure (building)	der binyen	been-yehn	דער בנין
struggle	dos gerangl	geh-rahng-l	דאָס געראַנגל
stubborn person	der akshn	ahksh-n	דער עקשן
stubborn	farakshnt	fah-rahksh-nt	פֿאַרעקשנט
student	der talmid	tahl-mid	דער תּלמיד
study, to	lernen	lehr-nehn	לערנען
	shtudirn	shtoo-deer-n	שטודירן
stuffed cabbage	di holebtses	haw-lehb-tsehs	די האָלעבצעס
	di prakes	prah-kehs	די פּראַקעס
stupid	narish	nah-rish	נאַריש

sturdy	kreftik	*krehf*-tik	קרעפטיק
stutter, to	farhiken zikh	fahr-*hee*-kehn zikh	פֿאַרהיקען זיך
	shtamlen	*shtahm*-lehn	שטאַמלען
substantial	hipsh	heepsh	היפּש
substitute, to	farbaytn	fahr-*beit*-n	פֿאַרבײַטן
subway	di unterban	*oon*-tehr-bahn	די אונטערבאַן
succeed, to	matsliakh zayn	mahts-*lee*-ahkh zein	מצליח זײַן
success	di hatslokhe	hahts-*law*-kheh	די הצלחה
successful	matsliakhdik	mahts-*lee*-ahkh-dik	מצליחדיק
such	azelkher	ah-*zehl*-khehr	אַזעלכער
such (of that kind)	aza	ah-*zah*	אַזאַ
suck, to	zoygn	*zoyg*-n	זויגן
sudden (un- expected)	plutsemdik	*ploo*-tsehm-dik	פּלוצעמדיק
suddenly	plutsling	*ploots*-leeng	פּלוצלינג
suede	dos shvedishe leder	*shveh*-dish-eh *leh*-dehr	דאָס שוועדישע לעדער
suffer, to	laydn	*leid*-n	לײַדן
suffice, to	genig zayn	geh-*neeg* zein	געניג זײַן
sugar	der tsuker	*tsoo*-kehr	דער צוקער
suggest, to	forshlogn	*fawr*-shlawg-n	פֿאַרשלאָגן
suggestion	der forshlog	*fawr*-shlawg	דער פֿאַרשלאָג
suicide	der zelbstmord	*zehblst*-mawrd	דער זעלבסטמאָרד
suit (clothing)	der kostyum	kawst-*yoom*	דער קאָסטיום
	der garniter	gahr-*nee*-tehr	דער גאַרניטער
suitable	pasik	*pah*-sik	פּאַסיק
suit, to	pasn	*pahs*-n	פּאַסן
suit, to (please)	tsufridn shteln	tsoo-*freed*-n *shtehl*-n	צופרידן שטעלן
suitcase	der tshemodan	cheh-*maw*-dahn	דער טשעמאָדאַן
summary	der kitser	*kee*-tsir	דער קיצור
summer	der zumer	*zoo*-mehr	דער זומער
summon, to	aroysrufn	ah-*royss*-roof-n	אַרויסרופֿן
sun	di zun	zoon	די זון
sunburn	der zunenbren	*zoo*-nehn-brehn	דער זונענברען
Sunday	der zuntik	*zoon*-tik	דער זונטיק
sunglasses	di zunbriln	*zoon*-breel-n	די זונברילן
sunlight	di zunlikht	*zoon*-leekht	די זונליכט
sunny	zunik	*zoo*-nik	זוניק
sunrise	der zunoyfgang	*zoon*-oyf-gahng	דער זונאויפֿגאַנג
sunset	der zun-untergang	*zoon*-oon-tehr-gahng	דער זון־אונטערגאַנג
sunshine	di zunenshayn	*zoo*-nehn-shein	די זונענשײַן

superstition	dos ayngleybenish	*ein*-glay-beh-nish	דאָס איַינגלייבעניש
supper	di vetshere	*veh*-cheh-reh	די וועטשערע
supply, to	tsushteln	*tsoo*-shtehl-n	צושטעלן
suppose, to	meshaer zayn	meh-*shah*-ehr zein	משער זיַין
suppress, to (sub-due)	farshtikn	fahr-*shteek*-n	פֿאַרשטיקן
supreme	hekhst	hehkhst	העכסט
sure	zikher	*zee*-khehr	זיכער
surgeon	der khirurg	khee-*roorg*	דער כירורג
surprise	der khidesh	*khee*-dish	דער חידוש
survive, to (remain alive)	blaybn lebn	*bleib*-n lehb-n	בליַיבן לעבן
suspenders	di shleykes	*shlay*-kehs	די שלייקעס
suspicion	der khshad	*kh-shahd*	דער חשד
swallow, to	shlingen	*shleeng*-en	שלינגען
swear, to (curse)	zidlen	*zeed*-lehn	זידלען
swear, to (vow)	shvern	*shvehr*-n	שווערן
sweat	der shveys	shvays	דער שווייס
sweater	der sveter	*sveh*-tehr	דער סוועטער
sweated	farshvitst	fahr-*shveetst*	פֿאַרשוויצט
sweep, to (clean)	oyskern	*oyss*-kehr-n	אויסקערן
sweet	zis	zeess	זיס
sweetheart	der gelibter	geh-*leeb*-tehr	דער געליבטער
	di gelibte	geh-*leeb*-teh	די געליבטע
sweetness	di ziskayt	*zeess*-keit	די זיסקייט
swim, to	shvimen	*shvee*-mehn	שווימען
swindler	der zhulik	*zhoo*-lik	דער זשוליק
swiss cheese	der shveytser kez	*shvay*-tsehr kez	דער שווייצער קעז
swollen	geshvoln	geh-*shvawl*-n	געשוואָלן
sympathy	dos mitgefil	*meet*-geh-feel	דאָס מיטגעפֿיל
symphony	di simfonye	sim-*fawn*-yeh	די סימפֿאָניע
symptom	der simptom	simp-*tawm*	דער סימפּטאָם
synagogue	di shul	shool	די שול

table	der tish	teesh	דער טיש
tablecloth	der tishtekh	*teesh*-tehkh	דער טישטעך
tact	der takt	tahkt	דער טאַקט

tactful	taktish	*tahk*-teesh	טאַקטיש
tail, end	der ek	ehk	דער עק
tailor	der shnayder	*shnei*-dehr	דער שנײַדער
take, to	nemen	*neh*-mehn	נעמען
talent	der talant	tah-*lahnt*	דער טאַלאַנט
talented	talantirt	tah-lahn-*teert*	טאַלאַנטירט
talk, to	redn	*rehd*-n	רעדן
tall	hoykh	hoykh	הױך
Talmudic scholar	der lamdn	*lahmd*-n	דער למדן
Talmudic academy	di yeshive	yeh-*shee*-vih	די ישיבֿה
tape recorder	der band-rekordirer	*bahnd*-reh-kawr-*dee*-rehr	דער באַנד־רעקאָרדירער
tardy	farshpetikt	fahr-*shpeh*-tikt	פֿאַרשפּעטיקט
taste	der taam	tahm	דער טעם
taste, to	farzukhn	fahr-*zookh*-n	פֿאַרזוכן
tasty	geshmak	geh-*shmahk*	געשמאַק
tavern	di shenk	shehnk	די שענק
tax	der shtayer	*shtei*-ehr	דער שטײַער
taxi	di taksi	*tahk*-see	די טאַקסי
tea	di tey	tay	די טײ
teach, to	lernen	*lehr*-nehn	לערנען
teacher (at highest level)	der rebe	*reh*-beh	דער רבי
teacher	der lerer	*leh*-rehr	דער לערער
teacher (elementary level)	der melamed	meh-*lah*-mehd	דער מלמד
teapot	der tshaynik	*chei*-nik	דער טשײַניק
teamster	der bale-gole	bah-leh-*gaw*-leh	דער בעל־עגלה
tear, to	raysn	*reis*-n	רײַסן
tear	di trer	trehr	די טרער
telegram	di telegram	teh-leh-*grahm*	די טעלעגראַם
telegraph, to	telegrafirn	teh-leh-grah-*feer*-n	טעלעגראַפֿירן
telephone	der telefon	teh-leh-*fawn*	דער טעלעפֿאָן
telephone, to	telefonirn	teh-leh-faw-*neer*-n	טעלעפֿאָנירן
television	di televisye	teh-leh-*veez*-yeh	די טעלעוויזיע
tell, to (inform)	zogn	*zawg*-n	זאָגן
tell, to (narrate)	dertseyln	dehr-*tsayl*-n	דערצײלן
temperament	der temperament	tehm-peh-rah-*mehnt*	דער טעמפּעראַמענט
temple (anat.)	di shleyf	shlayf	די שלייף
temporary	dervaylik	dehr-*vei*-lik	דערווײַליק

temptation	der nisoyen	nee-*soy*-yin	דער נסיון
ten	tsen	tsehn	צען
tennis	der tenis	*teh*-niss	דער טעניס
tension (anxiety)	di shpanung	*shpah*-noong	די שפּאַנונג
tenth	tsenter	*tsehn*-tehr	צענטער
terms (conditions)	di tnoim	t-*naw*-im	די תּנאים
terrace	di terace	teh-*rah*-seh	די טעראַסע
terrible	shreklekh	*shrehk*-lehkh	שרעקלעך
terrify, to	shrekn	*shrehk*-n	שרעקן
terror	der shrek	shrehk	דער שרעק
terror (political)	der teror	teh-*rawr*	דער טעראָר
test	di probe	*praw*-beh	די פּראָבע
testicles	di beytsim	*bay*-tsim	די בצים
testify, to	eydes zogn	*ay*-dis *zawg*-n	עדות זאָגן
thank, to	danken	*dahn*-kehn	דאַנקען
thank you	a dank	ah *dahnk*	אַ דאַנק
thankful	dankbar	*dahnk*-bahr	דאַנקבאַר
thanks	der dank	dahnk	דער דאַנק
that (conj.)	az	ahz	אַז
that (adj.)	der	dehr	דער
	di	dee	די
	dos	dawss	דאָס
	yener	*yeh*-nehr	יענער
that (rel. pron.)	vos	vawss	וואָס
the	dem	dehm	דעם
	der	dehr	דער
	di	dee	די
	dos	dawss	דאָס
theater	der teater	teh-*ah*-tehr	דער טעאַטער
their	zeyer	*zay*-ehr	זייער
theirs	zeyerer	*zay*-eh-rehr	זייערער
them	zey	zay	זיי
theme (topic)	di teme	*teh*-meh	די טעמע
themselves	zikh	zikh·	זיך
then (in that case)	oyb azoy	oyb ah-*zoy*	אויב אַזוי
then (at that time)	demolt	deh-*mawlt*	דעמאָלט
then (later)	vayter	*vei*-tehr	װײַטער
there	ahin	ah-*hin*	אַהין
there	dortn	*dawrt*-n	דאָרטן
thereafter	dernokhdem	dehr-*nawkh*-dehm	דערנאָכדעם

thereby	dermit	dehr-*meet*	דערמיט
therefore	derfar	dehr-*fahr*	דערפֿאַר
	deriber	deh-*ree*-behr	דעריבער
thereof	derfun	dehr-*foon*	דערפֿון
thermometer	der termometer	tehr-maw-*meh*-tehr	דער טערמאָמעטער
these	di	dee	די
they	zey	zay	זיי
thick	dik	deek	דיק
thief	der ganev	*gah*-nehv	דער גנבֿ
thievish	gneyvish	gah-*nay*-veesh	גנבֿיש
thigh	di dikh	deekh	די דיך
	di polke	*pawl*-keh	די פּאָלקע
thimble	der fingerhut	*feen*-gehr-hoot	דער פֿינגגערהוט
thin (not thick)	din	deen	דין
thin (not fat)	dar	dahr	דאַר
thing	di zakh	zahkh	די זאַך
think, to	trakhtn	*trahkht*-n	טראַכטן
think over, to	ibertrakhtn	*ee*-behr-trahkht-n	איבערטראַכטן
third	driter	*dree*-tehr	דריטער
thirsty	dorshtik	*dawrsh*-tik	דאָרשטיק
thirteen	draytsn	*dreits*-n	דרייצן
thirty	draysik	*drei*-sik	דרייסיק
this	dem	dehm	דעם
	der	dehr	דער
	di	dee	די
	dos	dawss	דאָס
thorough	gruntik	*groon*-tik	גרונטיק
thoroughly	durkh un durkh	*doorkh* oon *doorkh*	דורך און דורך
those (adj.) (pron.)	yene	*yeh*-neh	יענע
though	khotsh	khawch	כאָטש
thought	der gedank	geh-*dahnk*	דער געדאַנק
thoughtful (reflective)	fartrakht	fahr-*trahkht*	פֿאַרטראַכט
thousand	toyznt	*toy*-zint	טויזנט
thread	der fodem	*faw*-dehm	דער פֿאָדעם
threaten, to	strashen	*strah*-shehn	סטראַשען
three	dray	drei	דריי
thrifty	shporevdik	*shpaw*-rehv-dik	שפּאָרעוודיק
throat	der haldz	hahldz	דער האַלדז
	der gorgl	*gawrg*-l	דער גאָרגל

throughout	durkhoys	*doorkh*-oyss	דורכהויס
throw, to	varfn	*vahrf*-n	וואַרפֿן
thumb	der grober finger	*graw*-behr *feen*-gehr	דער גראָבער פֿינגער
thunder	der duner	*doo*-nehr	דער דונער
Thursday	der donershtik	*daw*-nehrsh-tik	דער דאָנערשטיק
thus (in this way)	azoy arum	ah-*zoy* ah-*room*	אַזוי אַרום
ticket	der bilet	bee-*leht*	דער בילעט
ticket office	di kase	*kah*-seh	די קאַסע
tickle, to	kitslen	*keets*-lehn	קיצלען
tidy	tsikhtik	*tseekh*-tik	ציכטיק
tie, to	bindn	*beend*-n	בינדן
tie (bond)	der bund	boond	דער בונד
tiger	der tiger	*tee*-gehr	דער טיגער
tight	eng	ehng	ענג
	shtayf	shteif	שטייַף
timber	dos gehilts	geh-*heelts*	דאָס געהילץ
time	di tsayt	tseit	די צייַט
timeless	eybik	*ay*-bik	אייביק
timetable	der forplan	*fawr*-plahn	דער פֿאָרפּלאַן
timid	shrekevdik	*shreh*-kehv-dik	שרעקעוודיק
tin	dos tsin	tsin	דאָס צין
tin can	di pushke	*poosh*-keh	די פּושקע
tiny	kleyntshik	*klayn*-chik	קלייַנטשיק
tip (top)	der shpits	shpeets	דער שפּיץ
tip (gratuity)	dos trinkgelt	*treenk*-gehlt	דאָס טרינקגעלט
tipsy	farshnoshket	fahr-*shnawsh*-keht	פֿאַרשנאָשקעט
tire	der reyf	rayf	דער רייף
tire, to	farmatern	fahr-*mah*-tehr-n	פֿאַרמאַטערן
tired	farmatert	fahr-*mah*-tehrt	פֿאַרמאַטערט
	mid	meed	מיד
to	tsu	tsoo	צו
to (destination) (enclosed area)	in	in	אין
to (bound for)	keyn	kayn	קיין
toast (bread)	der tost	tawst	דער טאָסט
tobacco	der tabak	*tah*-bahk	דער טאַבאַק
today	haynt	heint	הייַנט
toe	der finger fun fus	*feen*-gehr foon *fooss*	דער פֿינגער פֿון פֿוס
together	tsuzamen	tsoo-*zah*-mehn	צוזאַמען
toilet	der klozet	klaw-*zeht*	דער קלאָזעט

tolerate, to	tolerirn	taw-leh-*reer*-n	טאָלערירן
tomato	der pomidor	paw-mee-*dawr*	דער פּאָמידאָר
tomb	der keyver	*kay*-vehr	דער קבֿר
tomorrow	morgn	*mawrg*-n	מאָרגן
tongue	di tsung	tsoong	די צונג
tonight	haynt bay nakht	*heint* bei nahkht	הײַנט בײַ נאַכט
too (also)	oykh	oykh	אויך
too (excessively)	tsu	tsoo	צו
tool	der makhshir	*mahkh*-sheer	דער מכשיר
tooth	der tson	tsawn	דער צאָן
tooth paste	di tsonpaste	*tsawn*-pahss-teh	די צאָנפּאַסטע
toothache	der tsonveytik	*tsawn*-vay-tik	דער צאָנווייטיק
toothbrush	dos tsonbershtl	*tsawn*-behr-shtl	דאָס צאָנבערשטל
top (adj.)	hekhst	hehkhst	העכסט
top	der oybn	*oyb*-n	דער אויבן
top (tip)	der shpits	shpeets	דער שפּיץ
topmost	eybersht	*ay*-behrsh-t	אייבערשט
topsy-turvy	mitn kop arop	meet-n *kawp* ah-*rawp*	מיטן קאָפּ אַראָפּ
torment, to	mutshen	*moo*-chehn	מוטשען
	matern	*mah*-tehr-n	מאַטערן
torment	dos maternish	*mah*-tehr-nish	דאָס מאַטערניש
tormented	oysgemutshet	*oyss*-geh-moo-cheht	אויסגעמוטשעט
torture	di paynikung	*pei*-nee-koong	די פּײַניקונג
total (whole)	gants	gahnts	גאַנץ
total	der sakhakl	sah-*khah*-kil	דער סך־הכּל
touch, to	onrirn	*awn*-reer-n	אָנרירן
	tshepn	*cheh*-pehn	טשעפּען
touched (mentally)	gerirt	geh-*reert*	גערירט
tough	hart	hahrt	האַרט
toupe	der paruk	pah-*rook*	דער פּאָרוק
tourist	der turist	too-*reest*	דער טוריסט
toward	tsu	tsoo	צו
towel	dos hantekh	*hahn*-tehkh	דאָס האַנטעך
town	dos shtetl	*shteht*-l	דאָס שטעטל
toy	dos shpilekhl	*shpeel*-ehkh-l	דאָס שפּילעכל
	di tsatske	*tsahts*-keh	די צאַצקע
trace	di shpur	shpoor	די שפּור
trade, to	handlen	*hahnd*-lehn	האַנדלען
tradition	di traditsye	trah-*deets*-yeh	די טראַדיציע
tragedy	di tragedye	trah-*gehd*-yeh	די טראַגעדיע
tragic	tragish	*trah*-gish	טראַגיש

trail	der veg	vehg	דער וועג
train (railroad)	der tsug	tsoog	דער צוג
traitor	der farreter	fahr-*reh*-tehr	דער פֿאַררעטער
trample, to	tsetretn	tseh-*treht*-n	צעטרעטן
tranquility	di zakhtkayt	*zahkht*-keit	די זאַכטקייט
tranquilize, to	baruikn	bah-*roo*-eek-n	באַרויִקן
transform, to	ibermakhn	ee-behr-mahkh-n	איבערמאַכן
translate, to	iberzetsn	ee-behr-zehts-n	איבערזעצן
translation	di iberzetsung	ee-behr-zeh-tsoong	די איבערזעצונג
travel, to	arumforn	ah-*room*-fawr-n	אַרומפֿאָרן
travel bureau	der rayze-byuro	*rei*-zeh-boo-raw	דער רייַזע־ביוראָ
tray	di tats	tahts	די טאַץ
treasure	der oytser	*oy*-tsehr	דער אוצר
tree	der boym	boym	דער בוים
tremble, to	tsitern	*tsee*-tehr-n	ציטערן
trial (court)	der mishpet	*meesh*-pit	דער מישפּט
trick	di kunts	koonts	די קונץ
trifle	di kleynikayt	*klay*-nee-keit	די קלייניקייט
trinket	di tsatske	*tsahts*-keh	די צאַצקע
trip	di nesie	neh-*see*-ih	די נסיעה
trouble	di tsore	*tsaw*-reh	די צרה
troubled	umruik	*oom*-roo-ik	אומרויִק
trousers	di hoyzn	*hoyz*-n	די הויזן
trout	di forel	faw-*rehl*	די פֿאָרעל
truck	der lastoyto	*lahst*-oy-taw	דער לאַסטאויטאָ
true	emes	*eh*-mehs	אמת
trunk (baggage)	der kufert	*koo*-fehrt	דער קופֿערט
trust	der tsutroy	*tsoo*-troy	דער צוטרוי
trust, to	getroyen	geh-*troy*-en	געטרויען
truth	der emes	*eh*-mehs	דער אמת
try, to	pruvn	*proov*-n	פּרוּוון
Tuesday	der dinstik	*deen*-stik	דער דינסטיק
tulip	der tulpan	tool-*pahn*	דער טולפּאַן
tumor	der tumor	*too*-mawr	דער טומאָר
tuna fish	der tunfish	*toon*-fish	דער טונפֿיש
tune	der nign	*neeg*-n	דער ניגון
tunnel	der tunel	*too*-nehl	דער טונעל
turkey	der indik	*een*-dik	דער אינדיק
turn	der ker	kehr	דער קער
	der drey	dray	דער דריי
turn, to	dreyen	*dray*-en	דרייען

turnip	di brukve	*brook*-veh	די ברוקװע
turtle	di tsherepakhe	cheh-reh-*pah*-kheh	די טשערעפּאַכע
twelfth	tsvelfter	*tsvehlf*-tehr	צװעלפֿטער
twelve	tsvelf	tsvehlf	צװעלף
twenty	tsvantsik	*tsvahn*-tsik	צװאַנציק
twenty-one	eyn un tsvantsik	*ayn* oon *tsvahn*-tsik	איין און צװאַנציק
twice	tsvey mol	*tsvay* mawl	צװײ מאָל
twin	der tsviling	*tsvee*-ling	דער צװילינג
two	tsvey	tsvay	צװײ
type (kind)	der tip	teep	דער טיפּ
type, to (typewrite)	tipirn	tee-*peer*-n	טיפּירן
typewriter	di shraybmashin	*shreib*-mah-shin	די שרײַבמאַשין

ugly	mies	*mee*-ehs	מיאוס
ulcer	dos mogn-geshvir	*mawg*-n-geh-*shveer*	דעס מאָגן־געשװיר
ultimately	lesof	leh-*sawf*	לסוף
umbrella	der shirem	*shee*-rehm	דער שירעם
uncle	der feter	*feh*-tehr	דער פֿעטער
unconscious	farkhalesht	fahr-*khah*-lehsht	פֿאַרחלשט
uncouth	megushemdik	meh-*goo*-shehm-dik	מגושמדיק
under	unter	*oon*-tehr	אונטער
underclothes	dos untervesh	*oon*-tehr-vesh	דאָס אונטערװעש
underneath (prep.)	unter	*oon*-tehr	אונטער
underneath (adv.)	untn	*oont*-n	אונטן
underpants	di gatkes	*gaht*-kehs	די גאַטקעס
understand, to	farshteyn	fahr-*shtayn*	פֿאַרשטײן
undertaking	di unternemung	*oon*-tehr-neh-moong	די אונטערנעמונג
underwear	dos untervesh	*oon*-tehr-vehsh	דאָס אונטערװעש
unfortunate	umgliklekh	*oom*-gleek-lehkh	אומגליקלעך
unhappy	umgliklekh	*oom*-gleek-lehkh	אומגליקלעך
university	der universitet	oo-nee-vehr-see-*teht*	דער אוניװערסיטעט
unjust	umgerekht	*oom*-geh-rehkht	אומגערעכט
unknown	umbakant	*oom*-bah-kahnt	אומבאַקאַנט
unless	saydn	*seid*-n	סײַדן

unlike	nit-enlekh	nit-*ehn*-lehkh	ניט־ענלעך
unlucky	shlimazldik	shlee-*mahz*-l-dik	שלימזלדיק
unlucky person	der shlimazl	shlee-*mahz*-l	דער שלימזל
unmarried	nit khasene gehat	nit *khah*-seh-neh geh-*haht*	ניט חתונה געהאַט
unnecessary	umneytik	*oom*-nay-tik	אומנייטיק
unpaid (due)	nit batsolt	*nit* bah-tsawlt	ניט באַצאָלט
unrest	di umruikayt	*oom*-roo-ik-eit	די אומרויִקייט
until	biz	beez	ביז
unusual	umgevyntlekh	*oom*-geh-vaynt-lehkh	אומגעוויינטלעך
unwillingly	umgern	*oom*-gehr-n	אומגערן
unworthy	umverdik	*oom*-vehr-dik	אומווערדיק
up	aroyf	ah-*royf*	אַרויף
upon	oyf	oyf	אויף
uproar	der yerid	yah-*reed*	דער יריד
upset, to	iberkern	ee-behr-kehr-n	איבערקערן
upside down	mitn kop arop	*meet*-n kawp ah-*rawp*	מיטן קאָפּ אַראָפּ
upstairs	der oybn	*oyb*-n	דער אויבן
upward	aroyf	ah-*royf*	אַרויף
urge	der kheyshek	*khay*-shehk	דער חשק
urgent	dringlekh	*dreeng*-lehkh	דרינגלעך
us	undz	oonds	אונדז
use	der nuts	noots	דער נוץ
use, to	nutsn	*noots*-n	נוצן
used to (accus-tomed)	tsugevoynt	*tsoo*-geh-voynt	צוגעוווינט
useful	nutsik	*noo*-tsik	נוציק
useless	on a nutsn	*awn* ah *noots*-n	אָן אַ נוצן
usual	geveyntlekh	geh-*vaynt*-lehkh	געוויינטלעך
utmost	maksimal	ṃahk-see-*mahl*	מאַקסימאַל

vacant	leydik	*lay*-dik	ליידיק
vacation	di vakatsye	vah-*kahts*-yeh	די וואַקאַציע
vacuum cleaner	der shtoybzoyger	*shtoyb*-zoyg-ehr	דער שטויבזויגער
vagina	di vagine	vah-*gee*-neh	די וואַגינע
vain, in (futile)	aroysgevorfn	ah-*royss*-geh-vawrf-n	אַרויסגעוואָרפֿן

vain (conceited)	gayvedik	*gei*-ve-dik	גאווה׳דיק
valuable	vertful	*vehrt*-fool	ווערטפֿול
value	di/der vert	vehrt	די/דער ווערט
vanish, to	nelm vern	*nehl*-im vehr-n	נעלם ווערן
vanity (self-conceit)	dos gadles	*gahd*-lis	דאָס גדלות
various	farsheydn	fahr-*shee*-dn	פֿאַרשיידן
vary, to	zayn andersh	zein *ahn*-dehrsh	זײַן אַנדערש
vase	di vaze	*vah*-zeh	די וואַזע
veal	dos kalbfleysh	*kahlb*-flaysh	דאָס קאַלבפֿלייש
vegetable	dos grins	greens	דאָס גרינס
vegetable or fruit stew	der tsimes	*tsee*-mehs	דער צימעס
vein	di vene	*veh*-neh	די ווענע
vein (anat.)	di oder	*aw*-dehr	די אָדער
velvet	der samet	*sah*-meht	דער סאַמעט
vengeance	di nekome	neh-*kaw*-meh	די נקמה
verdict	der psak	*psahk*	דער פסק
very	zeyer	*zay*-ehr	זייער
vessel (ship)	di shif	sheef	די שיף
vest	dos vestl	*vehst*-l	דאָס וועסטל
victim	der korbn	*kawrb*-n	דער קרבן
view (sight)	der oysblik	*oyss*-blik	דער אויסבליק
view (opinion)	di meynung	*may*-noong	די מיינונג
vigor	di kraft	krahft	די קראַפֿט
vigorous	kraftik	*krahf*-tik	קראַפֿטיק
village	dos dorf	dawrf	דאָס דאָרף
villain	der roshe	*raw*-shih	דער רשע
vinegar	der esik	*eh*-sik	דער עסיק
violence	di gvald	g-*vahld*	די גוואַלד
violet (flower)	di fyalke	fee-*ahl*-keh	די פֿיאַלקע
violin	der fidl	*feed*-l	דער פֿידל
virgin	di bsule	b-*soo*-lih	די בתולה
virus	der virus	*vee*-roos	דער ווירוס
visible	kentik	*kehn*-tik	קענטיק
visit, to (go to view)	bazukhn	bah-*zukh*-n	באַזוכן
visiting the sick	mevaker khoyle zayn	meh-*vah*-kehr *khoy*-leh zein	מבקר חולה זײַן
visitor	der bazukher	bah-*zookh*-ehr	דער באַזוכער
vitamin	der vitamin	vee-tah-*meen*	דער וויטאַמין
vivid	lebedik	*leh*-beh-dik	לעבעדיק

voice	dos kol	kawl	דאָס קול
	di shtime	*shtee*-meh	די שטימע
void	posl	*paws*-l	פּסול
vomit, to	(oys)brekhn	(*oyss*) *brehkh*-n	(אויס)ברעכן
voter	der veyler	*vay*-lehr	דער ווײלער
vow	der neyder	*nay*-dehr	דער נדר
voyage	di nesie	neh-*see*-ih	די נסיעה

whack	der khmal	kh-*mahl*	דער כמאַל
wages	der loyn	loyn	דער לוין
waist	di talye	*tahl*-yeh	די טאַליע
wait, to	vartn	*vahrt*-n	וואַרטן
waiter	der kelner	*kehl*-nehr	דער קעלנער
waitress	di kelnerin	*kehl*-nehr-in	די קעלנערין
wake, to	oyfvekn	*oyf*-vehk-n	אויפֿוועקן
walk, to	shpatsirn	shpah-*tseer*-n	שפּאַצירן
	geyn	gayn	גיין
wall	di vant	vahnt	די וואַנט
wallop	der khmalye	kh-*mahl*-yeh	דער כמאַליע
walnut	der veltshener nus	*vehl*-cheh-nehr noos	דער וועלטשענער נוס
wander, to	vandern	*vahn*-dehr-n	וואַנדערן
want, to	veln	*vehl*-n	וועלן
war	di milkhome	mil-*khaw*-mih	די מלחמה
wardrobe (apparel)	der garderob	gah-deh-*rawb*	דער גאַדעראָב
warm	varem	*vah*-rehm	וואַרעם
warm, to	(on)varemen	(*awn*)*vah*-reh-mehn	(אָנ)וואַרעמען
warmth	di varemkayt	*vah*-rehm-keit	די וואַרעמקייט
warn, to	vorenen	*vaw*-reh-nehn	וואָרענען
wash, to	vashn	*vahsh*-n	וואַשן
wasp	di vesp	vehsp	די וועספּ
waste	der opfal	*awp*-fahl	דער אָפּפֿאַל
watch (clock)	dos zeygerl	*zay*-gehr-l	דאָס זייגערל
watch, to	tsukukn zikh	*tsoo*-kook-n zikh	צוקוקן זיך
watchmaker	der zeyger-makher	*zay*-gehr-*mah*-khehr	דער זייגער־מאַכער
water	dos vaser	*vah*-sehr	דאָס וואַסער
watermelon	di kavene	*kah*-veh-neh	די קאַוועננע

waterproof	vaser-zikher	*vah*-sehr-zee-khehr	וואַסער-זיכער
wave	di khvalye	kh-*vahl*-yeh	די כוואַליע
wax	der vaks	vahks	דער וואַקס
way (road)	der veg	vehg	דער וועג
we	mir	meer	מיר
weak	shvakh	shvahkh	שוואַך
weakness	di shvakhkayt	*shvahkh*-keit	די שוואַכקייט
wealth	di raykhkayt	*reikh*-keit	די רײַכקייט
	dos ashires	ah-*shee*-rehs	דאָס עשירות
wealthy	raykh	reikh	רײַך
wear, to	trogn	*trawg*-n	טראָגן
weary	farmatert	fahr-*mah*-tehrt	פֿאַרמאַטערט
weather	der veter	*veh*-tehr	דער וועטער
wedding	di khasene	*khah*-seh-nih	די חתונה
Wednesday	der mitvokh	*meet*-vawkh	דער מיטוואָך
wee bit	dos pitsl	*peets*-l	דאָס פּיצל
week	di vokh	vawkh	די וואָך
weekend	der sof-vokh	*sawf*-vokh	דער סוף-וואָך
weep, to	veynen	*vay*-nehn	וויינען
weigh, to	vegn	*vehg*-n	וועגן
weight	di vog	vawg	די וואָג
weird	tshudne	*chood*-neh	טשודנע
welcome	dos kaboles-ponem	kah-*baw*-lehs *paw*-nihm	דאָס קבלת-פּנים
welcome, to	bagrisn	bah-*grees*-n	באַגריסן
well (anyhow)	meyle	*may*-leh	מילא
well (good health) (adj.)	gezunt	geh-*zoont*	געזונט
well (impatient) (interj.)	nu	noo	נו
west	der mayrev	*mei*-rehv	דער מערב
western	mayrevdik	*mei*-rehv-dik	מערבֿדיק
wet, to	aynnetsn	*ein*-nehts-n	אײַננעצן
wet	nas	nahss	נאַס
whale	der valfish	*vahl*-fish	דער וואַלפֿיש
what (pron.)	vos	vawss	וואָס
what (which) (pron.)	velkher	*vehl*-khehr	וועלכער
whatever (pron.)	vos nor	*vawss*-nawr	וואָס נאָר
whatever	velkher	*vehl*-khehr	וועלכער
wheat	der veyts	*vayts*	דער ווייץ
wheel	di rod	rawd	די ראָד

when	ven	vehn	וועז
	az	ahz	אַז
whenever	ven nor	*vehn*-nawr	וועז נאָר
where	vu	voo	וווּ
where (whither)	vuhin	voo-*heen*	וווּהין
wherever	vu nor	*voo* nawr	וווּ נאָר
whether	tsi	tsee	צי
which	vos	vawss	וואָס
	velkher	*vehl*-khehr	וועלכער
whichever	velkher	*vehl*-khehr	וועלכער
while (conj.)	beshas	beh-*shahss*	בשעת
while	di vayle	*vei*-leh	די ווײַלע
whim	der kapritz	kah-*preez*	דער קאַפּריז
whip, to	shmaysn	*shmeis*-n	שמײַסן
whiskey	der bronfn	*brawn*-fn	דער בראָנפֿן
	der shnaps	shnahps	דער שנאַפּס
whisper, to	sheptshen	*shehp*-chehn	שעפּטשען
	shushken	*shoosh*-kehn	שושקען
whistle, to	fayfn	*feif*-n	פֿײַפֿן
white	vays	veis	ווײַס
who	ver	vehr	ווער
whoever	ver nor	*vehr* nawr	ווער נאָר
whole	dos gantse	*gahn*-tseh	דאָס גאַנצע
wholeheartedly	mitn gantsn hartsn	meet-n *gahnts*-n *hahrts*-n	מיטן גאַנצן האַרצן
whom	vemen	*veh*-mehn	וועמען
whore	di kurve	*koor*-veh	די קורווע
whose	vemes	*veh*-mehs	וועמעס
why	far vos	fahr *vawss*	פֿאָר וואָס
wicked	beyz	bayz	בייז
wide	breyt	brayt	ברייט
widow	di almone	ahl-*maw*-neh	די אַלמנה
widower	der almen	*ahl*-mehn	דער אַלמן
wife	di froy	froy	די פֿרוי
	dos vayb	veib	דאָס ווײַב
wig	di paruk	pah-*rook*	די פּאַרוק
wig, traditional womens'	dos shaytl	*shei*-til	דאָס שייטל
wild	vild	veeld	ווילד
will	vel	vehl	וועל
will (testament)	di tsavoe	tsah-*vaw*-ih	די צוואה

willingly	gern	*gehr*-n	גערן
win, to	gevinen	geh-*vee*-nehn	געווינען
wind	der vint	veent	דער ווינט
window	der fentster	*fehnts*-tehr	דער פֿענצטער
window pane	di shoyb	shoyb	די שויב
windshield	di vintshoyb	*veent*-shoyb	די ווינטשויב
windy	vintik	*veen*-tik	ווינטיק
wine	der vayn	vein	דער ווײַן
wing	der fligl	*fleeg*-l	דער פֿליגל
wink, to	vinken	*veen*-kehn	ווינקען
winter	der vinter	*veen*-tehr	דער ווינטער
wipe, to	vishn	*veesh*-n	ווישן
wire	der drot	drawt	דער דראָט
wisdom	di khokhme	*khawkh*-mih	די חכמה
wise	klug	kloog	קלוג
wise man	der khokhem	*khaw*-khim	דער חכם
wise woman	di khakhkome	khah-*khaw*-mih	די חכמה
wish, to	vintshn	*veench*-n	ווינטשן
wit	di vitsikayt	*vee*-tsee-keit	די וויציקייט
witch	di makhsheyfe	mahkh-*shay*-feh	די מכשפה
with	mit	meet	מיט
withdraw, to (take back)	tsuriktsien	tsoo-*reek*-tsee-en	צוריקציִען
within (prep.)	in	in	אין
without	on	awn	אָן
witness	der eydes	*ay*-dehs	דער עדות
witty	vitsik	*vee*-tsik	וויציק
woe	di tsore	*tsaw*-reh	די צרה
wolf	der volf	vawlf	דער וואָלף
woman	di froy	froy	די פֿרוי
womb	di trakht	trahkht	די טראַכט
wonder, to (ask oneself)	fregn zikh	*frehg*-n zikh	פֿרעגן זיך
wonderful	vunderlekh	*voon*-dehr-lehkh	וווּנדערלעך
woods (forest)	der vald	vahld	דער וואַלד
wood (lumber)	dos holts	hawlts	דאָס האָלץ
wool	di vol	vawl	די וואָל
word	dos vort	vawrt	דאָס וואָרט
work	di arbet	*ahr*-beht	די אַרבעט
work, to	arbetn	*ahr*-beht-n	אַרבעטן

worker	der arbeter	*ahr*-beh-tehr	דער אַרבעטער
world	di velt	vehlt	די וועלט
worm	der vorem	*vaw*-rehm	דער וואָרעם
worried	bazorgt	bah-*zawrg*-t	באַזאָרגטט
worry, to	zorgn zikh	*zawrg*-n zikh	זאָרגן זיך
	daygen	*dei*-gehn	דאגהן
worry	di dayge	*dei*-geh	די דאגה
worse	erger	*ehr*-gehr	ערגער
worst	ergst	ehrgst	ערגסט
worth	di/der vert	vehrt	די/דער ווערט
worthless	nishtik	*neesh*-tik	נישטיק
	on a vert	*awn* ah vehrt	אָן אַ ווערט
would	volt	vawlt	וואָלט
wound, to	farvundikn	fahr-*voon*-dik-n	פאַרוווּנדיקן
wound	di vund	voond	די ווונד
wrap, to	aynviklen	*ein*-vik-lehn	איַינוויקלען
wretched	tsoredik	*tsaw*-reh-dik	צרהדיק
wrinkle	der kneytsh	*knaych*	דער קנייטש
wrist	dos hantgelenk	*hahnt*-geh-lehnk	דאָס האַנטגעלענק
write, to	shraybn	*shreib*-n	שרײַבן
writer (author)	der shrayber	*shrei*-behr	דער שרײַבער
wrong	umgerekht	*oom*-geh-rehkht	אומגערעכט
wrong (amiss)	kalye	*kahl*-yeh	קאַליע
wrong (injustice)	di avle	*ahv*-leh	די עוולה

x-ray	der rentgen(bild)	*rehnt*-gehn(bild)	דאָס רענטגען(בילד)

yarn	der garn	*gahr*-n	דער גאָרן
yawn, to	genetsn	*geh*-nehts-n	גענעצן
year	dos yor	yawr	דאָס יאָר
yearly	yerlekh	*yehr*-lehkh	יערלעך
	ale yor	*ah*-leh yawr	אַלע יאָר

yeast	di heyvn	*hayv*-n	די הייוון
yellow	gel	gehl	געל
yes	yo	yaw	יא
yesterday	nekhtn	*nehkht*-n	נעכטן
yet (after all)	dokh	dawkh	דאָך
yet (still)	nokh (alts)	nawkh (ahlts)	נאָך (אַלץ)
yield, to	nokhgebn	*nawkh*-gehb-n	נאָכגעבן
you	dir, dikh, aykh	deer, deekh, eikh	דיר, דיך, אײך
you (familiar, sing.)	du	doo	דו
you (formal, sing. and pl.)	ir	eer	איר
young	yung	yoong	יונג
youngster	dos bokherl	*baw*-khehr-l	דאָס בחורל
your (familiar sing.)	dayn	dein	דײן
your (formal sing and pl.)	ayer	*ei*-ehr	אײַער
yours	dayner	*dei*-nehr	דײַנער
	ayere	*ah*-yeh-reh	אײַערע
yourself	zikh	zikh	זיך
yourselves	zikh	zikh	זיך
zeal	der bren	brehn	דער ברען
zero	der nul	nool	דער נול
zipper	dos blitsshlesl	*blits*-shlehs-l	דאָס בליצשלעסל

YIDDISH-ENGLISH DICTIONARY

YIDDISH

a	ah	a	אַ
a dank	ah *dahnk*	thank you	אַ דאַנק
a mol	ah *mawl*	formerly once	אַ מאָל
a sakh	ah *sahkh*	many much	אַ סך
a sakh mer	ah *sahkh* mehr	a lot more	אַ סך מער
a vayle	ah-*vei*-leh	awhile	אַ ווײַלע
abi	ah-*bee*	any as long as	אַבי
abi gezunt	ah-*bee* geh *zoont*	as long as you're healthy	אַבי געזונט
abi velkher	ah-*bee* vehl-khehr	any (whatever)	אַבי וועלכער
abi ver	ah-*bee* vehr	anybody (anybody whatsoever)	אַבי ווער
abi vos	ah-*bee* vawss	anything (anything whatever)	אַבי וואָס
adres, der	*ah*-drehs	address	אַדרעס, דער
advokat, der	ahd-vaw-*kaht*	attorney	אַדוואָקאַט, דער
aeroplan, der	ah-eh-raw-*plahn*	airplane	אַעראָפּלאַן, דער
afile	ah-*fee*-leh	even in spite of	אַפֿילו
agev	ah-*gehv*	incidentally by the way	אַגבֿ
agune, di	ah-*goo*-neh	abandoned wife	עגונה, די
aher	ah-*hehr*	here to this place	אַהער
aheym	ah-*haym*	homeward	אַהיים
ahin	ah-*hin*	there to that place	אַהין
ahin un tsurik	ah-*hin* oon tsoo-*reek*	back and forth	אַהין און צוריק
akhrayes, dos	ahkh-*rah*-yehs	responsibility liability	אחריות, דאָס
akht	ahkht	eight	אַכט
akhter	*ahkh*-tehr	eighth	אַכטער
akhtsik	*ahkh*-tsik	eighty	אַכציק
akhtsn	*ahkhts*-n	eighteen	אַכצן

147

(a)khuts	(ah)*khoots*	except for besides	(אַ)חוץ
akhzoryesdik	ahkh-*zawr*-yehs-dik	cruel	אַכזריותדיק
akorsht	ah-*kawrsht*	a moment ago just now	אַקאָרשט
akshn, der	*ahksh*-n	stubborn person	עקשן, דער
aksl, der	*ahks*-l	shoulder	אַקסל, דער
akt, der	ahkt	act deed	אַקט, דער
aktiv	ahk-*teev*	active	אַקטיוו
aktrise, di	akh-*tree-seh*	actress	אַקטריסע, די
aktsent, der	akh-*tsehnt*	accent	אַקצענט, דער
aktyor, der	akh-*tyawr*	actor	אַקטאָר, דער
akusherke, di	ah-koo-*shehr*-keh	midwife	אַקושערקע, די
ale	*ah*-leh	all (every)	אַלע
ale yor	*ah*-leh *yawr*	yearly	אַלע יאָר
ale mol	*ah*-leh mawl	always	אַלע מאָל
alergye, di	ah-*lehrg*-yeh	allergy	אַלערגיע,די
aleyn	ah-*layn*	alone	אַליין
algemeyn	*ahl*-geh-mayn	generally general	אַלגעמיין
aliirter, der	ah-lee-*eer*-tehr	ally	אַליִיִרטער, דער
almen, der	*ahl*-mehn	widower	אַלמן, דער
almone, di	ahl-*maw*-neh	widow	אַלמנה, די
alt	ahlt	old	אַלט
altfrenkish	ahlt-*frehn*-kish	old-fashioned quaint	אַלטפרענקיש
alt-gebakn	*ahlt*-geh-*bahk*-n	stale	אַלטᴬגעבאַקן
alte moyd, di	*ahl*-teh moyd	old maid	אַלטע מויד, די
alter-kaker, der	*ahl*-tehr-*kah*-kehr	lecherous old man; person unwilling to participate	אַלטער קאַקער, דער
alts	ahlts	all everything	אַלץ
altsding	ahlts-*deeng*	everything	אַלצדינג
ambityse, di	ahm-*beets*-yeh	ambition	אַמביציע, די
ambitsyez	ahm-beets-*yehz*	ambitious	אַמביציעז
ambulans, der	ahm-boo-*lahnss*	ambulance	אַמבולאַנס, דער

amerike, di	ah-*meh*-ree-keh	America	אַמעריקע, די
am-orets, der	ahm-*aw*-rehts	ignorant person ignoramus	עם־האָרץ, דער
an	ahn	an	אַן
analfabet, der	ahn-*ahlf*-ah-beht	illiterate person	אַנאַלפאַבעט, דער
ananas, der	ah-nah-*nahs*	pineapple	אַנאַנאַס, דער
an ander	ahn *ahn*-dehr	another	אַן אַנדער
anderer	*ahn*-deh-rehr	other	אַנדערער
andersh	*ahn*-dehrsh	different else otherwise	אַנדערש
andersh vu	*ahn*-dehrsh voo	somewhere else elsewhere	אַנדערש וווּ
andersh, zayn	zein *ahn*-dehrsh	to differ to vary	אַנדערש זײַן
anit	ah-*neet*	else otherwise	אַניט
anives, dos	ah-*nee*-vehs	humility	עניוות, דאָס
anivesdik	ah-*nee*-vehs-dik	humble	עניוותדיק
anshtot	ahn-*shtawt*	instead of by way of	אַנשטאָט
antibiotek, der	ahn-tee-bee-*aw*-tik	antibiotic	אַנטיביאָטיק, דער
antik, der	ahn-*teek*	antique	אַנטיק, דער
antkegn	ahnt-*kehg*-n	opposite (adv.)(prep.) across from	אַנטקעגן
antkegnshteln zikh	ahnt-*kehg*-n-shtehl-n zikh	to defy to oppose	אַנטקעגנשטעלן זיך
antlayen	ahnt-*lei*-en	to borrow (from) to loan (to)	אַנטלײַען
antloyfn	ahnt-*loyf*-n	to escape to flee	אַנטלויפֿן
antshuldikn	ahnt-*shool*-deek-n	to pardon to excuse	אַנטשולדיקן
antoyshn	ahn-*toysh*-n	to disappoint	אַנטוישן
antoyshung, di	anh-*toy*-shoong	disappointment	אַנטוישונג, די
anumlt	ah-*noom*-lt	recently the other day	אַנומלט
aparat, der	ah-pah-*raht*	apparatus camera	אַפּאַראַט, דער

apelirn	ah-peh-*leer*-n	to appeal	אַפּעלירן
apetit, der	ah-peh-*teet*	appetite	אַפּעטיט, דער
aplodirn	ah-plaw-*deer*-n	to applaud	אַפּלאָדירן
aprikos, der	ahp-ree-*kaws*	apricot	אַפּריקאָס, דער
april, der	ahp-*reel*	April	אַפּריל, דער
apteyk, di	ahp-*tayk*	pharmacy	אַפּטייק, די
apteyker, der	ahp-*tay*-kehr	pharmacist	אַפּטייקער, דער
arayn	ah-*rein*	in (adv.)	אַרײַן
		into	
arayn, in	ah-*rein* in	into (adv.)	אַרײַן אין
araynbrekher, der	ah-*rein*-breh- khehr	burglar	אַרײַנברעכער, דער
arayngang, der	ah-*rein*-gahng	entrance	אַרײַנגאַנג, דער
arayngeyn	ah-*rein*-gayn	to go in	אַרײַנגיין
		to enter	
araynmishn zikh	ah-*rein*-meesh-n zikh	to interfere	אַרײַנמישן זיך
araynnemen	ah-*rein*-neh-mehn	to take in	אַרײַננעמען
		to include	
araynlozn	ah-*rein*-lawz-n	to let in	אַרײַנלאָזן
		to admit	
arbes, der	*ahr*-behs	pea	אַרבעס, דער
arbet, di	*ahr*-beht	work	אַרבעט, די
arbeter, der	*ahr*-beh-tehr	worker	אַרבעטער, דער
arbetn	*ahr*-beht-n	to work	אַרבעטן
arbl, der	*ahrb*-l	sleeve	אַרבל, דער
arestirn	ah-rehs-*teer*-n	to arrest	אַרעסטירן
ariber	ah-*ree*-behr	across	אַריבער
		over	
aribergeyn	ah-*ree*-behr-gayn	to cross over	אַריבערגיין
arkhitekt, der	ahr-khee-*tehkt*	architect	אַרכיטעקט, דער
armey, di	ahr-*may*	army	אַרמיי, די
arn	*ahr*-n	to bother	אַרן
		to care	
aromat, der	ah-raw-*maht*	flavor	אַראָמאַט, דער
arop	ah-*rawp*	down	אַראָפּ
		downstairs	
arop fun zinen	ah-*rawp* foon zee- nehn	out of one's mind	אַראָפּ פון זינען
aropvarfn	ah-*rawp*-vahrf-n	to shed	אַראָפּוואַרפן

aroyf	ah-*royf*	up	אַרויף
		upward	
aroyfkrikhn	ah-*royf*-kreekh-n	to climb	אַרויפֿקריכן
aroys	ah-*royss*	out	אַרויס
		forth	
aroysgang, der	ah-*royss*-gahng	exit	אַרויסגאַנג, דער
aroysgebn	ah-*royss*-gehb-n	to surrender	אַרויסגעבן
		to betray	
aroysgebn	ah-*royss*-gehb-n	to issue	אַרויסגעבן
		to publish	
aroysgevorfn	ah-*royss*-geh-	in vain	אַרויסגעוואָרפֿן
	vawrf-n	useless	
aroysgeyn	ah-*royss*-gayn	to depart (on foot)	אַרויסגיין
aroyskuk, der	ah-*royss*-kook	outlook	אַרויסקוק, דער
		expectation	
aroysrufn	ah-*royss*-roof-n	to summon	אַרויסרופֿן
aroysshikn	ah-*royss*-sheek-n	to mail	אַרויסשיקן
		to send out	
aroystraybn	ah-*royss*-treib-n	to expel	אַרויסטרײַבן
		to banish	
arterye, di	ahr-*tehr*-yeh	artery	אַרטעריע, די
artrit, der	ahr-*treet*	arthritis	אַרטריט, דער
arum	ah-*room*	around	אַרום
arumblonken	ah-*room*-blawn-kehn	to roam	אַרומבלאָנקען
		to ramble	
arumforn	ah-*room*-fawr-n	to travel	אַרומפֿאָרן
		to cruise	
arumnemen	ah-*room*-neh-mehn	to clasp	אַרומנעמען
		to embrace	
arunter	ah-*roon*-tehr	downward(s)	אַרונטער
ashires, dos	ah-*shee*-rehs	fortune	עשירות, דאָס
		riches	
		wealth	
ashtetsl, dos	*ahsh*-teh-tsil	ash tray	אַשטעצל, דאָס
aspirin, di	ahss-pee-*reen*	aspirin	אַספּירין, די
atom, der	ah-*tawm*	atom	אַטאָם, דער
atomishe bombe,	ah-*taw*-mee-sheh	atomic bomb	אַטאָמישע באָמבע, די
di	bawm-beh		
avade	ah-*vah*-deh	certainly	אָודאי
		of course	

avek	ah-*vehk*	gone away off	אַװעק
avekforn	ah-*vehk*-fawr-n	to depart (by vehicle)	אַװעקפֿאָרן
avekgeyn	ah-*vehk*-gayn	to leave	אַװעקגײן
avekleygn	ah-*vehk*-layg-n	to put to set down	אַװעקלײגן
avekshikn	ah-*vehk*-sheek-n	to send away	אַװעקשיקן
avekvarfn	ah-*vehk*-vahrf-n	to discard to abandon	אַװעקװאַרפֿן
aveyre, di	ah-*vay*-reh	sin	עבֿירה, די
avle, di	*ahv*-leh	wrong injustice	עװלה, די
ayer	*ei*-ehr	your (formal sing. or pl.)	אײַער
ayere	*ah*-yeh-reh	yours	אײַערע
aykh	eikh	you	אײַך
ayln zikh	*eil*-n zikh	to hurry to rush	אײַלן זיך
aynfal, der	*ein*-fahl	notion idea	אײַנפֿאַל, דער
ayngemakhts, dos	*ein*-geh-mahkhts	jelly jam	אײַנגעמאַכטס, דאָס
ayngleybenish, dos	*ein*-glay-beh-nish	superstition	אײַנגלײבעניש, דאָס
aynhaltn	*ein*-hahlt-n	to hold to restraint	אײַנהאַלטן
aynkoyfn	*ein*-koyf-n	to buy to shop for	אײַנקױפֿן
aynkukn zikh	*ein*-kook-n zikh	to look to peer at	אײַנקוקן זיך
aynmonen	*ein*-maw-nehn	to collect a debt	אײַנמאָנען
aynnetsn	*ein*-nehts-n	to moisten to wet	אײַננעצן
aynordenen	*ein*-awr-deh-nehn	to arrange	אײַנאָרדענען
(ayn)pakn	(*ein*)*pahk*-n	to pack	(אײַנ)פּאַקן
aynredn	*ein*-rehd-n	to coax to convince	אײַנרעדן
aynshlingen	*ein*-shleen-gehn	to devour to gobble	אײַנשלינגען

aynshtelenish, dos	*ein*-shteh-leh-nish	gamble risk	אײַנשטעלעניש, דאָס
ayntsol, der	*ein*-tsawl	payment deposit	אײַנצאָל, דער
aynvendn	*ein*-vehnd-n	to object to mind	אײַנווענדן
aynvendung, di	*ein*-vehn-doong	objection	אײַנווענדונג, די
(ayn)veykn	(*ein*)*vayk*-n	to soak	(אײַן)ווייקן
aynviklen	*ein*-vik-lehn	to wrap to bundle up	אײַנוויקלען
ayz, dos	eiz	ice	אײַז, דאָס
ayzik	*ei*-zik	icy	אײַזיק
ayzkrem, der	*eiz*-krehm	ice cream	אײַזקרעם, דער
ayzn, dos	*eiz*-n	iron	אײַזן, דאָס
az	ahz	that (conj.) if when	אַז
aza	ah-*zah*	such a kind of	אַזאַ
azelkher	ah-*zehl*-khehr	such	אַזעלכער
azoy	ah-*zoy*	so thus in such a way	אַזוי
azoy arum	ah-*zoy* ah-*room*	thus (in this way)	אַזוי אַרום
azoy fil	ah-*zoy*-feel	so much	אַזוי פֿיל
azoy vi	ah-*zoy* vee	as (in the same way)	אַזוי ווי
baamter, der	bah-*ahm*-tehr	officer official	באַאַמטער, דער
bafaln	bah-*fahl*-n	to assault to attack	באַפֿאַלן
bafel, der	bah-*fehl*	command order	באַפֿעל, דער
bafrayen	bah-*frei*-en	to free to liberate	באַפֿרײַען

bafridikn	bah-*free*-deek-n	to satisfy	באַפֿרידיקן
bafridikt	bah-*free*-dikt	satisfied	באַפֿרידיקט
bagazh, der	bah-*gahzh*	baggage luggage	באַגאַזש, דער
bagazlen	bah-*gahz*-lehn	to rob	באַגזלען
bagleyter, der	bah-*glay*-tehr	companion	באַגלייטער, דער
bagrayfn	bah-*greif*-n	to comprehend	באַגרײַפֿן
bagrenetsn	bah-*greh*-nehts-n	to restrict to qualify	באַגרענעצן
bagrenetsn	bah-*greh*-nehts-n	to limit to confine	באַגרענעצן
bagrisn	bah-*grees*-n	to greet to welcome	באַגריסן
bagrisung, di	bah-*gree*-soong	greeting welcome	באַגריסונג, די
bagrobn	bah-*grawb*-n	to bury	באַגראָבן
bahaltn	bah-*hahlt*-n	to hide to conceal	באַהאַלטן
baheftn	bah-*hehft*-n	to join	באַהעפֿטן
bak, di	bahk	cheek	באַק, די
bakant	bah-*kahnt*	familiar acquainted	באַקאַנט
bakanter, der	bah-*kahn*-tehr	acquaintance	באַקאַנטער, דער
bakenen	bah-*keh*-nehn	to introduce	באַקענען
bakenen zikh mit	bah-*keh*-nehn zikh mit	to meet be introduced to	באַקענען זיך מיט
bakleydn	bah-*klayd*-n	to clothe	באַקליידן
baklogn zikh	bah-*klawg*-n zikh	to complain	באַקלאָגן זיך
bakn	*bahk*-n	to bake	באַקן
bakoshe, di	bah-*kaw*-sheh	plea request	בקשה, די
bakumen	bah-*koo*-mehn	to receive	באַקומען
bakvem	bahk-*vehm*	comfortable convenient	באַקוועם
balagan, der	bah-lah-*gahn*	mess bedlam	באַלאַגאַן, דער
bal-khoyv, der	bahl-*khoyv*	debtor	בעל-חוב, דער
bal-melokhe, der	bahl-meh-*law*- kheh	craftsman artisan	בעל-מלאָכה, דער

bal-tsdoke, der	bahl-tseh-*daw*-keh	philanthropist charitable person	בעל־צדקה, דער
bal-toyve, der	bahl-*toy*-veh	benefactor	בעל־טובֿה, דער
balaybt	bah-*leibt*	portly stout	באַלײַבט
bald	bahld	soon shortly	באַלד
bale-bos, der	bah-leh-*bawss*	master boss host	בעל־הבית, דער
bale-boste, di	bah-leh-*bawss*-teh	housewife hostess	בעל־הביתטע, די
bale-gole, der	bah-leh-*gaw*-leh	coachman teamster	בעל־עגלה, דער
baleydikn	bah-*lay*-deek-n	to offend insult	באַליידיקן
baleydikung, di	bah-*lay*-dee-koong	insult	באַליידיקונג, די
balibt	bah-*leebt*	beloved favorite	באַליבט
bamerkn	bah-*mehrk*-n	to notice	באַמערקן
bamerkung, di	bah-*mehr*-koong	comment remark	באַמערקונג, די
ban, di	bahn	railroad train	באַן, די
banane, di	bah-*nah*-neh	banana	באַנאַנע, די
band-rekordirer, der	*bahnd*-reh-kawr-*dee*-rehr	tape recorder	באַנד־רעקאָרדירער, דער
bande, di	*bahn*-deh	gang pack	באַנדע, די
bandazh, der	bahn-*dahzh*	bandage	באַנדאַזש, דער
bandit, der	bahn-*deet*	bandit gangster	באַנדיט, דער
bandzho, der	*bahn*-jaw	banjo	באַנדזשאָ, דער
bank, di	bahnk	bench	באַנק, די
bank, der	bahnk	bank (fin.)	באַנק, דער
bankes, di	*bahn*-kehs	cupping-glasses (med.)	באַנקעס, די
banket, der	bahn-*keht*	banquet	באַנקעט, דער
bankir, der	bahn-*keer*	banker	באַנקיר, דער

bankrot, der	bahnk-*rawt*	bankruptcy	באַנקראָט, דער
baputsn	bah-*poots*-n	to decorate	באַפּוצן
		to embellish	
bar, der	bahr	bar	באַר, דער
		saloon	
baratung, di	bah-*rah*-toong	conference	באַראָטונג, די
		consultation	
barekhtikn	bah-*rehkh*-teek-n	to justify	באַרעכטיקן
		to warrant	
barg, der	bahrg	mountain	באַרג, דער
barimen zikh	bah-*ree*-mehn zikh	to brag	באַרימען זיך
		to boast	
barimer, der	bah-*ree*-mehr	braggart	באַרימער, דער
barimt	bah-*reemt*	famous	באַרימט
barman, der	*bahr*-mahn	bartender	באַרמאַן, דער
bar-menen, der	*bahr*-meh-nahn	corpse	בר־מינן, דער
barne, di	*bahr*-neh	pear	באַרנע, די
barsht, di	bahrsht	brush	באַרשט, די
baruikn	bah-*roo*-eek-n	to calm	באַרויִקן
		to tranquilize	
bashafn	bah-*shahf*-n	to create	באַשאַפֿן
bashefenish, dos	bah-*sheh*-feh-nish	creature	באַשעפֿעניש, דאָס
bashert	bah-*shehrt*	inevitable	באַשערט
		destined	
basheydnkayt, di	bah-*shayd*-n-keit	modesty	באַשיידנקייט, די
bashitsn	bah-*sheets*-n	to protect	באַשיצן
		to shelter	
bashlisn	bah-*shlees*-n	to decide	באַשליסן
		to determine	
bashlus, der	bah-*shloos*	decision	באַשלוס, דער
		resolution	
bashtelung, di	bah-*shteh*-loong	order (for merchandise)	באַשטעלונג, די
bashtetikn	bah-*shteh*-teek-n	to confirm	באַשטעטיקן
		to acknowledge	
bashtimt	bah-*shteemt*	definite	באַשטימט
bashuldikn	bah-*shool*-deek-n	to accuse	באַשולדיקן
		to blame	
bashuldikung, di	bah-*shool*-dee-koong	charge	באַשולדיקונג, די
		accusation	
batamt	bah-*tahmt*	tasty	באַטעמט
		delicious	

bataytik	bah-*tei*-tik	significant relevant	באַטײַטיק
baterye, di	bah-*tehr*-yeh	battery	באַטעריע, די
batrakht, nit	nit bah-*trahkht*	reckless	באַטראַכט, ניט
batrakhtn	bah-*trahkht*-n	to consider to contemplate	באַטראַכטן
batrefn	bah-*trehf*-n	to amount to	באַטרעפֿן
batsirn	bah-*tseer*-n	to adorn to decorate	באַצירן
(ba)tsoln	(*bah*)tsawl-n	to pay	(בא)צאָלן
batrakhtung, di	bah-*trahkh*-toong	deliberation consideration	באַטראַכטונג, די
bavayzn	bah-*veiz*-n	to demonstrate to prove	באַווײַזן
bavayzn zikh	bah-*veiz*-n zikh	to appear to show up	באַווײַזן זיך
bavl, der	*bahv*-l	cotton	באָוול, דער
bavust	bah-*voost*	well known eminent	באַוווּסט
bavustzinik	bah-*voost*-zee-nik	conscious of one's cause	באַוווּסטזיניק
bay	bei	at by beside	בײַ
baym zinen	beim *zee*-nehn	sane	בײַם זינען
baysenish, dos	*bei*-sehn-ish	itch	בײַסעניש, דאָס
bayshtayer, der	*bei*-shtei-ehr	contribution donation	בײַשטײַער, דער
baysn	*beis*-n	to bite	בײַסן
baytl, dos	*beit*-l	purse wallet	בײַטל, דאָס
baytn	*beit*-n	to change to vary	בײַטן
bazorgt	bah-*zawrg*-t	worried anxious	באַזאָרגט
bazukher, der	bah-*zoo*-kehhr	visitor	באַזוכער, דער
bazukhn	bah-*zookh*-n	to visit	באַזוכן
bazunder	bah-*zoon*-dehr	separate apart	באַזונדער
bazaytikung, di	bah-*zei*-tee-koong	removal disposition	באַזײַטיקונג, די
bebl, dos	*behb*-l	bean	בעבל, דאָס

beemes	beh-*eh*-mehs	indeed	באמת
		really	
beheyme, di	beh-*hay*-meh	cow	בהמה, די
beheyme, di	beh-*hay*-meh	fool	בהמה, די
behole, di	beh-*haw*-leh	turmoil	בהלה, די
		bedlam	
beker, der	*beh*-kehr	baker	בעקער, דער
bekeray, di	beh-keh-*rei*	bakery	בעקעריַי, די
bekhavono	beh-kha-*voh*-noh	on purpose	בכוונה
		intentionally	
bekovedik	beh-*kaw*-veh-dik	honorable	בכבודיק
		respectable	
benken nokh	*behn*-kehn nawkh	to long for	בענקען נאָך
		to be homesick	
bentshn	*behnch*-n	to bless	בענטשן
ber, der	behr	bear	בער, דער
bergele, dos	*behr*-geh-leh	mound	בערגעלע, דאָס
bergl, dos	*behrg*-l	hill	בערגל, דאָס
		knoll	
berye, di/der	*behr*-yeh	skillful person	בריה, די/דער
		efficient person	
beryesh	*behr*-yehsh	skillful	בריהש
		efficient	
beser	*beh*-sehr	better	בעסער
beshas	beh-*shahs*	as (conj.)	בשעת
		during (prep.)	
		while	
besholem	beh-*shaw*-lehm	safely	בשלום
		unharmed	
best	behsst	best	בעסט
bet, di	beht	bed	בעט, די
betgevant, dos	*beht*-geh-vahnt	bedding	בעטגעוואַנט, דאָס
betler, der	*beht*-lehr	beggar	בעטלער, דער
betn	*beht*-n	to ask for	בעטן
		to request	
betn zikh (bay)	*beht*-n zikh (bei)	to beseech	בעטן זיך (ביַי)
		to beg	
betn mekhile	*beht*-n meh-*khee*-leh	to apologize	בעטן מחילה
betn rakhmim	*beht*-n *rahkh*-meem	to implore	בעטן רחמים

beyde	*bay*-deh	both	ביידע
beygl, der	*bay*-gil	bagel	בייגל, דער
beygn	*bayg*-n	to bend	בייגן
beykon, der	*bay*-kawn	bacon	בייקאָן, דער
beyn, der	bayn	bone	ביין, דער
beys-oylem, der	bays-*oy*-lehm	cemetery	בית־עולם, דער
beysbol, der	*bays*-bawl	baseball	בייסבאָל, דער
beytsim, di	*bay*-tsim	testicles	בצים, די
beyz	bayz	bad angry wicked evil	בייז
bez, der	behz	lilac	בעז, דער
bezem, der	*beh*-zehm	broom	בעזעם, דער
bibl, di	*beeb*-l	bible	ביבל, די
bibliotek, di	bib-lee-aw-*tehk*	library	ביבליאָטעק, די
bifsteyk, der	*beef*-stayk	steak	ביפֿסטייק, דער
bik, der	beek	bull	ביק, דער
biks, di	beeks	gun rifle	ביקס, די
bild, dos	beeld	picture	בילד, דאָס
bildung, di	*beel*-doong	education	בילדונג, די
bilet, der	bee-*leht*	ticket	בילעט, דער
bilik	*bee*-lik	cheap inexpensive	ביליק
bilkher	*beel*-khehr	preferred preferable	בילכער
biln	*beel*-n	to bark	בילן
bime, di	*bee*-meh	pulpit	בימה, די
bin	been	am (first person sing.)	בין
bin, di	been	bee	בין, די
bindn	*beend*-n	to bind to tie	בינדן
bine, di	*bee*-neh	stage	בינע, די
binshtok, der	*been*-shtawk	beehive	בינשטאָק, דער
bintl, dos	*beent*-l	bundle bunch	בינטל, דאָס
binyen, der	*been*-yehn	building structure	בנין, דער
bio, di	*bee*-aw	sexual intercourse	ביאה, די
bir, dos	beer	beer	ביר, דאָס

birger, der	*beer*-gehr	citizen	בירגער, דער
birger-mayster, der	*beer*-gehr-*mei*-stehr stehr	mayor	בירגער־מײַסטער, דער
bis, der	beess	bite	ביס, דער
bisl, dos	*bees*-l	a few a little	ביסל, דאָס
bisl, a	ah *bees*-l	some somewhat	ביסל, אַ
bislekhvayz	*bees*-lehkh-veiz	gradually little by little	ביסלעכווײַז
bisn, der	*bees*-n	morsel of food	ביסן, דער
bist	beest	(you) are	ביסט
biter	*bee*-tehr	bitter	ביטער
bitl, der	*bee*-tl	contempt scorn	ביטול, דער
bitokhn, der	bee-*tawkh*-n	faith confidence	בטחון, דער
biz	beez	by (prior to) until	ביז
biz aher	beez ah-*hehr*	previously	ביז אַהער
bizoyen, der	bee-*zoy*-en	shame disgrace	בזיון, דער
blas	blahss	pale pallid	בלאַס
blat, der	blaht	leaf	בלאַט, דער
blat, der	blaht	sheet of paper	בלאַט, דער
blaybn	*bleib*-n	to stay to remain	בלײַבן
blaybn lebn	*bleib*-n *lehb*-n	to survive	בלײַבן לעבן
blaybn shteyn	*bleib*-n *shtayn*	to pause	בלײַבן שטיין
blayer, der	*blei*-ehr	pencil	בלײַער, דער
bleykhn	*blaykh*-n	to bleach	בלײַכן
blezlen (zikh)	*blehz*-lehn (zikh)	to bubble	בלעזלען (זיך)
blien	*blee*-en	to flourish to bloom	בליִען
bliendik	*blee*-ehn-dik	prosperous flourishing	בליִענדיק
blik, der	bleek	look glance	בליק, דער
blind	bleend	blind	בלינד
blintse, di	*bleen*-tseh	stuffed crepe	בלינצע, די

blits, der	bleets	lightning flash	בליץ, דער
blitsshlesl, dos	*blits*-shlehs-l	zipper	בליצשלעסל, דאָס
blond	blawnd	blond	בלאָנד
blondzhen	*blawn*-jehn	to stray to ramble	בלאָנדזשען
blote, di	*blaw*-teh	mud filth	בלאָטע, די
bloy	bloy	blue	בלוי
bloyz	bloyz	just merely only	בלויז
blozn	*blawz*-n	to blow	בלאָזן
blum, di	bloom	flower	בלום, די
blut, dos	bloot	blood	בלוט, דאָס
blutikn	*bloo*-teek-n	to bleed	בלוטיקן
bluze, di	bloo-zeh	blouse	בלוזע, די
blyakirn	blah-*keer*-n	to fade to bleach	בליאַקירן
bobe, di	*baw*-beh	grandmother	באָבע, די
bobe mayse, di	*baw*-beh *mei*-seh	old wive's tale	באָבע-מעשה, די
bobkes, di	*bawb*-kehs	a meaningless amount a trifle	באָבקעס, די
bod, di	bawd	bathhouse	באָד, די
bodkostyum, der	*bawd*-kawst-yoom	bathing suit	באָדקאָסטיום, דער
bodn zikh	*bawd*-n zikh	to bathe	באָדן זיך
bodkhalat, der	*bawd*-khah-laht	bathrobe	באָדכאַלאַט, דער
bokher, der	*baw*-khehr	bachelor	בחור, דער
bokherl, dos	*baw*-khehr-l	youngster	בחורל, דאָס
bombe, di	*bawm*-beh	bomb	באָמבע, די
bord, di	bawrd	beard	באָרד די
borgn	*bawrg*-n	to borrow (from)	באָרגן
borsht, der	bawrsht	beet soup	באָרשט, דער
borukh-hashem	baw-*rookh*- hah-*shehm*	Thank God!	ברוך־השם
borves	*bawr*-vehs	barefoot	באָרוועס
boydem, der	*boy*-dehm	attic	בוידעם, דער
boyen	*boy*-en	to build to construct	בויען
boykh, der	boykh	abdomen belly	בויך, דער

boykhveytik, der	*boykh*-vay-tik	stomach ache	בויכווייטיק, דער
boylet	*boy*-leht	outstanding	בולט
boyml, der	*boym*-l	edible oil	בוימל, דער
boym, der	boym	tree	בוים, דער
braslet, der	brahss-*leht*	bracelet	בראַסלעט, דער
breg, der	brehg	bank	ברעג, דער
		border	
		edge	
brekhn	*brehkh*-n	to break	ברעכן
brekl, dos	*brehk*-l	scrap	ברעקל, דאָס
		crumb	
brem, di	brehm	eyebrow	ברעם, די
bren, der	brehn	burn	ברען, דער
		zeal	
brengen	*brehn*-gehn	to bring	ברענגען
brenvarg, dos	*brehn*-vahrg	fuel	ברענוואַרג, דאָס
bret, di/dos	breht	board	ברעט, די/דאָס
		plank	
breyt	brayt	broad	ברייט
		extensive	
		wide	
breythartsik	*brayt*-hahr-tsik	generous	ברייטהאַרציק
		magnanimous	
breyt shmeykhlen	*brayt shmaykh*-lehn	to grin	ברייט שמייכלען
brik, di	breek	bridge	בריק, די
brike, der	*bree*-keh	kick	בריקע, דער
briken	*bree*-kehn	to kick	בריקען
briln, di	*breel*-n	eyeglasses	ברילן, די
		spectacles	
brilyant, der	bril-*yahnt*	jewel	בריליאַנט, דער
brilyant	bril-*yahnt*	brilliant	בריליאַנט
bris, der	brees	circumcision ceremony	ברית, דער
briv, der	breev	letter	בריוו, דער
brivl, dos	*breev*-l	note	בריוול, דאָס
		message	
brivn-treger, der	*breev*-n-*trehg*-ehr	postman	בריוון־טרעגער, דער
brokh, der	brawkh	fracture	בראָך, דער
		rupture	
brokhe, di	*braw*-kheh	blessing	ברכה, די
bronfn, der	*brawn*-fn	whiskey	בראָנפֿן, דער
brosh, di	brawsh	brooch	בראָש, די

broshur, di	braw-*shoor*	booklet	בראָשור, די
brotn	*brawt*-n	to roast	בראָטן
		to broil	
broygez	*broy*-gehz	angry	ברוגז
		cross	
broyn	broyn	brown	ברוין
broyt, dos	broyt	bread	ברויט, דאָס
bruder, der	*broo*-dehr	brother	ברודער, דער
brudik	*broo*-dik	foul	ברודיק
		filthy	
brukve, di	*brook*-veh	turnip	ברוקווע, די
brunet	broo-*neht*	brunette	ברונעט
brust, di	broost	breast	ברוסט, די
brustkastn, der	*broost*-kahsst-n	chest (anat.)	ברוסטקאַסטן, דער
bsule, di	b-*soo*-lih	virgin	בתולה, די
		maiden	
budzhet, der	boo-*jeht*	budget	בודזשעט, דער
bufloks, der	*boof*-lawks	buffalo	בופלאָקס, דער
bukh, dos	bookh	book	בוך, דאָס
bulbe, di	*bool*-beh	potato	בולבע, די
bulke, di	*bool*-keh	bread roll	בולקע, די
bulvan, der	bool-*vahn*	blockhead	בולוואַן, דער
		oaf	
bund, der	boond	tie	בונד, דער
		bond	
burik, der	*boo*-rik	beet	בוריק, דער
burtshen	*boor*-chehn	to grumble	בורטשען
		to mutter	
bushe, di	*boo*-sheh	shame	בושה, די
buzem, der	*boo*-zehm	bosom	בוזעם, דער
byuro, dos	byoo-*raw*	bureau	ביוראָ, דאָס
		office	
dafke	*dahf*-keh	only	דווקא
		necessarily	
dakh, der	dahkh	roof	דאַך, דער
dakhtn zikh	*dahkht*-n zikh	to seem to one, to perceive	דאַכטן זיך
dales, der	*dah*-lehs	poverty	דלות, דער

dales-hayzer, di	*dah*-lehs-*hei*-zehr	slums	די דלות־הײַזער,
dame, di	*dah*-meh	lady	דאַמע, די
dank, der	dahnk	thanks	דאַנק, דער
dankbar	*dahnk*-bahr	grateful thankful	דאַנקבאַר
danken	*dahn*-kehn	to thank	דאַנקען
dar	dahr	thin lean	דאַר
darfn	*dahrf*-n	to need	דאַרפֿן
darfn	*dahrf*-n	have to ought to	דאַרפֿן
date, di	*dah*-teh	date (calendar)	דאַטע, די
davenen	*dah*-veh-nehn	to pray	דאַוועגען
dayge, di	*dei*-geh	worry anxiety	דאגה, די
daygen	*dei*-gehn	to worry	דאגהן
dayn	dein	your (familiar sing.)	דײַן
dayner	*dei*-nehr	yours	דײַנער
dekl, dos	*dehk*-l	cover	דעקל, דאָס
delikat	deh-lee-*kaht*	delicate dainty	דעליקאַט
dem	dehm	that this the	דעם
demokratish	deh-maw-*krah*-tish	democratic	דעמאָקראַטיש
demolt	deh-*mawlt*	since then (at that time)	דעמאָלט
denkmol, der	*dehnk*-mawl	memorial monument	דענקמאָל, דער
depresye, di	deh-*prehs*-yeh	depression (econ.)	דעפּרעסיע, די
der	dehr	the this that	דער
derekh-erets, der	*deh*-rehkh *eh*-rehts	respect esteem	דרך־ארץ, דער
derfar	dehr-*fahr*	therefore then	דערפֿאַר
derfreyen	dehr-*fray*-en	to gladden to delight	דערפֿרייען

derfun	dehr-*foon*	thereof hereof	דערפֿון
dergeyn di yorn	dehr-*gayn* dee-*yawr*-n	to pester	דערגיין די יאָרן
(der)hargenen	(*dehr*) *hahr*-geh-nehn	to kill	(דער)הרגענען
deriber	dehr-*ee*-behr	consequently therefore	דעריבער
derkenen	dehr-*keh*-nehn	to recognize	דערקענען
derklern	dehr-*klehr*-n	to explain to account for	דערקלערן
derklerung, di	dehr-*kleh*-roong	explanation	דערקלערונג, די
derlangen	dehr-*lahn*-gehn	to hand to serve	דערלאַנגען
derloybenish, dos	dehr-*loy*-beh-nish	permission	דערלויבעניש, דאָס
derloybn	dehr-*loyb*-n	to allow to permit	דערלויבן
derloybt mir	dehr-*loybt* meer	allow me	דערלויבט מיר
dermit	dehr-*meet*	herewith thereby	דערמיט
dermonen	dehr-*maw*-nehn	to mention to remind	דערמאָנען
dermonen zikh	dehr-*maw*-nehn zikh	to recall to remember	דערמאָנען זיך
dermonung, di	dehr-*maw*-noong	reminder remembrance	דערמאָנונג, די
dernerung, di	dehr-*neh*-roong	nourishment nutrition	דערנערונג, די
dernokhdem	dehr-*nawkh*-dehm	afterwards thereafter	דערנאָכדעם
dershlogn	dehr-*shlawg*-n	dejected depressed	דערשלאָגן
dershrokn	dehr-*shrawk*-n	frightenend afraid (of)	דערשראָקן
dershtekhn	dehr-*shtehkh*-n	to stab to death	דערשטעכן
dersthikn	dehr-*shteek*-n	to choke to strangle	דערשטיקן
dertrunken vern	dehr-*troon*-kehn *vehr*-n	to drown	דערטרונקען ווערן

dertseyln	dehr-*tsayl*-n	to tell to narrate	דערצײַלן
dertsu	dehr-*tsoo*	moreover furthermore	דערצו
dervaksn	dehr-*vahks*-n	grown adult	דערװאַקסן
dervaksener, der	dehr-*vahk*-sehn-ehr	adult grown-up	דערװאַקסענער, דער
dervartn	dehr-*vahrt*-n	to await to expect	דערװאַרטן
dervayl	dehr-*veil*	meanwhile for the present	דערװײַל
dervaylik	dehr-*vei*-lik	temporary provisional	דערװײַליק
dervayzn	dehr-*veiz*-n	to prove	דערװײַזן
dervayz, der	dehr-*veiz*	proof	דערװײַז, דער
derveyln	dehr-*vayl*-n	to elect	דערװײַלן
dervisn zikh	dehr-*vees*-n zikh	to learn to find out	דערװיסן זיך
detsember, der	deh-*tsehm*-behr	December	דעצעמבער, דער
doyfek, der	*doy*-fik	pulse	דופֿק, דער
di	dee	the (pl. & fem. sing. art.) these this that	די
diete, di	dee-*eh*-teh	diet	דיעטע, די
dik	deek	thick stout	דיק
dikh	deekh	you	דיך
dikh, di	deekh	thigh	דיך, די
diktirn	dik-*teer*-n	to dictate	דיקטירן
dil, der	dill	floor	דיל, דער
diment, der	*dee*-mehnt	diamond	דימענט, דער
din	deen	thin	דין
din, der	deen	religious law	דין, דער
diner, der	*dee*-nehr	servant	דינער, דער
dingen	*deen*-gehn	to rent to hire	דינגען
dingen zikh	*deen*-gehn zikh	to bargain to haggle	דינגען זיך
dinke, di	*deen*-keh	cantaloupe	דינקע, די

dinst, di	deenst	maid servant	דינסט, די
dinstik, der	*deen*-stik	Tuesday	דינסטיק, דער
dir	deer	you	דיר
dire, di	*dee*-reh	apartment dwelling	דירה, די
dire-gelt, dos	*dee*-reh-gehlt	rent	דירה-געלט, דאָס
disenterye, di	dee-sehn-*tehr*-yeh	dysentery	דיסענטעריע, די
disk, der	deesk	disk record	דיסק, דער
diskusye, di	diss-*koos*-yeh	discussion	דיסקוסיע, די
divan, der	dee-*vahn*	rug	דיוואָן, דער
divan, der	dee-*vahn*	sofa	דיוואָן, דער
dlonye, di	*dlawn*-yeh	palm (of hand)	דלאָניע, די
do	daw	here	דאָ
dokh	dawkh	yet still	דאָך
dokter, der	*dawk*-tehr	doctor	דאָקטער, דער
dolar, der	*daw*-lahr	dollar	דאָלאַר, דער
donershtik, der	*daw*-nehrsh-tik	Thursday	דאָנערשטיק, דער
dor, der	dawr	generation	דור, דער
dorem, der	*daw*-rim	south	דרום, דער
dorem-mayrevdik	*daw*-rim-*mei*- rehv-dik	southwestern	דרום-מערבדיק
dorem-mizrakhdik	*daw*-rim-*meez*- rahkh-dik	southeastern	דרום-מזרחדיק
doremdik	*daw*-rehm-dik	southern	דרומדיק
dorf, dos	dawrf	village	דאָרף, דאָס
dorfish	*dawr*-fish	rural	דאָרפיש
dorshtik	*dawr*-shtik	thirsty	דאָרשטיק
dortn	*dawrt*-n	there	דאָרטן
dos	dawss	the (neuter art.) this (pron.) that(adj.)	דאָס
doykhik, der	*doy*-kheek	lack scarcity	דוחק, דער
doyresdik	*doy*-rehs-dik	perpetual perennial	דורותדיק
doze, di	*daw*-zeh	dose	דאָזע, די
drame, di	*drah*-meh	drama	דראַמע, די
dray	drei	three	דרײַ

draysik	*drei*-sik	thirty	דרײַסיק
draytsn	*dreits*-n	thirteen	דרײַצן
drek, dos	drehk	human dung	דרעק, דאָס
		inferior merchandise (sl.)	
dremlen	*drehm*-lehn	to nap	דרעמלען
		to doze	
drey, der	dray	turn	דריי, דער
		twist	
dreyen	*dray*-en	to rotate	דרייען
		to turn	
dreyer, der	*dray*-ehr	finagler	דרייער, דער
dreykop, der	*dray*-kawp	pesty person	דרייקאָפּ, דער
dreyst	drayst	bold	דרייסט
drikn	*dreek*-n	to press	דריקן
		to oppress	
dringlekh	*dreeng*-lehkh	urgent	דרינגלעך
		pressing	
driter	*dree*-tehr	third	דריטער
droshe, di	*draw*-sheh	sermon	דרשה, די
		speech	
drot, der	drawt	wire	דראָט, דער
druk, der	drook	pressure	דרוק, דער
		stress	
druk, der	drook	print	דרוק, דער
druker, der	*droo*-kehr	printer	דרוקער, דער
drukn	*drook*-n	to print	דרוקן
du	doo	you (sing. familiar)	דו
duner, der	*doo*-nehr	thunder	דונער, דער
durkh	doorkh	through	דורך
		by (via)	
durkhveg, der	*doorkh*-vehg	shortcut	דורכוועג, דער
durkh un durkh	*doorkh* oon *doorkh*	thoroughly	דורך און דורך
durkhfaln	*doorkh*-fahl-n	to fall through	דורכפֿאַלן
		to fail	
durkhfirn	*doorkh*-feer-n	to carry out	דורכפֿירן
		to perform	
durkhhoys	*doorkh*-oyss	throughout	דורכויס
dzhentlman, der	*jehn*-til-mahn	gentlemen	דזשענטלמאַן, דער
dzhez, der	jehz	jazz	דזשעז, דער

efektiv	eh-fehk-*teev*	effective	עפֿעקטיוו
		efficient	
efenen	*eh*-feh-nehn	to open	עפֿענען
efenung, di	*eh*-feh-noong	opening	עפֿענונג, די
efsher	*ehf*-shehr	maybe	אפֿשר
		perhaps	
egoistish	eh-gaw-*ees*-tish	selfish	עגאָיסטיש
		egotistic	
ek, der	ehk	tail	עק, דער
ek, der	ehk	end	עק, דער
ekht	ehkht	genuine	עכט
		authentic	
ekl, der	*ehk*-l	disgust	עקל, דער
		aversion	
ekldik	*ehk*-l-dik	disgusting	עקלדיק
eksistirn	ehk-sis-*teer*-n	to exist	עקסיסטירן
ekskursye, di	ehks-*koors*-yeh	excursion	עקסקורסיע, די
		outing	
ekstrem	ehkst-*rehm*	extreme	עקסטרעם
ekstre	*ehks*-treh	extra	עקסטרע
		special	
elegant	eh-leh-*gahnt*	chic	עלעגאַנט
		elegant	
elektre, di	eh-*lehk*-treh	electricity	עלעקטרע, די
elektronik, di	eh-lehk-*traw*-nik	electronics	עלעקטראָניק, די
elf	ehlf	eleven	עלף
elfter	*ehlf*-tehr	eleventh	עלפֿטער
eliminirn	eh-*lee*-mi-neer-n	to eliminate	עלימינירן
elnboygn, der	*ehl*-n-boyg-n	elbow	עלנבױגן, דער
elnt	*ehl*-nt	lonely	עלנט
		lonesome	
elter	*ehl*-tehr	elder	עלטער
		senior	
elter-bobe, di	*ehl*-tehr-*baw*-beh	great-grandmother	עלטער־באָבע, די
elter-zeyde, der	*ehl*-tehr-*zay*-deh	great-grandfather	עלטער־זיידע, דער

emer, der	*eh*-mehr	bucket pail	עמער, דער
emes	*eh*-mehs	true real	אמת
emes, der	*eh*-mehs	truth	אמת, דער
emetser	*eh*-meh-tsehr	somebody someone	עמעצער
emotsye, di	eh-*mawts*-yeh	emotion	עמאָציע, די
emune, di	eh-*moo*-neh	faith creed	אמונה, די
endikn	*ehn*-deek-n	to finish to end	ענדיקן
eng	ehng	tight crowded	ענג
enlekh	*ehn*-lehkh	alike	ענלעך
enlekhkayt, di	*ehn*-lehkh-keit	similarity	ענלעכקייט, די
entfer, der	*ehnt*-fehr	reply answer	ענטפער, דער
entfern	*ehnt*-fehr-n	to answer to reply	ענטפערן
entuzyazm, der	ehn-tooz-*yah*-zim	enthusiasm	ענטוזיאַזם, דער
epes	*eh*-pehs	somewhat something anything	עפעס
epidemye, di	eh-pee-*dehm*-yeh	epidemic	עפידעמיע, די
epl, der	*eh*-pil	apple	עפל, דער
epl-tsimes, der	*eh*-pil-tsee-mehs	applesauce	עפל־צימעס, דער
er	ehr	he	ער
erd, di	ehrd	dirt earth ground	ערד, די
erd-tsiternish, dos	*ehrd*-tsee-tehr- nish	earthquake	ערד־ציטערניש, דאָס
erev	*eh*-rehv	before the day before on the eve of	ערב
erger	*ehr*-gehr	worse	ערגער
ergernish, dos	*ehr*-gehr-nish	grief	ערגערניש, דאָס

ergets	*ehr*-gehts	somewhere anywhere	ערגעץ
ergst	ehrgst	worst	ערגסט
erlekh	*ehr*-lehkh	honest virtuous	ערלעך
erlekhkayt, di	*ehr*-lehkh-keit	honesty	ערלעכקייט, די
erntst	*eh*-rintst	serious earnest	ערנסט
ersht	ehrsht	first	ערשט
ershter	*ehr*-shtehr	first	ערשטער
ershtik	*ehr*-shtik	original primary	ערשטיק
es	ehs	it	עס
es tut mir leyd	ehs *toot* meer layd	I'm sorry	עס טוט מיר לייד
esik, der	*eh*-sik	vinegar	עסיק, דער
eslefl, der	*ehs*-lehf-l	spoon tablespoon	עסלעפל, דער
esn	*ehs*-n	to eat	עסן
esnvarg, dos	*ehs*-n-vahrg	food	עסנוואַרג, דאָס
estsimer, der	*ehs*-tsee-mehr	dining room	עסצימער, דער
etiket, der	eh-tee-*keht*	etiquette	עטיקעט, דער
etlekhe	*eht*-leh-kheh	several a few	עטלעכע
evenu, di	*eh*-veh-noo	avenue	עוועניו, די
evyen, der	*ehv*-yin	pauper	אבֿיון, דער
ey, dos	ay	egg	איי, דאָס
eybersht	*ay*-behrsh-t	topmost	אייבערשט
eybershter, der	*ay*-behr-shtehr	God Almighty	אייבערשטער, דער
eybik	*ay*-bik	eternal everlasting	אייביק
eydem, der	*ay*-dehm	son-in-law	איידעם, דער
eyder	*ay*-dehr	before	איידער
eydes, der	*ay*-dis	witness	עדות, דער
eydes zogn	*ay*-dis *zawg*-n	to give evidence to testify	עדות זאָגן
eydl	*ayd*-l	genteel noble polite	איידל

eydlshteyn, der	*ayd*-l-shtayn	gem jewel	איידלשטיין, דער
eyferzikhtik	*ay*-fehr-zikh-tik	jealous	אייפערזיכטיק
eygener, der	*ay*-geh-nehr	own (one's own)	אייגענער, דער
eygn	*ayg*-n	own	אייגן
eyl, der	ayl	oil	אייל, דער
eyme, di	*ay*-meh	dread horror	אימה, די
eyn-ore, der	ayn-*ahw*-reh	evil eye	עין־הרע, דער
eymedik	*ay*-meh-dik	dreadful horrible	אימהדיק
eyn mol	*ayn* mol	once (one time)	איין מאָל
eyn un tsvantsik	*ayn* oon *tsvahn*-tsik	twenty-one	איין און צוואַנציק
eynikl, dos	*ay*-neek-l	grandchild	אייניקל, דאָס
eyns	ayns	one	איינס
eyntsik	*ayn*-tsik	one single only	איינציק
eynzam	*ayn*-zahm	lonesome solitary	איינזאַם
eytse, di	*ay*-tseh	advice counsel	עצה, די
eytsn	*ay*-tsehn	to advise to counsel	עצהן
eyver, der	*ay*-vir	limb	אבֿר, דער
eyzl, der	*ayz*-l	donkey	אייזל, דער
fabrik, di	fah-*breek*	factory plant	פֿאַבריק, די
fabrikant, der	fah-bree-*kahnt*	manufacturer maker	פֿאַבריקאַנט, דער
fakh, der	fahkh	trade vocation	פֿאַך, דער

fakt, der	fahkt	fact reality	פֿאַקט, דער
faktish	*fahk*-tish	actual real	פֿאַקטיש
faln	*fahl*-n	to fall to drop	פֿאַלן
falsh	fahlsh	wrong false	פֿאַלש
falshe shvue, di	*fahl*-sheh shvoo-eh	perjury	פֿאַלשע שבֿועה, די
fangen	*fahn*-gehn	to catch to capture	פֿאַנגען
fantazye, di	fahn-*tahz*-yeh	fantasy imagination	פֿאַנטאַזיע, די
far	fahr	before (prep.) for	פֿאַר
far vos	fahr *vawss*	why	פֿאַר וואָס
farakshnt	fahr-*ahksh*-nt	stubborn obstinate	פֿאַרעקשנט
faranen	fah-*rah*-nehn	available	פֿאַראַנען
farb, di	fahrb	color dye paint	פֿאַרב, די
farband, der	fahr-*bahnd*	association union	פֿאַרבאַנד, דער
farbay	fahr-*bei*	gone paint	פֿאַרביי
farbasyn, dos	fahr-*beis*-n	dessert	פֿאַרבייסן, דאָס
farbaytn	fahr-*beit*-n	to replace to substitute	פֿאַרבייטן
farbenkt	fahr-*behnkt*	homesick nostalgic	פֿאַרבענקט
farbesern	fahr-*beh*-sehr-n	to improve	פֿאַרבעסערן
farbetn	fahr-*beht*-n	to invite	פֿאַרבעטן
farbetung, di	fahr-*beh*-toong	invitation	פֿאַרבעטונג, די
farbisener, der	fahr-*bee*-sehn-ehr	embittered person	פֿאַרביסענער, דער
farbisn	fahr-*bees*-n	stubborn grim	פֿאַרביסן
farbitert	fahr-*bee*-tehrt	embittered	פֿאַרביטערט

farblonzhet	fahr-*blawn*-jeht	lost	פֿאַרבלאָנדזשעט
		confused	
farbn	*fahrb*-n	to color	פֿאַרבן
		to dye	
		to paint	
farborgn	fahr-*bawrg*-n	concealed	פֿאַרבאָרגן
		hidden	
farbrekhn, dos	fahr-*brehkh*-n	crime	פֿאַרברעכן, דאָס
farbrekher, der	fahr-*breh*-khehr	criminal	פֿאַרברעכער, דער
farbrenen	fahr-*breh*-nehn	to burn	פֿאַרברענען
farbrenter, der	fahr-*brehnt*-ehr	excited or ardent	פֿאַרברענטער, דער
		person	
fardamen	fahr-*dah*-mehn	to condemn	פֿאַרדאַמען
		to denounce	
fardart	fahr-*dahrt*	withered	פֿאַרדאַרט
fardinen	fahr-*dee*-nehn	to deserve	פֿאַרדינען
		to earn	
		to merit	
fardiner, der	fahr-*dee*-nehr	breadwinner	פֿאַרדינער, דער
farfaln	fahr-*fahl*-n	lost	פֿאַרפֿאַלן
		hopeless	
farfeln	fahr-*fehl*-n	to miss	פֿאַרפֿעלן
		to overlook	
farfirn	fahr-*feer*-n	to seduce	פֿאַרפֿירן
		to mislead	
farfl, di	*fahrf*-l	noodle flakes	פֿאַרפֿל, די
farfoylt	fahr-*foylt*	rotten	פֿאַרפֿוילט
		decayed	
farfroyrn	fahr-*froyr*-n	frozen	פֿאַרפֿרוירן
farfroyn vern	fahr-*froyr*-n *vehr*-n	to freeze	פֿאַרפֿרוירן ווערן
fargaft	fahr-*gahft*	amazed	פֿאַרגאַפֿט
fargenign, der	fahr-geh-*neeg*-n	joy	פֿאַרגעניגן, דער
		pleasure	
fargesn	fahr-*gehs*-n	to forget	פֿאַרגעסן
farginen	fahr-*gee*-nehn	to not begrudge	פֿאַרגינען
farginen zikh	fahr-*gee*-nehn zikh	to afford	פֿאַרגינען זיך
fargisn	fahr-*gees*-n	to spill	פֿאַרגיסן
farglaykh, der	fahr-*gleikh*	comparison	פֿאַרגלײַך, דער

farglaykhn	fahr-*gleikh*-n	to compare	פֿאַרגלײַכן
fargleybter, der	fahr-*glayb*-tehr	bigot	פֿאַרגלייבטער, דער
fargresern	fahr-*greh*-sehr-n	to enlarge	פֿאַרגרעסערן
		to increase	
fargvaldikn	fahr-g-*vahl*-dik-n	to rape	פֿאַרגוואַלדיקן
farhaltn	fahr-*hahlt*-n	to delay	פֿאַרהאַלטן
		to detain	
farhandlung, di	fahr-*hahnd*-loong	negotiation	פֿאַרהאַנדלונג, די
		proceedings	
farhiken zikh	fahr-*hee*-kehn zikh	to stammer	פֿאַרהיקען זיך
		to stutter	
farhitn	fahr-*heet*-n	to avert	פֿאַרהיטן
		to prevent	
faribl, hobn	*hawb*-n fahr-*reeb*-l	to resent	פֿאַראיבל, האָבן
		to take offense	
farkakt	fahr-*kahkt*	shitty	פֿאַרקאַקט
farkert	fahr-*kehrt*	opposite	פֿאַרקערט
		contrary	
farkhalesht	fahr-*khah*-lehsht	unconscious	פֿאַרחלשט
farkilung, di	fahr-*kee*-loong	cold (ailment)	פֿאַרקילונג, די
farkirtst	fahr-*keertst*	shortened	פֿאַרקירצט
farkirtsn	fahr-*keerts*-n	to shorten	פֿאַרקירצן
farklenern	fahr-*kleh*-nehr-n	to lessen	פֿאַרקלענערן
		to decrease	
farklert	fahr-*klehrt*	thoughtful	פֿאַרקלערט
		absorbed in thought	
farlobn	fahr-*lawb*-n	to betroth	פֿאַרלאָבן
farlobt	fahr-*lawbt*	engaged	פֿאַרלאָבט
		betrothed	
farlobsung, di	fah-*law*-b soong	engagement	פֿאַרלאָבנג, די
		betrothal	
farkoyf-tsetl, der	fahr-*koyf*-tseht-l	bill of sale	פֿאַרקויף-צעטל, דער
farkoyfer, der	fahr-*koy*-fehr	clerk	פֿאַרקויפֿער, דער
		salesperson	
farkoyflekh	fahr-*koyf*-lehkh	negotiable	פֿאַרקויפֿלעך
farkoyfn	fahr-*koyf*-n	to sell	פֿאַרקויפֿן
farkrimen	fahr-*kree*-mehn	to distort	פֿאַרקרימען
		to deform	

farkrimt	fahr-*krimt*	distorted sour-faced	פֿאַרקרימט
farkukn	fahr-*kook*-n	to overlook	פֿאַרקוקן
farlangen	fahr-*lahn*-gehn	to desire to require	פֿאַרלאַנגען
farleygn	fahr-*layg*-n	to mislay	פֿאַרלייגן
farlirn	fahr-*leer*-n	to misplace to lose	פֿאַרלירן
farloyrn	fahr-*loy*-rin	lost	פֿאַרלוירן
farlozlekh	fahr-*lawz*-lehkh	reliable dependable	פֿאַרלאָזלעך
farlozn	fahr-*lawz*-n	to neglect to forsake	פֿאַרלאָזן
farlozn zikh	fahr-*lawz*-n zikh	to rely on to depend on	פֿאַרלאָזן זיך
farm, di	*fahr*-m	farm	פֿאַרם, די
farmakhn	fahr-*mahkh*-n	to close to shut	פֿאַרמאַכן
farmatern	fahr-*mah*-tehr-n	to tire	פֿאַרמאַטערן
farmatert	fahr-*mah*-tehrt	weary tired	פֿאַרמאַטערט
farmegn, dos	fahr-*mehg*-n	possession holdings	פֿאַרמעגן, דאָס
farminern	fahr-*mee*-neh-rin	to diminish to lessen	פֿאַרמינערן
farmishpetn	fahr-*meesh*- peht-n	to doom to sentence	פֿאַרמישפּטן
farmogn	fahr-*mawg*-n	to own to possess	פֿאַרמאָגן
farnakht, der	fahr-*nahkht*	dusk evening	פֿאַרנאַכט, דער
farnemen	fahr-*neh*-mehn	to occupy to take possession of	פֿאַרנעמען
farnumen	fahr-*noo*-mehn	busy occupied	פֿאַרנומען
farratn	fahr-*raht*-n	to betray	פֿאַרראַטן
farreter, der	fahr-*reh*-tehr	traitor	פֿאַררעטער, דער
farrekhn- konte, di	fahr-*rehkh*-n- *kawn*-teh	charge account	פֿאַררעכן־קאָנטע, די

farrikhtn	fahr-*reekh*-tin	to fix to mend	פֿאַרריכטן
farsamen	fahr-*sah*-mehn	to poison	פֿאַרסמען
farshemen	fahr-*sheh*-mehn	to embarrass to disgrace	פֿאַרשעמען
farshemt	fahr-*shehmt*	ashamed	פֿאַרשעמט
farshidn	fahr-*sheed*-n	miscellaneous various	פֿאַרשיידן
farshiltn	fahr-*sheelt*-n	to damn to curse	פֿאַרשילטן
farshimlt	fahr-*shee*-mlt	moldy	פֿאַרשימלט
farshlisn	fahr-*shlees*-n	to lock up to lock in	פֿאַרשליסן
farshnoshket	fahr-*shnawsh*- keht	tipsy	פֿאַרשנאָשקעט
farshpetikt	fahr-*shpeh*-tikt	late tardy	פֿאַרשפּעטיקט
farshpreytn	fahr-*shprayt*-n	to spread to distribute	פֿאַרשפּרייטן
farshtelung, di	fahr-*shteh*-loong	disguise	פֿאַרשטעלונג, די
farshtelung, di	fahr-*shtehl*- oong	obstruction	פֿאַרשטעלונג, די
farshteyn	fahr-*shtayn*	to understand to realize	פֿאַרשטיין
farshtikn	fahr-*shteek*-n	to suppress to muffle	פֿאַרשטיקן
farshtopung, di	fahr-*shtaw*- poong	constipation	פֿאַרשטאָפּונג, די
farshvitst	fahr-*shveetst*	perspired sweaty	פֿאַרשוויצט
farshvundn vern	fahr-*shvoond*-n *vehr*-n	to disappear	פֿאַרשוווּנדן ווערן
fartekh, der	*fahr*-tehkh	apron	פֿאַרטעך, דער
farteyln	fahr-*tayl*-n	to distribute	פֿאַרטיילן
fartik	*fahr*-tik	ready finished	פֿאַרטיק
fartrakht	fahr-*trahkht*	thoughtful pensive	פֿאַרטראַכט

fartrakhtn	fahr-*trahkht*-n	to contrive	פֿאַרטראַכטן
fartrakhtn zikh	fahr-*trahkht*-n zikh	to reflect	פֿאַרטראַכטן זיך
fartrogn	fahr-*trawg*-n	absent minded	פֿאַרטראָגן
fartrogn	fahr-*trawg*-n	to bear to endure	פֿאַרטראָגן
fartsaytik	fahr-*tsei*-tik	antique ancient	פֿאַרצײַטיק
fartsveyflt	fahr-*tsvay*-flt	desperate	פֿאַרצווייפֿלט
farumert	fah-*roo*-mehrt	gloomy despondent	פֿאַראומערט
farvayln	fahr-*veil*-n	to entertain to amuse	פֿאַרווײַלן
farvaylung, di	fahr-*vei*-loong	pastime entertainment	פֿאַרווײַלונג, די
farver, dos	fahr-*vehr*	prohibition ban	פֿאַרווער, דאָס
farvern	fahr-*vehr*-n	to forbid to prohibit	פֿאַרווערן
farvert	fahr-*vehrt*	forbidden prohibited	פֿאַרווערט
farvolknt	fahr-*vawl*-knt	cloudy overcast	פֿאַרוואָלקנט
farvundikn	fahr-*voon*-dik-n	to wound	פֿאַרוווּנדיקן
farzamlung, di	fahr-*zahm*-loong	assembly meeting	פֿאַרזאַמלונג, די
farze, der	fahr-*zeh*	oversight slip	פֿאַרזע, דער
farzesene moyd, di	fahr-*zehs*-eh-neh moyd	spinster	פֿאַרזעסענע מויד, די
farzhavert	fahr-*zhah*-vehrt	rusty	פֿאַרזשאַווערט
farzikhern	fahr-*zee*-khehr-n	to assure	פֿאַרזיכערן
farzikhert	fahr-*zee*-khehrt	insured	פֿאַרזיכערט
farzikherung, di	fahr-*zee*-kheh--roong	insurance	פֿאַרזיכערונג, די
farzorgn	fahr-*zawrg*-n	to provide to supply to care for	פֿאַרזאָרגן

farzukhn	fahr-*zookh*-n	to taste	פֿאַרזוכן
		to sample	
fas	fahss	barrel	פֿאַס, די
fasolye, di	fah-*sawl*-yeh	bean	פֿאַסאָליע, די
fastn	*fahst*-n	to fast	פֿאַסטן
fayer	*fei*-ehr	fire	פֿײַער, דאָס
		ardor	
fayerlekh	*fei*-ehr-lehkh	solemn	פֿײַערלעך
		ceremonial	
		celebrative	
fayer-lesher, der	*fei*-ehr *leh*-shehr	fireman	פֿײַער־לעשער, דער
fayfn	*feif*-n	to whistle	פֿײַפֿן
fayfn	*feif*-n	to hold in contempt	פֿײַפֿן
fayg, di	feig	fig	פֿײַג, די
faykht	feikht	damp	פֿײַכט
		moist	
		humid	
fayn	fein	fine	פֿײַן
		nice	
faynd, der	feind	enemy	פֿײַנד, דער
		foe	
fayndlekh	*feind*-lehkh	hostile	פֿײַנדלעך
faynkukhn, der	*fein*-kookh-n	omelet	פֿײַנקוכן, דער
faynt hobn	*feint* hawb-n	to hate	פֿײַנט האָבן
		to despise	
februar, der	*fehb*-roo-ahr	February	פֿעברואַר, דער
feder, di	*feh*-dehr	feather	פֿעדער, די
fefer, der	*feh*-fehr	pepper	פֿעפֿער, דער
fel, di	fehl	hide	פֿעל, די
		pelt	
feld, dos	fehld	field	פֿעלד, דאָס
felik	*feh*-lik	payable	פֿעליק
		due	
feln	*fehl*-n	to be missing	פֿעלן
		to be lacking	
felndik	*feh*-lin-dik	absent	פֿעלנדיק
		missing	
fendl, dos	*fehnd*-l	saucepan	פֿענדל, דאָס
		pot	

fentster, der	*fehnts*-tehr	window	פֿענצטער, דער
ferd, dos	fehrd	horse	פֿערד, דאָס
fershke, di	*fehrsh*-keh	peach	פֿערשקע, די
ferter	*fehr*-tehr	fourth	פֿערטער
fertl, dos	*fehrt*-l	quarter (one-fourth)	פֿערטל, דאָס
fertsik	*fehr*-tsik	forty	פֿערציק
fertsn	*fehrts*-n	fourteen	פֿערצן
fest	fehst	firm steady	פֿעסט
festshteln	*fehst*-shtehl-n	to assert to state	פֿעסטשטעלן
fet	feht	fat	פֿעט
feter, der	*feh*-tehr	uncle	פֿעטער, דער
fets, dos	fehts	fat grease	פֿעטס, דאָס
feye, di	*feh*-yeh	fairy	פֿעע, די
feyik	*feh*-yeek	able capable	פֿעיִק
feyikayt, di	*feh*-yee-keit	ability aptitude	פֿעיִקייט, די
fiber, der	*fee*-behr	fever	פֿיבער, דער
fidl, der	*feed*-l	violin	פֿידל, דער
figur, di	fee-*goor*	figure	פֿיגור, די
fikh, dos	feekh	cattle	פֿיך, דאָס
fil	feel	many much	פֿיל
film, der	feelm	film	פֿילם, דער
filosofye, di	fee-law-*sawf*- yeh	philosophy	פֿילאָסאָפֿיע, די
finf	feenf	five	פֿינף
finfter	*feenf*-tehr	fifth	פֿינפֿטער
finger, der	*feen*-gehr	finger	פֿינגער, דער
finger fun fus, der	*feen*-gehr foon foos	toe	פֿינגער פֿון פֿוס, דער
fingerhut, der	*feen*-gehr-hoot	thimble	פֿינגערהוט, דער
fingerl, dos	*feeng*-ehr-l	ring (jewelry)	פֿינגערל, דאָס
finklen	*feenk*-lehn	to sparkle	פֿינקלען
fintster	*feents*-tehr	dark	פֿינצטער
fintsternish, dos	*feents*-tehr-nish	darkness	פֿינצטערניש, דאָס

fir	feer	four	פיר
firer, der	*fee*-rehr	leader guide	פירער, דער
firlitsents, der	*feer*-lee-tsehnts	driver's license	פירליצענץ, דער
firme, di	*feer*-meh	company firm	פירמע, די
firn	*feer*-n	to drive (a vehicle) to lead to manage	פירן
firn zikh	*feer*-n zikh	to conduct oneself	פירן זיך
firung, di	*fee*-roong	practice custom	פירונג, די
fish, der	feesh	fish	פיש, דער
fisher, der	*fee*-shehr	fisher	פישער, דער
fishn	*feesh*-n	to fish	פישן
fistashke, di	fee-*shtahsh*-keh	peanut	פיסטאַשקע, די
flam, der	flahm	flame	פלאַם, דער
flanken, dos	*flahn*-kehn	meat from cow's flank	פלאַנקען, דאָס
flash, di	flahsh	bottle	פלאַש, די
flaterl, dos	*flah*-tehr-l	butterfly	פלאַטערל, דאָס
flaysik	*flei*-sik	diligent industrious	פלײַסיק
fledermoyz, di	*fleh*-dehr-moyz	bat (animal)	פלעדערמויז, די
flek, der	flehk	blot spot stain	פלעק, דער
fleysh, der	flaysh	flesh meat	פלייש, דאָס
fleyshik	*flay*-shik	made of meat	פליישיק
fleyt, di	flayt	flute	פלייט, די
flien	*flee*-en	to fly	פליִען
flier, der	*flee*-ehr	aviator	פליִער, דער
flig, di	fleeg	fly	פליג, די
fligl, der	*fleeg*-l	wing	פליגל, דער
flikn	*fleek*-n	to pluck	פליקן
fliplats, der	*flee*-plahts	airport	פליפּלאַץ, דער
flishlang, di	*flee*-shlahng	kite	פלישלאַנג, די
flokn, der	*flawk*-n	club pole	פלאָקן, דער

floym, di	floym	plum	פלוים, די
floym, (getriknte) di	(geh-*treek*-n-teh) floym	prune	פלוים, (געטריקנטע), די
fodem, der	*faw*-dehm	thread	פֿאָדעם, דער
fodern	*faw*-dehr-n	to demand to call for	פֿאָדערן
folgn	*fawlg*-n	to obey to take advice	פֿאָלגן
folk, dos	fawlk	people nation	פֿאָלק, דאָס
fon, di	fawn	flag	פֿאָן, די
fonar, der	faw-*nahr*	headlight	פֿאָנאַר, דער
fone, di	*faw*-neh	banner	פֿאָנע, די
fonfen	*fawn*-fehn	to double talk	פֿאָנפֿען
for, der	fawr	ride	פֿאָר, דער
forel, di	faw-*rehl*	trout	פֿאָרעל, די
forgelt, dos	*fawr*-gehlt	fare	פֿאָרגעלט, דאָס
forhang, der	*fawr*-hahng	curtain drape	פֿאָרהאַנג, דער
forn	*fawr*-n	to drive to go ride	פֿאָרן
fornt, der	*fawr*-nt	front	פֿאָרנט, דער
foroys	faw-*royss*	forward (adj.) ahead onward	פֿאָרויס
foroyszogn	faw-*royss*-zawg-n	to predict to forecast	פֿאָרויסזאָגן
forplan, der	*fawr*-plahn	timetable schedule	פֿאָרפּלאַן, דער
forshlog, der	*fawr*-shlawg	suggestion proposal offer	פֿאָרשלאָג, דער
forshlogn	*fawr*-shlawg-n	to suggest to propose	פֿאָרשלאָגן
forshpayz, der	*fawr*-shpeiz	appetizer	פֿאָרשפּײַז, דער
forshteln	*fawr*-shtehl-n	to present to introduce	פֿאָרשטעלן
fortz, der	*fawrtz*	fart	פֿאָרץ, דער
forurtl, der	*faw*-roor-tl	prejudice	פֿאָראורטל, דער

foter, der	*faw*-tehr	father	פֿאָטער, דער
fotografye, di	faw-taw-*grahf*-yeh	photograph photography	פֿאָטאָגראַפֿיע, די
foygl, der	*foyg*-l	bird	פֿױגל, דער
foyl	foyl	sluggish lazy	פֿױל
foyler, der	*foy*-lehr	lazy person	פֿױלער, דער
foyln	*foyl*-n	to rot	פֿױלן
foyst, di	foyst	fist	פֿױסט, די
frage, di	*frah*-geh	question	פֿראַגע, די
frask, der	frahsk	powerful smack	פֿראַסק, דער
fray	frei	free independent	פֿרײַ
frayhayt, di	*frei*-heit	freedom liberty	פֿרײַהײט, די
fraylin	*frei*-lin	Miss	פֿרײַלין
fraynd, der	freind	friend	פֿרײַנד, דער
frayndlekh	*freind*-lehkh	friendly kind	פֿרײַנדלעך
frayndlekhkayt, di	*freind*-lehkh-keit	kindness friendliness	פֿרײַנדלעכקײט, די
frayndshaft, di	*freind*-shahft	friendship	פֿרײַנדשאַפֿט, די
fraytik, der	*frei*-tik	Friday	פֿרײַטיק, דער
fraye tsayt, di	*frei*-eh tseit	leisure	פֿרײַע צײַט, די
fregn	*frehg*-n	to ask to inquire	פֿרעגן
fregn zikh	*frehg*-n zikh	to wonder to ask oneself	פֿרעגן זיך
fremd	frehmd	strange foreign	פֿרעמד
fremder, der	*frehm*-dehr	stranger	פֿרעמדער, דער
fresn	*frehs*-n	to eat greedily to devour	פֿרעסן
freser, der	*frehs*-ehr	big eater	פֿרעסער, דער
freyd, di	frayd	joy delight	פֿרייד, די
freydik	*fray*-dik	joyful joyous	פֿריידיק
freyen zikh	*fray*-en zikh	to be glad to rejoice	פֿרייען זיך

freylekh	*fray*-lehkh	cheerful gay	פריילעך
fridlekh	*freed*-lehkh	peaceful amicable	פרידלעך
fridzhider, der	free-jee-*dehr*	refrigerator	פרידזשידער, דער
fri	free	early	פרי
frier	*free*-ehr	before (adv.) earlier	פריִער
friling, der	*free*-ling	spring	פריילינג, דער
frimorgn, der	free-*mawrg*-n	morning	פרימאָרגן, דער
frirn	*freer*-n	to freeze	פרירן
frish	freesh	fresh	פריש
frishtik, der	*freesh*-tik	breakfast	פרישטיק, דער
frosh, der	frawsh	frog	פראָש, דער
frost, der	frawst	freezing temperature	פראָסט, דער
froy, di	froy	wife woman	פרוי, די
frukht, di	frookht	fruit	פרוכט, די
frukhtayz, der	*frookht*-eiz	sherbert	פרוכטאײַז, דער
frum	froom	pious devout	פרום
fuftsik	*foof*-tsik	fifty	פופֿציק
fuftsn	*foof*-tsin	fifteen	פופֿצן
fuks, der	fooks	fox	פוקס, דער
ful	fool	full (of)	פול
fulshtendik	*fool*-shtehn-dik	entire complete	פולשטענדיק
fun	foon	of from out of	פון
funanderklaybn	foo-*nahn*-dehr- kleib-n	to analyze	פונאַנדערקלײַבן
fundestvegn	foon-*dehst*- *vehg*-n	nevertheless however	פונדעסטוועגן
fun itst on	foon *eetst* awn	henceforth	פון איצט אָן
funt, der	foont	pound	פונט, דער
fus, der	fooss	foot leg	פוס, דער
fusbol, der	*fooss*-bawl	soccer soccer ball	פוסבאָל, דער

futer, der	*foo*-tehr	fur fur coat	פוטער, דער
fyalke, di	fee-*ahl*-keh	violet (flower)	פיאלקע, די

gadles, dos	*gahd*-lis	greatness vanity	גדלות, דאָס
gavedik	*gei*-vi-dik dik	arrogant vain	גאווה׳גולן
gal, di	gahl	gall gall bladder	גאַל, די
galakh, der	*gah*-lahkh	Christian priest	גלח, דער
galaret, der	gah-lah-*reht*	jelly	גאַלאַרעט, דער
galon, der	gah-*lawn*	gallon	גאַלאָן, דער
gandz, di	gahndz	goose	גאַנדז, די
ganev, der	*gah*-nehv	thief crook	גנב, דער
gan-eydn, der	gah-*nayd*-n	the Garden of Eden paradise	גן־עדן, דער
gang, der	gahng	walk pace	גאַנג, דער
gang, der	gahng	errand	גאַנג, דער
ganik, der	*gah*-nik	porch stoop	גאַניק, דער
gants	gahnts	whole entire complete	גאַנץ
gantse, dos	*gahn*-tseh	whole total	גאַנצע, דאָס
gantsn, in	in *gahnts*-n	altogether all	גאַנצן, אין
ganvenen	*gahn*-veh-nehn	to steal	גנבענען
garantirn	gah-rahn-*teer*-n	to guarantee	גאַראַנטירן
garazh, der	gah-*rahzh*	garage	גאַראַזש, דער
garderob, der	gahr-deh-*rawb*	wardrobe cloak room	גאַרדעראָב, דער

garn, der	*gahr*-n	yarn	גאָרן, דער
garn noch	*gahr*-n nawkh	to crave	גאָרן נאָך
garniter, der	gahr-*nee*-tehr	outfit suit	גאָרניטער, דער
gartl, der	*gahrt*-l	belt	גאָרטל, דער
gas, di	gahss	street	גאַס, די
gast, der	gahst	visitor guest	גאַסט, דער
gastgeber, der	*gahst*-geh-behr	host	גאַסטגעבער, דער
gastgeberin, di	*gahst*-geh-behr-in	hostess	גאַסטגעבערין, די
gatkes, di	*gaht*-kehs	underpants drawers	גאַטקעס, די
gayst, der	geist	ghost spirit	גײַסט, דער
gaystlekher, der	*geist*-leh-khehr	Gentile clergyman minister	גײַסטלעכער, דער
gaz, der	gahz	gas fume	גאַז, דער
gazlen, der	*gahz*-lehn	robber bandit	גזלן, דער
gazolin, di	gah-zaw-*leen*	gasoline	גאַזאָלין, די
gebeks, dos	geh-*behks*	pastry	געבעקס, דאָס
gebn	*gehb*-n	to give	געבן
gebn tsu far-shteyn	*gehb*-n tsoo fahr-*shtayn*	to indicate to suggest	געבן צו פֿאַרשטיין
gebot, dos	geh-*bawt*	commandment	געבאָט, דאָס
geboyrn	geh-*boyr*-n	to give birth to	געבוירן
geboyrn	geh-*boyr*-n	born	געבוירן
geboyrener, der	geh-*boy*-reh-nehr	native	געבוירענער, דער
geboyrn vern	geh-*boyr*-n *vehr*-n	to be born	געבוירן ווערן
geboyrn-tog, der	geh-*boyr*-n-tawg	birthday	געבוירן־טאָג, דער
gebrotns, dos	geh-*brawt*-ns	roast	געבראָטנס, דאָס
geburt, di	geh-*boort*	birth	געבורט, די
gedank, der	geh-*dahnk*	idea thought	געדאַנק, דער
gedayen	geh-*dei*-en	to prosper	געדײַען
gedenken	geh-*dehn*-kehn	to remember	געדענקען

gederem, di	geh-*deh*-rehm	bowels intestines	געדערעם, די
gedikht	geh-*deekht*	thick dense	געדיכט
geduld, dos	geh-*doold*	patience temper	געדולד, דאָס
geduldik	geh-*dool*-dik	patient	געדולדיק
gefar, di	geh-*fahr*	danger peril	געפֿאַר, די
gefeln	geh-*fehl*-n	to please to appeal to	געפֿעלן
geferlekh	geh-*fehr*-lehkh	dangerous terrible	געפֿערלעך
gefil, dos	geh-*feel*	feeling sensation	געפֿיל, דאָס
gefinen	geh-*fee*-nehn	to find to locate	געפֿינען
gegnt, di	*geh*-gint	area locality region	געגנט, די
gehakte	geh-*hahk*-teh	chopped	געהאַקטע
gehenem, dos	geh-*heh*-nehm	hell inferno	גיהנום, דאָס
geherik	geh-*heh*-rik	appropriate proper	געהעריק
gehern	geh-*hehr*-n	to belong to possess	געהערן
gehilts, dos	geh-*heelts*	lumber timber	געהילץ, דאָס
gel	gehl	yellow	געל
gelegnhayt, di	geh-*lehg*-n-heit	occasion chance	געלעגנהייט, די
gelekhter, dos	geh-*lehkh*-tehr	laugh laughter	געלעכטער, דאָס
gelerenter, der	geh-*lehr*-n-tehr	scholar scientist	געלערנטער, דער
geleymt	geh-*laymt*	paralyzed numb	געליימט
gelibte, di	geh-*leeb*-teh	sweetheart (fem.) lover	געליבטע, די

gelibter, der	geh-*leeb*-tehr	sweetheart (masc.) lover	דער ,געליבטער
gelt, dos,	gehlt	money funds	דאָס ,געלט
geltshtrof, di	*gehlt*-shtrawf	fine	די ,געלטשטראָף
gemel, dos	geh-*mehl*	illustration painting	דאָס ,געמעל
genetsn	*geh*-nehts-n	to yawn	געענעצן
genug	geh-*noog*	enough sufficient	גענוג
genugik, nit	*neet* geh-*noog*-ik	insufficient	ניט ,גענוגיק
gepregelte	geh-*prehg*-elt	fried	געפּרעגלט
ger, der	gehr	convert (to Judaism)	דער ,גר
gerangl, dos	geh-*rahng*-l	struggle conflict	דאָס ,געראַנגל
gerekhtikayt, di	geh-*rehkh*-tee-keit	justice	די ,גערעכטיקייט
gerirt	geh-*reert*	touched (mentally)	גערירט
gern	*gehr*-n	gladly willingly	גערן
gertner, der	*gehrt*-nehr	gardener	דער ,גערטנער
geruder, dos	geh-*roo*-dehr	commotion disturbance	דאָס ,גערודער
gesheft, dos	geh-*shehft*	business	דאָס ,געשעפֿט
geshikhte, di	geh-*sheekh*-teh	history story	די ,געשיכטע
geshlekht, dos	geh-*shlehkht*	sex	דאָס ,געשלעכט
geshmak	geh-*shmahk*	tasty delicious	געשמאַק
geshrey, dos	geh-*shray*	shout cry	דאָס ,געשריי
geshvir, dos	geh-*shveer*	abscess boil	דאָס ,געשוויר
geshvoln	geh-*shvawl*-n	swollen	געשוואָלן
gest, der	gehst	guest	דער ,געסט
get, der	geht	divorce	דער ,גט
getlekh	*geht*-lehkh	divine	געטלעך

getrank, dos	geh-*trahnk*	beverage drink	געטראַנק, דאָס
getray	geh-*trei*	devoted faithful	געטרײַ
getroyen	geh-*troy*-en	to trust to confide in	געטרויען
gech, der	gehts	idol	געץ, דער
geule, di	geh-*oo*-leh	salvation deliverance	גאולה, די
gevet, dos	geh-*veht*	bet wager	געוועט, דאָס
geveyntlekh	geh-*voynt*-lehkh	usual common	געוויינטלעך
geviks, dos	geh-*veeks*	plant	געוויקס, דאָס
gevinen	geh-*vee*-nehn	to gain to win	געווינען
gevirts, dos	geh-*veerts*	spice	געווירץ, דאָס
gevis	geh-*veess*	certain sure	געוויס
gevisn, dos	geh-*vees*-n	conscience	געוויסן, דאָס
gevoynhayt, di	geh-*voyn*-heit	habit	געווווינהייט, די
		heroism	
geyn	gayn	to walk to go to depart	גיין
geyn leydik	gayn *lay*-dik	to loaf	גיין ליידיק
gezets, dos	geh-*zehts*	law statute	געזעץ, דאָס
gezunt	geh-*zoont*	healthy sound	געזונט
gezunt vern	geh-*zoont vehr*-n	to recover (get well)	געזונט ווערן
gezunt, zay (t)	*zei* (t) geh-*zoont*	good-bye be healthy	געזונט, זײַט
gikh	geekh	fast quick	גיך
gikhkayt, di	*geekh*-keit	speed	גיכקייט, די
gintsik	*geen*-tsik	favorable opportune	גינציק

girik	*gee*-rik	greedy avid	גיריק
(on) gisn	(*awn*) *gees*-n	to pour	(אָן) גיסן
gitare, di	gee-*tah*-reh	guitar	גיטאַרע, די
glat(ik)	*glaht*(ik)	smooth even	גלאַט(יק)
glaykh	gleikh	straight level equal	גליַיך
glaykhgiltik	*gleikh*-gil-tik	casual indifferent	גליַיכגילטיק
glentsndik	*glehn*-tsin-dik	splendid magnificent	גלענצנדיק
gletling, der	*gleht*-leeng	pet	גלעטלינג, דער
gletn	*gleht*-n	to caress to stroke	גלעטן
gleybn	*glayb*-n	to believe	גלייבן
glik, dos	gleek	good fortune happiness	גליק, דאָס
glik, tsum	tsoom *gleek*	fortunately luckily	גליק, צום
gliklekh	*gleek*-lehkh	happy	גליקלעך
glitshik	*glee*-chik	slippery slick	גליטשיק
glok, der	glawk	bell	גלאָק, דער
glotsn	*glawts*-n	to stare	גלאָצן
gloybn, der	*gloyb*-n	belief	גלויבן, דער
gloz, di	glawz	glass	גלאָז, די
gneyvish	gah-*nay*-veesh	thievish sneaky	גנביש
goen, der	*gaw*-oyn	genius	גאָון, דער
gold, dos	gawld	gold	**גאָלד, דאָס**
goles, dos	*gaw*-lehs	exile diaspora	גלות, דאָס
golf, der	gawlf	golf	גאָלף, דער
golfshtekn, der	*gawlf*-shtehk-n	golf club	גאָלפֿשטעקן, דער
golmesser, der	*gawl*-meh-sehr	razor	גאָלמעסער, דער
golmesserl, dos	*gawl*-meh-sehr-l	razor blade	גאָלמעסערל, דאָס
gombe, di	*gawm*-beh	chin	גאָמבע, די
gopl, der	*gawp*-l	fork (eating utensil)	גאָפּל, דער
gopl-lefl, di	*gawp*-l-*lehf*-l	silverware	גאָפּל-לעפֿל, די

gorgl, der	*gawrg*-l	throat larynx	גאָרגל, דער
gorn, der	*gawr*-n	floor upper story	גאָרן, דער
gornit, gornisht	*gawr*-nit	nothing (not) at all	גאָרניט
gortn, der	*gawrt*-n	garden	גאָרטן, דער
got, der	gawt	God	גאָט, דער
got tsu danken	*gawt* tsoo *dahnk*- en	thank God	גאָט צו דאַנקען
got zol ophitn	*gawt* zawl *awp*- heet-n	God forbid	גאָט זאָל אָפּהיטן
gotenu	*gawt*-eh-nyoo	dear God	גאָטעניו
goy, der	goy	Gentile (masc.)	גוי, דער
goye, di	*goy*-eh	Gentile (fem.)	גויע, די
goylem, der	*goy*-lehm	dolt blockhead	גולם, דער
goyresh, der	*goy*-rehsh	divorced man	גרוש, דער
goyrl, der	*goy*-rl	fate destiny	גורל, דער
gragern	*grah*-gehr-n	to rattle	גראַגערן
gram, der	grahm	rhyme	גראַם, דער
gratsyez	*grahtz*-yehz	graceful	גראַציעז
gratulirn	grah-too-*leer*-n	to congratulate	גראַטולירן
grayz, der	greiz	error mistake	גרײַז, דער
grayzl, dos	*greiz*-l	curl	גרײַזל, דאָס
grenets, der	*greh*-nehts	boundary border	גרענעץ, דער
grepts, der	grehpts	belch	גרעפּץ, דער
greykhn	*graykh*-n	to reach to extend	גרייכן
greypfrut, der	*grayp*-froot	grapefruit	גרייפּפֿרוט, דער
greys, di	grays	extent size	גרייס, די
greyt	grayt	ready willing	גרייט
grin	green	green	גרין
gring	greeng	easy light	גרינג
grins, dos	greens	vegetable	גרינס, דאָס

grivines, di	*gree*-vee-nehs	rendered chicken skin	גריװענעס, די
grizhen	*gree*-zhehn	to nibble to gnaw	גריזשען
grizhen	*gree*-zhehn	to nag	גריזשען
grob	grawb	thick fat	גרָאב
grob	grawb	crude rude	גרָאב
grober finger, der	*graw*-behr *feen*-gehr	thumb	גרָאבער פֿינגער, דער
grober-yung, der	*graw*-behr- yoong	boor ignoramus	גרָאבער־יונג, דער
grobn	*grawb*-n	to dig	גרָאבן
groy	groy	gray	גרוי
groylik	*groy*-lik	appalling horrible	גרויליק
groys	groyss	great big large	גרויס
groyskayt, di	*groyss*-keit	greatness	גרויסקייט, די
groz, dos	grawz	grass	גרָאז, דָאס
grub, di	groob	pit	גרוב, די
grunteygns, dos	*groont*-ayg-nss	real estate	גרונטאייגנס, דָאס
gruntik	*groon*-tik	thorough	גרונטיק
grus, der	groos	greeting	גרוס, דער
grushe, di	*groo*-sheh	divorced woman	גרושה, די
guf, der	goof	body (anat.)	גוף, דער
gume, di	*goo*-meh	rubber elastic	גומע, די
gut	goot	good	גוט
gut durkhgekokht	*goot doorkh*-geh- kawkht	cooked well done	גוט דורכגעקָאכט
guthartsikayt, di	goot-*hahr*-tsi-keit	benevolence kindness	גוטהַארציקייט, די
gut-morgn	goot-*mawrg*-n	good morning	גוט־מָארגן
gutn-ovnt	*goot*-n-*awv*-nt	good evening	גוטן־אָװנט
gutskayt, di	*goots*-keit	goodness	גוטסקייט, די
guzme, di	*gooz*-meh	exaggeration	גוזמא, די
gvald!	g-*vahld*	Help!	גװאַלד!

gvald, di	g-*vahld*	violence force	גוואַלד, די
gvaldeven	g-*vahld*-eh-vehn	to scream to rave	גוואַלדעוועּן
gvaldik	g-*vahl*-dik	immense mighty	גוואַלדיק
gvir, der	g-*veer*	rich man	גבֿיר, דער
gvul, der	g-*vool*	bounds limit	גבֿול, דער
gvure, di	*gvoo*-reh	prowress heroism	גבֿורה, די

hagam	hah-*gahm*	although	הגם
hak, di	hahk	axe hatchet	האַק, די
hakfleysh, dos	*hahk*-flaysh	chopmeat	האַקפֿלייש, דאָס
hakhnose, di	hahkh-*naw*-seh	income revenue	הכנסה, די
hakhnose-shtayer, der	hahkh-*naw*-seh-*shtei*-ehr	income tax	הכנסה־שטײַער, דער
hakmeser, der	*hahk*-meh-sehr	cleaver chopper	האַקמעסער, דער
halb	hahlb	half	האַלב
halb durkhgekokht	*hahlb doorkh*-geh-kawkht	cooked medium	האַלב דורכגעקאָכט
halboshe, di	hahl-*baw*-sheh	clothing attire	הלבשה, די
haldz, der	hahldz	neck throat	האַלדז, דער
haldzband, di	*hahldz*-bahnd	necklace	האַלדזבאַנד, די
haldzn	*hahldz*-n	to hug to embrace	האַלדזן
haldzveytik, der	*hahldz*-vay-tik	sore throat	האַלדזווייטיק, דער
halevay	hah-leh-*vei*	hopefully	הלוואַי
haltn	*hahlt*-n	to hold to keep	האַלטן

haltn fun	*hahlt*-n foon	to approve to believe in	האַלטן פֿון
haltn fun zikh	*hahlt*-n foon zikh	conceited	האַלטן פֿון זיך
halvoe, di	hahl-*vaw*-eh	loan	הלוואה, די
hamer, der	*hah*-mehr	hammer	האַמער, דער
hamoyn, der	hah-*moyn*	mob rabble	המון, דער
handlen	*hahnd*-lehn	to act to deal to trade	האַנדלען
hanoe, di	hah-*naw*-ih	fun, benefit	הנאה, די
hanoe hobn fun	hah-*naw*-ih *hawb*-n foon	to enjoy	הנאה האָבן פֿון
hanokhe, di	hah-*naw*-khih	discount	הנחה, די
hant, di	hahnt	hand arm	האַנט, די
hantekh, dos	*hahn*-tehkh	hand towel towel	האַנטעך, דאָס
hantgelenk, dos	*hahnt*-geh-lehnk	wrist	האַנטגעלענק, דאָס
harb	hahrb	difficult harsh	האַרב
harbst, der	hahrbst	fall autumn	האַרבסט, דער
hargenen	*hahr*-geh-nehn	to kill	הרגענען
hart	hahrt	tough hard	האַרט
harts, dos	hahrts	heart	האַרץ, דאָס
hartsik	*hahr*-tsik	cordial hearty	האַרציק
harts-brenenish, dos	*hahrts*-breh-neh- neesh	heartburn	האַרץ־ברענעניש, דאָס
hartsveytik, der	*hahrts*-vay-tik	heartache	האַרצווייטיק, דער
has, der	hahss	hate hatred	האַס, דער
hashpoe, di	hah-*shpaw*-eh	influence	השפעה, די
haskalah, di	hahs-*kah*-lah	the Jewish enlighten- ment movement	השׂכּלה, די
haskome, di	hahss-*kaw*-meh	approval	הסכּמה, די
hastik	*hahs*-tik	impetuous	האַסטיק
hatslokhe, di	hahts-*law*-kheh	success	הצלחה, די
havtokhe, di	hahv-*taw*-kheh	pledge	הבטחה, די

haynt	heint	today	הײַנט
haynt bay nakht	*heint* bei nahkht	tonight	הײַנט בײַ נאַכט
haynttsaytik	*heint*-tsei-tik	contemporary modern	הײַנטצײַטיק
hayzl, dos	*heiz*-l	brothel	הײַזל, דאָס
hebreish, dos	heh-*breh*-ish	Hebrew	העברעיִש, דאָס
heflekh	*hehf*-lehkh	courteous polite	העפֿלעך
heflekhkayt, di	*hehf*-lehkh-keit	courtesy	העפֿלעכקייט, די
heft, di	hehft	notebook	העפֿט, די
hekdish, dos	*hehk*-deesh	poorhouse decrepit place (sl.)	הקדש, דאָס
hekher	heh-khehr	higher taller above	העכער
hekherung, di	*heh*-kheh-roong	promotion rise	העכערונג, די
hekhst	hehkhst	supreme top	העכסט
hel	hehl	fair blond	העל
held, der	hehld	hero	העלד, דער
heldin, di	*hehl*-din	heroine	העלדין, די
heldish	*hehl*-dish	brave heroic	העלדיש
helfand, der	*hehl*-fahnd	elephant	העלפֿאַנד, דער
helfn	*hehlf*-n	to aid to help	העלפֿן
helft, di	hehlft	half	העלפֿט, די
hemd, dos	hehmd	shirt	העמד, דאָס
hendler, der	*hehnd*-lehr	dealer merchant	הענדלער, דער
hengen	*hehn*-gehn	to hang	הענגען
hentl, dos	*hehnt*-l	handle	הענטל, דאָס
hentshke, di	*hehnch*-keh	glove	הענטשקע, די
her	hehr	gentleman Mister	הער
hern	*hehr*-n	to hear to obey	הערן
hering, der	*heh*-reeng	herring	הערינג, דער

heskem, der	*hehs*-kim	accord agreement	הסכּם, דער
hesped, der	*hehs*-pid	funeral oration eulogy	הספּד, דער
hey, dos	hay	hay	היי, דאָס
heybn	*hayb*-n	to lift to heave	הייבן
heykh, di	haykh	height altitude	הייך, די
heylik	*hay*-lik	sacred holy	הייליק
heyln	*hayl*-n	to heal	היילן
heym, di	haym	home	היים, די
heymish	*hay*-mish	homey cozy	היימיש
heypekh, der	*hay*-pehkh	opposite reverse	היפּוך, דער
heys	hays	hot	הייס
heytsn	*hayts*-n	to heat	הייצן
heyvn, di	*hayv*-n	yeast	הייוון, די
heyzerik	*hay*-zeh-rik	hoarse	הייזעריק
hilf, di	heelf	assistance aid help	הילף, די
himl, der	*heem*-l	sky heaven	הימל, דער
hinken	heen-kehn	to limp to hobble	הינקען
hinter	heen-tehr	behind (prep.) in back of	הינטער
hintn, der	*heent*-n	buttocks	הינטן, דער
hipotek, di	hee-paw-*tehk*	mortgage	היפּאָטעק, די
hipsh	heepsh	considerable substantial	היפּש
hirsh, der	heersh	deer stag	הירש, דער
hitl, dos	*heet*-l	hat cap	היטל, דאָס
hitn	*heet*-n	to guard to watch	היטן

hitn zikh far	*heet*-n zikh fahr	to beware of	היטן זיך פֿאַר
hits, di	heets	heat fever	היץ, די
hitsik	*hee*-tsik	feverish excitable	היציק
hit zikh	*heet* zikh	Watch out!	היט זיך
hobn	*hawb*-n	to have	האָבן
hobn in zinen	*hawb*-n in *zee*-nehn	to have in mind	האָבן אין זינען
hodeven	*haw*-deh-vehn	to grow to cultivate	האָדעווען
hofenung, di	*haw*-feh-noong	hope	האָפֿענונג, די
hofenung, ful mit	*fool* mit *haw*-feh-noong	hopeful	האָפֿענונג, פֿול מיט
hofenung, on	*awn haw*-feh-noong	hopeless	האָפֿענונג, אָן
hofn	*hawf*-n	to hope	האָפֿן
hogl, der	*hawg*-l	hail	האָגל, דער
holebtses, di	*haw*-lehb-tsehs	stuffed cabbage	האָלעבצעס, די
holts, dos	hawlts	wood	האָלץ, דאָס
homar, der	haw-*mahr*	lobster	האָמאַר, דער
hon, der	hawn	cock rooster	האָן, דער
honik, der	*haw*-nik	honey	האָניק, דער
hopken	*hawp*-kehn	to hop	האָפּקען
hor, di	hawr	hair	האָר, די
horb, der	hawrb	hump	האָרב, דער
hotel, der	haw-*tehl*	hotel	האָטעל, דער
hoyker, der	*hoy*-kehr	hump hunchback	הױקער, דער
hoykh	hoykh	high tall	הױך
hoykh	hoykh	loud	הױך
hoypt	hoypt	chief major	הױפּט
hoyt, di	hoyt	skin	הױט, די
hoytkrem, der	*hoyt*-krehm	cold cream	הױטקרעם, דער
hoyz, dos	hoyz	house	הױז, דאָס
hoyzn, di	*hoyz*-n	trousers pants	הױזן, די
humor, der	hoo-*mawr*	humor	הומאָר, דער

hun, di	hoon	hen chicken	הון, די
hundert	*hoon*-dert	hundred	הונדערט
hunger, der	*hoon*-gehr	hunger	הונגער, דער
hungerik	*hoon*-geh-rik	hungry	הונגעריק
hunt, der	hoont	dog	הונט, דער
hust, der	hoost	cough	הוסט, דער
hut, der	hoot	hat	הוט, דער

iber	*ee*-behr	above (prep.) over	איבער
iberbaysn, dos	*ee*-behr-beis-n	breakfast refreshments	איבערבײַסן, דאָס
iberbaytn	*ee*-behr-beit-n	to change to alter	איבערבײַטן
iberbetn zikh	*ee*-behr-beht-n zikh	to be reconciled	איבערבעטן זיך
iberik	*ee*-beh-rik	superfluous needless	איבעריק
iberkern	*ee*-behr-kehr-n	to overturn to upset	איבערקערן
iberkhazern	*ee*-behr-khah- zehr-n	to repeat to reiterate	איבערחזרן
iberkukn	*ee*-behr-kook-n	to examine to review	איבערקוקן
iberlozn	*ee*-behr-lawz-n	to leave behind	איבערלאָזן
ibermakhn	*ee*-behr-mahkh-n	to change to transform	איבערמאַכן
iberraysn	*ee*-behr-reis-n	to interrupt	איבעררײַסן
iberredn	*ee*-behr-rehd-n	to persuade	איבעררעדן
ibershrekn	*ee*-behr-shrehk-n	to scare to frighten	איבערשרעקן
ibertrakhtn	*ee*-behr-trahkht-n	to think over to be apprehensive	איבערטראַכטן
ibertsaygung, di	*ee*-behr-tsei-goong	conviction belief	איבערצײַגונג, די

ibervog	*ee*-behr-vawg	overweight	איבערוואָג
iberyogn	*ee*-behr-yawg-n	to pass to overtake	איבעריאָגן
iberzetsn	*ee*-behr-zehts-n	to translate	איבערזעצן
iberzetsung, di	*ee*-behr-zeh-tsoong	translation	איבערזעצונג, די
idee, di	ee-*day*-eh	idea	אידעע, די
identifitsirn	ee-dehn-tee-fee-*tseer*-n	to identify	אידענטיפֿיצירן
idiot, der	ee-dee-*awt*	idiot	אידיאָט, דער
iker, der	ee-kehr	chiefly mainly	עיקר, דער
ikerdik	ee-kehr-dik	basic essential	עיקרדיק
ikh	eekh	I	איך
ilustratsye, di	ee-loo-*strahts*-yeh	illustration	אילוסטראַציע, די
im	eem	him it	אים
imigrant, der	eem-ee-*grahnt*	immigrant	אימיגראַנט, דער
im-yirtse-hashem	eem-*yeer*-tseh-hah-*shehm*	God willing	אם־ירצה־השם
in	in	in (prep.) at to inside within	אין
in droysn	in *droyss*-n	outdoors outside	אין דרויסן
in ergets nit	een *ehr*-gehts nit	nowhere	אין ערגעץ ניט
in oysland	in *oyss*-lahnd	abroad	אין אויסלאַנד
indik, der	*een*-dik	turkey	אינדיק, דער
indzl, der	*eendz*-l	island	אינדזל, דער
ineveynik	*een*-eh-vay-nik	indoors inside	אינעווייניק
infektsye, di	een-*fehk*-tsyeh	infection	אינפֿעקציע, די
inflatsye, di	in-*flahts*-yeh	inflation	אינפֿלאַציע, די
informatsye, di	in-fawr-*mahts*-yeh	information	אינפֿאָרמאַציע, די
influentsye, di	in-floo-*ehn*-tsyeh	influenza	אינפֿלוענציע, די
ingber, der	*eeng*-behr	ginger	אינגבער, דער
inhalt, der	*een*-hahlt	contents subject	אינהאַלט, דער

inlendish	*een*-lehn-dish	domestic interior	אינלענדיש
insekt, der	in-*sehkt*	insect	אינסעקט, דער
inspiratsye, di	in-spee-*rahts*-yeh	inspiration	אינספּיראַציע, די
inteligent	in-teh-lee-*gehnt*	intelligent	אינטעליגענט
inteligents, di	in-teh-lee-*gehnts*	intelligence	אינטעליגענץ, די
interesant	in-teh-reh-*sahnt*	interesting	אינטערעסאַנט
investirn	in-vehs-*teer*-n	to invest	אינוועסטירן
inyen, der	*een*-yihn	affair matter	עניָן, דער
inzhenir, der	een-zheh-*neer*	engineer	אינזשעניר, דער
ir	eer	her you (sing. formal and pl.)	איר
itst	eetst	now at present	איצט
itst on, fun	foon *eetst* awn	henceforth	איצט אָן, פֿון
itstik	*eets*-tik	present (adj.)	איצטיק
itstikayt, di	*eets*-tee-keit	(the) present	איצטיקייט, די
iz	eez	is	איז

kaas, der	kahss	anger	כּעס, דער
kabinet, der	kah-bee-*neht*	cabinet (of ministers)	קאַבינעט, דער
kabinet, der	kah-bee-*neht*	study office	קאַבינעט, דער
kaboles-ponem, dos	kah-*baw*-lehs- *paw*-nim	welcome	קבלת־פּנים, דאָס
kabole, di	kah-*baw*-leh	receipt (bus.)	קבלה, די
kabtsn, der	*kahb*-tsehn	pauper poor man	קבצן, דער
kadish, der	*kah*-dish	mourner's doxology	קדיש, דער
kakao, der	kah-*kah*-aw	cocoa	קאַקאַאָ, דער
kaker, der	*kah*-kehr	shit-head	קאַקער, דער
kakn	*kahk*-n	to defecate	קאַקן

kalb, dos	kahlb	calf	קאַלב, דאָס
kalbfleysh, dos	*kahlb*-flaysh	veal	קאַלבפלייש, דאָס
kale, di	*kah*-leh	bride (to be) fiancée	כּלה, די
kalendar, der	kah-lehn-*dahr*	calendar	קאַלענדאַר, דער
kalifyor, der	kah-leef-*yawr*	cauliflower	קאַליפיאָר, דער
kalike, der/di	*kah*-lee-keh	cripple an incompetent (sl.)	קאַליקע, דער/די
kalorye, di	kah-*lawr*-yeh	calorie	קאַלאָריע, די
kaloshn, di	kah-*lawsh*-n	galoshes rubbers	קאַלאָשן, די
kalt	kahlt	cold	קאַלט
kaluzhe, di	kah-*loo*-zheh	pool puddle	קאַלוזשע, די
kalye	*kahl*-yeh	out of order spoiled	קאַליע
kalye makhn	*kahl*-yeh *mahkh*-n	to spoil	קאַליע מאַכן
kam, der	kahm	comb	קאַם, דער
kamin, der	kah-*meen*	fireplace	קאַמין, דער
kamtsn, der	*kahmts*-n	miser	קמצן, דער
kamtsonish	kahm-*tsaw*-neesh	niggardly	קמצניש
kanape, di	kah-*nah*-peh	couch sofa	קאַנאַפּע, די
kanarik, der	kah-*nah*-rik	canary	קאַנאַריק, דער
kandidat, der	kahn-dee-*daht*	candidate	קאַנדידאַט, דער
kane, di	*kah*-neh	enema	קאַנע, די
kapelye di	kah-*pehl*-yeh	band gang	קאַפּעליע, די
kapriz, der	kah-*preez*	caprice whim	קאַפּריז, דער
kaprizik	kah-*pree*-zik	capricious	קאַפּריזיק
karg	kahrg	stingy	קאַרג
karg	kahrg	short almost	קאַרג
kark, der	kahrk	neck	קאַרק, דער
karlik, der	*kahr*-lik	dwarf midget	קאַרליק, דער
karsh, di	kahrsh	cherry	קאַרש, די
karte, di	*kahr*-teh	map	קאַרטע, די

kartl, dos	*kahrt*-l	card	קאַרטל, דאָס
kartofl, der	kahr-*tawf*-l	potato	קאַרטאָפֿל, דער
kase, di	*kah*-seh	ticket office	קאַסע, די
kase, di	*kah*-seh	cashbox strongbox	קאַסע, די
kashe, di	*kah*-sheh	cereal porridge	קאַשע, די
kashres, dos	*kahsh*-rehs	Jewish dietary laws	כּשרות, דאָס
kasirer, der	kah-*see*-rehr	cashier	קאַסירער, דער
kastn, der	*kahsst*-n	box chest	קאַסטן, דער
katastrofe, di	kah-tah-*straw*-feh	catastrophe	קאַטאַסטראָפֿע, די
katoves, der	kah-*taw*-vehs	jest	קאַטאָוועס, דער
kats, di	kahts	cat	קאַץ, די
katsev, der	*kah*-tsehv	butcher	קצבֿ, דער
katshke, di	*kahch*-keh	duck	קאַטשקע, די
kave, di	*kah*-veh	coffee	קאַווע, די
kavene, di	*kah*-veh-neh	watermelon	קאַוונע, די
kavenik, der	*kah*-veh-nik	coffee pot	קאַוועניק, דער
kayen	*kei*-en	to chew	קײַען
kayer, der	*kei*-ehr	jaw	קײַער, דער
kaygume, di	*kei*-goo-meh	chewing gum	קײַגומע, די
kaykhn	*keikh*-n	to gasp	קײַכן
kayklen	*keik*-lehn	to roll	קײַקלען
kaylekhik	*kei*-leh-khik	round circular	קײַלעכיק
kayn (see keyn)	kein		קײַן
kayor, der	kah-*yawr*	dawn	קאַיאָר, דער
kayute, di	kah-*yoo*-teh	stateroom cabin	קאַיוטע, די
kedey	kih-*day*	so that in order to	כּדי
kedey nit	kih-*day* nit	lest	כּדי ניט
kegener, der	*keh*-geh-nehr	adversary opponent	קעגענער, דער
kegn	*kehg*-n	against versus	קעגן
keler, der	*keh*-lehr	cellar basement	קעלער, דער
kelner, der	*kehl*-nehr	waiter	קעלנער, דער
kelnerin, di	*kehl*-nehr-in	waitress	קעלנערין, די

kelt, di	kehlt	cold chill	קעלט, די
kenen	*keh*-nehn	to be able to to know how to	קענען
kentik	*kehn*-tik	apparent evident	קענטיק
ker, der	kehr	turn	קער, דער
kereven	*keh*-reh-vehn	to steer	קערעווען
kerper, der	*kehr*-pehr	body (anat.)	קערפּער, דער
keseyderdik	keh-*say*-dehr-dik	constant continuous	כּסדרדיק
keshene, di	*keh*-sheh-neh	pocket	קעשענע, די
kesl, der	*kehs*-l	kettle boiler	קעסל, דער
kestl, dos	*kehst*-l	box	קעסטל, דאָס
ketsl, dos	*kehts*-l	kitten	קעצל, דאָס
keylim, di	*kay*-lim	dishes	כּלים, די
keyn	kayn	to (bound for)	קיין
keyn . . . nit	*kayn* . . . neet	no (not any)	קיין . . . ניט
keyn eyn-ore	*kayn* eyne *haw*-reh	no evil eye	קיין עין־הרע
keyn mol nit	*kayn* mawl nit	never	קיין מאָל ניט
keyn zakh nit	*kayn* zahkh neet	nothing not anything	קיין זאַך ניט
keyner nit	*kay*-nehr neet	not anyone nobody	קיינער ניט
keyser, der	*kay*-sehr	emperor	קייסער, דער
keyserine, di	*kay*-seh-ri-neh	empress	קייסערינע, די
keyt, di	kayt	chain shackle	קייט, די
keyver, der	*kay*-vehr	tomb grave	קבֿר, דער
kez, der	kehz	cheese	קעז, דער
khabar, der	khah-*bahr*	bribe	כּאַבאַר, דער
khakhome, di	khah-*khaw*-mih	wise woman	חכמה, די
khalat, der	khah-*laht*	robe smock housecoat	כאַלאַט, דער
khale, di	*khah*-lih	Sabbath bread	חלה, די
khaleshn	*khah*-leh-shn	to faint	חלשן
khaloshesdik	khah-*law*-shehs- dik	nauseating disgusting	חלשותדיק

kham, der	khahm	boor cad	כאַם, דער
khaneles eygele, dos	*khah*-neh-lehs *ay*- geh-leh	pansy	חנהלעס אייגעלע, דאס
khanfenen	*khahn*-feh-nehn	to flatter to cajole	חנפֿענען
khapn	*khahp*-n	to grab to catch	כאַפּן
kharakter, der	khah-*rahk*-tehr	character	כאַראַקטער, דער
kharote, di	khah-*raw*-tih	regret remorse	חרטה, די
kharote hobn	khah-*raw*-tih *hawb*-n	to repent	חרטה האָבן
kharpe, di	*khahr*-peh	disgrace shame	חרפה, די
khasene, di	*khah*-seh-nih	wedding	חתונה, די
khasene gehat	*khah*-seh-nih geh- *haht*	married	חתונה געהאַט
khasene gehat, nit	*neet*-khah-seh-nih geh-*haht*	unmarried	חתונה געהאַט, ניט
khaver, der	*khah*-vir	pal friend	חבֿר, דער
khaye, di	*khah*-yeh	animal beast	חיה, די
khazer, der	*khah*-zehr	hog pig	חזיר, דער
khazer-fleysh, dos	*khah*-zehr-flaysh	pork	חזיר־פֿלייש, דאָס
khazer-kotlet, der	*khah*-zehr-kawt- *leht*	pork chop	חזיר־קאָטלעט, דער
khazeray, dos	khah-zehr-*ei*	junk food (coll.) junk mess	חזירײַ, דאָס
khazn, der	*khahz*-n	cantor	חזן, דער
khemye, di	*khehm*-yeh	chemistry	כעמיע, די
khet, der	kheht	sin offense	חטא, דער
khevre-man, der	*khehv*-reh-mahn	finagler guy	חבֿרה־מאַן, דער
kheyder, der	*khay*-dehr	room religious school (traditional Jewish)	חדר, דער

kheyfets, der	*khay*-fehts	article object	חפֿץ, דער
kheylek, der	*khay*-lehk	portion share	חלק, דער
kheyn, der	khayn	charm grace	חן, דער
kheyrem, der	*khay*-rehm	excommunication	חרם, דער
kheyshek, der	*khey*-shehk	eagerness urge	חשק, דער
khezhbn, der	*khehzh*-bn	account bill calculation	חשבון, דער
khezhbn-firer, der	*khehzh*-bn-*fee*-rehr	accountant	חשבון־פֿירער, דער
khidesh, der	*khee*-dehsh	surprise astonishment	חידוש, דער
khirurg, der	khee-*roorg*	surgeon	כירורג, דער
khisorn, der	khee-*sawr*-n	fault defect	חסרון, דער
khitre	*kheet*-reh	cunning sly	כיטרע
khlipen	*khlee*-pehn	to sob	כליפּען
khmal, der	kh-*mahl*	wack	כמאַל, דער
khmalye, der	kh-*mahl*-yeh	wallop	כמאַליע, דער
khmarne	kh-*mahr*-neh	cloudy dreary	כמאַרנע
khokhem, der	*khaw*-khim	smart person wise man	חכם, דער
khokhme, di	*khawkh*-mih	wisdom	חכמה, די
kholem, der	*khaw*-lim	dream	חלום, דער
kholemen	*khaw*-lih-mehn	to dream	חלומען
kholere, di	khaw-*leh*-reh	cholera	כאָלערע, די
kholile	khaw-*lee*-lih	God forbid!	חלילה
khomets, der	*khaw*-mehts	leavened food (not kosher for Passover)	חמץ, דער
khorev makhn	*khaw*-rehv *mahkh*-n	to ruin	חרובֿ מאַכן
khosn, der	*khaws*-n	bridegroom fiancé	חתן, דער
khotsh	khawch	though although	כאָטש
khoydesh, der	*khoy*-dehsh	month	חודש, דער

khoyle, der	*khoy*-leh	sick person patient	חולה, דער
khoyv, der	khoyv	debt duty	חוב, דער
khoyzek, der	*khoy*-zehk	mockery ridicule	חוזק, דער
khoyzek, makhn fun	*mahkh*-n *khoy*- zehk foon	to mock to ridicule	חוזק, מאַכן פֿון
khraken	*khrah*-kehn	to clear one's throat	כראַקען
khreyn, der	khrayn	horseradish	כריין, דער
khropen	*khraw*-pehn	to snore	כראָפּען
khshad, der	kh-*shahd*	suspicion	חשד, דער
khupe, di	*khoo*-peh	wedding canopy	חופּה, די
khurbn, der	*khoor*-bn	destruction ruin	חורבן, דער
khuts	khoots	except (prep.) besides apart from	חוץ
khuts dem	*khoots* dehm	besides (adv.)	חוץ דעם
khutspe, di	*khoots*-peh	brazenness	חוצפּה, די
khvalye, di	kh-*vahl*-yeh	wave	כוואַליע, די
kibed, der	*kee*-behd	refreshment	כּיבוד, דער
kikh, di	keekh	kitchen	קיך, די
kikhl, dos	*keekh*-l	cookie	קיכל, דאָס
kil	keel	cool chilly	קיל
kile, di	*kee*-leh	hernia	קילע, די
kiln	*keel*-n	to cool	קילן
kimat	kee-*maht*	almost nearly	כּמעט
kiml, der	*keem*-l	caraway (seed)	קימל, דער
kin, der	kin	chin jaw	קין, דער
kind, dos	keend	child kid	קינד, דאָס
kinder-gortn, der	*keen*-dehr- *gawrt*-n	kindergarten	קינדער־גאָרטן, דער
kinder-tsimer, der	*keen*-dehr-*tsee*- mehr	nursery	קינדער־צימער, דער

kindhayt, di	*keend*-heit	childhood	קינדהייט, די
kindskinder, di	*keends*-keen-dehr	descendants	קינדסקינדער, די
kine, di	*kee*-neh	envy	קנאה, די
		jealousy	
kinig, der	*kee*-nig	king	קיניג, דער
kinigin, di	*keh*-nig-in	queen	קיניגין, די
kinigl, dos	*kee*-neeg-l	rabbit	קיניגל, דאָס
kino, der	*kee*-naw	movie theatre	קינאָ, דער
		the movies	
kinstlekh	*keenst*-lehkh	artificial	קינצלעך
		man-made	
kinstler, der	*keenst*-lehr	artist	קינסטלער, דער
kiosk, der	kee-*awsk*	newsstand	קיאָסק, דער
kishef, der	*kee*-shehf	enchantment	כישוף, דער
		magic	
kishef-makher, der	kee-shehf-*mah*-khehr	magician	כישוף־מאַכער, דער
kishke, di	*keesh*-keh	stuffed derma	קישקע, די
		intestine	
kishn, der	*keesh*-n	pillow	קישן, דער
		cushion	
kitser, der	*keet*-sehr	summary	קיצור, דער
		digest	
kitslen	*keets*-lehn	to tickle	קיצלען
klal, a	ah *klahl*	in short	כלל, אַ
		in sum	
klal, der	klahl	the public	כלל, דער
		community at large	
klang, der	klahng	sound	קלאַנג, דער
		rumor	
klap, der	klahp	blow	קלאַפֿ, דער
		hit	
klapn	*klahp*-n	to knock on	קלאַפֿן
		to rap	
klarnet, der	klahr-*neht*	clarinet	קלאַרנעט, דער
klas, der	klahss	class	קלאַס, דער
		grade	
klastsimer, der	*klahss*-tsee-mehr	classroom	קלאַסצימער, דער
klaybn	*kleib*-n	to gather	קלײַבן
		to collect	

klekn	*klehk*-n	to be enough	קלעקן
		to suffice	
klern	*klehr*-n	to think	קלערן
		to contemplate	
kley, der	klay	glue	קליי, דער
kleyd, dos	klayd	dress	קלייד, דאָס
		gown	
kleyn	klayn	little	קליין
		small	
kleynikayt, di	*klay*-nee-keit	trifle	קלייניקייט, די
kleyntshik	*klayn*-chik	tiny	קליינטשיק
klezmer, der	*klehz*-mehr	musician	קלעזמער, דער
klimat, der	*klee*-maht	climate	קלימאַט, דער
klingen	*kleeng*-en	to ring	קלינגען
klipe, di	*klee*-pih	nag (sl.)	קליפּה, די
		shrew	
klole, di	*klaw*-lih	curse	קללה, די
		oath	
klor	klawr	clear	קלאָר
		apparent	
klore diburim, di	*klaw*-reh dee-*boo*-reem	plain talk	קלאָרע דיבורים, די
klor vi der tog	*klawr* vee dehr *tawg*	obvious	קלאָר ווי דער טאָג
		clear as day	
klots, der	klawts	log	קלאָץ, דער
		wooden beam	
		ungraceful, awkward person (sl.)	
kloyster, der	*kloyss*-tehr	church	קלויסטער, דער
klozet, der	klaw-*zeht*	toilet	קלאָזעט, דער
klub, der	kloob	club	קלוב, דער
		society	
klug	kloog	wise	קלוג
		clever	
knaker, der	k-*nah*-kehr	big shot (sl.)	קנאַקער, דער
knakn	k-*nahk*-n	to crack	קנאַקן
		to snap	
knaknisl, dos	k-*nahk*-nees-l	nutcracker	קנאַקניסל, דאָס
knaypn	k-*neip*-n	to pinch	קניַיפּן
		to nip	

knekhl, dos	k-*nehkh*-l	ankle	קנעכל, דאָס
knekhl, dos	k-*nehkh*-l	nuckle	קנעכל, דאָס
knepl, dos	k-*nehp*-l	button	קנעפּל, דאָס
kneydl, dos	k-*nayd*-l	matzoh ball dumpling	קניידל, דאָס
kneytsh, der	k-*naych*	wrinkle fold crease	קנייטש, דער
kni, der	k-*nee*	knee	קני, דער
knien	k-*nee*-en	to kneel	קניִען
knobl, der	k-*nawb*-l	garlic	קנאָבל, דער
knup, der	k-*noop*	knot	קנופּ, דער
kokhlefl, der	*kawkh*-leh-fehl	busybody (sl.) cooking spoon	קאָכלעפֿל, דער
kokhn	*kawkh*-n	to boil to cook to seethe	קאָכן
kokoshes, di	kaw-*kaw*-shehs	popcorn	קאָקאָשעס, די
kokosnus, der	*kaw*-kawss-noos	coconut	קאָקאָסנוס, דער
koks, der	kawks	coke	קאָקס, דער
kokteyl, der	*kawk*-tayl	cocktail	קאָקטייל, דער
kol-boynik, der	kawl-*boy*-nik	rascal	כּל-בוניק, דער
kol, dos	kawl	voice	קול, דאָס
koldre, di	*kawld*-reh	blanket	קאָלדרע, די
koldre, geshtepte, di	geh-*shtehp*-teh *kawld*-reh	quilt	קאָלדרע, געשטעפּטע, די
kolir, der	kaw-*leer*	color	קאָליר, דער
kolner, der	*kawl*-nehr	collar	קאָלנער, דער
kol-zman	kawl-*zmahn*	as long as	כּל-זמן
komar, der	kaw-*mahr*	mosquito	קאָמאַר, דער
kombinatsye, di	kawm-bee-*nahts*-yeh	combination	קאָמבינאַציע, די
komiker, der	*kaw*-mee-kehr	comic (jester)	קאָמיקער, דער
komish	*kaw*-mish	comical funny	קאָמיש
komod, der	kaw-*mawd*	dresser bureau	קאָמאָד, דער
kompetent	kawm-peh-*tehnt*	competent	קאָמפּעטענט
kompliment, der	kawm-plee-*mehnt*	compliment	קאָמפּלימענט, דער
kompot, der	kawm-*pawt*	fruit dessert	קאָמפּאָט, דער

komunist, der	kaw-moo-*neest*	communist	קאָמוניסט, דער
komunizm, der	kaw-moo-*nee*-zim	communism	קאָמוניזם, דער
kongregatsye, di	kawn-greh-*gahts*-yeh	congregation	קאָנגרעגראַציע, די
konkurent, der	kawn-koo-*rehnt*	competitor rival	קאָנקורענט, דער
konkurs, der	*kawn*-koors	contest	קאָנקורס, דער
kontsert, der	kawn-*tsehrt*	concert recital	קאָנצערט, דער
konvert, der	kawn-*vehrt*	envelope	קאָנווערט, דער
konvulsye, di	kawn-*vool*-syeh	convulsion	קאָנוווּלסיע, די
konyak, der	*kawn*-yahk	brandy	קאָניאַק, דער
kop, der	kawp	head	קאָפּ, דער
kopete, di	*kaw*-peh-teh	hoof	קאָפּעטע, די
kopveytik, der	*kawp*-vay-tik	headache	קאָפּווייטיק, דער
kopye, di	*kawp*-yeh	copy	קאָפּיע, די
korb, der	kawrb	basket	קאָרב, דער
korbn, der	*kawrb*-n	sacrifice victim	קרבן, דער
korespondirn	kaw-rehs-pawn-*deer*-n	to correspond with	קאָרעספּאָנדירן
korev, der	*kaw*-riv	relation relative	קרובֿ, דער
koridor, der	kaw-ree-*dawr*	hall corridor	קאָרידאָר, דער
korik, der	*kaw*-rik	fuse; cork	קאָריק, דער
korporatsye, di	kawr-paw-*rahts*-yeh	corporation	**קאָרפּאָראַציע, די**
korset, der	kawr-*se*	corset	קאָרסעט, דער
kort, di	kawrt	playing card	קאָרט, די
kosher	*kaw*-shir	food conforming to dietary laws (adj.)	כּשר
kosmetik, di	kaw-*smeh*-tik	cosmetic	קאָסמעטיק, די
kostn	*kawsst*-n	to cost	קאָסטן
kostyum, der	kawst-*yoom*	suit costume	קאָסטיום, דער
kotlet, der	kawt-*leht*	cutlet hamburger	קאָטלעט, דער
koved, der	*kaw*-vid	honor	כּבֿוד, דער
koved, opgebn	*awp*-gehb-n *kaw*-vid vehd	to honor	כּבֿוד, אָפּגעבן

koyakh, der	*koy*-ihkh	force strength power	כּח, דער
koyfn	*koyf*-n	to buy	קויפֿן
koyln, di	*koyl*-n	coal	קוילן, די
koym	koym	barely hardly	קוים
koymen, der	*koy*-mehn	chimney smokestack	קוימען, דער
koyne, der	*koy*-neh	customer purchaser	קונה, דער
koyshbol, der	*koysh*-bawl	basketball	קוישבאָל, דער
krab, der	krahb	crab	קראַב, דער
kraft, di	krahft	power vigor	קראַפֿט, די
kraftik	*krahf*-tik	vigorous	קראַפֿטיק
kramf, der	krahmf	cramp	קראַמף, דער
kran, der	krahn	faucet	קראַן, דער
krank	krahnk	sick ill	קראַנק
krankayt, di	*krahn*-keit	disease illness	קראַנקייט, די
krankn-shvester, di	*krahnk*-n-*shvehs*- tehr	nurse	קראַנקן-שוועסטער, די
kratsn	*krahts*-n	to scratch	קראַצן
kravat, der	krah-*vaht*	necktie	קראַוואַט, דער
kraytekhts, dos	*krei*-tehkhts	herb	קרײַטעכץ, דאָס
krayz, der	kreiz	circle	קרײַז, דער
kredit, der	kreh-*deet*	credit	קרעדיט, דער
kreftik	*krehf*-tik	strong sturdy	קרעפֿטיק
krekhtsn	*krehkhts*-n	to groan	קרעכצן
krel, di	krehl	claw	קרעל, די
krenk, di	krehnk	sickness disease	קרענק, די
kretshme, di	*krehch*-meh	tavern inn	קרעטשמע, די
krigeray, dos	*kree*-geh-rei	quarrel brawl	קריגערײַ, דאָס
krign	*kreeg*-n	to get to receive to obtain	קריגן

krign zikh	*kreeg*-n zikh	to quarrel	קריגן זיך
krik	k-*reek*	return (adj.) back	קריק
krikhn	*kreekh*-n	to creep	קריכן
krimen zikh	*kree*-mehn zikh	to scowl to frown	קרימען זיך
krishildik	*kreesh*-l-dik	brittle	קרישלדיק
krist, der	kreest	Christian	קריסט, דער
kritikirn	kree-tee-*keer*-n	to criticize	קריטיקירן
krizhes, di	*kree*-zhehs	lower back	קריזשעס, די
krizis, der	*kree*-ziss	crisis	קריזיס, דער
krokhmal, der	*krawkh*-mahl	starch	קראָכמאַל, דער
krom, di	krawm	shop store	קראָם, די
kroyt, dos	kroyt	cabbage	קרױט, דאָס
krug, der	kroog	pitcher jug	קרוג, דער
kruk, der	krook	hook peg	קרוק, דער
krukhle	*krookh*-leh	crisp	קרוכלע
krum	kroom	crooked	קרום
ksube, di	k-*soo*-beh	marriage contract	כּתובֿה, די
ku, di	koo	cow	קו, די
kubik, der	*koo*-bik	cup	קוביק, דער
kufert, der	*koo*-fehrt	trunk chest	קופֿערט, דער
kugl, der	*koog*-l	pudding	קוגל, דער
kuk, der	kook	look	קוק, דער
kukher, der	*koo*-khehr	cook	קוכער, דער
kukn	*kook*-n	to look	קוקן
kulikl, dos	*koo*-leek-l	mitten	קוליקל, דאָס
kultur, di	kool-*toor*	culture	קולטור, די
kulye, di	*kool*-yeh	crutch	קוליע, די
kumen	*koo*-mehn	to come to arrive	קומען
kumen tsu gast tsu	*koo*-mehn tsoo *gahst* tsoo	to visit	קומען צו גאַסט צו
kuni-leml, der	*koo*-nee-lehm-l	simpleton good-hearted fool	קוני־לעמל, דער
kunst, di	koonst	art	קונסט, די

kunstzayd, dos	*koonst*-zeid	rayon	קונסטזײַד, דאָס
kunts, di	koonts	trick stunt	קונץ, די
kupe, di	*koo*-peh	pile heap	קופּע, די
kuper, dos	*koo*-pehr	copper	קופּער, דאָס
kupon, der	koo-*pawn*	coupon	קופּאָן, דער
kurts	koorts	brief short	קורץ
kurve, di	*koor*-veh	whore	קורװע, די
kush, der	koosh	kiss	קוש, דער
kuzin, der	koo-*zeen*	cousin (masc.)	קוזין, דער
kuzine, di	koo-*zee*-neh	cousin (fem.)	קוזינע, די
kvalpen, di	k-*vahl*-pehn	fountain pen	קװאַלפּען, די
kveln	k-*vehl*-n	to beam with pride	קװעלן
kvenklen zikh	k-*vehnk*-lehn zikh	to hesitate	קװענקלען זיך
kvetsh, der	*kvehch*	complainer (sl.)	קװעטש, דער
kvetshn	k-*vehch*-n	to squeeze to complain (sl.) to whine (sl.)	קװעטשן
kveyt, der	k-*vayt*	blossom	קװײט, דער
kvitshen	k-*vee*-chehn	to scream to shriek	קװיטשען
kvote, di	k-*vaw*-teh	quota	קװאָטע, די
kvure, di	k-*voo*-reh	burial	קבֿורה, די
lakhn	*lahkh*-n	to laugh	לאַכן
laks, der	lahks	salmon	לאַקס, דער
lam, di	lahm	lamb	לאַם, די
lamdn, der	*lahm*-dn	learned man Talmudic scholar	למדן, דער
land, dos	lahnd	land country	לאַנד, דאָס
landshaft, di	*lahnd*-shahft	landscape	לאַנדשאַפֿט, די
landsman, der	*lahnds*-mahn	countryman compatriot	לאַנדסמאַן, דער

lang	lahng	long	לאַנג
lape, di	*lah*-peh	paw large hand (sl.)	לאַפּע, די
lastoyto, der	*lahst*-oy-taw	truck	לאַסטאָויטאָ, דער
late, di	*lah*-teh	patch	לאַטע, די
latke, di	*laht*-keh	pancake	לאַטקע, די
layb, dos	leib	flesh	לײַב, דאָס
laydn	*leid*-n	to suffer	לײַדן
layen	*lei*-en	to lend	לײַען
laykhter, der	*leikh*-tehr	candlestick	לײַכטער, דער
laylekh, der	*lei*-lehkh	bedsheet	לײַלעך, דער
laym, der	leim	lime	לײַם, דער
layt, di	leit	people	לײַט, די
laytish	*lei*-tish	decent respectable	לײַטיש
lebedik	*leh*-beh-dik	alive vivid living	לעבעדיק
leber, di	*leh*-behr	liver	לעבער, די
lebediker, der	*leh*-beh-deek-ehr	lively person	לעבעדיקער, דער
lebn, dos	*lehb*-n	life lifetime	לעבן, דאָס
lebn	*lehb*-n	to live	לעבן
lebn	*lehb*-n	near beside by	לעבן
leder, di	*leh*-dehr	leather	לעדער, די
ledl, dos	*lehd*-l	eyelid	לעדל, דאָס
lefele, dos	*leh*-feh-leh	teaspoon	לעפעלע, דאָס
lefl, der	*lehf*-l	tablespoon	לעפל, דער
legende, di	leh-*gehn*-deh	legend	לעגענדע, די
lehabe	leh-*hah*-beh	hereafter	להבא
lekekh, der	leh-kehkh	cake	לעקעך, דער
lekhayim	leh-*khah*-yeem	To life!	לחיים
lekherlekh	*leh*-khehr-lehkh	ridiculous	לעכערלעך
lekn	*lehk*-n	to lick	לעקן
lektsye, di	*lehkts*-yeh	lecture lesson	לעקציע, די
lemeshke, der	*leh*-mehsh-keh	non-assertive person	לעמישקע, דער
leml, dos	*lehm*-l	lamb	לעמל, דאָס

lemoshl	leh-*mawsh*-l	for example	למשל
lempert, der	*lehm*-pehrt	leopard	לעמפּערט, דער
lempl, dos	*lehmp*-l	lightbulb	לעמפּל, דאָס
lend, di	lehnd	hip	לענד, די
leng, di	lehng	length	לענג, די
lerer, der	*leh*-rehr	teacher	לערער, דער
lernen	*lehr*-nehn	to teach	לערנען
		to instruct	
		to study	
lernen zikh	*lehr*-nehn zikh	to learn	לערנען זיך
lesof	leh-*sawf*	ultimately	לסוף
		finally	
lets, der	lehts	jester	לץ, דער
letst	lehtst	last	לעצט
		final	
		ultimate	
levaye, di	leh-*vah*-yeh	funeral	לוויה, די
levone, di	leh-*vaw*-neh	moon	לבֿנה, די
levone-likht, dos	leh-*vaw*-neh-likht	moonlight	לבֿנה־ליכט, דאָס
leyb, der	layb	lion	לייב, דער
leydik	*lay*-dik	empty	ליידיק
		vacant	
leydik, geyn	*gayn lay*-dik	to loaf	ליידיק, גיין
leyenen	*lay*-eh-nehn	to read	לייענען
leygn	*layg*-n	to lay	לייגן
leykenen	*lay*-keh-nehn	to deny	לייקענען
		to disavow	
leyter, der	*lay*-tehr	ladder	לייטער, דער
libe, di	*lee*-beh	love	ליבע, די
libhober, der	*leeb*-haw-behr	lover (unromantic)	ליבהאָבער, דער
		amateur	
lib hobn	*leeb hawb*-n	to love	ליב האָבן
		to like	
lib hobn, nit	nit *leeb hawb*-n	to dislike	ליב האָבן, ניט
libshaft, di	*leeb*-shahft	affection	ליבשאַפֿט, די
		love	
liblekh	*leeb*-lehkh	affectionate	ליבלעך
lid, dos	leed	song	ליד, דאָס
litke, di	*leet*-keh	calf (anat.)	ליטקע, די
lift, der	leeft	elevator	ליפֿט, דער

Yiddish Dictionary Sourcebook

lign, der	*leeg*-n	falsehood lie	ליגן, דער
lign	*leeg*-n	to lie (be located)	ליגן
lign zogn	*leeg*-n *zawg*-n	to lie (prevaricate)	ליגן זאָגן
ligner, der	*leeg*-nehr	liar	ליגנער, דער
likht, dos	leekht	candle	ליכט, דאָס
likhtik	*leekh*-tik	light bright	ליכטיק
lila	*lee*-lah	purple	לילאַ
lilye, di	*leel*-yeh	lily	ליליע, די
limene, di	*lee*-meh-neh	lemon	לימענע, די
limenad, der	lee-meh-*nahd*	lemonade	לימענאַד, דער
links	leenks	left	לינקס
linolyen, der	lee-*nawl*-yehn	linoleum	לינאָלייען, דער
lip, di	leep	lip	ליפ, די
lipnshtift, der	*leep*-n-shtift	lipstick	ליפנשטיפט, דער
lise	*lee*-seh	bald	ליסע
lodn	*lawd*-n	to sue	לאָדן
lokh, di	lawkh	hole	לאָך, די
lokshn, di	*lawksh*-n	noodles	לאָקשן, די
lom	lawm	lame	לאָם
lombard, der	*lawm*-bahrd	pawnshop	לאָמבאַרד, דער
lomir	*law*-meer	let us	לאָמיר
lomp, der	lawmp	lamp	לאָמפ, דער
lonke, di	*lawn*-keh	lawn meadow	לאָנקע, די
lontsh, der	lawntsh	lunch	לאָנטש, דער
loshn, dos	*lawsh*-n	language	לשון, דאָס
loshn-koydesh, dos	*lawsh*-n-*koy*-desh	the holy language	לשון־קודש, דאָס
loshn-ashkenazim, dos	*lawsh*-n-ahsh-keh- *nah*-zim	the language of the Ashkenaz	לשון אַשְכְּנזים, דאָס
loybn	*loyb*-n	to praise	לויבן
loyfn	*loyf*-n	to run to flow	לויפֿן
loyn, der	loyn	wages	לוין, דער
loyz	loyz	loose	לויז
lozn	*lawz*-n	to leave to allow	לאָזן
luakh, der	*loo*-ahkh	calendar (Jewish)	לוח, דער
luft, di	looft	air	לופֿט, די
luftkilung, di	*looft*-kee-loong	air conditioning	לופֿטקילונג, די
luftpost, di	*looft*-pawst	air mail	לופֿטפּאָסט, די
luksus, der	*looks*-oos	luxury	לוקסוס, דער

lung, di	loong	lung	לונג, די
lyalke, di	*lahl*-keh	doll	ליאַלקע, די
lyulke, di	*lyool*-keh	tobacco pipe	ליולקע, די

mabl, der	*mahb*-l	deluge torrent	מבול, דער
mageyfe, di	mah-*gay*-feh	plague pestilence	מגפה, די
make, di	*mah*-keh	plague	מכּה, די
make, di	*mah*-keh	abcess	מכּה, די
makherayke, di	mah-kheh-*rei*-keh	contraption	מאַכעריַיקע, די
makhmes	*mahkh*-mehs	because of	מחמת
makhn	*mahkh*-n	to make	מאַכן
makhsheyfe, di	mahkh-*shay*-feh	witch	מכשפה, די
makhshir, der	*mahkh*-sheer	tool	מכשיר, דער
maksimal, der	mahk-see-*mahl*	utmost greatest possible	מאַקסימאַל, דער
malakh, der	*mah*-lakh	angel	מלאך, דער
malakh-amoves, der	*mah*-lahkh-ah- *maw*-vehs	angel of death	מלאך־המוות, דער
malbush, dos	*mahl*-boosh	garment piece of clothing	מלבוש, דאָס
mal zayn	*mahl*-zein	to circumcise	מל זיַין
malene, di	*mah*-leh-neh	raspberry	מאַלענע, די
malke, di	*mahl*-keh	queen	מלכּה, די
malpe, di	*mahl*-peh	monkey	מאַלפּע, די
malyer, der	*mahl*-yehr	(house) painter	מאַליער, דער
mame-loshn, dos	*mah*-meh-*lawsh*-n	mother tongue the Yiddish language (coll.)	מאַמע־לשון, דאָס
mamshikh zayn	*mahm*-shikh zein	to continue	ממשיך זיַין
mamzer, der	*mahm*-zehr	bastard	ממזר, דער
man, der	mahn	husband man	מאַן, דער
mandl, der	*mahnd*-l	almond	מאַנדל, דער
mandlbroyt, dos	*mahnd*-l broyt	almond bread	מאַנדלברויט, דאָס

manikur, der	*mah*-nee-koor	manicure	מאַניקור, דער
manirn, di	mah-*neer*-n	manners	מאַנירן, די
mantl, der	*mahnt*-l	coat	מאַנטל, דער
		overcoat	
		cloak	
mape, di	*mah*-peh	map	מאַפע, די
mapole, di	mah-*paw*-leh	defeat	מפלה, די
		failure	
marants, der	mah-*rahnts*	orange	מאַראַנץ, דער
marantsn-zaft, der	mah-*rahnts*-n-zahft	orange juice	מאַראַנצן-זאַפֿט, דער
margarin, der	mahr-gah-*reen*	margarine	מאַרגאַרין, דער
margeritke, di	mahr-geh-*reet*-keh	daisy	מאַרגעריטקע, די
mark, der	mahrk	market	מאַרק, דער
marke, di	*mahr*-keh	postage stamp	מאַרקע, די
marshrut, der	mahrsh-*root*	route	מאַרשרוט, דער
marts, der	mahrts	March	מאַרץ, דער
masazh, der	mah-*sahzh*	massage	מאַסאַזש, דער
mase, di	*mah*-seh	mass	מאַסע, די
		load	
mashin, di	mah-*sheen*	machine	מאַשין, די
mashmoes	mahsh-*maw*-ehs	probably	משמעות
mashmoes, dos	mahsh-*maw*-ehs	probability	משמעות, דאָס
maskil, der	*mahs*-kil	an adherent of the Haskalah (Jewish Enlightenment) movement	משׂכּיל, דער
maskim zayn	*mahss*-kim zein	to agree	מסכּים זײַן
		to consent	
masline, di	*mahss*-lee-neh	olive	מאַסלינע, די
matbeye, di	maht-*bay*-eh	coin	מטבע, די
matern	*mah*-tehr-n	to torment	מאַטערן
maternish, dos	*mah*-tehr-nish	torment	מאַטערניש, דאָס
materyal, der	mah-tehr-*yahl*	material	מאַטעריאַל, דער
materye, di	mah-*tehr*-yeh	matter	מאַטעריע, די
		substance	
matone, di	mah-*taw*-neh	gift	מתּנה, די
		present	
matrats, der	maht-*rahts*	mattress	מאַטראַץ, דער
matsev, der	*mah*-tsihv	status	מצבֿ, דער
matsliahkdik	mahts-*lee*-ahkh-dik	successful	מצליחדיק
matsliakh zayn	mahts-*lee*-ahkh zein	to prosper	מצליח זײַן

may, der	mei	May	מײַ
maykhl, dos	*mei*-khl	food (dish)	מאכל, דאָס
		treat	
		delight	
mayle, di	*mei*-leh	merit	מעלה, די
		advantage	
mayn	mein	my	מײַן
mayner	*mei*-nehr	mine	מײַנער
mayrev, der	*mei*-rehv	evening prayer	מעריב, דער
mayrev, der	*mei*-rehv	west	מערב, דער
mayrevdik	*mei*-rehv-dik	western	מערבֿדיק
mayse, di	*mei*-seh	story	מעשה, די
		tale	
maysele, dos	*mei*-seh-leh	fairy tale	מעשהלע, דאָס
		little story	
mazl, dos	*mahz*-l	fortune	מזל, דאָס
		luck	
mazl-tov	*mahz*-l-tawv	Congratulations!	מזל־טובֿ
mazldik	*mahz*-l-dik	lucky	מזלדיק
		fortunate	
me	meh	one (someone)	מע
		you	
		they	
		people	
me vet zikh zen	meh *veht* zikh *zehn*	See you again!	מע וועט זיך זען
mebl, dos	*mehb*-l	furniture	מעבל, דאָס
medine, di	meh-*dee*-neh	country	מדינה, די
		state	
meditsin, di	meh-dee-*tseen*	drug	מעדיצין, די
		medicine	
megazem zayn	meh-*gah*-zehm zein	to exaggerate	מגזם זײַן
megn	*mehg*-n	to be permitted	מעגן
megushemdik	meh-*goo*-shehm-dik	crude	מגושמדיק
		uncouth	
mehuderdik	meh-*hoo*-dehr-dik	exquisite	מהודרדיק
		superb	
mehume, di	meh-*hoo*-meh	turmoil	מהומה, די
		riot	
mekane zayn	meh-*kah*-neh zein	to envy	מקנא זײַן

mekayem zayn	meh-*kah*-yehm zein	to fulfill	מקיים זײַן
meker, der	*meh*-kehr	eraser	מעקער, דער
mekhaber, der	meh-*khah*-behr	author	מחבר, דער
mekhaniker, der	meh-*khah*-nee-kehr	mechanic	מעכאַניקער, דער
mekhaye zayn	meh-*khah*-yeh zein	to delight	מחיה זײַן
mekheteneste, di	meh-kheh-*teh*-nehs-teh	one's child's spouse's parent (fem.)	מחותּנסטע, די
mekhile, di	meh-*khee*-lih	forgiveness pardon	מחילה, די
mekhutn, der	meh-*khoot*-n	one's child's spouse's parent (masc.)	מחותּן, דער
mekler, der	*meh*-klehr	broker	מעקלער, דער
mekn	*mehk*-n	to erase	מעקן
mel, di	mehl	flour	מעל, די
melamed, der	meh-*lah*-mehd	teacher (elementary level)	מלמד, דער
melankholish	meh-lahn-*khawl*-eesh	melancholy	מעלאַנכאָליש
melon, der	meh-*lawn*	melon	מעלאָן, דער
men	mehn	one (someone) you they people	מען
menie, di	meh-*nee*-eh	difficulty impediment	מניעה, די
menlekh	*mehn*-lehkh	masculine	מענלעך
menoyre, di	meh-*noy*-reh	candelabra (religious)	מנורה, די
mentsh, der	mehnch	person human being	מענטש, דער
mentshhayt, di	*mehnch*-heit	humanity mankind	מענטשהײט, די
mentshlekh	*mehnch*-lehkh	humane human	מענטשלעך
menyu, der	*mehn*-yoo	menu	מעניו, דער
mer, di	mehr	carrot	מער, די
mer	mehr	more	מער
merder, der	*mehr*-dehr	murderer	מערדער, דער
merste	*mehr*-steh	most	מערסטע

merstns	*mehr*-stns	mostly	מערסטנס
mes, der	mehs	corpse	מת, דער
meser, der	*meh*-sehr	knife	מעסער, דער
meshaer zayn zikh	meh-*shah*-ehr zein zikh	to suppose	משער זײַן זיך
meshiakh, der	meh-*shee*-ahkh	Messiah	משיח, דער
meshugaas, dos	meh-shoo-*gahss*	madness insanity	משוגעת, דאָס
meshuge	meh-*shoo*-geh	crazy mad	משוגע
meshumed, der	meh-*shoo*-mid	apostate (Jewish)	משומד, דער
mesik	*meh*-sik	moderate	מעסיק
mes-les, der	mehs-*lehs*	day (24-hour period)	מעת־לעת, דער
mestn	*mehst*-n	to measure	מעסטן
metrese, di	meht-*reh*-seh	mistress lover	מעטרעסע, די
metsie, di	meh-*tsee*-ih	bargain	מציאה, די
mevaker khoyle zayn	meh-*vah*-kehr *khoy*-leh zein	visiting the sick	מבֿקר חולה זײַן
mevater zayn oyf	meh-*vah*-tehr zein oyf	to sacrifice	מוותֿר זײַן אויף
mevayesh zayn	meh-*vah*-yehsh zein	to humiliate	מבֿייש זײַן
meyashev zayn zikh mit	meh-*yah*-shehv zein zikh mit	to consult	מישבֿ זײַן זיך מיט
meydl, di/dos	*mayd*-l	girl	מיידל, די/דאָס
meyle	*may*-leh	never mind forget it anyhow	מילא
meynen	*may*-nehn	to mean to stand for	מיינען
meynung, di	*may*-noong	opinion	מיינונג, די
meysim, di	*may*-seem	the dead	מתים, די
meyvin, der	*may*-vin	expert	מבֿין, דער
mezumen, dos	meh-*zoo*-mehn	cash	מזומן, דאָס
mezuze, di	meh-*zoo*-zeh	doorpost scroll (Jewish)	מזוזה, די
mid	meed	tired	מיד
midber, di	*meed*-behr	desert	מידבר, די
midkayt, di	*meed*-keit	fatigue	מידקייט, די
mies	*mee*-ehs	ugly	מיאוס
meglehk	*meeg*-lehkh	possible	מיגלעך

mikh	meekh	me	מיך
mikve, di	*meek*-veh	ritual bathhouse	מיקווה, די
milkh, di	meelkh	milk	מילך, די
milkhik	*meelkh*-eek	dairy (adj.)	מילכיק
milkhikeray, di	mil-khee-keh-*rei*	dairy	מילכיקעריַי, די
milkhome, di	mil-*khaw*-mih	war	מלחמה, די
milts, di	meelts	spleen	מילץ, די
milyon, der	mil-*yawn*	million	מיליאָן, דער
minern	mee-nehr-n	to reduce	מינערן
		to diminish	
minervertik	*mee*-nehr-*vehr*-tik	inferior	מינערווערטיק
		minor	
minkhe, di	*meen*-khih	afternoon prayer	מינחה, די
minut, di	mee-*noot*	minute	מינוט, די
mir	meer	we	מיר
		me	
mishmash, der	*mish*-mahsh	hodge podge	מישמאַש, דער
mishn	*meesh*-n	to mix	מישן
mishn zikh	*meesh*-n zikh	to meddle	מישן זיך
mishpet, der	*meesh*-piht	courtroom trial	מישפּט, דער
		judgement	
mishpetn	*meesh*-piht-n	to judge	מישפּטן
mishpokhe, di	mish-*paw*-khih	family	משפּחה, די
mist, dos	meest	manure	מיסט, דאָס
		rubbish	
		garbage	
misterye, di	mees-*tehr*-yeh	mystery	מיסטעריע, די
misteryez	mees-*tehr*-yehz	mysterious	מיסטעריעז
mistome	mee-*staw*-meh	probably	מסתמא
mit	meet	with	מיט
mitgefil, dos	*meet*-geh-feel	sympathy	מיטגעפֿיל, דאָס
mitlshul, di	*meet*-l-shool	high school	מיטלשול, די
mitn, der	*meet*-n	middle	מיטן, דער
mitn gantsn hartsn	meet-n *gahnts*-n *hahrts*-n	wholeheartedly	מיטן גאַנצן האַרצן
mitn kop arop	*meet*-n kawp ah-*rawp*	upside down topsy-turvy	מיטן קאָפּ אַראָפּ
mitog, der	*mee*-tawg	dinner	מיטאָג, דער
mitogtsayt, di	*mee*-tawg-tseit	noon	מיטאָגצײַט, די

mitsve, di	*mits*-veh	commandment good deed	מיצווה, די
mitvokh, der	*meet*-vawkh	Wednesday	מיטוואָך, דער
mizrakh, der	*meez*-rahkh	east	מיזרח, דער
mizrakhdik	*meez*-rahkh-dik	eastern	מיזרחדיק
mode, di	*maw*-deh	style fashion	מאָדע, די
modern	maw-*dehr*-n	modern	מאָדערן
modern	maw-*dehr*-n	fashionable ʼstylish	מאָדערן
modne	*mawd*-neh	strange odd	מאָדנע
moger	*maw*-gehr	lean slender	מאָגער
mogn, der	*mawg*-n	stomach	מאָגן, דער
mogn-geshvir, dos	*mawg*-n-geh- *shveer*	ulcer	מאָגן־געשוויר, דאָס
moker, der	*maw*-kehr	source origin	מקור, דער
mol, der	mawl	moth	מאָל, דער
moler, der	*maw*-lehr	painter (artist)	מאָלער, דער
mole-tam	*maw*-leh-tahm	luscious delicious	מלא־טעם
moln	*mawl*-n	to paint (a picture)	מאָלן
moltsayt, der	*mawl*-tseit	meal	מאָלצײַט, דער
moment, der	maw-*mehnt*	moment	מאָמענט, דער
monashke, di	maw-*nahsh*-keh	nun	מאָנאַשקע, די
montik, der	*mawn*-tik	Monday	מאָנטיק, דער
moral, di	maw-*rahl*	morals morale	מאָראַל, די
moralish	maw-*rah*-leesh	moral (adj.)	מאָראַליש
mord, der	mawrd	murder	מאָרד, דער
more-shkhoyre, di	maw-reh-*shkhoy*- reh	depression (sadness)	מרה־שחורה, די
morgn	*mawrg*-n	tomorrow	מאָרגן
mos, di	mawss	measure	מאָס, די
moshl, der	*mawsh*-l	example	משל, דער
motiv, der	maw-*teev*	motive	מאָטיוו, דער
motor, der	maw-*tawr*	motor	מאָטאָר, דער

moyd, di	moyd	maiden	מויד, די
moyde zayn	*moy*-deh-zein	to admit	מודה זײַן
moyde zayn zikh	*moy*-deh zein zikh	to confess	מודה זײַן זיך
moyekh, der	*moy*-ehkh	mind brain	מוח, דער
moyel, der	*moy*-ehl	ritual circumciser	מוהל, דער
moykhl zayn	*moykh*-l-zein	to forgive to pardon	מוחל זײַן
moyl, dos	moyl	mouth	מויל, דאָס
moyre, di	*moy*-reh	fear apprehension	מורא, די
moyre hobn	*moy*-reh hawb-n	to fear to be afraid of	מורא האָבן
moyredik	*moy*-reh-dik	timid fearful	מוראדיק
moyshe kapoyr	*moy*-sheh kah-*poyr*	upside down backwards wrong end first	משה קאַפּויער
moyz, di	moyz	mouse	מויז, די
mozlen, di	*mawz*-lehn	measles	מאָזלען, די
mume, di	*moo*-meh	aunt	מומע, די
mumkhe, der	*moom*-kheh	expert specialist	מומחה, דער
murashke, di	moo-*rahsh*-keh	ant	מוראַשקע, די
musern	moo-*sehr*-n	to reproach to scold	מוסרן
mushkat, der	*moosh*-kaht	nutmeg	מושקאַט, דער
muskl, der	*moosk*-l	muscle	מוסקל, דער
mut, der	moot	courage boldness	מוט, דער
muter, di	*moo*-tehr	mother	מוטער, די
mutshen	*moo*-chehn	to torment to torture	מוטשען
muzey, der	moo-*zay*	museum	מוזיי, דער
muzhik, der	moo-*zheek*	Russian peasant	מוזשיק, דער
muzik, di	moo-*zeek*	music	מוזיק, די
muzn	*mooz*-n	must	מוזן

nadn, der	*nahd*-n	dowry	נדן, דער
naft, der	nahft	petroleum kerosene	נאַפֿט, דער
nafke, di	*nahf*-keh	prostitute	נפֿקע, די
nahit, der	nah-*heet*	chick pea	נאַהיט, דער
naiv	nah-*eev*	naive	נאַיװ
naket	*nah*-keht	bare naked	נאַקעט
nakhes, dos	*nah*-khihs	pleasure (mixed with pride) satisfaction proud enjoyment	נחת, דאָס
nakht, di	nahkht	night	נאַכט, די
nakht, halbe, di	*hahl*-beh *nahkht*	midnight	נאַכט, האַלבע, די
nakhthemd, dos	*nahkht*-hehmd	nightgown	נאַכטהעמד, דאָס
nakn, der	*nahk*-n	neck	נאַקן, דער
nar, der	nahr	fool	נאַר, דער
narish	*nah*-rish	foolish silly	נאַריש
narishkayt, di	*nah*-rish-keit	foolishness stupidity	נאַרישקייט, די
nartlen zikh	*nahrt*-lehn zikh	to ski	נאַרטלען זיך
nas	nahss	wet	נאַס
nash, der	nahsh	snack	נאַש, דער
nashn	*nahsh*-n	to nibble (on)	נאַשן
natirlekh	nah-*teer*-lehkh	natural	נאַטירלעך
nay	nei	new	נײַ
nayes, di	*nei*-ehs	news	נײַעס, די
naygerik	*nei*-geh-rik	curious inquisitive	נײַגעריק
naygerikayt, di	*nei*-geh-ree-keit	curiosity	נײַגעריקייט, די
naylon, der	*nei*-lawn	nylon	נײַלאָן, דער
nayn	nein	nine	נײַן
naynter	*nein*-tehr	ninth	נײַנטער
nayntsn	*neints*-n	nineteen	נײַנצן

nayntsik	*nein*-tsik	ninety	נײַנציק
nebekh	*neh*-behkh	unfortunate poor	נעבעך
nebekhl, dos	*neh*-behkh-l	helpless person dupe	נעבעכל, דאָס
nebish, dos	*neh*-beesh	helpless person	נעביש, דאָס
nedove, di	neh-*daw*-vih	donation (alms)	נדבה, די
nekhome, di	neh-*khaw*-mih	consolation solace	נחמה, די
nekhtn	*nehkht*-n	yesterday	נעכטן
nekome, di	neh-*kaw*-mih	retribution revenge	נקמה, די
nekrolog, der	nehk-raw-*lawg*	obituary notice	נעקראָלאָג, דער
nelm vern	*nehl*-im- vehr-n	to disappear to vanish	נעלם ווערן
nemen	*neh*-mehn	to take	נעמען
nepl, der	*nehp*-l	fog mist	נעפּל, דער
nerv, der	nehrv	nerve (anat.)	נערוו, דער
nervez	*nehr*-vehz	nervous	נערוועז
nes, der	nehs	miracle	נס, דער
neshome, di	neh-*shaw*-mih	soul	נשמה, די
nesie, di	neh-*see*-ih	voyage trip	נסיעה, די
nets, di	nehts	network	נעץ, די
nets, di	nehts	wetness moisture	נעץ, די
neyder, der	*nay*-dihr	vow	נדר, דער
neyen	*nay*-en	to sew	נייען
neymashin, di	*nay*-mah-shin	sewing machine	ניימאַשין, די
neyn	nayn	no (nay)	ניין
neytik	*nay*-tik	necessary	נייטיק
neytikayt, di	*nay*-tee-keit	need necessity	נייטיקייט, די
neytral	nay-*trahl*	neutral	נייטראַל
niderik	*nee*-deh-rik	low	נידעריק
nief, der	*nee*-ihf	adultery	ניאוף, דער
nief, der	*nee*-ihf	debauchery lechery	ניאוף, דער

nifter, der	*neef*-tihr	deceased person	ניפטר, דער
nign, der	*neeg*-n	melody tune	ניגון, דער
nikhter	*neekh*-tehr	sober	ניכטער
nir, di	neer	kidney	ניר, די
nishkoshe	nish-*kaw*-shih	bearable passable acceptable	נישקשה
nishkoshedik	nish-*kaw*-shih-dik	equitable fair	נישקשהדיק
nisimdik	*nees*-im-dik	miraculous	נסימדיק
nisht	neesht	not	נישט
nishtik	*neesh*-tik	insignificant negligible	נישטיק
nisn	*nees*-n	to sneeze	ניסן
nisoyen, der	nee-*soy*-yihn	temptation	נסיון, דער
nit	neet	not	ניט
nit der, nit yener	nit *dehr*, nit *yeh*-nehr	neither one	ניט דער, ניט יענער
nit batsolt	nit bah-*tsawlt*	unpaid	ניט באַצאָלט
nit derkokht	nit dehr-*kawkht*	cooked rare	ניט דערקאָכט
nit-enlekh	nit-*ehn*-lehkh	unlike	ניט־ענלעך
nit-fardayung, di	nit-fahr-*dei*-oong	indigestion	ניט־פֿאַרדײַונג, די
nit farginen	nit fahr-*gee*-nehn	to begrudge to envy	ניט פֿאַרגינען
nit folgn	nit *fawlg*-n	to disobey	ניט פֿאָלגן
nit khasene gehat	nit *khah*-seh-nih geh-*haht*	unmarried	ניט חתונה געהאַט
nit-rikhtik	nit *reekh*-tik	incorrect	ניט־ריכטיק
nit tsu fartrogn	nit tsoo fahr-*trawg*-n	intolerable	ניט צו פֿאַרטראָגן,
nito	nee-*taw*	absent gone away	ניטאָ
nito far vos	nee-*taw* fahr *vawss*	You're welcome.	ניטאָ פֿאַר וואָס
nitsn	*neets*-n	to use	ניצן
nodl, di	*nawd*-l	needle	נאָדל, די
noent	*naw*-ehnt	close near	נאָענט

nogid, der	*naw*-gid	rich man	נגיד, דער
nogl, der	*nawg*-l	nail spike	נאָגל, דער
nogl, der	*nawg*-l	fingernail toenail	נאָגל, דער
nokh	nawkh	yet (adv.) still more after (prep.)	נאָך
nokh a	*nawkh* ah	another one more	נאָך אַ
nokhgebn	*nawkh*-gehb-n	to yield to give in (to)	נאָכגעבן
nokhgeyn	*nawkh*-gayn	to follow to pursue	נאָכגיין
nokhmakhn	*nawkh*-mahkh-n	to imitate to copy	נאָכמאַכן
nokhmitog, der	nawkh-*mee*-tawg	afternoon	נאָכמיטאָג, דער
nokhyogn	*nawkh*-yawg-n	to pursue to chase	נאָכיאָגן
nomen, der	*naw*-mehn	name	נאָמען, דער
nor	nawr	only merely just	נאָר
normal	nawr-*mahl*	normal standard	נאָרמאַל
not, di	nawt	seam	נאָט, די
november, der	naw-*vehm*-behr	November	נאָוועמבער, דער
novi, der	*naw*-vee	prophet	נבֿיא, דער
noyt, di	noyt	need distress hardship	נויט, די
noytfal, der	*noyt*-fahl	emergency	נויטפֿאַל, דער
noz, di	nawz	nose	נאָז, די
nozlokh, di	*nawz*-lawkh	nostril	נאָזלאָך, די
noztikhl, dos	*nawz*-teekh-l	handkerchief	נאָזטיכל, דאָס
nu	noo	Go on! Well? Come on!	נו

nudne	*nood*-neh	dull boring	נודנע
nudnik, der	*nood*-nik	pest bore	נודניק, דער
nudzhen	*noodj*-en	to bore, badger	נודזשען
nul, der	nool	zero nil	נול, דער
numer, der	*noo*-mehr	number	נומער, דער
numer, der	*noo*-mehr	size of apparel, clothes	נומער, דער
nus, der	noos	nut	נוס, דער
nuts, der	noots	use benefit profit	נוץ, דער
nutsik	*noo*-tsik	helpful useful	נוציק
nutsn	*noots*-n	to use	נוצן
nutsn, on a	*awn* ah *noots*-n	useless	נוצן, אָן אַ

ober	*aw*-behr	but (conj.) however	אָבער
oder	*aw*-dehr	or	אָדער
oder . . . oder	*aw*-dehr . . . *aw*- dehr	either . . . or	אָדער . . . אָדער
oder, di	*aw*-dehr	blood vessel vein	אָדער, די
of, dos	oyf	fowl poultry	עוף, דאָס
ofitsir, der	aw-fee-*tseer*	military officer	אָפֿיציר, דער
ofn	*awf*-n	open overt	אָפֿן
ofn	*awf*-n	blunt frank	אָפֿן
oft	awft	often frequent	אָפֿט

ofter	*awf*-tehr	more often	אָפֿטער
oks, der	awks	ox	אָקס, דער
oktober, der	awk-*taw*-behr	October	אָקטאָבער, דער
oley-hasholem	aw-lay-hoh hah-*shaw*-lehm	May she rest in peace.	עליה־השלום
oliv-hashalom	aw-leev-hah-*shaw*-lehm	May he rest in peace.	עליו־השלום
omlet, der	awm-*leht*	omelette	אָמלעט, דער
on	awn	without	אָן
ondenk, der	awn-dehnk	momento souvenir	אָנדענק, דער
onfirn	*awn*-feer-n	to direct to manage	אָנפֿירן
onfreg, der	*awn*-frehg	inquiry	אָנפֿרעג, דער
ongeblozn	*awn*-geh-blawz-n	overblown conceited	אָנגעבלאָזן
ongeshtopt	*awn*-geh-shtawpt	very wealthy (coll.)	אָנגעשטאָפּט
ongisn	*awn*-gees-n	to pour	אָנגיסן
ongreytn zikh	*awn*-grayt-n zikh	to get ready to prepare	אָנגרייטן זיך
onheyb, der	*awn*-hayb	beginning start	אָנהייב, דער
onheybn	*awn*-hayb-n	to begin to start	אָנהייבן
onkhapn	*awn*-khahp-n	to get hold of to grasp to sieze	אָנכאַפּן
onkumen	*awn*-koo-mehn	to arrive	אָנקומען
onkumen tsu	*awn*-koo-mehn tsoo	to be dependent on	אָנקומען צו
onkukn	*awn*-kook-n	to look at to gaze	אָנקוקן
onlenen zikh	*awn*-lehn-en zikh	to recline to lean	אָנלענען זיך
onrirn	*awn*-reer-n	to touch	אָנרירן
onshteln tsu	*awn*-shtehl-n tsoo	to employ to hire	אָנשטעלן צו
onshtendik	*awn*-shtehn-dik	decent honorable respectable	אָנשטענדיק

onton zikh	*awn*-tawn zikh	to dress	אָנטאָן זיך
ontsindn	*awn*-tsind-n	to kindle to spark to light	אָנצינדן
ontsindung, di	*awn*-tsin-doong	inflammation	אָנצינדונג, די
onvern	*awn*-vehr-n	to lose	אָנווערן
onzogn	*awn*-zawg-n	to announce to inform	אָנזאָגן
onvayzn	*awn*-veiz-n	to indicate to instruct	אָנווײַזן
operatsye, di	aw-peh-*rahts*-yeh	operation (mil. or med.)	אָפּעראַציע, די
operirn	aw-peh-*reer*-n	to operate	אָפּערירן
opfal, der	*awp*-fahl	garbage refuse	אָפּפֿאַל, דער
opflien	*awp*-flee-en	to depart (by plane)	אָפּפֿליִען
opgehit	*awp*-geh-heet	cautious careful	אָפּגעהיט
opgelozn	*awp*-geh-lawz-n	neglected careless	אָפּגעלאָזן
opgeshepte milkh, di	*awp*-geh-shehp- teh meelkh	skimmed milk	אָפּגעשעפּטע מילך, די
opgeteyt	*awp*-geh-tayt	numb	אָפּגעטייט
opgos, der	*awp*-gawss	sink	אָפּגאָס, דער
ophaltn	*awp*-hahlt-n	to stop to prevent to deter	אָפּהאַלטן
ophitn	*awp*-heet-n	to take care of to cherish	אָפּהיטן
ophentik	*awp*-hehn-tik	helpless discouraged	אָפּהענטיק
opklekn	*awp*-klehk-n	to blot	אָפּקלעקן
opleyger, der	*awp*-lay-gehr	procrastinator	אָפּלייגער, דער
opleygn	*awp*-layg-n	to put off to postpone	אָפּלייגן
oplozn	*awp*-lawz-n	to abandon to release	אָפּלאָזן
opnar, der	*awp*-nahr	deceit hoax	אָפּנאַר, דער
opnarer, der	*awp*-nah-rehr	faker	אָפּנאַרער, דער

opnarn	*awp*-nahr-n	to deceive	אָפּנאַרן
		to cheat	
opozitsye, di	aw-paw-*zeets*-yeh	opposition	אָפּאָזיציע, די
opruen	*awp*-roo-en	to rest	אָפּרוען
		to relax	
opruf, der	*awp*-roof	reaction	אָפּרוף, דער
		response	
opshatsn	*awp*-shahts-n	to value	אָפּשאַצן
		to appreciate	
opshmaysn	*awp*-shmeis-n	to spank	אָפּשמײַסן
opshporn	*awp*-shpawr-n	to save (put away)	אָפּשפּאָרן
opshteln	*awp*-shtehl-n	to halt	אָפּשטעלן
		to stop	
opteyln	*awp*-tayl-n	to separate	אָפּטײלן
optimistish	awp-tee-*mees*-tish	optimistic	אָפּטימיסטיש
optret, der	*awp*-treht	restroom	אָפּטרעט, דער
		privy	
optretn	*awp*-treht-n	to defer	אָפּטרעטן
		to yield	
optsapn	*awp*-tsahp-n	to drain	אָפּצאַפּן
		to tap	
optsol, der	*awp*-tsawl	charge	אָפּצאָל, דער
		fee	
opvegn	*awp*-vehg-n	to weigh	אָפּוועגן
opzogn	*awp*-zawg-n	to dismiss	אָפּזאָגן
		to refuse	
oranzh	aw-*rahnzh*	orange (color)	אָראַנזש
ordenung, di	*awr*-deh-noong	order	אָרדענונג, די
		arrangement	
orem, der	aw-rehm	arm	אָרעם, דער
orem	aw-rehm	poor	אָרעם
oreman, der	aw-reh-*mahn*	poor man	אָרעמאַן, דער
oremkayt, di	aw-rehm-keit	poverty	אָרעמקייט, די
orev, der	aw-rehv	guarantor	ערב, דער
orevnik, der	*awr*-ehv-nik	hostage	ערבניק, דער
organ, der	awr-*gahn*	organ (anat.)	אָרגאַן, דער
orkester, der	awr-*kehs*-tehr	orchestra	אָרקעסטער, דער
orkhidee, di	awr-khee-*day*-eh	orchid	אָרכידעע, די
orn, der	*awr*-n	coffin (Jewish)	אָרון, דער

orntlekh	*aw*-rint-lehkh	respectable honest fair	אָרנטלעך
ort, dos	awrt	room space place	אָרט, דאָס
os, der/dos	awss	letter (alphabet) character	אות, דער/דאָס
ot	awt	here there	אָט
otem, der	*aw*-tehm	breath	אָטעם, דער
otemen	*aw*-teh-mehn	to breathe	אָטעמען
oves, di	*aw*-vehs	ancestors	אבֿות, די
ovnt, der	*awv*-nt	evening	אָוונט, דער
oy	oy	Oh! Ouch!	אוי
oyb	oyb	if	אויב
oyb azoy	oyb ah-*zoy*	then (in that case)	אויב אַזוי
oybn, der	*oyb*-n	top	אויבן, דער
oybn	*oyb*-n	above upstairs	אויבן
oyer, der	*oy*-ehr	ear	אויער, דער
oyer-veytik, der	*oy*-ehr-vay-tik	earache	אויער־ווייטיק, דער
oyf	oyf	up upon on at(occasion)	אויף
oyf an emes	oyf ahn *eh*-mehs	seriously; truthfully	אויף אַן אמת
oyf eybik	oyf *ay*-bik	forever	אויף אייביק
oyf tselokhes	oyf tseh-*law*-khehs	for spite	אויף צו להכעיס
oyfdekn	*oyf*-dehk-n	to uncover to discover	אויפֿדעקן
oyfes, di	*oy*-fehs	poultry	עופֿות, די
oyffir	*oyf*-feer	conduct behaviour	אויפֿפיר, דער
oyfgekokht	*oyf*-geh-kawkht	furious exasperated	אויפֿגעקאָכט
oyfhern	*oyf*-hehr-n	to stop to cease	אויפֿהערן

oyfheybn	*oyf*-hayb-n	to raise	אויפֿהייבן
		to lift up	
oyfhitn	*oyf*-heet-n	to preserve	אויפֿהיטן
oyfn kol	*oyf*-n kawl	aloud	אויפֿן קול
oyfraysn	*oyf*-reis-n	to burst	אויפֿרײַסן
		to explode	
oyfrikhtik	*oyf*-rikh-tik	sincere	אויפֿריכטיק
oyfrikhtikayt, di	*oyf*-rikh-ti-keit	sincerety	אויפֿריכטיקייט ,די
oyfshteln	*oyf*-shtehl-n	to erect	אויפֿשטעלן
		to establish	
oyfshteyn	*oyf*-shtayn	to rise	אויפֿשטיין
		to stand up	
oyftretn	*oyf*-treht-n	to perform	אויפֿטרעטן
oyftsitern	*oyf*-tsee-tehr-n	to shudder	אויפֿציטערן
		to thrill	
oyf tsurik	oyf tsoo-*reek*	backward	אויך צוריק
oyfvaksn	*oyf*-vahks-n	to grow up	אויפֿוואַקסן
oyfvekn	*oyf*-vehk-n	to awaken	אויפֿוועקן
		to arouse	
oyg, dos	oyg	eye	אויג, דאָס
oygust, der	oy-*goost*	August	אויגוסט, דער
oykh	oykh	also	אויך
		too	
		furthermore	
oylem, der	*oy*-lehm	audience	עולם, דער
		crowd	
oyrekh, der	*oy*-rehkh	guest	אורח, דער
oyringl, dos	*oy*-ring-l	earring	אויירינגל, דאָס
oys	oyss	no more (adv.)	אויס
		through	
oysbahaltn	*oyss*-bah-hahlt-n	to hide	אויסבאַהאַלטן
		to conceal	
oysbaytn	*oyss*-beit-n	to change	אויסבײַטן
		to exchange	
oysblik, der	*oyss*-blik	outlook	אויסבליק, דער
		view	
oysbrekhn	*oyss*-brehkh-n	to break out	אויסברעכן
		to erupt	
oysbrekhn	*oyss*-brehkh-n	to vomit	אויסברעכן

oysdruk, der	*oyss*-drook	expression	אויסדרוק, דער
oysenveynik	*oys*-sehn-*vay*-nik	outside externally	אויסנווייניק
oysenveynik	*oys*-sehn-*vay*-nik	by heart	אויסנווייניק
oysfirn	*oyss*-feer-n	to execute to accomplish	אויספֿירן
oysforshn	*oyss*-fawrsh-n	to investigate to explore	אויספֿאָרשן
oysforshung, di	*oyss*-fawr-shoong	investigation inquiry	אויספֿאָרשונג, די
oysgedart	*oyss*-geh-dahrt	haggard emaciated	אויסגעדאַרט
oysgefinen	*oyss*-geh-fee-nehn	to learn to discover to invent	אויסגעפֿינען
oysgefins, dos	*oyss*-geh-finss	invention	אויסגעפֿינס, דאָס
oysgelasn	*oyss*-geh-lahs-n	lewd	אויסגעלאַסן
oysgematert	*oyss*-geh-mah- tehrt	exhausted	אויסגעמאַטערט
oysgemutshet	*oyss*-geh-moo- cheht	tormented	אויסגעמוטשעט
oysgeputst	*oyss*-geh-pootst	dressed up flamboyant	אויסגעפּוצט
oysgeshept	*oyss*-geh-shehpt	drained	אויסגעשעפּט
óysglaykhn	*oyss*-glyeikh-n	to straighten to even off	אויסגלײַכן
oysgletn	*oyss*-gleht-n	to smooth	אויסגלעטן
oyshaltn	*oyss*-hahlt-n	to endure to maintain	אויסהאַלטן
oyshitn	*oyss*-heet-n	to protect	אויסהיטן
oyskern	*oyss*-kehr-n	to sweep to turn inside out	אויסקערן
oysklaybn	*oyss*-kleib-n	to select to choose	אויסקלײַבן
oyskuk, der	*oyss*-kook	outlook prospect	אויסקוק, דער
oyslender, der	*oyss*-lehn-dehr	foreigner alien	אויסלענדער, דער
oysleyzgelt, dos	*oyss*-layz-gehlt	ransom	אויסלייזגעלט, דאָס

oysleyzn	*oyss*-layz-n	to ransom	אויסלייזן
oysloz, der	*oyss*-lawz	ending	אויסלאָז, דער
		conclusion	
oyslozn	*oyss*-lawz-n	to end	אויסלאָזן
		to omit	
oysmaydn	*oyss*-meid-n	to avoid	אויסמײַדן
(oys)mekn	*(oyss)*-mehk-n	to erase	אויס)מעקן)
oysnem, der	*oyss*-nehm	exception	אויסנעם, דער
oysn zayn	*oyss*-n zein	to mean	אויסן זײַן
		to intend	
oysreynikn	*oyss*-ray-neek-n	to clean	אויסרייניקן
oysrinen	*oyss*-ree-nehn	to leak out	אויסרינען
		to trickle	
oysshrayen	*oyss*-shrei-en	to exclaim	אויסשרײַען
oystaytshn	*oyss*-teich-n	to interpret	אויסטײַטשן
oysterlish	*oyss*-tehr-lish	quaint	אויסטערליש
		queer	
oysvorf, der	*oyss*-vawrf	outcast	אויסוואָרף, דער
		scoundrel	
oyszogn	*oyss*-zawg-n	to reveal	אויסזאָגן
		to disclose	
oyto, der	*oy*-taw	car	אויטאָ, דער
oytobus, der	oy-taw-*booss*	bus	אויטאָבוס, דער
oytomobil, der	oy-taw-maw-*beel*	automobile	אויטאָמאָביל, דער
oytser, der	*oy*-tsehr	treasure	אוצר, דער
		hoard	
oyver-botl	*oy*-vehr-*bawt*-l	senile	עובֿר-בטל
oyvn, der	*oyv*-n	oven	אויוון, דער
		stove	
		furnace	
ozere, di	*aw*-zeh-reh	lake	אָזערע
ozhene, di	*aw*-zheh-neh	blackberry	אָזשענע, די

padeshve, di	pah-*dehsh*-veh	(shoe) sole	פּאַדעשוע, די
padloge, di	pahd-*law*-geh	floor	פּאַדלאָגע די
pakhdn, der	*pahkh*-din	coward	פּחדן, דער

pakn	*pahk*-n	to pack	פּאַקן
pamelekh	pah-*meh*-lehkh	slow tardy	פּאַמעלעך
panik, di	*pah*-neek	panic	פּאַניק, די
pap, der	pahp	paste pulp	פּאַפּ, דער
papir, dos	pah-*peer*	paper	פּאַפּיר, דאָס
papiros, der	pah-pee-*rawss*	cigarette	פּאַפּיראָס, דער
papugay, der	pah-poo-*gei*	parrot	פּאַפּוגײ, דער
parev(e)	*pah*-rehv(-eh)	food (neither dairy nor meat) (adj.)	פּאַרעוו(ע)
parfum, der	pahr-*foom*	perfume	פּאַרפֿום, דער
park der	pahrk	park	פּאַרק, דער
parkh, der	pahrkh	scalp disease	פּאַרך, דער
parnose, di	pahr-*naw*-seh	livelihood substinence	פּרנסה, די
parshoyn, der	pahr-*shoyn*	person character (in a play)	פּאַרשוין, דער
paruk, der	pah-*rook*	wig	פּאַרוק, דער
pas, der	pahss	pass passport	פּאַס, דער
pasazhir, der	pah-sah-*zheer*	passenger	פּאַסאַזשיר, דער
pasik	*pah*-sik	fit suitable	פּאַסיק
pasirn	pah-*seer*-n	to happen to occur	פּאַסירן
pasirung, di	pah-*see*-roong	event occurrence	פּאַסירונג, די
paskenen	*pahs*-keh-nehn	to judge to rule	פּסקענען
paskudne	pahs-*kood*-neh	loathsome	פּאַסקודנע
paskudnyak, der	pahs-kood-*nyahk*	scoundrel	פּאַסקודניאַק, דער
pasn	*pahs*-n	to be fitting to be proper	פּאַסן
pastekh, der	*pahs*-tehkh	shepherd	פּאַסטעך, דער
patern	*pah*-tehr-n	to waste	פּטרן
patsh, der	pahch	slap	פּאַטש, דער
patshn	*pahch*-n	to slap to clap	פּאַטשן
patsyent, der	pahts-*yehnt*	patient	פּאַציענט, דער

pay, der	pei	pie	פּײַ, דער
payn, di	pein	anguish	פּײַן, די
paynikung, di	*pei*-nee-koong	torture	פּײַניקונג, די
pazronish	pahz-*raw*-neesh	lavish extravagant	פּזרניש
pekl, dos	*pehk*-l	package bundle	פּעקל, דאָס
peklfleysh, dos	*peh*-kil-flaysh	corned beef	פּעקלפֿלייש, דאָס
peklpost, di	*peh*-kil-pawst	parcel post	פּעקלפּאָסט, די
pelts, der	pehlts	fur pelt	פּעלץ, דער
pen, di	pehn	pen	פּען, די
penets, der	*peh*-nehts	section slice	פּענעץ, דער
penis, der	*peh*-niss	penis	פּעניס, דער
penkher, der	*pehn*-khehr	bladder	פּענכער, דער
pensye, di	*pehns*-yeh	pension	פּענסיע, די
perene, di	*peh*-reh-neh	featherbed	פּערענע, די
perfekt	pehr-*fehkt*	perfect	פּערפֿעקט
perl, der	*pehr*-l	pearl	פּערל, דער
perzenlekh	pehr-*zehn*-lehkh	personal personally	פּערזאָנלעך
perzon, di	pehr-*zawn*	person	פּערזאָן, די
peshl, dos	*pehsh*-l	deck of cards	פּעשל, דאָס
pesimistish	peh-see-*mees*-tish	pessimistic	פּעסימיסטיש
petitsye, di	peh-*teets*-yeh	petition	פּעטיציע, די
peye, di	*pay*-eh	earlock	פּאה, די
peygern	*pay*-gehr-n	to die (animals)	פּגרן
pil, di	peel	pill	פּיל, די
pileven	*pee*-leh-vehn	to nurse (give treatment) to pamper	פּילעווען
pilke, di	*peel*-keh	toy ball	פּילקע, די
pilot, der	pee-*lawt*	pilot	פּילאָט, דער
pinktlekh	*peenkt*-lehkh	accurate prompt	פּינקטלעך
pintele, dos	*peen*-teh-leh	dot	פּינטעלע, דאָס
pirsum, der	*peer*-soom	publicity	פּירסום, דער
pishekhts, dos	*peesh*-ehkhts	urine	פּישעכץ, דאָס

pisher, der	*peesh*-ehr	a nobody a little squirt (male)	פּישער, דער
pisherke, di	*peesh*-ehr-keh	a nobody a little squirt (female)	פּישערקע, די
pishn	*peesh*-n	to urinate	פּישען
pisk, der	pisk	animal's mouth loudmouth (sl.)	פּיסק, דער
pistoyl, der	pis-*toyl*	pistol	פּיסטויל, דער
pitsl, dos	*peets*-l	tiny bit shred	פּיצל, דאָס
pizhame, di	pee-*zhah*-meh	pajamas	פּיזשאַמע, די
plan, der	plahn	plan schedule blueprint	פּלאַן, דער
planeven	*plah*-neh-vehn	to plan	פּלאַנעווען
plaplen	*plahp*-lehn	to jabber to chatter	פּלאַפּלען
plastik, der	*plahss*-tik	plastic	פּלאַסטיק, דער
plate, di	*plah*-teh	slab	פּלאַטע, די
plate, di	*plah*-teh	record (mus.)	פּלאַטע, די
platforme, di	*plaht*-fawr-meh	platform	פּלאַטפֿאָרמע, די
plats, der	plahts	place space location	פּלאַץ, דער
platsn	*plahts*-n	to crack to burst	פּלאַצן
plazhe, di	*plahzh*-eh	beach	פּלאַזשע, די
pleytse, di	*play*-tseh	shoulder back	פּלייצע, די
plimenik, der	plee-*meh*-nik	nephew	פּלימעניק, דער
plimenitse, di	plee-*meh*-neet-seh	niece	פּלימעניצע, די
plukte, di	*plook*-teh	controversy issue	פּלוגתּא, די
plutsemdik	*ploo*-tsehm-dik	sudden abrupt	פּלוצעמדיק
plutsling	*ploots*-leeng	suddenly abruptly	פּלוצלינג
plyukhen	*plyoo*-khehn	to rain heavily	פּליוכען

plyushken	*plyoosh*-kehn	to splash	פליושקען
pokn, di	*pawk*-n	smallpox	פּאָקן, די
polir, der	paw-*leer*	polish	פּאָליר, דער
polirn	paw-*leer*-n	to polish to shine	פּאָלירן
polit, der	*paw*-leet	refugee	פּליט, דער
politse, di	*paw*-lee-tseh	shelf	פּאָליצע, די
politsey, di	paw-lee-*tsay*	police	פּאָליציי, די
politsey-stantsye, di	paw-lee-*tsay*-*stahnts*-yeh	police station	פּאָליציי־סטאַנציע, די
politsyant, der	paw-leets-*yahnt*	policeman	פּאָליציאַנט, דער
polke, di	*pawl*-keh	thigh	פּאָלקע, די
pomidor, der	paw-mee-*dawr*	tomato	פּאָמידאָר, דער
poms	pawms	crimson	פּאָמס
ponim, dos	*paw*-nim	countenance face	פּנים, דאָס
por, di	pawr	couple pair	פּאָר, די
porets, der	*paw*-rehts	nobleman landowner	פּריץ, דער
porn zikh	*pawr*-n zikh	to mate to copulate	פּאָרן זיך
portret, der	pawr-*treht*	portrait	פּאָרטרעט, דער
portselay, dos	pawr-tseh-*lei*	porcelain	פּאָרצעלײַ, דאָס
poshet	*paw*-sheht	simple plain	פּשוט
posl	*paws*-l	void invalid	פּסול
post, di	pawst	mail	פּאָסט, די
postamt, der	*pawst*-ahmt	post office	פּאָסטאַמט, דער
postgelt, dos	*pawst*-gehlt	postage	פּאָסטגעלט, דאָס
postn, der	*pawst*-n	position post	פּאָסטן, דער
poter vern fun	*paw*-tehr *vehr*-n foon	to dispose of	פּטור ווערן פֿון
pots, der	pawts	penis insulting characterization	פּאָץ, דער
poyer, der	*paw*-yehr	peasant farmer	פּויער, דער
poyk, di	poyk	drum	פּויק, די
pozitsye, di	paw-*zeets*-yeh	position	פּאָזיציע, די

prakes, di	*prah*-kehs	stuffed cabbage	פּראַקעס, די
praktish	*prahk*-tish	practical	פּראַקטיש
prayz, der	preiz	price	פּרײַז, דער
preglen	*prehg*-lehn	to fry	פּרעגלען
prekhtik	*prehkh*-tik	superb	פּרעכטיק
		gorgeous	
preplen	*prehp*-lehn	to mumble	פּרעפּלען
		to mutter	
presayzn, dos	*prehs*-eiz-n	pressing iron	פּרעסאײַזן, דאָס
presn	*prehs*-n	to press	פּרעסן
		to iron	
pretendirn	preh-tehn-*deer*-n	to pretend	פּרעטענדירן
prazhenitse, di	*preh*-zheh-nee-tseh'	scrambled eggs	פּרעזשעניצע, די
prister, der	*prees*-tehr	priest	פּריסטער, דער
privat	pree-*vaht*	private	פּריוואַט
privilegye, di	pree-vee-*lehg*-yeh	privilege	פּריווילעגיע, די
probe, di	*praw*-beh	test	פּראָבע, די
		tryout	
problem, di	prawb-*lehm*	problem	פּראָבלעם, די
profesor, der	praw-*feh*-sawr	professor	פּראָפֿעסאָר, דער
prost	prawst	common	פּראָסט
		ordinary	
		coarse	
prostitutke, di	*praws*-tee-*toot*-keh	prostitute	פּראָסטיטוטקע, די
protestirn	praw-tehs-*teer*-n	to protest	פּראָסטעסטירן
provints, di	praw-*veents*	province	פּראָװינץ, די
pruvn	*proov*-n	to attempt	פּרוּוון
		to try	
psak, der	psahk	judgement	פּסק, דער
		verdict	
pshat, der	p-shaht	literal meaning	פּשט, דער
		sense	
psikhiatrye, di	p-see-khee-*aht*-ree-yeh	psychiatry	פּסיכיאַטריע, די
psikhoanaliz, der	p-see-khaw-*ahn*-ah-leez	psychoanalysis	פּסיכאָאַנאַליז, דער
psikhkologye, di	p-see-khaw-*lawg*-yeh	psychology	פּסיכאָלאָגיע, די
puder, der	*poo*-dehr	powder (cosmetic)	פּודער, דער

pukhke	*pookh*-keh	fluffy	פּוכקע
punkt	poonkt	exactly	פּונקט
		just	
		punctually	
pupik, der	*poo*-pik	navel	פּופיק, דער
		gizzard	
pushke, di	*poosh*-keh	tin can	פּושקע, די
		alms box	
pust	poost	empty	פּוסט
		blank	
pust un pas	*poost* oon *pahss*	idle	פּוסט און פּאַס
puter, di	*poo*-tehr	butter	פּוטער, די
pyane, di	pee-*ah*-neh	piano	פּיאַנע, די
pyate, di	pee-*ah*-teh	sole	פּיאַטע, די
		heel	

radikal, der	*rah*-dee-kahl	radical	ראַדיקאַל, דער
radyo, der	*rahd*-yaw	radio	ראַדיאָ, דער
rak, der	rahk	cancer	ראַק, דער
rakhmones, dos	rahkh-*maw*-nehs	mercy	רחמנות, דאָס
		pity	
		compassion	
rakl, dos	*rahk*-l	shrimp	ראַקל, דאָס
rateven	*rah*-teh-vehn	to save	ראַטעווען
		to rescue	
raybn	*reib*-n	to rub	רײַבן
		to grate	
raye, di	*rei*-eh	piece of evidence	ראיה, די
raykh	reikh	rich	רײַך
		wealthy	
raykhkayt, di	*ryeikh*-keit	wealth	רײַכקייט, די
raysn	*reis*-n	to rip	רײַסן
		to tear	
rayz, der	reiz	rice	רײַז, דער
rayze-byuro, der	*rei*-zeh-boo-raw	travel bureau	רײַזע־ביוראָ, דער

razirn zikh	rah-*zeer*-n zikh	to shave	ראזירן זיך
razirzeyf, di	rah-*zeer*-zayf	shaving cream	ראזירזייף, די
reb	rehb	mister (Jewish)	רב
rebe, der	*reh*-beh	Hasidic rabbi	רבי, דער
		teacher (at highest level)	
rebetsn, di	*reh*-beh-tseen	rabbi's wife	רביצין, די
rede, di	*reh*-deh	speech	רעדע, די
		oration	
redn	*rehd*-n	to speak	רעדן
		to talk	
redner, der	*rehd*-nehr	speaker	רעדנער, דער
		orator	
refue, di	reh-*foo*-eh	drug	רפואה, די
		remedy	
rege, di	*reh*-geh	moment	רגע, די
		instant	
regenen	*reh*-geh-nehn	to rain	רעגענען
regirung, di	reh-*gee*-roong	government	רעגירונג, די
registrirt	reh-giss-*treert*	registered	רעגיסטרירט
		registered mail	
regn, der	*rehg*-n	rain	רעגן, דער
		rainfall	
regn-boygn, der	*rehg*-n-*boyg*-n	rainbow	רעגן־בויגן, דער
regn-mantl, der	*rehg*-n-*mahnt*-l	raincoat	רעגן־מאַנטל, דער
regndik	*rehg*-n-dik	rainy	רעגנדיק
regndl, dos	*rehg*-n-dil	drizzle	רעגנדל, דאָס
		shower	
rekhenen	*reh*-kheh-nehn	to calculate	רעכענען
		to reckon	
rekhiles, dos	reh-*khee*-lehs	slander	רכילות, דאָס
		gossip	
rekht, dos	rehkht	right	רעכט, דאָס
		due	
rekhts	rehkhts	right (direction)	רעכטס
rekl, dos	*rehk*-l	jacket	רעקל, דאָס
		skirt	
rekomendirn	reh-kaw-mehn-*deer*-n	to recommend	רעקאָמענדירן
		to advise	
religyez	reh-*leeg*-yehz	religious	רעליגיעז
religye, di	reh-*leeg*-yeh	religion	רעליגיע, די

rentgen-bild, dos	*rehnt*-gehn-bild	x-ray	רענטגען־בילד, דאָס
rer, di	rehr	pipe	רער, די
		tube	
reshime, di	reh-*shee*-meh	list	רשימה, די
resht, der	rehsht	rest	רעשט, דער
		remainder	
restoran, der	rehs-taw-*rahn*	restaurant	רעסטאָראַן, דער
retekh, der	*reh*-tehkh	radish	רעטעך, דער
retenish, dos	*reh*-teh-nish	riddle	רעטעניש, דאָס
		puzzle	
retsept, der	reh-*tsehpt*	prescription	רעצעפּט, דער
		recipe	
reyakh, der	*ray*-ahkh	odor	ריח, דער
		smell	
		scent	
reyf, der	rayf	hoop	רייף, דער
		tire	
reykhern	*ray*-khehr-n	to smoke	רייכערן
		to fume	
reyn	rayn	clean	ריין
		pure	
reynikn	*ray*-neek-n	to clean	רייניקן
		to purify	
reynkayt, di	*rayn*-keit	cleanliness	רייניקייט, די
		purity	
reytlen zikh	*rayt*-lehn zikh	to blush	רייטלען זיך
reytsn zikh mit	*rayts*-n zikh meet	to bait	רייצן זיך מיט
		to tease	
rezervatsye, di	reh-zehr-*vahts*-yeh	reservation	רעזערוואַציע, די
ridl, der	*reed*-l	shovel	רידל, דער
		spade	
rigl, der	*reeg*-l	bolt	ריגל, דער
rikhter, der	*rikh*-tehr	judge	ריכטער, דער
		magistrate	
rikhtik	*reekh*-tik	correct	ריכטיק
		right	
rikhtn zikh oyf	*rikht*-n zikh oyf	to anticipate	ריכטן זיך אויף
		to expect	
rikhtung, di	*reekh*-toong	direction	ריכטונג, די

rinderns, dos	*reen*-dehrns	beef	רינדערנס, דאָס
rinen	*ree*-nehn	to leak	רינען
		to run	
ring, der	reeng	ring	רינג, דער
rip, di	reep	rib	ריפּ, די
rirevdik	*ree*-rehv-dik	agile	רירעוודיק
		lively	
rirn	*reer*-n	to touch	רירן
		to move	
riz, der	reez	giant	ריז, דער
rod, dos	rawd	wheel	ראָד, דאָס
roman, der	raw-*mahn*	romance	ראָמאַן, דער
		love affair	
roman, der	raw-*mahn*	novel	ראָמאַן, דער
rosh, der	rawsh	chief	ראָש, דער
		head	
roshe, der	*raw*-shih	villain	רשע, דער
roslfleysh, der	*raws*-l-flaysh	pot roast	ראָסלפֿלייש, דער
rot, der	rawt	council	ראָט, דער
		board	
rov, der	rawv	rabbi	רבֿ, דער
roy	roy	raw	רוי
		crude	
roykh, der	roykh	smoke	רויך, דער
		fume	
royt	royt	red	רויט
royz, di	·royz	rose	רויז, די
rozeve	raw-zeh-veh	pink	ראָזעווע
		rosy	
rozhinke, di	raw-zhin-keh	raisin	ראָזשינקע, די
ru, di	roo	calm	רו, די
		rest	
		quiet	
ruakh, der	*roo*-ahkh	ghost	רוח, דער
		devil	
rufn	*roof*-n	to call	רופֿן
ruik	*roo*-ik	calm	רויִק
		quiet	
rukn, der	*rook*-n	back	רוקן, דער
ruknbeyn, der	*rook*-n-bayn	spine	רוקנביין, דער

sakhakl, der	sah-*khah*-kil	sum total	סך־הכּל, דער
sakone, di	sah-*kaw*-neh	danger threat	סכּנה, די
sakonedik	sah-*kaw*-neh-dik	dangerous	סכּנהדיק
salat, der	sah-*laht*	salad lettuce	סאַלאַט, דער
sam, der	sahm	poison venom	סם, דער
samet, der	*sah*-meht	velvet	סאַמעט, דער
sardinke, di	sahr-*deen*-keh	sardine	סאַרדינקע, די
saydn	*seid*-n	unless but	סײַדן
say vi say	*sei* vee *sei*	anyway in any case	סײַ ווי סײַ
sekunde, di	seh-*koon*-deh	second (time unit)	סעקונדע, די
selerye, di	seh-*lehr*-yeh	celery	סעלעריע, די
sendvitsh, der	*sehnd*-vitch	sandwich	סענדוויטש, דער
september, der	sehp-*tehm*-behr	September	סעפּטעמבער, דער
servetke, di	sehr-*veht*-keh	napkin	סערוועטקע, די
seyfer, der	*say*-fehr	religious book	ספֿר, דער
seykhl, der	*saykh*-l	reason sense intellect	שׂכל, דער
sgule, di	s-*goo*-leh	remedy solution	סגולה, די
sha!	shah	Hush! Quiet!	שאַ!
shabes, der	*shah*-behs	Saturday	שבת, דער
shadkhn, der	*shahd*-khn	marriage broker	שדכן, דער
shafe, di	*shah*-feh	closet cupboard	שאַפֿע, די
shakhris, der	*shahkh*-riss	morning prayer	שחרית, דער
shal, di	shahl	scarf shawl	שאַל, די
shames, der	*shah*-mehs	sexton, Jewish	שמשׂ, דער
shampu, der	shahm-*poo*	shampoo	שאַמפּו, דער

shande, di	*shahn*-deh	shame	שאַנדע, די
sharbn, der	*shahrb*-n	skull	שאַרבּי דער
sharf	shahrf	sharp keen	שאַרף
shatn	*shaht*-n	to harm to hurt	שאַטן
shatsn	*shahts*-n	to estimate to appraise	שאַצן
shayern	*shei*-ehr-n	to scrub to scour	שײַערן
shaynen	*shei*-nehn	to shine to glow	שײַנען
shefe, di	*sheh*-feh	plenty abundance	שפֿע, די
shefedik	*sheh*-feh-dik	abundant prolific	שפֿעדיק
shemevdik	*sheh*-mehv-dik	shy bashful	שעמעוודיק
shenk, di	shehnk	tavern	שענק, די
shenken	*shehnk*-en	to donate	שענקען
shenken	*shehnk*-en	to pardon to forgive	שענקען
sheps, der	ʂhehps	sheep	שעפּס, דער
shepsnfleysh, dos	*shehps*-n-flaysh	mutton	שעפּסנפֿלייש, דאָס
shepsn-kotlet, der	*shehps*-n-kawt- leht	lamb chop	שעפּסן־קאָטלעט, דער
sheptshen	*shehp*-chehn	to whisper	שעפּטשען
sher, di	shehr	scissors	שער, די
sherer, der	*sheh*-rehr	barber	שערער, דער
shern	*shehr*-n	to cut to shear	שערן
sheygets, der	*shay*-gehts	Gentile (young male)	שייגעץ, דער
sheyden zikh	*shayd*-n zikh	to part	שיידן זיך
sheyln	*shayl*-n	to peel	שיילן
sheytl, dos	*shay*-til	wig, traditional Jewish woman's wig	שייטל, דאָס
sheyn	shayn	beautiful handsome pretty	שיין
sheynkayt, di	*shayn*-keit	beauty	שיינקייט, די
sheynkayt-salon, der	*shayn*-keit-sah- lawn	beauty parlor	שיינקייט־סאַלאָן, דער

shidekh, der	*shee*-dehkh	marriage match	שידוך, דער
shif, di	sheef	ship vessel	שיף, די
shifl, dos	*sheef*-l	boat	שיפֿל, דאָס
shiker	*shee*-kehr	drunk	שיכּור
shiker, der	*shee*-kehr	drunkard	שיכּור, דער
shikn	*sheek*-n	to send	שיקן
shikse, di	*sheek*-seh	Gentile (young fem.)	שיקסע, די
shilshl, der	*sheel*-shl	diarrhea	שילשול, דער
shiltn	*shelt*-n	to curse	שילטן
shirem, der	*shee*-rehm	umbrella	שירעם, דער
shisl, di	*shees*-l	bowl	שיסל, די
shisn	*shees*-n	to shoot	שיסן
shive, di	*shee*-veh	mourning period (Jewish)	שבֿעה, די
shkheyne, di	*shkhay*-neh	neighbor (fem.)	שכנה, די
shkheyneshaft, di	*shkhay*-neh-shahft	neighborhood	שכנישאַפֿט, די
shklaf, der	shklahf	slave	שקלאַף, דער
shklaferay, dos	shklah-feh-*rei*	slavery	שקלאַפֿעריַי, דאָס
shlang, di	shlahng	snake	שלאַנג, די
shlank	shlahnk	slender slim	שלאַנק
shlaydern	*shlei*-dehr-n	to hurl to fling	שליַידערן
shlayfn	*shleif*-n	to polish to sharpen	שליַיפֿן
shlekht	shlehkht	bad evil	שלעכט
shlepn	*shlehp*-n	to pull to drag	שלעפּן
shleper, der	*shleh*-pehr	tramp (sl.) incompetent and hopeless person (sl.)	שלעפּער, דער
shleyf, di	shlayf	temple (anat.)	שלייף, די
shleykes, di	*shlay*-kehs	suspenders	שלייקעס, די
shlimazl, der	shli-*mahz*-l	unlucky person ne'er do well	שלימזל, דער
shlimiel, der	shli-*meel*	inept person	שלימיעל, דער
shlimazldik	shlee-*mahz*-l-dik	unlucky	שלימזלדיק
shlingen	*shleeng*-en	to swallow to devour	שלינגען

shlisl, der	*shlees*-l	key	שליסל, דער
shlisn	*shlees*-n	to close	שליסן
shlof, der	shlawf	sleep	שלאָף, דער
shlofn	*shlawf*-n	to sleep	שלאָפֿן
shlofrok, der	*shlawf*-rawk	robe	שלאָפֿראָק, דער
		housecoat	
shloftsimer, der	*shlawf*-tsee-mehr	bedroom	שלאָפֿצימער, דער
shlogn	*shlawg*-n	to hit	שלאָגן
		to strike	
		to beat	
shlos, der	shlawss	lock	שלאָס, דער
shlump, der	shloomp	slob	שלומפֿ, דער
shmadn	*shmahd*-n	to convert to Christianity	שמדן
shmalts, dos	shmahlts	animal fat (as food)	שמאַלץ, דאָס
shmant, der	shmahnt	sweet cream	שמאַנט, דער
shmate, di	*shmah*-teh	rag	שמאַטע, די
shmaysn	*shmeis*-n	to thrash	שמײַסן
		to whip	
shmegege, der	shmeh-*geh*-geh	fool (sl.)	שמעגעגע, דער
shmekn	*shmehk*-n	to smell	שמעקן
shmendrik, der	*shmehn*-drik	nincompoop (sl.)	שמענדריק, דער
		fool (sl.)	
shmeykhl, der	*shmay*-khil	smile	שמייכל, דער
shmeykhlen	*shmaykh*-lehn	to smile	שמייכלען
		to grin	
shmid, der	shmeed	blacksmith	שמיד, דער
shminke, di	*shmeen*-keh	make-up	שמינקע, די
		rouge	
shmirkez, der	*shmeer*-kehz	cream cheese	שמירקעז, דער
shmirekhts, dos	*shmeer*-ehkhts	lubricant	שמירעכטס, דאָס
		lotion	
		grease	
shmirn	*shmeer*-n	to smear	שמירן
		to grease	
shmitz, der	shmeets	lash	שמיץ, דער
		spank	
shmok, der	shmawk	penis	שמאָק, דער
		self made fool	
shmue, di	*shmoo*-eh	rumor	שמועה, די
shmues, der	*shmoo*-ehs	chat	שמועס, דער

shmuesn	*shmoo*-ehs-n	to talk to chat	שמועסן
shmuts, dos	shmoots	dirt filth	שמוץ, דאָס
shmutsik	*shmoo*-tsik	filthy dirty smutty	שמוציק
shnapn	*shnahp*-n	to sniff around to spy	שנאַפן
shnaps, der	shnahps	liquor whiskey	שנאַפּס, דער
shnayder, der	*shnei*-dehr	tailor	שנײַדער, דער
shnaydn	*shneid*-n	to cut	שנײַדן
shnel	shnehl	quick	שנעל
shney, der	shnay	snow	שניי, דער
shnips, der	shneeps	necktie	שניפּס, דער
shnorer, der	*shnaw*-rehr	beggar cheapskate (sl.)	שנאָרער, דער
shnuk, der	shnook	snout jerk (sl.)	שנוק, דער
shnur, di	shnoor	daughter-in-law	שנור, די
sho, di	shaw	hour	שעה, די
shofer, der	shaw-*fehr*	driver chauffeur	שופר, דער
shokhn, der	*shawkh*-n	neighbor (masc.)	שכן, דער
shoklen	*shawk*-lehn	to rock to shake	שאָקלען
shokolad, der	shaw-kaw-*lahd*	candy bar chocolate	שאָקאָלאַד, דער
sholekhts, di	*shaw*-lehkhts	shell peel skin	שאָלעכץ, די
sholem, der	*shaw*-lehm	peace	שלום, דער
sholem-aleykhem	shaw-lehm-ah-*lay*-khehm	hello	שלום־עליכם
sholiakh, der	shaw-*lee*-ahkh	messenger	שליח, דער
shos, der	shawss	shot discharge burst	שאָס, דער

shosey, der	shaw-*say*	highway	שאָסיי, דער
shotn, der	*shawt*-n	shadow shade	שאָטן, דער
shoyb, di	shoyb	window pane	שויב, די
shoykhet, der	*shoy*-kheht	ritual slaughterer	שוחט, דער
shoymer, der	*shoy*-mehr	guard	שומר, דער
shoyn	shoyn	already	שוין
shoyte, der	*shoy*-teh	fool blockhead	שוטה, דער
shpaltn	*shpahlt*-n	to split to crack	שפּאַלטן
shpan, der	shpahn	span	שפּאַן, דער
shpanung, di	*shpah*-noong	strain tension suspense	שפּאַנונג, די
shpas, der	shpahs	joke gag	שפּאַס, דער
shpatsirn	shpah-*tseer*-n	to walk to stroll	שפּאַצירן
shpayen	*shpei*-en	to spit	שפּײַען
shpayzkamer, di	*shpeiz*-kah-mehr	pantry	שפּײַזקאַמער, די
shpayzkrom, di	*shpeiz*-krawm	grocery food store	שפּײַזקראָם, די
shpet	shpeht	late	שפּעט
shpeter	*shpeh*-tehr	later afterwards	שפּעטער
shpigl, der	*shpeeg*-l	mirror	שפּיגל, דער
shpiler, der	*shpee*-lehr	player	שפּילער, דער
shpilke, di	*shpeel*-keh	pin	שפּילקע, די
shpilekhl, dos	*shpee*-lehkh-l	toy plaything	שפּילעכל, דאָס
shpiln	*shpeel*-n	to play to act (perform)	שפּילן
shpinat, der	shpee-*naht*	spinach	שפּינאַט, דער
shpitol, der	shpee-*tawl*	hospital	שפּיטאָל, דער
shpits, der	shpeets	tip top	שפּיץ, דער
shpogl nay	*shpawg*-l nei	brand-new spick and span	שפּאָגל נײַ

shporevdik	*shpaw*-rehv-dik	thrifty	שפּאָרעװודיק
shporn	*shpawr*-n	to save	שפּאָרן
		to economize	
shprakh, di	shprahkh	language	שפּראַך, די
shpringen	*shpreen*-gehn	to jump	שפּרינגען
		to leap	
shprits, der	shpreets	squirt	שפּריץ, דער
		shower	
shpritsn	*shpreets*-n	to splash	שפּריצן
		to sprinkle	
		to squirt	
shpur, di	shpoor	trace	שפּור, די
		track	
		footprint	
shpyon, der	*shpee*-awn	spy	שפּיאָן, דער
shrayber, der	*shrei*-behr	writer	שרײַבער, דער
shraybmashin, di	*shreib*-mah-shin	typewriter	שרײַבמאַשין, די
shraybn	*shreib*-n	to write	שרײַבן
shraybtish, der	*shreib*-tish	desk	שרײַבטיש, דער
shrayen	*shrei*-en	to shout	שרײַען
		to cry out	
		to yell	
shrek, di	shrehk	fear	שרעק, די
		terror	
		alarm	
shrekevdik	*shreh*-kehv-dik	timid	שרעקעװודיק
		fearful	
shreklekh	*shrehk*-lehkh	terrible	שרעקלעך
		frightening	
shrekn	*shrehk*-n	to frighten	שרעקן
		to terrify	
shroyf, der	shroyf	screw	שרויף, דער
		bolt	
shroyfn-tsier, der	*shroyf*-n-*tsee*-ehr	screwdriver	שרויפֿן־ציִער, דער
shtamlen	*shtahm*-lehn	to stammer	שטאַמלען
		to stutter	
shtarbn	*shtahr*-bn	to die	שטאַרבן
shtarbn fun hunger	*shtahr*-bn foon *hoon*-gehr	to starve	שטאַרבן פֿון הונגער

shtark	shtahrk	strong	שטאַרק
shtayer, der	*shtei*-ehr	tax	שטײַער, דער
shtayf	shteif	rigid stiff tight	שטײַף
shtayg, di	shteig	cage	שטײַג, די
shtaygn	*shteig*-n	to ascend to advance	שטײַגן
shteg, der	shtehg	path lane trail	שטעג, דער
shtekhn	*shtehkh*-n	to sting to stab	שטעכן
shtekn, der	*shtehk*-n	stick cane	שטעקן, דער
shtekshukh, der	*shtehk*-shookh	slipper	שטעקשוך, דער
shtele, di	*shteh*-leh	job position	שטעלע, די
shteln	*shtehl*-n	to put to set to place	שטעלן
shtendik	*shtehn*-dik	steady permanent	שטענדיק
shtern, der	*shtehr*-n	star	שטערן, דער
shtern, der	*shtehr*-n	forehead brow	שטערן, דער
shtetl, dos	*shteht*-l	small town	שטעטל, דאָס
shteyn, der	shtayn	stone rock	שטיין, דער
shteyn	shtayn	to stand	שטיין
shtiferay, dos	*shtee*-feh-rei	mischief	שטיפֿערײַ, דאָס
shtiferish	*shtee*-feh-rish	mischievous playful	שטיפֿעריש
shtifmame, di	*shteef*-mah-meh	stepmother	שטיפֿמאַמע, די
shtiftate, der	*shteef*-tah-teh	stepfather	שטיפֿטאַטע, דער
shtiftokhter, di	*shteef*-tawkh-tehr	stepdaughter	שטיפֿטאָכטער, די
shtifzun, der	*shteef*-zoon	stepson	שטיפֿזון, דער
shtik, dos	shteek	piece	שטיק, דאָס
shtikl, dos	*shteek*-l	bit	שטיקל, דאָס

shtiklekhvayz	*shteek*-lehkh-veiz	piecemeal (adv.)	שטיקלעכווײַז
shtil	shteel	quiet	שטיל
		silent	
		still	
shtilkayt, di	*shteel*-keit	quiet	שטילקייט, די
		silence	
shtime, di	*shtee*-meh	voice	שטימע, די
shtimen	*shtee*-mehn	to agree	שטימען
shtimen	*shtee*-mehn	to vote	שטימען
shtimtsetl, dos	*shteem*-tseht-l	ballot	שטימצעטל, דאָס
shtimung, di	*shtee*-moong	mood	שטימונג, די
		spirits	
shtinken	*shteen*-kehn	to stink	שטינקען
shtitsn	*shteets*-n	to support	שטיצן
		to countenance	
shtivl, der	*shteev*-l	boot	שטיוול, דער
shtof, der	shtawf	matter	שטאָף, דער
		fabric	
		cloth	
shtokh, der	shtawkh	prick	שטאָך, דער
		sting	
		stitch	
shtokh, der	shtawkh	sarcastic dig	שטאָך, דער
shtolts, der	shtawlts	pride	שטאָלץ, דער
shtolts	shtawlts	proud	שטאָלץ
shtot, di	shtawt	city	שטאָט, די
shtoyb, der	shtoyb	dust	שטויב, דער
		pollen	
shtoybzoyger, der	*shtoyb*-zoyg-ehr	vacuum cleaner	שטויבזויגער, דער
shtrebn	*shtrehb*-n	to strive	שטרעבן
shtreng	shtrehng	severe	שטרענג
		strict	
shtrengkayt, di	*shtrehng*-keit	severity	שטרענגקייט, די
		rigor	
shtrik, der	shtreek	rope	שטריק, דער
shtrikl, dos	*shtreek*-l	string	שטריקל, דאָס
		leash	
shtrikeray, dos	shtree-keh-*rei*	knitting	שטריקערײַ, דאָס
shtrikn	*shtreek*-n	to knit	שטריקן

shtrof, di	shtrawf	punishment penalty	שטראָף, די
shtrofn	*shtrawf*-n	to punish	שטראָפֿן
shtshur, der	sh-*choor*	rat	שטשור, דער
shtub, di	shtoob	house home	שטוב, די
shtudirn	shtoo-*deer*-n	to study	שטודירן
shtul, di	shtool	chair	שטול, די
shtum	shtoom	mute dumb	שטום
shtunk, der	shtoonk	stinker	שטונק, דער
shtup, der	shtoop	sexual intercourse (sl.)	שטופּ, דער
shtupn	*shtoop*-n	to push to shove	שטופּן
shturem, der	*shtoo*-rehm	storm	שטורעם, דער
shtus, der	shtoos	folly nonsense	שטות, דער
shtusik	*shtoo*-sik	foolish ludicrous	שטותיק
shuflod, der	*shoof*-lawd	drawer	שופֿלאָד, דער
shukh, der	shookh	shoe	שוך, דער
shukhbendl, dos	*shookh*-behnd-l	shoelace	שוכבענדל, דאָס
shul, di	shool	synagogue school	שול, די
shuld, di	shoold	guilt blame fault	שולד, די
shuldik	*shool*-dik	guilty	שולדיק
shuldikayt, di	*shool*-dee-keit	obligation	שולדיקייט, די
shushken	*shoosh*-kehn	to whisper	שושקען
shuster, der	*shoo*-stehr	shoemaker	שוסטער, דער
shutef, der	*shoo*-tehf	partner	שותּף, דער
shvakh	shvahkh	weak faint feeble	שוואַך
shvakhkayt, di	*shvahkh*-keit	weakness fraility	שוואַכקייט, די
shvakhkepik	*shvahkh*-keh-pik	feeble-minded	שוואַכקעפּיק

shvanger	shvahn-gehr	pregnant	שוואַנגער
shvants, der	shvahnts	person who behaves stupidly	שוואַנץ, דער
shvarts	shvahrts	black	שוואַרץ
shvebele, dos	shveh-beh-leh	match (for lighting)	שוועבעלע, דאָס
shvegerin, di	shveh-geh-rin	sister-in-law	שוועגעווין, די
shveml, dos	shvehm-l	mushroom	שוועמל, דאָס
shver, der	shvehr	father-in-law	שווער, דער
shver	shvehr	difficult	שווער
		heavy	
shvern	shvehr-n	to swear	שווערן
shvester, di	shvehs-tehr	sister	שוועסטער, די
shvesterkind, dos	shvehs-tehr-keend	cousin	שוועסטערקינד, דאָס
shveys, der	shvays	sweat	שווייס, דער
shveytser kez, der	shvayts-ehr kehz	swiss cheese	שווייצער קעז, דער
shviger, di	shvee-gehr	mother-in-law	שוויגער, די
shvimen	shvee-mehn	to swim	שווימען
shvindl, der	shveend-l	fraud	שווינדל, דער
		swindle	
shvitsbod, di	shveets-bawd	steam bath	שוויצבאָד, די
shvitsn	shveets-n	to sweat	שוויצן
		to perspire	
shvoger, der	shvaw-gehr	brother-in-law	שוואָגער, דער
shvom, der	shvawm	sponge	שוואָם, דער
		mushroom	
shvue, di	shvoo-ih	oath	שבֿועה, די
sibe, di	see-bih	cause	סיבה, די
		reason	
sider, der	see-dihr	Jewish daily prayer book	סידור, דער
sikhsekh	seekh-sihkh	conflict	סיכסוך, דער
		controversy	
		feud	
simen, der	see-mihn	mark	סימן, דער
		sign	
simfonye, di	sim-fawn-yeh	symphony	סימפֿאָניע, די
simkhe, di	seem-kheh	joyous celebration	שמחה, די
simptom, der	simp-tawm	symptom	סימפּטאָם, דער
sine, di	see-nih	hatred	שנאה, די
		hate	
sinyak, der	seen-yahk	bruise	סיניאַק, דער

skale, di	*skah*-leh	scale (of measurement)	סקאַלע, די
skalp, der	skahlp	scalp	סקאַלפֿ, דער
skandal, der	skahn-*dahl*	scandal	סקאַנדאַל, דער
		outrage	
skhar, der	skhahr	reward	שׂכר, דער
skhires, di	*skhee*-rehs	salary	שכירות, די
		pay	
skhoyre, di	*skhoy*-reh	wares	סחורה, די
		goods	
		commodity	
skore, di	*skaw*-reh	crust	סקאָרע, די
skovrode, di	*skawv*-raw-deh	frying pan	סקאָוואָראָדע, די
sloy, der	sloy	jar	סלוי, דער
slup, der	sloop	pole	סלופֿ, דער
		post	
smetene, di	*smeh*-teh-neh	sour cream	סמעטענע, די
snobish	*snaw*-beesh	snobbish	סנאָביש
sod, der	sawd	orchard	סאָד, דער
sod, der	sawd	secret	סוד, דער
sof, der	sawf	conclusion	סוף, דער
		end	
sof-vokh, der	sawf-*vawkh*	weekend	סוף־וואָך, דער
sof, on a	*awn* ah *sawf*	endless	סוף, אָן אַ
sofe, di	*saw*-feh	sofa	סאָפֿע, די
sofek, der	*saw*-fehk	doubt	ספֿק, דער
sofek, on	*awn saw*-fehk	doubtless	ספֿק, אָן
sofekdik	*saw*-fehk-dik	doubtful	ספֿקדיק
		dubious	
soldat, der	sawl-*daht*	soldier	סאָלדאַט, דער
sort, der	sawrt	kind	סאָרט, דער
		sort	
		brand	
sotn, der	*sawt*-n	Satan	שטן, דער
sos, der	sawss	sauce	סאָוס, דער
		dressing	
soykher, der	*soy*-khihr	dealer	סוחר, דער
		merchant	
soyne, der	*soy*-neh	enemy	שׂונא, דער
		foe	
sparzhe, di	*spahr*-zheh	asparagus	ספּאַרזשע, די

spektakl, der	spehk-*tahk*-l	spectacle sight	ספּעקטאַקל, דער
spetsyel	spehts-*yehl*	special especially	ספּעציעל
spodik, der	*spaw*-dik	fur hat (traditional)	ספּאָדיק, דער
stade, di	*stah*-deh	herd flock	סטאַדע, די
stanik, der	*stah*-nik	brassiere	סטאַניק, דער
stantsye, di	*stahnts*-yeh	station	סטאַנציע, די
statue, di	*stah*-too-eh	statue	סטאַטוע, די
staytsh	steitch	How come? How is that possible?	סטײַטש
stav, der	stahv	pond pool	סטאַװ, דער
stelye, di	*stehl*-yeh	ceiling	סטעליע, די
stolyer, der	*stawl*-yehr	carpenter cabinet maker	סטאָליער, דער
strakhirung, di	strah-*khee*-roong	insurance	סטראַכירונג, די
strashen	*strah*-shehn	to threaten	סטראַשען
sude, di	*soo*-deh	repast feast banquet	סעודה, די
sufit, der	soo-*feet*	ceiling	סופֿיט, דער
sveter, der	*sveh*-tehr	sweater	סװעטער, דער
taam, der	tahm	taste zest	טעם, דער
tabak, der	*tah*-bahk	tobacco	טאַבאַק, דער
take	*tah*-keh	indeed really	טאַקע
takhlis, der	*tahkh*-lis	result practical purpose	תּכלית
takhrikhim, di	tahkh-*ree*-kheem	burial shrouds (Jewish)	תּכריכים, די
taksi, der	*tahk*-see	taxicab	טאַקסי, דער

takt, der	tahkt	tact	טאַקט, דער
taktish	*tahk*-teesh	tactical	טאַקטיש
		tactful	
talant, der	tah-*lahnt*	talent	טאַלאַנט, דער
		gift	
talantirt	tah-lahn-*teert*	talented	טאַלאַנטירט
		gifted	
talis, der	*tah*-lis	prayer shawl (Jewish)	טלית, דער
talmid, der	*tahl*-mid	student	תלמיד, דער
		pupil	
talmid-khokhem, der	*tahl*-mid-*khaw*-khehm	learned man Jewish scholar	תלמיד־חכם, דער
talye, di	*tahl*-yeh	waist	טאַליע, די
tam, der	tahm	naive person	תּם, דער
		moron	
		half-wit	
tamevate	*tah*-meh-vah-teh	foolish	תּמעוואַטע
		half-witted	
tante, di	*tahn*-teh	aunt	טאַנטע, די
tantsn	*tahnts*-n	to dance	טאַנצן
tapn	*tahp*-n	to feel	טאַפּן
		to touch	
tareram, der	tah-reh-*rahm*	fuss	טאַרעראַם, דער
tash, di	tahsh	bag	טאַש, די
		purse	
tate, der	*tah*-teh	father	טאַטע, דער
		dad	
tate-mame, di	*tah*-teh-*mah*-meh	parents	טאַטע־מאַמע, די
tats, di	tahts	platter	טאַץ, די
		tray	
tayer	*tei*-ehr	dear	טײַער
		adorable	
		expensive	
		beloved	
tayer haltn	*tei*-ehr *hahlt*-n	to cherish	טײַער האַלטן
taykh, der	teikh	river	טײַך, דער
taykhl, dos	*teikh*-l	stream	טײַכל, דאָס
		creek	
tayne, di	*tei*-nih	claim	טענה, די
		complaint	

tayneg, der	*tei*-nehg	pleasure delight zest	תענוג, דער
taynen	*tei*-nehn	to maintain to argue to contend	טענהן
taynes, hobn	*haw*-bin *tei*-nehs	to reproach	טענות, האָבן
taytsh, der/di	teich	meaning; the Yiddish language; translation into Yiddish	טײַטש, דער/די
tayve, di	*tei*-veh	passion lust	תּאווה, די
tayvl, der	*teiv*-l	devil fiend	טײַוול, דער
teater, der	teh-*ah*-tehr	theater	טעאַטער, דער
teke, di	*teh*-keh	file folder briefcase	טעקע, די
telefon, der	teh-leh-*fawn*	telephone	טעלעפֿאָן, דער
telefonirn	teh-leh-faw- *neer*-n	to telephone	טעלעפֿאָנירן
telegrafirn	teh-leh-grah- *feer*-n	to telegraph	טעלעגראַפֿירן
telegram, di	teh-leh-*grahm*	telegram	טעלעגראַם, די
teler, der	*teh*-lehr	plate	טעלער, דער
televizye, di	teh-leh-*vzez*-yeh	television	טעלעוויזיע, די
teme, di	*teh*-meh	topic theme	טעמע, די
temperament, der	tehm-peh-rah- *mehnt*	temperament	טעמפּעראַמענט, דער
tenis, der	*teh*-niss	tennis	טעניס, דער
tepekh, der	*teh*-pehkh	carpet rug	טעפּעך, דער
tepl, dos	*tehp*-l	cup	טעפּל, דאָס
terase, di	teh-*rah*-seh	terrace	טעראַסע, די
terets, der	*teh*-rehts	pretext justification	תּירוץ, דער
termometer, der	tehr-maw-*meh*- tehr	thermometer	טערמאָמעטער, דער
teror, der	teh-*rawr*-	terror (political)	טעראָר, דער
tetsl, dos	*tehts*-l	saucer	טעצל, דאָס
tey, di	tay	tea	טיי, די

teyg, dos	tayg	dough batter	טייג, דאָס
teykef	*tay*-kehf	at once immediately	תּיכּף
teyl, der	tayl	part division	טייל, דער
teylefl, der	*tey*-lehf-l	teaspoon	טיילעפֿל, דער
teyln zikh	*tayl*-n zikh	to divide to share	טיילן זיך
teytl, der	*tayt*-l	date (fruit)	טייטל, דער
tfile, di	t-*fee*-leh	prayer	תּפֿילה, די
tif	teef	deep intense profound	טיף
tifkayt, di	*teef*-keit	depth profundity	טיפֿקייט, די
tiger, der	*tee*-gehr	tiger	טיגער, דער
tint, di	teent	ink	טינט, די
tip, der	teep	type kind	טיפּ, דער
tipesh, der	*tee*-pehsh	dolt fool	טיפּש, דער
tipirn	tee-*peer*-n	to type	טיפּירן
tipshes, dos	*teep*-shihs	folly foolishness	טיפּשות, דאָס
tir, di	teer	door	טיר, די
tish, der	teesh	table	טיש, דער
tishtekh, der	*teesh*-tehkh	tablecloth	טישטעך, דער
tnoim, di	t-*naw*-im	terms conditions	תּנאָים, די
toes, der	*taw*-ehs	error mistake	טעות, דער
tog, der	tawg	day	טאָג, דער
toglikht, dos	*tawg*-likht	daylight	טאָגליכט, דאָס
tokhes, der	*taw*-khehs	buttocks	תּחת, דער
tokhes-leker, der	*taw*-khehs-*leh*-kehr	ass-kisser	תּחת-לעקער, דער
tokhter, di	*tawkh*-tehr	daughter	טאָכטער, די
tolerirn	taw-leh-*reer*-n	to tolerate	טאָלערירן
tombank, der	*tawm*-bahnk	work counter	טאָמבאַנק, דער

tomer	*taw*-mehr	if perhaps	טאָמער
tomid	*taw*-mid	always ever invariably	תמיד
ton	tawn	to do to do to	טאָן
top, der	tawp	pot	טאָפּ, דער
tormoz, der	*tawr*-mawz	brake	טאָרמאָז, דער
torn nit	*tawr*-n nit	to not be permitted to	טאָרן ניט
tost, der	tawst	toast	טאָסט, דער
toy, der	toy	dew	טוי, דער
toyb, di	toyb	dove pigeon	טויב, די
toyb	toyb	deaf	טויב
toyer, der	*taw*-yehr	gate	טויער, דער
toygn	*toyg*-n	to be adequate	טויגן
toyt	toyt	dead	טויט
toyve, di	*toy*-veh	favor kindness	טובה, די
toyznt	*toy*-zint	thousand	טויזנט
traditsye, di	trah-*deets*-yeh	tradition	טראַדיציע, די
tragedye, di	trah-*gehd*-yeh	tragedy	טראַגעדיע, די
tragish	*trah*-gish	tragic	טראַגיש
trakht, di	trahkht	womb	טראַכט, די
trakhtn	*trahkht*-n	to think	טראַכטן
traybn	*treib*-n	to drive	טרײַבן
trefn	*trehf*-n	to meet to encounter	טרעפֿן
trefn	*trehf*-n	to guess	טרעפֿן
trefshpil, di	*trehf*-shpeel	puzzle	טרעפֿשפּיל, די
treger, der	*trehg*-ehr	porter	טרעגער, דער
trenen	*treh*-nehn	to rip	טרענען
trenen	*treh*-nehn	to fornicate (sl.)	טרענען
trep, di	trehp	stairs	טרעפּ, די
trepl, dos	*trehp*-l	step stair	טרעפּל, דאָס
trer, di	trehr	tear	טרער, די

tretar, der	treh-*tahr*	sidewalk	טרעטאַר, דער
tretn	*treht*-n	to step to tread	טרעטן
treyf	trayf	non-kosher, not conforming to dietary laws (adj.)	טרייף
treyslen	*trayss*-lehn	to shake	טרייסלען
treyst, di	trayst	consolation comfort	טרייסט, די
trikenen	*tree*-keh-nehn	to dry to drain	טריקענען
trinken	*treen*-kehn	to drink	טרינקען
trinkgelt, dos	*treenk*-gehlt	tip gratuity	טרינקגעלט, דאָס
trogn	*trawg*-n	to wear to bear to carry	טראָגן
trombenik, der	*trawm*-beh-nik	ne'er-do-well (sl.) bum (sl.)	טראָמבעניק, דער
trop, der	trawp	stress emphasis	טראָפּ, דער
trop, der	trawp	musical accents	טראָפּ, דער
troyer, der	*traw*-yehr	grief sorrow mourning	טרויער, דער
troyerik	*traw*-yeh-rik	sad mournful sorrowful	טרויעריק
troyern	*traw*-yeh-rin	to grieve for to mourn	טרויערן
trukn	*trook*-n	dry	טרוקן
trumeyt, der	troo-*mayt*	trumpet bugle	טרומייט, דער
truskavke, di	troos-*kahv*-keh	strawberry	טרוסקאַווקע, די
tsaar, der	tsahr	grief sorrow	צער, דער
tsadik, der	*tsah*-dik	pious/saintly man	צדיק, דער
tsamen	*tsah*-mehn	to tame to restrain	צאַמען

tsatske, di	*tsahts*-keh	plaything toy trinket	צאַצקע, די
tsavoe, di	tsah-*vaw*-ih	will testament	צוואה, די
tsayt, di	tseit	time season	צײַט, די
tsaytik	*tsei*-tik	ripe mature	צײַטיק
tsaytung, di	*tsei*-toong	newspaper	צײַטונג, די
tsdoke, di	tseh-*daw*-keh	charity alms	צדקה, די
tsebrekhn	tseh-*brehkh*-n	to smash to break up	צעברעכן
tsebreklen	tseh-*brehk*-lehn	to crumble	צעברעקלען
tsedreyt	tseh-*drayt*	mixed up emotionally ally	צעדרייט
tselokhes, oyf	oyf tseh-*law*-khehs	for spite	צו להכעיס, אויף
tsehitsn	tseh-*heets*-n	to warm up to excite	צעהיצן
tsement, der	tseh-*mehnt*	cement	צעמענט, דער
tsemishn	tseh-*meesh*-n	to mix up to confuse	צעמישן
tsemisht	tseh-*meesht*	mixed up	צעמישט
tsemishung, di	tseh-*mee*-shoong	mix up confusion	צעמישונג, די
tsemoln	tseh-*mawl*-n	to grind up	צעמאָלן
tsen	tsehn	ten	צען
tsenter	*tsehn*-tehr	tenth	צענטער
tseremonye, di	tesh-reh-*mawn*- yeh	ceremony	צערעמאָניע, די
tsesarke, di	tseh-*sahr*-keh	honeydew	צעסאַרקע, די
tsesheydung, di	tseh-*shay*-doong	separation	צעשיידונג, די
tseshitn	tseh-*sheet*-n	to scatter	צעשיטן
tseshnaydn	tseh-*shneid*-n	to cut	צעשנײַדן
tseshpreytn	tseh-*shprayt*-n	to spread to disperse	צעשפּרייטן
tseteyln	tseh-*tayl*-n	to divide to separate	צעטיילן

tsetl, der	*tseht*-l	note slip tag	צעטל, דער
tsetretn	tseh-*treht*-n	to trample to crush	צעטרעטן
tsetumlen	tseh-*toom*-lehn	to confuse to bewilder	צעטומלען
tsetumlt	tseh-*toom*-lt	confused bewildered	צעטומלט
tseykhenen	*tsay*-kheh-nehn	to draw to design	צייכענען
tseylem, der	*tsay*-lehm	cross	צלם, דער
tseyln	*tsayl*-n	to count to number	ציילן
tsezetst vern	tseh-*zehtst* vehrn-n	to burst	צעזעצט ווערן
tshaynik, der	*chei*-nik	teapot	טשײַניק, דער
tshek, der	chehk	bank check	טשעק, דער
tshemodan, der	cheh-*maw*-dahn	suitcase	טשעמאָדאַן, דער
tshepen	*cheh*-pehn	to touch to handle	טשעפּען
tshepen zikh tsu	*cheh*-pehn zikh tsoo	to annoy to bother	טשעפּען זיך צו
tsherepakhe, di	cheh-reh-*pah*- kheh	turtle	טשערעפּאַכע, די
tshernitse, di	*chehr*-nee-tseh	huckleberry	טשערניצע, די
tsholent, der	*chawl*-nt	traditional Sabbath stew	טשאָלנט, דער
tshudne	*chood*-neh	uncanny queer bizarre	טשודנע
tshvok, der	chvawk	nail	טשוואָק, דער
tsi	tsee	whether if	צי
tsibele, di	*tsee*-beh-leh	onion	ציבעלע, די
tsibur, der	*tsee*-boor	community group	ציבור, דער
tsien	*tsee*-en	to pull to draw to tug	ציִען
tsig, di	tseeg	goat	ציג, די

tsigar, der	tsee-*gahr*	cigar	ציגאַר, דער
tsigl, der	*tseeg*-l	brick	ציגל, דער
tsikhtik	*tseekh*-tik	clean tidy neat	ציכטיק
tsil, der	tseel	purpose aim goal	ציל, דער
tsimer, der	*tsee*-mehr	room	צימער, דער
tsimering, der	*tsee*-meh-ring	cinnamon	צימערינג, דער
tsimes, der	*tsee*-mehs	vegetable or fruit stew a big deal (sl.)	צימעס, דער
tsin, dos	tsin	tin	צין, דאָס
tsireven	*tsee*-reh-vehn	to darn to mend	צירעווען
tsirk, der	tseerk	circus	צירק, דער
tsirung, di	*tsee*-roong	jewelry	צירונג, די
tsitern	*tsee*-tehr-n	to tremble to shiver to quake	ציטערן
tsivilizatsye, di	tsee-vee-lee-*zahts*-yeh	civilization	ציוויליזאַציע, די
tsofn, der	*tsawf*-n	north	צפֿון, דער
tsofn-mayrevdik	*tsawf*-n-*mei*-rehv-dik	northwestern	צפֿון־מערבֿדיק
tsofn-mizrakhdik	*tsawf*-n-*meez*-rahkh-dik	northeastern	צפֿון־מיזרחדיק
tsofndik	*tsawf*-n-dik	northern	צפֿונדיק
tsol, di	tsawl	number	צאָל, די
tsolfray	*tsawl*-frei	duty-free	צאָלפֿרײַ
tsoln	*tsawl*-n	to pay	צאָלן
tsolung, di	*tsaw*-loong	payment	צאָלונג, די
tson, der	tsawn	tooth	צאָן, דער
tsonbershtl, dos	*tsawn*-behr-shtl	toothbrush	צאָנבערשטל, דאָס
tsondokter, der	*tsawn*-dawk-tehr	dentist	צאָנדאָקטער, דער
tsonpaste, di	*tsawn*-pahss-teh	tooth paste	צאָנפּאַסטע, די
tsonveytik, der	*tsawn*-vay-tik	toothache	צאָנווייטיק, דער
tsore, di	*tsaw*-reh	trouble woe	צרה, די

tsoredik	*tsaw*-reh-dik	lamentable	צרהדיק
		miserable	
		wretched	
tsores, di	*tsaw*-rehs	misery; troubles	צרות, די
tsoye, di	*tsoy*-eh	excrement	צואה, די
tsu	tsoo	at (time)	צו
		toward	
		at (for the price of)	
		to	
		too	
tsu der tsayt	*tsoo* dehr tseit	on time	צו דער צײַט
tsu gezunt	tsoo geh-*zoont*	To health!	צו געזונט
		God bless you! (coll.)	
tsuayln	*tsoo*-eil-n	to hasten	צואײַלן
		to urge on	
tsubindn	*tsoo*-beend-n	to tie	צובינדן
		to lash	
tsudekn	*tsoo*-dehk-n	to cover	צודעקן
tsufal, der	*tsoo*-fahl	accident	צופֿאַל, דער
		chance	
tsu fil	*tsoo* fil	too much	צו פֿיל
tsufridn shteln	tsoo-*freed*-n	to suit (please)	צופֿרידן שטעלן
	shtehl-n		
tsufridn	tsoo-*freed*-n	glad	צופֿרידן
		content	
		pleased	
tsufridnkayt, di	tsoo-*freed*-n-keit	satisfaction	צופֿרידנקייט, די
		gratification	
		contentment	
tsug, der	tsoog	train	צוג, דער
tsugevoynt	*tsoo*-geh-voynt	used to	צוגעוווינט
		accustomed to	
tsugreytn	*tsoo*-grayt-n	to prepare	צוגרייטן
		to arrange	
tsuker, der	*tsoo*-kehr	sugar	צוקער, דער
tsukerkrenk, di	*tsoo*-kehr-krehnk	diabetes	צוקערקרענק, די
tsukerl, dos	*tsoo*-kehr-l	piece of candy	צוקערל, דאָס
tsukuker, der	*tsoo*-koo-kehr	viewer	צוקוקער, דער
		spectator	

tsukukn zikh	*tsoo*-kook-n zikh	to watch	צוקוקן זיך
		to pay attention	
tsulib	tsoo-*leeb*	because of	צוליב
		on account of	
tsum bayshpil	tsoom *bei*-shpil	for example	צום בײַשפּיל
tsunemen	*tsoo*-neh-mehn	to take away	צונעמען
		to remove (from)	
tsunemenish, dos	*tsoo*-neh-meh-nish	nickname	צונעמעניש, דאָס
tsung, di	tsoong	tongue	צונג, די
tsurik	tsoo-*reek*	back	צוריק
tsurikkrign	tsoo-*reek*-kreeg-n	to retrieve	צוריקקריגן
		to recover	
tsurikkumen	tsoo-*reek*-koo-mehn	to come back	צוריקקומען
		to return	
tsuriktsien	tsoo-*reek*-tsee-en	to withdraw	צוריקציִען
		to pull back	
tsuriktsien zikh	tsoo-*reek*-tsee-en zikh	to retire	צוריקציִען זיך
		to retreat	
tsushtayer, der	*tsoo*-shtei-ehr	contribution	צושטײַער, דער
		donation	
tsushteln	*tsoo*-shtehl-n	to add	צושטעלן
		to provide	
tsutroy, der	*tsoo*-troy	trust	צוטרוי, דער
		confidence	
tsutshepenish, dos	*tsoo*-cheh-peh-nish	nuisance	צוטשעפּעניש, דאָס
		pest	
tsutsien	*tsoo*-tsee-en	to attract	צוציִען
		to lure	
tsuzamen	tsoo-*zah*-mehn	together	צוזאַמען
tsuzog, der	*tsoo*-zawg	promise	צוזאָג, דער
		pledge	
tsuzogn	*tsoo*-zawg-n	to promise	צוזאָגן
		to pledge	
tsvang, di	tsvahng	pliers	צוואַנג, די
tsvantsik	*tsvahn*-tsik	twenty	צוואַנציק
tsvayg, di	tsveig	branch	צווײַג, די
		bough	
tsvelf	tsvehlf	twelve	צוועלף
tsvelfter	*tsvehlf*-tehr	twelfth	צוועלפטער
tsvey	tsvay	two	צוויי

tsvey mol	*tsvay* mawl	twice	צוויי מאָל
tsveyendik	*tsvay*-ehn-dik	double dual	צוויייענדיק
tsveyter	*tsvay*-tehr	second	צווייטער
tsvies, dos	*tsvee*-ehs	hypocrisy	צביעות, דאָס
tsviling, der	*tsvee*-ling	twin(s)	צווילינג, דער
tsvishn	*tsveesh*-n	among between	צווישן
tsvuak, der	tsvoo-*ahk*	hypocrite	צבֿועק, דער
tulpan, der	tool-*pahn*	tulip	טולפּאַן, דער
tuml, der	*toom*-l	noise din	טומל, דער
tumldik	*toom*-l-dik	noisy boisterous	טומלדיק
tumor, der	*too*-mawr	tumor	טומאָר, דער
tunel, der	too-*nehl*	tunnel	טונעל, דער
tunfish, der	*toon*-fish	tuna fish	טונפֿיש, דער
tunken	*toon*-kehn	to dip	טונקען
tunkl	*toonk*-l	dark obscure	טונקל
turist, der	too-*reest*	tourist	טוריסט, דער
turme, di	*toor*-meh	jail prison	טורמע, די
tuts, der	toots	dozen	טוץ, דער
tuung, di	*too*-oong	action act	טוונג, די
tvue, di	*tvoo*-ih	grain cereal	תּבֿואה, די
ugerke, di	*oo*-gehr-keh	cucumber	אוגערקע, די
umbakant	*oom*-bah-kahnt	unknown obscure	אומבאַקאַנט
umet, der	*oo*-meht	sadness gloom	אומעט, דער

umetik	*oo*-meh-tik	sad lonesome	אומעטיק
umetum	*oo*-meh-toom	everywhere	אומעטום
umgeduld, di	*oom*-geh-doold	impatience	אומגעדולד, די
umgeduldik	*oom*-geh-dool-dik	impatient	אומגעדולדיק
umgelumpert	*oom*-geh-*loom*-pehrt	awkward clumsy	אומגעלומפּערט
umgerekht	*oom*-geh-rehkht	wrong unjust	אומגערעכט
umgern	*oom*-gehr-n	unwilling grudgingly	אומגערן
umgeveyntlekh	*oom*-geh-*vaynt*-lehkh	unusual extraordinary	אומגעוויינטלעך
umglik, dos	*oom*-gleek	accident misfortune	אומגליק, דאָס
umgliklekh	*oom*-gleek-lehkh	unfortunate unhappy	אומגליקלעך
umkern	*oom*-kehr-n	to return to restore	אומקערן
umklor	*oom*-klawr	obscure unclear	אומקלאָר
umkoved, der	*oom*-kaw-vihd	disgrace dishonor	אומכּבֿוד, דער
umkovedik	*oom*-*kaw*-vih-dik	derogatory	אומכּבֿודיק
ummiglekh	*oom*-*mehg*-lehkh	impossible	אוממיגלעך
umneytik	*oom*-nay-tik	unnecessary	אומנייטיק
umreyn	*oom*-rayn	unclean impure	אומריין
umru, di	*oom*-roo	anxiety uneasiness	אומרו, די
umruik	*oom*-roo-ik	restless anxious	אומרויִק
umruikayt, di	*oom*-roo-i-keit	anxiety	אומרויִקייט, די
umshuldik	*oom*-shool-dik	innocent	אומשולדיק
umveg, der	*oom*-vehg	roundabout way detour	אומוועג, דער
umverdik	*oom*-vehr-dik	unworthy	אומווערדיק
umvisndik	*oom*-*vees*-n-dik	ignorant	אומוויסנדיק
umzikher	*oom*-zee-khehr	precarious	אומזיכער

umzin, der	*oom*-zin	nonsense	אומזין, דער
umzist	oom-*zeest*	free	אומזיסט
umzist	oom-*zeest*	fruitless futile	אומזיסט
un	oon	and	און
undz	oonds	us	אונדז
undzer	*oon*-dzehr	our	אונדזער
undzerer	*oon*-dzeh-rehr	ours	אונדזערער
universal-krom, di	oo-nee-vehr-*sahl*- krawm	department store	אוניווערסאַל־קראָם, די
universitet, der	oo-nee-vehr-see- *teht*	university	אוניווערסיטעט, דער
unter	*oon*-tehr	under (prep.) beneath below underneath	אונטער
unterban, di	*oon*-tehr-bahn	subway	אונטערבאַן, די
unterhern	*oon*-tehr-*hehr*-n	to overhear	אונטערהערן
unterhern zikh	*oon*-tehr-*hehr*-n zikh	to eavesdrop	אונטערהערן זיך
unterkleyd, dos	*oon*-tehr klayd	slip petticoat	אונטערקלייד, דאָס
unterkoyfn	*oon*-tehr-koyf-n	to bribe	אונטערקויפֿן
unternemung, di	*oon*-tehr-neh- moong	undertaking enterprise	אונטערנעמונג, די
untersheyd, der	*oon*-tehr-shayd	difference	אונטערשייד, דער
untershlak, der	*oon*-tehr-shlahk	lining	אונטערשלאַק, דער
untertraybn	*oon*-tehr-treib-n	to urge on to goad	אונטערטרײַבן
untervesh, dos	*oon*-tehr-vehsh	underclothes underwear	אונטערוועש, דאָס
unterzogn	*oon*-tehr-*zawg*-n	to breathe into another's ear; to prompt	אונטערזאָגן
untn	*oont*-n	below (adv.) underneath bottom downstairs	אונטן
ureyniklekh, di	*oor*-ay-nik-lehkh	great-grandchildren	אוראייניקלעך, די

vagine, di	vah-*gee*-neh	vagina	װאַגינע, די
vakatsye, di	vah-*kahts*-yeh	vacation	װאַקאַציע, די
vaklen zikh	*vahk*-lehn zikh	to shake to wobble	װאַקלען זיך
vaks, der	vahks	wax	װאַקס, דער
vaksn	*vahks*-n	to grow	װאַקסן
vald, der	vahld	forest	װאַלד, דער
valfish, der	*vahl*-fish	whale	װאַלפיש, דער
valn, dos	*vahl*-n	election	װאַלן, דאָס
vandern	*vahn*-dehr-n	to wander	װאַנדערן
vane, di	*vah*-neh	bathtub	װאַנע, די
vant, di	vahnt	wall	װאַנט, די
vants, di	vahnts	bedbug	װאַנץ, די
varem	*vah*-rehm	warm affectionate	װאַרעם
varemen	*vah*-reh-mehn	to warm	װאַרעמען
varemkayt, di	*vah*-rehm-keit	warmth	װאַרעמקײט, די
varfn	*vahrf*-n	to throw to pitch	װאַרפן
vartn	*vahrt*-n	to wait (for)	װאַרטן
varum	vah-*room*	why	װאַרום
vaser, dos	*vah*-sehr	water	װאַסער, דאָס
vaser-zikher	*vah*-sehr-zee- khehr	waterproof	װאַסער־זיכער
vashn	*vahsh*-n	to wash to launder	װאַשן
vashtsimer, der	*vahsh*-tsee-mehr	lavatory bathroom	װאַשצימער, דער
vate, di	*vah*-teh	cotton	װאַטע, די
vatrones, dos	vah-*traw*-nehs	generosity	װאַתרונות, דאָס
vayb, dos	veib	wife	װײַב, דאָס
vayblekh	*veib*-lehkh	female feminine	װײַבלעך
vayl	veil	as long as since because	װײַל
vayle, di	*vei*-leh	while	װײַלע, די
vayn, der	vein	wine	װײַן, דער
vayn, vilder, der	*veel*-dehr vein	ivy	װײַן, װילדער, דער

vayntroyb, di	*vein*-troyb	grape	ווײַנטרויב, די
vays	veis	white	ווײַס
vayt	veit	far away	ווײַט
		distant	
		remote	
vayter	*vei*-tehr	farther	ווײַטער
		next	
		further	
		then	
vayter fun	*vei*-tehr foon	beyond	ווײַטער פֿון
vayzn	*veiz*-n	to show	ווײַזן
vaze, di	*vah*-zeh	vase	וואָזע, די
veg, der	vehg	way	וועג, דער
		path	
		road	
vegele, dos	*veh*-geh-leh	carriage (baby buggy)	וועגעלע, דאָס
vegn	*vehg*-n	to weigh	וועגן
vegn	*vehg*-n	about	וועגן
		regarding	
vel	vehl	shall	וועל
		will	
velkher	*vehl*-khehr	which	וועלכער
		what	
		whatever	
		whichever	
veln	*vehl*-n	to want	וועלן
		to wish	
velosiped, der	veh-law-see-*pehd*	bicycle	וועלאָסיפּעד, דער
veltshener nus, der	*vehl*-cheh-nehr noos	walnut	וועלטשענער נוס, דער
velt, di	vehlt	world	וועלט, די
vemen	*veh*-mehn	whom	וועמען
vemens	*veh*-mehns	whose	וועמענס
ven	vehn	when	ווען
		whenever	
vèn es iz	vehn ehs *eez*	ever (any time)	ווען עס איז
		sometimes	
ven nor	*vehn* nawr	whenever	ווען נאָר
vene, di	*veh*-neh	vein	וועגע, די
ventilator, der	vehn-tee-*lah*-tawr	electric fan	ווענטילאַטאָר, דער
ver	vehr	who	ווער

ver es iz	*vehr* ehs eez	anyone anybody	ווער עס איז
ver nor	*vehr* nawr	whoever	ווער נאָר
vern	*vehr*-n	to become	ווערן
vert, di/der	vehrt	value worth merit	ווערט, די/דער
vert, on a	*awn* ah *vehrt*	worthless	ווערט, אָן אַ
vertful	*vehrt*-fool	valuable	ווערטפֿול
vesh, dos	vehsh	wash laundry	וועש, דאָס
vesp, di	vehsp	wasp	וועספּ, די
vestl, dos	vehst-l	vest	וועסטל, דאָס
veter, der	*veh*-tehr	weather	וועטער, דער
vetn zikh	*veht*-n zikh	to bet to wager	וועטן זיך
vetshere, di	*veh*-cheh-reh	supper	וועטשערע, די
veverke, di	*veh*-vehr-keh	squirrel	וועווערקע, די
vey ton	*vay* tawn	to ache to hurt	וויי טאָן
veykh	vaykh	soft tender	ווייך
veykhn	*vayhk*-n	to soak	ווייכן
veyler, der	*vay*-lehr	voter constituent	ווײלער, דער
veynen	*vay*-nehn	to cry to weep	וויינען
veyniker	*vay*-nee-kehr	less	ווייניקער
veytik, der	*vay*-tik	pain ache hurt	ווייטיק, דער
veytikdik	*vay*-tik-dik	painful sore	ווייטיקדיק
veyts, der	vayts	wheat	ווייץ, דער
vi	vee	how as like than	ווי
vi es iz	*vee* ehs *eez*	somehow	ווי עס איז
vider	*vee*-dehr	again	ווידער

viderkol, dos	*vee*-dehr-kawl	echo	ווידערקול, דאָס
vie, di	*vee*-eh	eyelash	וויִע, די
vifl	vifl	how much	וויפֿל
		how many	
vig, di	veeg	cradle	וויג, די
		crib	
viglid, dos	*veeg*-lid	lullaby	וויגליד, דאָס
vikhtik	*veekh*-tik	important	וויכטיק
		major	
vild	veeld	wild	ווילד
		savage	
vinken	*veen*-kehn	to wink	ווינקען
vinken	*veen*-kehn	to beckon	ווינקען
vinkl, der	*veenk*-l	angle	ווינקל, דער
		corner	
vint, der	veent	wind	ווינט, דער
vinter, der	*veen*-tehr	winter	ווינטער, דער
vintik	*veen*-tik	windy	ווינטיק
vintl, dos	*veent*-l	breeze	ווינטל, דאָס
vintshn	*veench*-n	to wish	ווינטשן
vintshn zikh	*veench*-n zikh	to wish for	ווינטשן זיך
vintshoyb, di	*veent*-shoyb	windshield	ווינטשויב, די
vintsik	*veen*-tsik	few	ווינציק
vintsiker	*veen*-tsee-kher	less	ווינציקער
virus, der	*vee*-roos	virus	ווירוס, דער
visikayt, di	*vee*-see-keit	awareness	וויסיקייט, די
vishn	*veesh*-n	to dry	ווישן
		to wipe	
visn	*vees*-n	to know (knowledge)	וויסן
visndik	*vees*-n-dik	knowingly	וויסנדיק
visnshaft, di	*vees*-n-shahft	science	וויסנשאַפֿט, די
		scholarship	
vist	veest	deserted	וויסט
		dismal	
vitamin, der	vee-tah-*meen*	vitamin	וויטאַמין, דער
vits, der	veets	joke	וויץ, דער
		jest	
vitsik	*vee*-tsik	witty	וויציק
		funny	
vitsikayt, di	*vee*-tsee-keit	wit	וויציקייט, די

vitslen zikh	*veets*-lehn zikh	to joke	וויצלען זיך
vog, di	vawg	weight scale	וואָג, די
vogn, der	*vawg*-n	cart buggy	וואָגן, דער
vokh, di	vawkh	week	וואָך, די
vokhedik	*vaw*-kheh-dik	everyday commonplace	וואָכעדיק
vol, di	vawl	wool	וואָל, די
volf, der	vawlf	wolf	וואָלף, דער
volkn, der	*vawlk*-n	cloud	וואָלקן, דער
volt	vawlt	should would	וואָלט
volvl	*vawlv*-l	cheap	וואָלוול
vontses, di	*vawnt*-sehs	moustache	וואָנצעס, די
vorenen	*vaw*-reh-nehn	to caution to warn	וואָרענען
vorem, di	*vaw*-rehm	worm	וואָרעם, די
vort, dos	vawrt	word	וואָרט, דאָס
vortshen	*vawr*-chehn	to grumble to growl	וואָרטשען
vos	vawss	what that which	וואָס
vos es iz	vawss ehs *eez*	anything something	וואָס עס איז
vos gikher	vawss gee-khehr	as soon as possible	וואָס גיכער
vos makht ir	vawss *mahkt* eer	How are you?	וואָס מאַכט איר
vos nor	vawss nawr	whatever	וואָס נאָר
vos tustu	vawss *toos*-too	What are you doing?	וואָס טוסטו
voyl	voyl	good nice	ווויל
voynen	*voy*-nehn	to live to reside	וווינען
voynort, dos	*voyn*-awrt	residence	וווינאָרט, דאָס
voynung, di	*voy*-noong	dwelling apartment	וווינונג, די
vu	voo	where	ווו
vu es iz	voo ehs *eez*	anywhere	ווו עס איז

vu nor	voo *nawr*	wherever	וווּ נאָר
vuhin	voo-*heen*	Where to?	וווּהין
vund, di	voond	wound injury	וווּנד, די
vunder, der	*voon*-dehr	wonder marvel	וווּנדער, דער
vunderlekh	*voon*-dehr-lehkh	marvelous wonderful	וווּנדערלעך
vursht, der	voorsht	sausage salami	ווורשט, דער
yagde, di	*yahg*-deh	berry blueberry	יאַגדע, די
yak, di	yahk	jacket	יאַק, די
yakhne, di	*yahkh*-neh	gossip, coarse (sl.)	יאַכנע, די
yam, der	yahm	sea	ים, דער
yam-krank	*yahm*-krahnk	seasick	ים־קראַנק
yanuar, der	*yah*-noo-ahr	January	יאַנואַר, דער
yarshenen	*yahr*-sheh-nehn	to inherit to be heir to	ירשענען
yasher-koyakh!	*yah*-shehr-*koy-* ahkh	Well done!	ישר־כּח!
yasle, di	*yahss*-leh	gum (anat.)	יאַסלע, די
yat, der	yaht	chap guy lad	יאַט, דער
yeder	*yeh*-dehr	each every	יעדער
yeder eyner	*yeh*-dehr *ay*-nehr	everybody everyone each one	יעדער איינער
yedie, di	yeh-*dee*-eh	communication message	ידיעה, די
yene	*yeh*-neh	those	יענע
yener	*yeh*-nehr	that	יענער

yente, di	*yehn*-teh	gossip (sl.) busybody (sl.)	יענטע, די
yentsn	yehnts-n	to fornicate (sl.) to swindle (sl.)	יענצן
yerid, der	yah-*reed*	a fair	יריד, דער
yerid, der	yah-*reed*	uproar	יריד, דער
yerlekh	*yehr*-lehkh	yearly annual	יערלעך
yerushe, di	yeh-*roo*-shih	inheritance	ירושה, די
yeshive, di	yeh-*shee*-vih	Talmudic academy	ישיבה, די
yeshue, di	yeh-*shoo*-ih	salvation	ישועה, די
yesoyme, di	yeh-*soy*-mih	orphan (fem.)	יתומה, די
yesurim, di	ye-*soo*-rim	agony suffering	יסורים, די
yeytser-hore, der	*yay*-tsehr *haw*-rih	inclination to evil	יצר-הרע, דער
yeytser-tov, der	*yay*-tsehr *tawv*	inclination to good	יצר-טוב, דער
yid, der	yeed	Jew	ייִד, דער
yiddish	*yee*-dish	Jewish	ייִדיש
yiddishkayt, dos	*yee*-dish-keit	Jewishness Judaism	ייִדישקייט, דאָס
yikhes, der	*yee-khihs*	pedigree lineage	ייִחוס, דער
yinger	*yeen*-gehr	younger junior	ייִנגער
yingl, der	*yeeng*-l	boy	ייִנגל, דער
yires-hakoved, der	*yee*-rihs-hah-*kaw*-vihd	awe	ייִראת-הכּבוד, דער
yisroel, dos	yis-*raw*-ihl	Israel	ישראל, דאָס
yo	yaw	yes	יאָ
yog, di	yawg	chase pursuit	יאָג, די
yogenish, dos	*yaw*-geh-nish	haste rush	יאָגעניש, דאָס
yold, der	yawld	simpleton dupe	יאָלד, דער
yontev, der	*yawn*-tiv	holiday festival	יום-טוב, דער
yor, dos,	yawr	year	יאָר, דאָס
yorgelt, dos	*yawr*-gehlt	annuity	יאָרגעלט, דאָס
yorik	*yaw*-rik	year-long yearly	יאָריק

yortog, der	*yawr*-tawg	anniversary	יאָרטאָג, דער
yortsayt, der	*yawr*-tseit	anniversary of death	יאָרצײַט, דער
yosem, der	*yaw*-sihm	orphan (masc.)	יתום, דער
yoykh, di	yoykh	broth gravy	יויך, די
yoyresh, der	*yoy*-rihsh	heir	יורש, דער
yoysher, der	*yoy*-shir	justice fairness	יושר, דער
yoysherdik	*yoy*-shihr-dik	fair just	יושרדיק
yoyvlen	*yoyv*-lehn	to celebrate an anniversary	יובֿלען
yuli, der	*yoo*-lee	July	יולי, דער
yung	yoong	young	יונג
yungatsh, der	yoon-*gahch*	brat rascal	יונגאַטש, דער
yuni, der	*yoo*-nee	June	יוני, דער
zaft, der	zahft	juice	זאַפֿט, דער
zaftik	*zahf*-tik	juicy succulent fat (sl.)	זאַפֿטיק
zak, der	zahk	sack bag	זאַק, דער
zakh, di	zahkh	thing	זאַך, די
zakhtkayt, di	*zahkht*-keit	tranquility	זאַכטקייט, די
zal, der	zahl	hall auditorium	זאַל, דער
zalb, di	zahlb	salve ointment	זאַלב, די
zalts, di	zahlts	salt	זאַלק, די
zamd, dos	zahmd	sand	זאַמד, דאָס
zamlen	*zahm*-lehn	to gather to collect	זאַמלען
zamlung, di	*zahm*-loong	collection compilation	זאַמלונג, די
zat	zaht	satisfied full	זאַט

zaverukhe, di	zah-veh-*roo*-kheh	blizzard	זאַווערוכע, די
zayd, di	zeid	silk	זײַד, די
zayen	*zei*-en	to strain to filter	זײַען
zayern	*zah*-yehr-n	to pickle	זײַערן
zayn	zein	his its	זײַן
zayn	zein	to be	זײַן
zayner	*zei*-nehr	his its	זײַנער
zayt, di	zeit	side direction	זײַט, די
zayt, di	zeit	page	זײַט, די
zayt azoy gut	*zeit* ah-zoy goot	please	זײַט, אַזוי גוט
zayt gezunt	*zeit* geh-*zoont*	So long! Be well!	זײַט געזונט
zayt moykhl	*zeit* moykh-l	Pardon me!	זײַט מוחל
zeg, di	zehg	saw	זעג, די
zekhtsik	*zehkh*-tsik	sixty	זעכציק
zekhtsn	*zehkhts*-n	sixteen	זעכצן
zekl, dos	*zehk*-l	pouch	זעקל, דאָס
zeks	zehks	six	זעקס
zekster	*zehks*-tehr	sixth	זעקסטער
zelbik	*zehl*-bik	same	זעלביק
zelbstmord, der	*zehlbst*-mawrd	suicide	זעלבסטמאָרד, דער
zelner, der	*zehl*-nehr	soldier	זעלנער, דער
zeltn	*zehlt*-n	rare seldom	זעלטן
zeml, der	*zehm*-l	bread roll	זעמל, דער
zen	zehn	to see to behold	זען
zeneft, der	*zeh*-nehft	mustard	זענעפֿט, דער
zets, der	zehts	blow punch bump	זעץ, דער
zetsn zikh	*zehts*-n zikh	to sit down	זעצן זיך
zey	zay	they them	זיי
zeyde, der	*zay*-deh	grandfather	זיידע, דער
zeyde-bobe, di	*zay*-deh-*baw*-beh	grandparents	זיידע־באָבע, די

zeyer	*zay*-ehr	very greatly	זייער
zeyer	*zay*-ehr	their	זייער
zeyerer	*zay*-eh-rehr	theirs	זייערער
zeyf, di	zayf	soap	זייף, די
zeyger, der	*zay*-gehr	clock	זייגער, דער
zeygerl, dos	*zay*-gehr-l	watch (clock)	זייגערל, דאָס
zeyger-makher, der	*zay*-gehr-*mah*-khehr	watchmaker	זייגער־מאַכער, דער
zhabe, di	*zhah*-beh	toad	זשאַבע, די
zhargon, der	zhahr-*gawn*	jargon; Yiddish	זשאַרגאָן, דער
zhaver, der	*zhah*-vehr	rust	זשאַװער, דער
zhlob, der	zhlawb	clod boor	זשלאָב, דער
zhloken	*zhlaw*-kehn	to gulp to slurp	זשליאָקען
zhuk, der	zhook	bug beetle	זשוק, דער
zhuri, di	*zhoo*-ree	jury	זשורי, די
zhurnal, der	zhoor-*nahl*	magazine journal	זשורנאַל, דער
zi	zee	she	זי
zibeter	*zee*-beh-tehr	seventh	זיבעטער
zibetsik	*zee*-beh-tsik	seventy	זיבעציק
zibetsen	*zee*-behts-n	seventeen	זיבעצן
zibn	*zeeb*-n	seven	זיבן
zidn	*zeed*-n	to seethe to boil	זידן
zidlen	*zeed*-lehn	to swear to curse	זידלען
ziftsn	*zeefts*-n	to sigh	זיפצן
zikh	zikh	herself himself themselves yourselves self yourself myself itself ourselves	זיך

zikher	*zee*-khehr	certain sure	זיכער
zikher-shpilke, di	*zee*-khehr-*shpeel*-keh	safety pin	זיכער־שפּילקע, די
zikorn, der	zee-*kawr*-n	memory	זכּרון, דער
zilber, dos	*zeel*-behr	silver	זילבער, דאָס
zilzl, der	*zeelz*-l	defamation humiliation	זילזול, דער
zind, di	zeend	sin	זינד, די
zindiker, der	*zeen*-dee-kehr	sinner	זינדיקער, דער
zindikn	*zeen*-deek-n	to sin	זינדיקן
zingen	*zeen*-gehn	to sing	זינגען
zinger, der	*zeen*-gehr	singer	זינגער, דער
zinken	*zeen*-kehn	to sink	זינקען
zint	zeent	since	זינט
zis	zeess	sweet	זיס
ziskayt, di	*zeess*-keit	sweetness	זיסקייט, די
zitsn	*zeets*-n	to sit	זיצן
zitsort, dos	*zeets*-awrt	seat	זיצאָרט, דאָס
zitsung, di	zee-tsoong	meeting conference	זיצונג, די
zkhus, der	zkhoos	merit	זכות, דער
zogn	*zawg*-n	to say to tell	זאָגן
zok, der	zawk	sock stocking	זאָק, דער
zokher, der	*zaw*-khehr	male	זכר, דער
zokn, der	*zawk*-n	old man	זקן, דער
zokn-bendl, dos	*zawk*-n behnd-l	garter	זאָקן־בענדל, דאָס
zoknvarg, dos	*zawk*-n-vahrg	hosiery	זאָקנוואַרג, דאָס
zol zayn mit mazl	zawl zein mit *mahz*-l	Good luck!	זאָל זײַן מיט מזל
zol	zawl	should	זאָל
zorg, di	zawrg	care worry	זאָרג, די
zorgn zikh	*zawrg*-n zikh	to worry	זאָרגן זיך
zotl, der	*zawt*-l	saddle	זאָטל, דער
zoyer	*zoy*-ehr	sour	זויער

zoyershtof, der	*zoy*-ehr-shtawf	oxygen	זויערשטאָף, דער
zoyere ugerke, di	*zoy*-ehr-eh *oo*-gehr-keh	pickle	זויערע אוגערקע, די
zoygn	*zoyg*-n	to suck	זויגן
zoym, der	zoym	hem	זוים, דער
zoyne, di	*zoy*-neh	prostitute	זונה, די
zukhn	*zookh*-n	to look for to search	זוכן
zumer, der	*zoo*-mehr	summer	זומער, דער
zun, di	zoon	sun	זון, די
zun, der	zoon	son	זון, דער
zunenbren, der	*zoo*-nehn-brehn	sunburn	זונענברען, דער
zunbriln, di	*zoon*-breel-n	sunglasses	זונברילן, די
zunenshayn, di	*zoo*-nehn-shein	sunshine	זונענשײַן, די
zunik	*zoo*-nik	sunny	זוניק
zunlikht, di	*zoon*-leekht	sunlight	זונליכט, די
zunoyfgang, der	*zoon*-oyf-gahng	sunrise	זונאויפֿגאַנג, דער
zuntik, der	*zoon*-tik	Sunday	זונטיק, דער
zun-untergang, der	*zoon*-oon-tehr-gahng	sunset	זון־אונטערגאַנג, דער
zup, di	zoop	soup	זופּ, די
zupn	*zoop*-n	to guzzle to sip	זופֿן

POPULAR EXPRESSIONS

POPULAR EXPRESSIONS

Advice, Laments and Woes

A brokh tsu mir.
A curse on me.

A dayge hob ikh?
Is it my worry?

A dayge host du.
You shouldn't worry.
(A worry you have).

A klog iz mir.
Woe is me.

A moyre hob ikh?
Think I'm scared?
(I have a fear?)

A sof, an ek!
That's enough—stop it!

Alts vet zikh oysglaykhn.
Everything will smooth itself out.

Az a yor oyf mir,
I should have such good fortune.
(Such a year on me.)

Az ikh zog tog, zogt er nakht.
If I say day, he says night.

Az me redt tsu im, iz azoy vi me redt tsu a toyte vants.
Talking to him is like talking to a dead bedbug.

Azoy geyt es.
That's how it goes.

Du farkirtst mir di yorn.
You'll be the death of me.
(You're shortening my years.)

Er iz mir a beyn in haldz.
He's a bone in my throat.

Es iz nokh di khasene.
It's not important now.
(It's after the wedding.)

Es iz shoyn tsayt.
It's about time.
(It's already time.)

Es ligt mir in linke pyate.
I couldn't care less.
(It's lying in my left sole.)

Es ligt mir nit in zinen.
It's something I don't care about.
(It's not in my mind.)

Es vert mir finster in di oygn.
I am shocked.
(It's growing dark in my eyes.)

Es vert mir nit gut.
I am getting sick.

Es vet gornit helfn.
Nothing will help.

Es vet helfn vi a toytn bankes.
It's absolutely hopeless.
(It will help like blood-cupping a corpse.)

Eyder er krats zikh oys . . .
Until he gets started . . .
(Until he finishes scratching . . .)

Far dem zelbn gelt . . .
While you're at it . . .
(For the same money . . .)

Gey nit mit getseylte gelt.
Don't go without allowing for
    contingencies.
(Don't go with counted money.)

Gib zikh a shokl!
Go a little faster!
(Give yourself a shake!)

Host du bay mir an avle.
So I made a mistake.

Host es gedarft?
So you needed it? (sarcastic)

Kamandeve nit!
Stop giving orders!

Khap nit di lokshn far di fish.
Don't jump to conclusions.
(Don't grab the noodles before eating
    the fish.)

Kholile!
Perish the thought!

Klap mir nit in kop arayn!
Stop talking so much!
(Don't bang into my head!)

Kuk mir nit in moyl arayn!
Don't get so close!
(Don't look at me in my mouth!)

Kuk nor on!
Look at that!

Leyg dem klotz oyf mir.
I'll take the blame.
(Put the log on me.)

Loyf nit!
Don't hurry!
(Don't run!)

Loz im geyn.
Don't bother with him.
(Let him go.)

Makh a sof!
Stop it!
(Make an end!)

Makh es kaylekh un shpitsik!
Come to the point!
(Make it round and pointy!)

Makh es kurts un shnel!
Hurry up!
(Make it short and fast!)

Makh nit keyn tsimes fun dem.
Don't make a fuss about it.
(Don't make a fruit stew from it.)

Makh zikh nit visindik.
Make yourself unaware (and pretend
    you don't know.)

Me lebt a khazershn tog,
He's living it up.
(One lives a swinish day.)

**Mit eyn tokhes ken men nit zayn oyf
    tsvey yaridn.**
You can't do two things at one time.
(With one rear end you can't be at two
    fairs.)

Nit gefonfit.
Don't fake it.

Oy vey iz mir!
Woe is me!

Oyf mayn ergste sonim, vintsh ikh es nit.
I don't wish it on my worst enemies.

Oykh mir a lebn.
What a life.
(Also a life for me.)

Oykh mir a meyvn.
Look who's acting like an expert.
(Also an expert.)

Ruf mir knaknisl!
Call me a nut!
(Call me a nutcracker!)

Shlof gikher, me darf der kishn!
Speed it up; we're waiting!
(Sleep faster; we need the pillow!)

Shpilst zikh mit im?
You're associating with him?
(You're playing with him?)

Tokhes oyfn tish!
Get serious!
(Buttocks on the table!)

Vest zayn der zelbeker kabtsn.
You'll be the same pauper anyway, (so
    live it up).

Veys ikh vos!
That's nonsense!
(Do I know what!)

Veys nor vos du host tsu ton.
Keep your mind on what you're doing.
(Know only what you have to do.)

Zits nit mit leydike hent.
Keep yourself occupied.
(Don't sit with empty hands.)

Zukh nit keyn glikn.
Don't look for good luck.

Aphorisms

A khazer blaybt a khazer.
A greedy person is always a greedy
    person.
(A pig remains a pig.)

A nar blaybt a nar.
A fool remains a fool.

Abi gezunt.
As long as you're healthy.

Az me muz, ken men.
If you must, you can.

**Az me vil, ken men iberkern di gantse
    velt.**
If you want to, you can turn over the
    whole world.

Bist oyf eyn fus?
Are you in a hurry?
(Are you standing on one foot?)

Di gantse velt iz nit meshuge.
The whole world isn't crazy (so you
    could be wrong).

Es gefelt mir.
I like it.
(It pleases me.)

Es geyt nit.
It isn't working.
(It doesn't go.)

Es iz nit neytik.
It's not necessary.

Es iz nit oyf eybik.
It's not for an eternity.

Far di zelbe gelt . . .
For the same money . . .

Fun zogn vern, vert men nit trogn.
From talk alone you don't get pregnant.
(From talking, you don't carry.)

Gey shray gevald.
Yell for help (but it won't help at all).

Gezunthayt iz beser vi krankhayt.
Health is better than illness.

Gutskayt iz beser fun frumkayt.
Goodness is better than piety.

Gut gezogt.
Well said.

Ikh hob tsu dir a tayne.
I have a complaint to bring to you.

Khap es arayn.
Grab it (while you can).

Kum ikh nit haynt, kum ikh morgn.
I can't make up my mind.
(If I don't come today, I'll come
tomorrow.)

Lomir makhn nakht.
Let's call it a day.
(Let's make night.)

Lomir redn fun freylikher zakhn.
Let's talk about more cheerful things.

Lomir redn takhlis.
Let's talk with purpose.

Me darf lebn un lozn lebn.
Live and let live.

**Me darf nit zayn sheyn; me darf hobn
kheyn.**
You don't have to be pretty if you have
charm.

Me darf nor veln.
Where there's a will there's a way.
(You just have to want to.)

Me darf zayn shtark vi ayzn.
You have to be strong as iron.

Me dreyt zikh.
One manages.
(One keeps spinning.)

Me dreyt zikh, un me freyt zikh.
Keep on trying and you'll be happy.
(You keep spinning, and you become
happy.)

Me gefint zikh an eytse.
You can find a way out.
(You can find counsel.)

Me ken im getroyen vi a kats smetene.
You can trust him like you can trust a cat
with sour cream.

Meshugene gens, meshugene gribbenes.
Crazy parents, crazy children.
(Crazy fowl, bad cracklings.)

Mish zikh nit arayn.
Don't mix yourself in.

Nor a shteyn zol zayn aleyn.
Only a stone should be alone.

Nu, iz nit gefidelt.
So, it won't work out.
(So, there won't be any fiddling.)

Nu, krats zikh oys.
So, get going.
(So, scratch yourself.)

Oyf a mayse fregt men nit keyn kashes.
Don't interrupt with unnecessary
     details.
(About a story one asks no questions.)

Shem zikh nit.
Don't be bashful.

Tsum glik, tsum shlimazl.
For better, for worse.
(For good luck, for bad luck.)

**Vi azoy kumt men di kats iber dem
     vaser?**
How does one work this out?
(How does one get the cat over the
     water?)

Vi azoy vet es oyskukn?
How will it look?

Vos iz der untershte shure?
What's the bottom line?

Vos vet zayn, vet zayn.
What will be, will be.

Vos vilst du fun mir?
What do you want from me?

Yeder hot zayn eygene meshugaas.
Everyone has his own craziness.

Zol er zikh fardreyen zayn kop.
Let him be the one to get involved.
(Let him twist his head around.)

Zolst nit visn fun dem.
May you not know about that.

Conversational Expressions

A dank	Thank you	**Danken got**	Thank God
A gliklekh nay-yor	Happy New Year	**Derloybt mir**	Allow me
		Es fardrist mir	I am sorry
A gut yor	A good year	**Es tut mir leyd**	I am sorry
A gut vokh	A good week (Sabbath greeting)	**Farvos nit?**	Why not?
		Gut-morgn	Good morning
A gute nakht	Good night	**Gut shabes**	Good Sabbath
Aleykhem-sholem	Peace to you (the response to sholem-aleykhem)	**Gut yontev**	Good Holiday
		Gutn-ovnt	Good evening
		Ikh bin tsufridn	I am glad
Antshuldik mir	Excuse me	**Ikh volt veln . . .**	I would like . . .
Bakent zikh mit . . .	May I introduce . . .	**Me vet zikh zen**	See you again
		Nito far vos	You're welcome

Sholem-aleykhem	Hello (peace to you)	**Vos tust du?**	What are you doing?
Vi heyst dos?	What do you call this?	**Vos tut zikh?**	What's going on?
Vos makht dos oys?	What difference does it make?	**Vos volt ir gevolt?**	What do you wish?
Vos makht ir?	How are you?	**Zayt moykhl**	Excuse me
Vos nokh vilst du?	What more do you want?	**Zayt azoy gut**	Please

Curses

A brokh tsu dir!
A curse on you!

A fayer zol im trefn!
He should burn up!

A finstern yor oyf dir!
A dark year on you!

A klog oyf im!
A misery on him!

A kholyere oyf dir!
The cholera on you!

A klog tsu mayne sonim!
A blow to my enemies!

A mageyfe zol dikh trefn!
A plague should come to you!

A mise meshune oyf im!
May an ugly, strange thing befall him!

A ruakh in dayn tate's taten arayn!
A devil should be in your father's father!

A shvarts yor oyf im!
A black year on him!

An umglik oyf im!
A misfortune upon him!

Derharget zolst du vern!
You should get killed!

Dershtikt zol er vern!
He should be choked!

Di beyner zol im oysrinen!
May his bones be drained of marrow!

Er zol aynnemen a mise meshune!
He should meet with a strange death!

Er zol vaksn vi a tsibele mit dem kop in drerd!
He should grow like an onion with its head in the ground!

Finster zol dir vern!
A darkness should be yours!

Gebn im? A make vel ikh im gebn!
Give it to him? A plague I'll give him!

Geshvoln zol er vern!
May he swell up!

Gey in drerd arayn!
Go into the earth (and die)!

Gey klap zikh kop in vant!
Go bang your head against the wall!

Ikh hob dikh in drerd!
I have you buried in the earth (because you're nothing to me).

Ikh hob im in tokhes!
I have him in my rear end (because he's worth less than nothing)!

Klap kop in vant un shray gevald!
Go bang your head against the wall and yell for help!

Lig in drerd!
Go bury yourself.!

Tsebrekh a fus!
Break a leg!

Tsegezetst zol er vern!
May he explode!

Ver dershtikt!
You should be choked!

Zol er tsebrekhn a linke hant un a rekhte fus!
He should break a left hand and a right foot!

Zolst farlirn ale tseyner akhuts eynem, un der zol dir vey ton!
You should lose all your teeth except one, and that one should ache!

Zolst geshvoln vern vi a barg!
You should swell up like a mountain!

Zol im nit gut vern!
He should feel ill!

Zol im shtinkin fun kop!
May his head stink!

Peygern zol er!
He should die (like an animal)!

Zol im klapn in kop vi es hakt mir in oyer!
I hope his head aches as much as my ear does!

Descriptive Expressions

A fardreyenish
A mix-up

A farshlepenish
A long drawn-out matter

A farshlepte krenk
An unending annoyance
(A chronic ailment)

A gantse megile
A big deal (sarcastic)
(A whole story)

A gantse metsie
A great bargain (sarcastic)

A hekdish
A real mess
(A poorhouse)

A kleyner gornit
A little nothing

A lebedike velt
Things are happening
(A lively world)

A lek un a shmek
Only a little bit
(A taste and a smell)

A metsie fun a ganev.
It's really no bargain.
(It's a bargain from a thief.)

A nekhtiger tog
Impossible
(Yesterday's day)

A shande un a kharpe
A shame and a disgrace

A shenern bagrobt men.
They bury better-looking ones.

A sheyn gelekhter
Nothing to laugh about
(A pretty laughter)

A sheyne mayse
A likely tale (sardonic)
(A pretty tale)

A shtik nakhes
A great joy
(A piece of pleasure)

Ado ligt der hunt bagrobn.
Here is the source of the problem.
(Here's where the dog is buried.)

Ale montik un donershtik
Constantly
(Every Monday and Thursday)

Aroysgevorfine gelt
Wasted money
(Money thrown out)

Azoy vert dos kikhl tsebrokhn .
That's how the cookie crumbles .

Azoy vi du kukst mikh on
Just like that
(Just as you look at me)

Azoy zogst du.
That's what you say.

Bilik vi borsht
Very cheap
(Cheap as beet soup)

Bobe mayse
A far-fetched story
(A grandmother story)

Dos heyst gelebt.
That's what I call living.

Dos iz opgeret.
That goes without saying.
(That's talked out).

Drey mir nit keyn kop.
Don't bother me.
(Don't twist my head.)

Es art mikh vi der vant.
I don't care.
(It bothers me like the wall.)

Es brent nit.
It's not urgent.
(It's not burning.)

Es iz blote.
It's worthless.
(It's mud.)

Es iz mir arop a shteyn fun hartsn.
It's a great relief.
(It's a stone off my heart.)

Es iz nit geshtoygn un nit gefloygn.
It just doesn't make sense.
(It never rose and it never flew.)

Es iz vert a zets in drerd.
It has no value.
(It's worth a stomp on the earth.)

Es klapt mir in kop.
It's giving me a headache.
(It bangs in my head.)

Es lost zikh esn.
It's very tasty.
(It lets itself be eaten.)

Es past vi a khazer.
It's in very bad taste.
(It's as suitable as a pig.)

Es past zikh vi a patsh tsu gut shabes.
It's very unfitting.
(It's as appropriate as answering "Good
   Shabes" with a slap in the face.)

Es tsegeyt zikh in moyl.
It melts in your mouth.

Es vet nit shatn tsum shidekh.
It certainly won't hurt.
(It won't hurt in arranging a marriage.)

Eyn kleynikayt
A small matter

Folg mikh a gang.
It's not worth the trouble.
(Follow me on an errand).

Gefunene gelt
Found money

Gehakte tsores
Utter misery
(Chopped-up troubles)

Glat in der velt arayn
Totally unexpected
(Just into the world)

Goldene medine
Golden country (United States)

In mitn derinen
(Right) in the middle of everything

Kadokhes mit koshere fodem
Absolutely nothing
(Fever with kosher thread)

Kam derlebt
Narrowly achieved
(Barely lived through)

Kam mit tsores
Barely made it
(Barely with troubles)

Mayn bobe's tam
A terrible taste
(My grandmother's taste)

Me ken es in moyl nit nemen.
It's unpalatable.
(You can't put it in your mouth.)

Me ken nit farzorgn di gantse velt.
One can't provide for the whole world.

Me lebt a tog.
This is real enjoyment.
(One lives a day.)

Me makht a gantsn yontev fun dos.
They're making a "big deal" of this.
(They're making a whole holiday from
   this.)

Me vert tsugevoynt tsu di tsores.
One grows accustomed to troubles.

Shenere leygt men in drerd.
They bury better-looking ones.

Sheyn vi di zibn veltn.
Beautiful as the seven worlds.

Take a metsie
Really a bargain (sarcastic)

Vos gikher, alts beser.
The faster, the better.

Personal Descriptions

A fardarter
A cheerless type
(A dried-out one)

A farshloginer
A beaten-down person

A ganste knaker
An important person (sarcastic)

A gantse makher
An important person
(A big doer)

A goyisher kop
A "slow-witted" person
(A Gentile head)

A hipshe meydl
A hefty girl

A kalyiker
A spoiler

A "Khayim Yankel"
An undependable person

A langer loksh
A skinny, tall person
(A long noodle)

A hunt mit oygn
A mean character
(A dog with eyes)

A nokhshleper
A hanger-on

A shleper
A slob

A shtik fleysh mit oygn
A clod
(A hunk of meat with two eyes)

A tsudreyter
A mixed-up person

A vilde khaye
A very undisciplined person
(A wild animal)

A yid fun a gants yor
A constant Jew
(A Jew for a whole year.)

Frish, gezunt un meshuge
Hale, hearty but crazy
(Fresh, healthy and crazy)

Gezunt vi a ferd
Healthy as a horse

Gliklekh vi der velt
Happy as could be
(Fortunate as the world)

Klug vi der velt
Very smart
(Clever as the world)

Lebst a khazhershn tog
Really enjoying oneself
(Living a day as a pig would)

Pust un pas
Insipid and idle

Shtark vi a ferd
Strong as a horse

A glik hot mikh getrofn.
That's a stroke of luck.
(A stroke of luck has befallen me.)

Ale mayles hot er.
He has all the virtues.

Er est vi nokh a krenk.
He eats a lot.
(He eats as if he just recovered from an
    illness.)

Er firt im in bod arayn.
He's cheating him.
(He's leading him to the bathhouse.)

Er frest vi a ferd.
He eats like a horse.

Er geyt im in noz.
He's driving him insane.
(He's going into his nose.)

Er geyt im nokh.
He's backing him up.
(He follows him.)

Er git im a shtokh.
He's needling him.
(He's giving him a stitch.)

Er hot a farshtoptn kop.
He's thick-headed.
(He has a stuffed-up head.)

Er hot a kats in kop.
He can't remember a thing.
(He has a cat in his head.)

Er hot a kop oyf di pleytses.
He has a (good) head on his shoulders.

Er hot a kop vi a ferd.
He's really stupid.
(He has a head like a horse.)

**Er hot azoyfil gelt vifl a yid hot
    khazeyrim.**
He really has nothing at all.
(He has as much money as a Jew has
    pigs.)

Er hot kadokhes.
He has nothing at all.
(He has malarial fever.)

Er hot shpilkes.
He can't sit still.
(He has pins.)

Er iz a leyminer goylem.
He's a numbskull.
(He's a clay dummy.)

Er iz a shtik ferd.
He's a worthless clod.
(He's a hunk of horse.)

Er iz meshuge oyf toyt.
He's just really impossible.
(He's crazy to death.)

**Er iz nit keyn groyser khokhem, un nit
    keyn kleyner nar.**
He's not a great wise man and he's not a
    small fool.

Er iz shoyn oyf yener velt.
He just died.
(He's already in the other world.)

Er ken dikh tsen mol koyfn un farkoyfn.
He's a very wealthy man.
(He can buy and sell you ten times over.)

Er krikht in di hoykhe fenster.
He's a social climber.
(He climbs to high windows.)

Er krikht vi a vants.
He's very slow.
(He crawls like a bedbug.)

Er molt gemolene mel.
He repeats himself.
(He grinds flour that is already ground.)

Er rayst di hoyt.
He overcharges.
(He tears the skin.)

Er redt fun haynt biz morgn.
He talks from today until tomorrow.

Er redt in di velt arayn.
He speaks and it makes no sense.
(He speaks into the world.)

Er redt on a mos.
He talks endlessly.
(He speaks without measure.)

Er redt tsu der vant.
He's talking in vain.
(He talks to the wall.)

Er redt zikh arayn a krenk.
He talks himself into being sick.

Er shmekt nit un er shtinkt nit.
He's so-so.
(He doesn't smell (good) and he doesn't
    smell bad.)

Er toyg oyf kapores.
He's worthless.
(He's only suitable to be a sacrificial
    chicken.)

Er varft im a beyz oyg.
He's hexing him.
(He's throwing him a bad eye.)

Er vet shoyn keyn honik nit lekn.
Things won't be easy for him.
(He won't be licking honey.)

Er veyst fun bobkes.
He really knows nothing.
(He (only) knows about beans.)

Es iz bay im a lebidike velt.
Things are going well for him.
(With him it's a lively world.)

Es klept zikh tsu im.
Everything happens to him.
(It attaches itself to him.)

Kam vos er krikht.
He's barely crawling along.

Kam vos er lebt.
He's barely alive.

Mayn neshome iz nit keyn rozhinke.
I'm only human.
(My soul is not a raisin.)

Me tsurayst im di kishke.
They're giving him a difficult time.
(They're tearing his guts out.)

Nor er makht kalye.
All he does is ruin things.
(He just makes things crippled.)

**Shpay im in ponim, meynt er az es
    regnt.**
Spit in his face and he thinks it's raining.

Zi hot goldene hent.
She has golden hands.

Zey fardreyen im di yorn.
They're getting him all tangled up.
(They're tangling up his years.)

Put-Downs and Retorts

Bist meshuge?
Are you crazy?

Drey nit keyn spodik.
Don't confuse me.
(Don't turn the cap around.)

Es freyt mir zeyer tsu hern.
I'm very glad to hear it.

Es geyt mir in pupik arayn.
It doesn't hurt me at all.
(It goes into my belly-button.)

Er iz im shuldik di lokh fun beygl.
He owes him nothing.
(He owes him the hole in the bagel.)

Es art aykh?
Does it disturb you?

Es iz nito mit vemen tsu redn,
You just don't understand.
(There's no one with whom to talk.)

**Fardrey zikh dayn kop, vest du meynen
   az s'iz mayner.**
Drive yourself crazy and then you'll
   know how I feel.
(Twist your head around and you'll
   think it's mine.)

Freg mir bekheyrim.
No matter what, I can't answer.
(Ask me even under the threat of excom-
   munication.)

Freg mir nit keyn kashes.
Don't ask me any questions.

Gey strashe di gens.
Go threaten the geese (because you're
   not threatening me.)

Gib mir nit keyn eyn-ore.
Don't give me the evil eye.

Hak mir nit in kop.
Don't talk so much.
(Don't bang me on my head.)

Hak nit keyn tshaynik.
Don't be long-winded and boring.
(Don't bang on the tea kettle.)

Ikh darf es vi a lokh in kop.
I need it like a hole in the head.

Ikh darf es vi a lung un leber oyfn noz.
I need it like (I need) a lung and liver on
   my nose.

Ikh fayf oyf dir.
You're meaningless to me.
(I whistle on you.)

Ikh hob dikh in bod.
I don't care about you.
(I have you in the bathhouse.)

Ikh hob im lib fun der vaytn.
I don't like him.
(I like him from a distance.)

Ikh vel dir gebn kadokhes.
I'll give you nothing.
(I'll give you a malarial fever.)

Ikh vil es farn moyl nit brengen.
I don't want to discuss it.
(I don't want to bring it to my mouth.)

Ikh vil nit visn fun keyn khokhmes.
I don't want to hear any words of
   wisdom.

Ikh zol azoy lang lebn.
I should live so long.

Ikh zol azoy visn fun tsores.
I have no idea.
(I should know as little about trouble.)

Loz mikh tsu ru.
Leave me in peace.

Makh zikh nit narish.
Don't make yourself foolish.

Mayne sonim zoln azoy lang lebn.
My enemies should only live so long.

Me ken brekhn.
One could vomit.

Me krikht oyf di glaykhe vent.
You're asking the impossible.
(You're climbing on the straight wall.)

Me makht a tel fun dir.
He's making a shambles out of you.

Oyf mayne sonim gezogt gevorn.
It should be said about my enemies.

Redt mir nit arayn keyn krenk.
Don't talk me into illness.
(Don't talk a disease into me.)

Redt nit keyn narishkayt.
Don't talk nonsense.

Shem zikh in dayn vaytn haldz.
You should be ashamed of yourself.
(You should be ashamed to the bottom
of your throat.)

Shlog mikh nit, un lek mikh nit.
Do me no good and do me no evil.
(Don't hit me and don't lick me.)

Shlog zikh kop in vant.
Go bang your head against the wall (and
don't bother me).

Strashe mir nit!
Don't threaten me!

Tshepe zikh nit tsu mir.
Don't annoy me.
(Don't attach yourself to me.)

Ven ikh ess, hob ikh zey ale in drerd.
When I eat, they can all go to hell.

**Vet meshiakh geboyrn vern mit a tog
shpeter.**
Don't be in a hurry.
(So the Messiah will be born a day later.)

Vos dreyste mir a kop?
What are you bothering me about?
(What are you twisting my head about?)

Vu krikhst du mit dayn krume fis?
Since you're not capable, what are you
trying to accomplish?
(Where are you climbing with your
crooked feet?)

Zol ikh azoy visn fun tsores.
I'm not the least bit interested.
(I should know as much about troubles
as I want to know about this.)

Toasts and Wishes

A gezunt oyf dayn kop!
Be with good health!

A gezunt dir in pupik!
Thanks for the favor!
(Good health to your belly-button!)

A gezunt oyf ir piskele!
Well said!
(Health on her dear mouth!)

A lebn oyf dayn kop!
A long life upon your head!

A lebn oyf im!
Long may he live!
(A life on him!)

Az got vet helfn un mir veln lebn . . .
If God helps and we live . . .

Biz hundert un tsvantsik yor!
For a hundred and twenty years!

Borukh hashem .
Blessed be God (I'm all right).

Er kukt oys vi zayn taten, zol er lebn un zayn gezunt.
He looks like his father, may he live and be well.

Fun dayn moyl in got's oyern.
From your mouth into God's ears.

Gey gezunt un kum gezunt.
Go in health and come back in health.

Gezunt zolst du zayn!
May you be healthy!

Kayn eyn-ore zol nit zayn!
May there be no evil eye!

Lang lebn zolt ir!
Long may you live!

Lekhayim!
To life!

Lomir lebn un lakhn.
May we live and laugh.

Mazl-tov!
Congratulations!

Me zol nit darfn onkumen tsu kinder!
Pray that you may not be a burden to your children!

Me zol zikh bagegenen oyf simkhes.
May we meet on happy occasions.

Nit do gedakht!
May it never happen here!

Nit far dir gedakht!
May it never happen to you!

Nit oyf undz gedakht!
It shouldn't happen to us!

Nit oysgeredt zol es zayn!
May it never be spoken!

Oyf lange yorn!
May he have long years!

Oyf mir gezogt gevorn.
It should only happen to me.
(Let it be said about me.)

Oyf undz ale gezogtgevorn.
It should only happen to all of us.
(Let it be said about us.)

Tsu gezunt!
God bless you (after a sneeze)!
(To health!)

302 Yiddish Dictionary Sourcebook

Zayt gezunt!
So long!
(Be healthy!)

Zol dos zayn dayn ergste dayge.
That should be your worst worry.

Zolst lebn un zayn gezunt.
You should live and be well.

Zolst nit visn fun azelkhe tsores.
May you not know of such troubles.

Zolst nit visn fun keyn shlekhts.
You shouldn't know from bad.

Zol zayn mit mazl!
Good luck!

PROVERBS

PROVERBS

Common Sense and Ethics

A halber emes iz a gantser lign.
Half a truth is a whole lie.

A shlekhter sholem iz beser vi a guter krig.
A bad peace is better than a good war.

Ale mayles in eynem, iz nito bay keynem.
No one person possesses all the virtues.

Az a leyb shloft, loz im shlofn.
When a lion is sleeping, let him sleep.

Az es brent, iz a fayer.
When something's burning, there's a fire.

Beser a krumer fus eyder a krumer kop.
Better a crooked foot than a crooked mind.

Beser a yid on a bord, vi a bord on a yid.
Better a Jew without a beard, than a beard without a Jew.

Der emes iz der bester lign.
The truth is the best lie.

Der emes ken arumgeyn a naketer; dem lign darf men bakleydn.
The truth can walk around naked; the lie has to be clothed.

Der vos hot lib tsu nemen, hot nit lib tsu gebn.
He who likes to take does not like to give.

Di klenste nekome farsamt di neshome.
The smallest vengeance poisons the soul.

Emes iz nor in sider.
Truth is found only in the prayerbook.

Fun yidishe reyd ken men zikh nit opvashn in tsen vasern.
Ten washings will not cleanse you of Jewish talk.

Ganve nit un fast nit.
Steal not and repent not.

Host du, halt; veyst du, shvayg; kenst du, tu.
If you have it, hold it; if you know it, be silent; if you can do it, do it!

Krikh nit tsu hoykh, vest du nit darfn faln.
Don't climb too high and you won't have to fall.

Kuk arop, vest du visn vi hoykh du shteyst.
Look down and you'll know how high up you are.

Loyf nit nokh koved, vet es aleyn kumen.
Don't run after honor; it will come by itself.

Me darf nit zayn hoykh tsu zayn groys.
You don't have to be tall to be great.

Me ken makhn dem kholem greser vi di nakht.
One can make the dream bigger than
   the night.

Mit fremdn seykhl ken men nit lebn.
With another's common sense one
   cannot live.

Mit lign kumt men vayt, ober nit tsurik.
With lies one can go far—but not back
   again.

Oyf a vund tor men nit shitn zalts.
On a wound one should not pour salt.

Tsvishn yidn vert men nit farfaln.
One doesn't perish among Jews.

Ver es toyg nit far zikh, toyg nit far yenem.
Who is no good to himself, is no good
   to anyone.

Verter zol men vegn un nit tseyln.
Words should be weighed and not
   counted.

Ven mayn bobe volt gehat a bord, volt zi geven mayn zeyde.
If my grandmother had a beard, she
   would have been my grandfather.

Fools, Wise Men and Saints

A fremder nar iz a gelekhter, an eygener a shande.
A strange fool is laughable, but your
   own fool is shameful.

A gantser nar iz a halbe novi.
A whole fool is half a prophet.

A groyse oylem, un nito eyn mentsh.
A crowd of people and not one real
   person among them.

A kluger farshteyt fun eyn vort tsvey.
A wise man understands two words
   from one.

A kluger veyst vos er zogt, a nar zogt vos er veyst.
A smart man knows what he says; a fool
   says what he knows.

A nar blaybt a nar.
A fool remains a fool.

A nar ken a mol zogn a klug vort.
Sometimes even a fool can say a smart
   word.

A nar vakst on regn.
A fool grows without rain.

A tsadik vos veyst az er iz a tsadik iz keyn tsadik nit.
A saintly man who knows he is a saintly
   man is not a saintly man.

Az a nar shvaygt, veyst men nit tsi er iz a nar oder a khokhem.
When a fool keeps quiet, you can't tell
   whether he's foolish or clever.

**Az me redt a sakh, ken men zikh
   aynredn a narishkayt.**
If you talk a lot, you might talk
   foolishness.

Az mi's tsu klug, ligt men in drerd.
When you're too smart, you ruin
   yourself.

**Beser mit a klugn in gehenem eyder mit
   a nar in ganeydn.**
Better to be with a wise person in hell
   than with a fool in paradise.

**Beser mit a klugn tsu farlirn, eyder mit a
   nar tsu gevinen.**
Better to lose with a wise man than to
   win with a fool.

**Dem roshe geyt oyf der velt, dem tsadik
   oyf yener velt.**
The wicked person fares well in this
   world, the saint in the life to come.

**Der vos farshteyt zayn narishkayt iz a
   kluger mentsh.**
He who is aware of his own foolishness
   is a wise person.

**Di greste narishkayt fun a nar iz az er
   meynt az er iz klug.**
The greatest folly of the fool is when he
   thinks he is smart.

**Eyn nar ken mer fregn eyder tsen kluge
   ken entfern.**
One fool can ask more than ten smart
   men can answer.

Fun a nar hot men tsar.
From a fool one has grief.

**Got hot gegebn dem nar hent un fis, un
   im gelozt loyfn.**
God has given the fool hands and feet
   and allowed him to run.

Klugkayt iz beser fun frumkayt.
Wisdom is better than piety.

Mit a nar tor men nit handlen.
Don't do business with a fool.

Nor naronim farlozn zikh oyf nisem.
Only fools rely on miracles.

**Ofy a sheynem iz gut tsu kukn, mit a
   klugn iz gut tsu lebn.**
On a beautiful person it's good to look,
   with a smart person it's good to live.

Seykhl iz an eydele zakh.
Wisdom is a precious thing.

**Ven der nar volt nit geven mayn, volt ikh
   oykh gelakht.**
If the fool didn't belong to me, I'd be
   laughing too.

**Vos a nar ken kalye makhn, kenen tsen
   khakhomim nit farrikhtn.**
What a fool can spoil, ten wise men
   cannot repair.

**Vos bay a nikhtern oyfn lung, iz bay a
   shikern oyfn tsung.**
What a sober person has on his lung
   [mind], a drunk has on his tongue.

**Vos der mentsh farshteyt veyniker, iz alts
   far im beser.**
The less a person understands, the
   better off he is.

Yeder nar iz klug far zikh.
Every fool thinks he's smart.

**Zey zaynen undzere khakhomim vayl
   mir zaynen zeyere naronim.**
They are our sages because we are their
   fools.

God, Life and the Family

A gute tokhter iz a gute shnur.
A good daughter makes a good
   daughter-in-law.

A mentsh trakht un got lakht.
Man thinks and God laughs.

A mol iz di refue erger fun di make.
Sometimes the remedy is worse than the
   disease.

A shlekhte mame iz nito.
There is no such thing as a bad mother.

**Az der tate shenkt dem zun, lakhn
   beyde; az der zun shenkt dem taten,
   veynen beyde.**
When the father supports the son, both
   laugh; when the son supports the
   father, both cry.

**Az di muter shrayt oyfn kind "mamzer,"
   meg men ir gloybn.**
When a mother screams "bastard" at
   her child, you can believe her.

**Az got vil nit gebn, ken men zikh aleyn
   nit nemen.**
If God does not want to give, one
   cannot take.

Bay tog tsum get, bay nakht tsum bet.
By day they're ready to divorce, by night
   they're ready for bed.

**Beser oyf der velt nit tsu lebn, eyder
   onkumen tsu kinder.**
Better not to live than to become
   dependent on children.

Blut iz diker fun vaser.
Blood is thicker than water.

Di tsayt iz der bester doktor.
Time is the best doctor.

**Dos lebn iz di greste metsie, men krigt
   dos umzist.**
Life is the greatest bargain; we get it for
   nothing.

**Dos oybershte kleyd fardekt di untershe
   leyd.**
The outer dress hides the inner distress.

**Eltern kenen alts gebn, nor keyn mazl
   kenen zey nit gebn.**
Parents can provide everything, but they
   can't give good luck.

Eyn got un azoy fil soynim.
Only one God and so many enemies.

**Fun a muter's klap, vert dem kind nit
   keyn lokh in kop.**
A mother's slap won't give a child a hole
   in the head.

**Fun krume shiddukhim kumen aroys
   glaykhe kinder.**
From bad matches comes good
   children.

Fun nakhes lebt men nit; fun tsores shtarbt men nit.
From joy one doesn't live; from troubles one doesn't die.

Gezunt kumt far parnose.
Health comes before making a living.

Got iz eyner, vos er tut zet keyner.
God is the One; none can witness what He does.

Got shikt di refue far di make.
God sends the remedy before the plague.

Kinder brengen glik, kinder brengen umglik.
Children bring good fortune, children bring misfortune.

Kleyne kinder, kleyne freydn; groyse kinder, groyse zorgn.
Little children, little joys; big children, big worries.

Kleyne kinder trogt men oyf di hent; groyse kinder oyfn kop.
Little children are a load for the hands; big children are a load on the mind.

Leyg zikh nit mit a gezuntn kop in a krankn bet.
Don't lie down with a healthy head in a sick bed.

Nadn kenen eltern gebn, ober nit keyn mazl.
Parents can give a dowry, but not luck.

Nakhes fun kinder iz tayere fun gelt.
Joy from children is more precious than money.

Nokh di khupe iz shpet di kharote.
After the wedding it's late to have regrets.

Oyf eygene kinder iz yederer a blinder.
When it comes to one's own children, everyone is blind.

Oyf morgn zol got zorgn.
Let God worry about tomorrow.

Zint es iz oyfgekumen dos shtarbn, iz men nit zikher mitn lebn.
Ever since dying appeared, man has not been certain about life.

Zol er zayn yudel, zol er zayn nosen, abi a khosn.
Should he be Yudel or should he be Nosen, as long as he's a bridegroom.

Heaven, Destiny and Morality

A beyze tsung iz erger fun a shlekhter hant.
A wicked tongue is worse than an evil hand.

A sho in ganeydn iz oykh gut.
An hour in paradise is also good.

Alts iz gut, nor in der tsayt.
Everything is good, but only in its time.

Az me est nit keyn knobl, shtinkt nit fun moyl.
If you don't eat garlic, your mouth won't stink.

Az me vil nit alt vern, zol men zikh yungerheyt oyfhengen.
If you want to avoid old age, hang yourself when you're young.

Az men dermont zikh oyfn toyt, iz men nit zikher mitn lebn.
If you start thinking of death, you're not sure of life.

Biz zibetsik yor lernt men seykhl, un me shtarbt a nar.
Up to seventy we learn wisdom, yet die fools.

Der goy iz tsum goles nit gevoynt.
The Gentile is not used to exile.

Der iz klug vemes mazl geyt im nokh.
He is smart whose good luck accompanies him.

Der seykhl kumt nokh di yorn.
Wisdom comes with the years.

Di velt iz ful mit tsores, ober yederer filt nor zayne.
The world is full of troubles, but each person feels only his own.

Dos lebn iz nit mer vi a kholem, ober vek mikh nit oyf.
Life is no more than a dream, but don't wake me up.

Eynems mazl is an anderens shlimazl.
One's good luck is another's misfortune.

Far gelt ken men alts koyfn, nor keyn seykhl nit.
For money one can buy anything except good sense.

Farlorene yorn iz erger vi farlorene gelt.
Lost years are worse than lost dollars.

Fun glik tsum umglik iz nor a shpan; fun umglik tsum glik iz a shtik veg.
From fortune to misfortune is but a short span; from misfortune to fortune is a long way.

Gehakte leber iz beser vi gehakte tsores.
Chopped liver is better than chopped-up troubles.

Got iz a foter; doz mazl iz a shtif-foter.
God is a father; fortune a stepfather.

Gute tsoln, shlekhte monen.
The good ones pay up; the bad ones demand.

In a sheynem epl gefint zikh a mol a vorem.
In a nice apple you sometimes find a worm.

Keyner veyst nit vemes morgn es vet zayn.
No one knows whose tomorrow it will be.

Mit mazl ken men alts ton.
With luck one can do anything.

Nit yeden mesles treft zikh a nes.
Not everyday leads into a miracle.

Oyb er volt gehandelt mit likht, volt di zun nit untergegangen.
If he dealt in candles, the sun wouldn't set.

Oyf nisem tor men zikh nit farlozn.
One ought not depend upon miracles.

Tsores vil men nit tsunemen; mitsves ken men nit tsunemen.
Nobody wants to take away your troubles; nobody can take away your good deeds.

Tsu gut iz umgezunt.
Too good is unhealthy.

Tsum glik darf men keyn khokhme nit.
You don't have to be wise to be lucky.

Tsum shlimazl darf men oykh hobn mazl.
Even when you're unlucky you need good luck.

Ven es geyt glaykh, vert men raykh.
When things go right, you become rich.

Ven men fort aroys veyst men, ven men kumt tsurik veyst men nit.
We know the time of our setting out, but not of our return.

Vos vet zayn mit kol yisroel, vet zayn mit reb yisroel.
Whatever happens to all the Jews, will happen to each Jew.

Yeder morgn brengt zikh zorgn.
Every morning brings its own worries.

Relationships with Others

A geshvir iz a gute zakh bay yenem untern orem.
A boil is fine as long as it's under someone else's arm.

An alter fraynt iz beser vi naye tsvey.
Better an old friend than two new.

Az der meydl ken nit tantsn, zogt zi az di klezmer ken nit shpiln.
When a girl can't dance, she says the band can't play.

Az du kenst nit baysn, tsayg nit dayne tseyner.
If you can't bite, don't show your teeth.

Az du krigst zikh, krig zikh az du zolst zikh kenen iberbetn.
When you quarrel, do it in a manner that will allow you to make up.

Az me redt zikh arop fun hartsn, vert gringer.
When you speak from your heart, you feel better.

Beser a guter soyne eyder a shlekhter fraynd.
Better a good enemy than a bad friend.

Beser der soyne zol bay mir guts zen, eyder ikh bay im shlekhts.
It is better for my enemy to see good in me, than for me to see bad in him.

Beser zikh tsu vintshn, eyder yenem tsu shiltn.
Better to make a wish for oneself than to curse another.

Borgn makht zorgn.
Borrowing causes worrying.

Der ershter broygez iz der bester broygez.
The first quarrel is the best quarrel.

Far an akshn iz keyn refue nito.
For a stubborn person there is no cure.

Far got hot men moyre; far mentshn muz men zikh hitn.
Fear God but be wary of people.

Freg an eytse bay yenem, un hob dayn seykhl bay dir.
Ask advice of another, and keep your own counsel.

Fun kine vert sine.
From envy grows hate.

Fun vaytn nart men laytn, fun noent zikh aleyn.
At a distance you fool others, close at hand just yourself.

Gring iz tsu krign a soyne; shver iz tsu krign a fraynd.
It's easy to acquire an enemy; it's difficult to acquire a friend.

Hit zikh far di fraynd, nit far di faynd.
Beware of your friends, not your enemies.

Hob mikh veynik lib nor hob mikh lang lib.
Love me little but love me long.

Keyner iz nit azoy toyb vi der vos vil nit hern.
No one is as deaf as one who will not listen.

Khavershaft iz shtarker vi brudershaft.
Friendship is stronger than kinship.

Kratsn un borgn iz nor gut oyf a vayl.
Scratching and borrowing is only good for a while.

Mit fremdn seykhl ken men nit lebn.
One cannot live by another's wits.

Mit honik ken men khapn mer flign vi mit esik.
You can catch more flies with honey than with vinegar.

Nit keyn entfer iz oykh an entfer.
Having no answer is also an answer.

Oyf a fremder bord iz zikh gut tsu lernen shern.
It's good to learn to shave on someone else's beard.

Oyf a nar tor men nit faribl hobn.
Don't be offended by a fool.

Oyf yenems hintn iz gut tsu shmaysn.
On someone else's behind it's good to whip.

Redn iz gut, shvaygn iz beser.
Talking is good, but silence is better.

Redn iz zilber, shvaygn iz gold.
Speech is silver, but silence is gold.

Sheyn shvaygn iz shener vi sheyn redn.
Eloquent silence is better than eloquent speech.

Ven ale mentshn zoln tsien oyf eyn zayt, volt zikh di velt ibergekert.
If everyone pulled in one direction, the world would keel over.

Ver es toyg nit far zikh, toyg nit far yenem.
He who is no good to himself, is no good to another.

**Ver es varft oyf yenem shteyner, krigt
    tsurik in zayn eygene beyner.**
He who throws stones on another gets
    them back on his own bones.

**Ven men lakht ze'en ale; ven men veynt
    zet keyner nit.**
Laugh and everyone sees; cry and you
    cry alone.

**Vos der mentsh ken ibertrakhtn, kenen
    di ergste soyne im nit vintshin.**
What one can think up for himself, his
    worst enemy can't wish on him.

Vos veyniker me redt, iz alts beser.
The less you talk, the better everything
    is.

Vos vintsiker me fregt, iz alts gezunter.
The less you ask, the healthier you are.

The Human Condition

A biter harts redt a sakh.
An embittered heart talks a lot.

A hunt on tseyner iz oys hunt.
A dog without teeth is not a dog.

A mentsh iz nor a mentsh.
A human being is only human.

**A sheyne velt, a likhteke velt, nor vi far
    vemen?**
A beautiful world, a glorious world, but
    for whom?

A shpigl ken zayn der grester farfirer.
A mirror can be the greatest deceiver.

**Abi gezunt, dos lebn ken men zikh ale
    mol nemen.**
As long as you're healthy, you can
    always kill yourself.

An iberik vort hot nit keyn ort.
A superfluous word has no place.

**Az der mogn iz leydik, iz der moyekh
    oykhet leydik.**
When the stomach is empty, the brain is
    also empty.

**Az me hengt bay eyn fus, hengt men bay
    tsvey.**
If you're hanging by one foot, you
    might just as well be hanging by
    both.

**Az me ken nit aribergeyn, geyt men
    arunter.**
If you can't go over, go underneath.

**Az me ken nit vi me vil, tut men vi me
    ken.**
If you can't do what you want, do what
    you can.

Az me redt a sakh, redt men fun zikh.
If you talk a lot, you talk about yourself.

Der glaykhster veg iz ful mit shteyner.
The smoothest way is full of rocks.

Der mentsh iz tsu shtarbn geboyrn.
A human being is born to die.

Der mentsh iz vos er iz, nit vos er iz geven.
A man is what he is, not what he has been.

Der vos hot nit farzukht biters, veyst nit vos zis iz.
He who has not tasted the bitter does not know what is sweet.

Dortn iz gut vu mir zaynen nito.
Where we could be is better than where we are.

Dos mieste lebn iz beser fun dem shenster toyt.
The ugliest life is better than the nicest death.

Eynem dakht zikh az bay yenem lakht zikh.
One thinks to oneself that with another there is laughter.

Gut iz tsu hofn, shlekht iz tsu vartn.
It's good to hope; it's the waiting that's bad.

Ibergekumene tsores iz gut tsu dertseylen.
Bygone troubles are good to tell.

In der shpigl zet itlekher zayn bestn fraynd.
In the mirror everyone sees his best friend.

In shlof zindikt nit der mentsh, nor zayn khaloymes.
In sleep man doesn't sin; only his dreams do.

Keyner zogt nit "oy" az es tut nit vey.
One doesn't cry "ouch" if he's not in pain.

Libe iz vi puter; es iz gut mit broyt.
Love is like butter; it's good with bread.

Libe iz zis, nor zi iz gut mit broyt.
Love is sweet, but tastes best with bread.

Libe un hunger voynen nit in eynem.
Love and hunger don't dwell together.

Me falt nit vayl me iz shvakh, nor vayl me meynt az me iz shtark.
You don't stumble because you're weak, but because you think you're strong.

Me ken nit di gantse velt farzorgn.
You can't provide for the whole world.

Me vert alt vi a ku, un lernt zikh alts tsu.
You get old as a cow, but you still go on learning.

Nit yeder harts vos lakht iz freylekh.
Not every heart that laughs is really full of joy.

Nit yeder iz tsufridn mit zayn ponim, ober mit zayn seykhl iz yeder tsufridn.
Not everyone is satisfied with his looks, but everyone is satisfied with his intelligence.

Nor bay dem eygene tish ken men zat vern.
You can only eat your fill at your own table.

Oder me darf nit, oder es helft nit.
Either it isn't necessary, or it won't help.

Oyf a nikhtern mogn ken men keyn zakh nit fartrogn.
With an empty stomach nothing can be tolerated.

Tsores mit zup iz gringer tsu fartrogn vi tsores on zup.
Worries with soup are easier to bear than worries without soup.

Tsu broyt gefint men shoyn a meser.
If you have the bread, you can always find a knife.

Tsufil koved iz a halbe shande.
Too much honor is half a shame.

Tsu shtarbn darf men nit keyn luakh.
To die one doesn't need a calendar.

Umzist krigt men nor mist.
For free one gets only garbage.

Ven der harts iz biter, helft nit keyn tsuker.
When the heart is bitter, sugar doesn't help.

Vos klener der oylem, alts greser di simkhe.
The smaller the crowd, the greater the joy.

Vos men hot, vil men nit; vos men vil, hot men nit.
What one has, one doesn't want; what one wants, one doesn't have.

Yeder barg aroyf hot zayn barg arop.
Every uphill has its downhill.

Yeder mentsh hot zayn eygene meshugaas.
Every person has his own madness.

Yeder mentsh hot zayn eygene pekl.
Every person has his own burden.

Yeder trakht zikh az bay yenem lakht zikh.
One always thinks that others are happy.

Zey hobn zikh beyde lib; er zikh un zi zikh.
They both have love, he for himself and she for herself.

Zingen ken ikh nit, ober a mayvn bin ikh.
I can't sing a note, but I know all about it.

Work, Money and Poverty

A dank ken men in keshene nit leygn.
You can't put "thank you" in your pocket.

A kabtsn blaybt a kabtsn.
A pauper remains a pauper.

A kats meg oykh kukn oyfn keyser.
Even a cat may look at a king.

Ale shusters geyn borves.
All shoemakers go barefoot.

An opgeshelte ey falt oykh nit aleyn in moyl.
Even a shelled egg won't fall into your mouth by itself.

An oreman vil oykh lebn.
A poor man also wants to live.

Az an oreman est a hun, is oder er iz krank, oder di hun iz krank.
When a poor man eats a chicken, either he is sick or the chicken is sick.

Az es kumt tsu arbet, iz keyner nito.
When it comes to work, nobody's
around.

**Az es regnt mit gold, shteyt yeder unter
a dakh.**
When it's raining gold, everyone is
standing inside.

Az me leygt arayn, nemt men aroys.
What you put in, you take out.

Az me shmirt di reder, fort der vogn.
When you grease the wheels, the wagon
goes.

Az mi'iz foyl, hot men nit in moyl.
If you're lazy, you'll have nothing to eat.

Der dales farshemt di khokhme,
Poverty gets in the way of wisdom.

**Der doktor hot a refue far alts, ober nit
far dales.**
The doctor has a remedy for everything,
but not for poverty.

**Der oreman hot veynik faynt, der
raykher hot veyniker fraynd.**
The poor man has few enemies; the rich
man has fewer friends.

**Der rekhening iz do, ober dos gelt iz
nito.**
The bill is here, but the money is not.

**Di kats hot lib fish, nor zi vil di fis nit
aynetsn.**
The cat loves fish, but doesn't want to
wet its feet.

**Di shvereste arbet iz arum tsu geyn
leydik.**
The hardest work is to be idle.

**Dray zakhn ken men nit bahaltn: libe,
hustn un dales.**
Three things cannot be hidden: love,
coughing and poverty.

**Es iz nit azoy gut mit gelt, vi es iz shlekht
on gelt.**
It is not so much that it's good to have
money, as it's bad to be without it.

Es tut zikh nit azoy gut vi es redt zikh.
Easier said than done.

**Far gelt ken men alts koyfn, nor keyn
seykhl nit.**
For money one can buy anything except
good sense.

Gelt tsu fardinen iz gringer vi tsu haltn.
It's easier to earn money than to hold
on to it.

Gornit mit gornit iz alts gornit.
Nothing added to nothing is still
nothing.

**Got hot lib der oreman un helft der
nogid.**
God loves the poor and helps the rich.

**Me ken nit tantsn oyf tsvey khasenes mit
eyn mol.**
You can't dance at two weddings at the
same time.

**Me zol zikh kenen oyskoyfn fun toyt,
voltn di oreme layt gehat parnose.**
If the rich could hire others to die for
them, the poor could make a living.

**Nayn rabonim kenen keyn minyen nit
makhn, ober tsen shusters yo.**
Nine rabbis don't make a *minyen,* but
ten cobblers do.

Nit mit shiltn un nit mit lakhn ken men di velt ibermakhn.

Neither with curses nor with laughter can you change the world.

Orem un raykh, in bod zaynen zey beyde glaykh.

The poor and the rich, in the bath they are both equal.

Oremkayt iz nit keyn shande, ober keyn groyse koved iz dos oykh nit.

Poverty is no disgrace, but it's also not a great honor.

Oyf dray zakhn shteyt di velt; oyf gelt, oyf gelt un oyf gelt.

The world stands on three things: money, money and money.

Oyf gelt shteyt di velt.

Money supports the world.

Oyf "volt ikh" un "zolt ikh," borgt men nit keyn gelt.

With an "I would" and an "I should," one can not borrow money.

Shlofn shpet brengt oremkayt.

Sleeping late brings poverty.

Shpor, shpor, kumt der shvarts yor un nemt alts gor.

You save and you save, and then a lean year comes and takes away every-thing.

Takhrikhim makht men on keshenes.

Burial shrouds are made without pockets.

Tsvey mol a yor iz shlekht dem oreman: zumer un vinter.

Twice a year the poor are badly off: summer and winter.

THE AUTHORS

Herman Galvin is a business man who teaches Yiddish and lectures on Yiddish humor.

Stan Tamarkin received his Ph.D. from Yale University in American Studies. He has taught American social and cultural history at Yale, Connecticut College, and the University of Rhode Island.